NE능률 영어교과서

대한민국 고등학생 **10명 중 4.7명**이 보는 교과서

영어 고등 교과서 점유율 1위
(7차, 2007 개정, 2009 개정, 2015 개정)

능률보카

그동안 판매된
능률VOCA 1,100만 부

대한민국 박스오피스
천만명을 넘은 영화 단 28개

리딩튜터

그동안 판매된
리딩튜터 1,900만 부
차곡차곡 쌓으면 19만 미터

에베레스트 21배 높이

190,000m

에베레스트 8,848m

그래머존

그동안 판매된 450만 부의 그래머존을 바닥에 쭉 ~ 깔면

1000km 서울-부산 왕복가능

서울

부산

GRAMMAR Inside

LEVEL 1

지은이	NE능률 영어교육연구소
선임연구원	김지현
연구원	박효빈, 가민아
영문교열	Curtis Thompson, Angela Lan
디자인	민유화
맥편집	허문희

Let's grow together

NE능률이
미래를
창조합니다.

건강한 배움의 고객가치를 제공하겠다는 꿈을 실현하기 위해
40년이 넘는 시간 동안 열심히 달려왔습니다.

앞으로도 끊임없는 연구와 노력을 통해
당연한 것을 멈추지 않고

고객, 기업, 직원 모두가 함께 성장하는 NE능률이 되겠습니다.

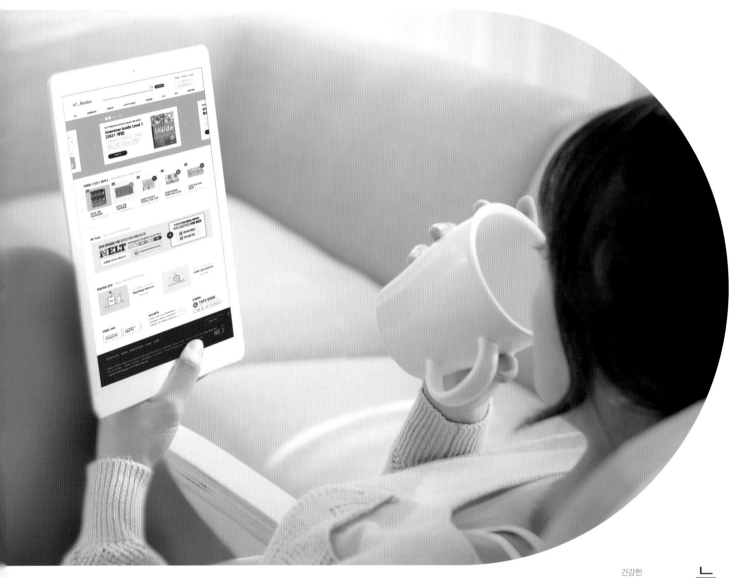

GRAMMAR
Inside

LEVEL 1

UNIT 02 be동사의 부정문과 의문문

A be동사의 부정문

1 be동사 현재형의 부정문(~가 아니다, (~에) 없다): am/are/is + not

주어	be동사 + not		줄임말	
I	am not		I'm not	
You	are not	You're not	You aren't	
He/She/It	is not	He's/She's/It's not	He/She/It isn't	
We/You/They	are not	We're/You're/They're not	We/You/They aren't	

He's not in the office. / **He isn't** in the office.

2 be동사 과거형의 부정문: was/were + not

It **wasn't[was not]** cold yesterday.
We **weren't[were not]** at home last week.

B be동사의 의문문

1 be동사 현재형의 의문문(~입니까?, (~에) 있습니까?): Am/Are/Is + 주어 ~?

be동사 + 주어 ~?	긍정의 대답	부정의 대답
Am I ~?	Yes, you are.	No, you aren't.
Are you ~?	Yes, I am.	No, I'm not.
Is he/she/it ~?	Yes, he/she/it is.	No, he/she/it isn't.
Are we/you/they ~?	Yes, you/we/they are.	No, you/we/they aren't.

A: **Is he** American?
B: **Yes, he is. / No, he isn't.**

cf. 긍정의 대답을 할 때는 주어와 be동사를 줄여 쓰지 않는다.
Yes, I'm. Yes, he's.

2 be동사 과거형의 의문문: Was/Were + 주어 ~?

A: **Was she** at the party yesterday?
B: **Yes, she was. / No, she wasn't.**

CHECK UP 빈칸에 알맞은 말을 고르시오.

1 She _____ my sister.
ⓐ am not   ⓑ aren't   ⓒ isn't

2 _____ they in the room?
ⓐ Be   ⓑ Are   ⓒ Is

✦ PLUS : There is/are의 부정문과 의문문

부정문: There is/are + not ~
의문문: Is/Are there ~?

There aren't many stars in the sky.
Is there a bank near here?

14

PRACTICE

🔍 Answer Key p-2

STEP 1 밑줄 친 부분을 줄여 쓰시오.

1 I <u>am not</u> a liar. _____
2 You <u>are not</u> a kid. _____
3 He <u>is not</u> on vacation. _____
4 She <u>was not</u> in the cafeteria. _____
5 They <u>are not</u> interested in science. _____

STEP 2 빈칸에 be동사의 부정형을 써서 문장을 완성하시오. (줄임말로 쓸 것)

1 China is a big country. It _____ small.
2 We are in Seoul now. We _____ in Busan.
3 The dogs were in the yard. They _____ in the house.
4 Tom and I are baseball fans. We _____ soccer fans.
5 Bob was a member of a book club. He _____ a member of a movie club.

STEP 3 ( ) 안의 말과 be동사를 이용하여 의문문을 완성하시오.

1 A: _____ a cook? (you)
  B: No, I'm not.
2 A: _____ too loud? (I)
  B: No, you aren't.
3 A: _____ with you? (Peter)
  B: No, he isn't.
4 A: _____ nice to you? (they)
  B: Yes, they were.

STEP 4 우리말과 일치하도록 ( ) 안의 말을 이용하여 문장을 완성하시오. (부정문은 줄임말로 쓸 것)

1 식사는 맛있지 않다. (the meal)
  → _____ delicious.
2 우리는 지금 바쁘지 않다. (busy)
  → We _____ now.
3 A: 그 영화 무서웠니? B: 응, 무서웠어. (the movie)
  → A: _____ scary?
     B: Yes, it _____.

GRAMMAR POINT

1 GRAMMAR POINT

해당 Unit에서 배워야 할 핵심 문법들을 명확한 설명과 실용적인 예문으로 체계적으로 정리했습니다.

2 CHECK UP

핵심을 묻는 문제를 통해 Grammar Point에서 배운 내용을 이해했는지 확인할 수 있습니다.

3 PLUS

Grammar Point에서 제시한 핵심 문법 외의 추가 정보를 담았습니다.

PRACTICE

1 Grammar Point에서 학습한 내용을 다양한 유형의 문제를 통해 자연스럽게 익힐 수 있습니다.

2 학교 내신 시험에 자주 등장하는 서술형 쓰기 연습문제를 매 Unit마다 경험할 수 있도록 하였습니다.

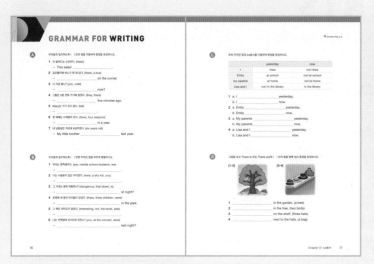

GRAMMAR FOR WRITING

다양한 형태의 쓰기 문제를 풀어봄으로써 Grammar Point를 반복 학습하며 sentence writing의 기초를 마련할 수 있습니다.

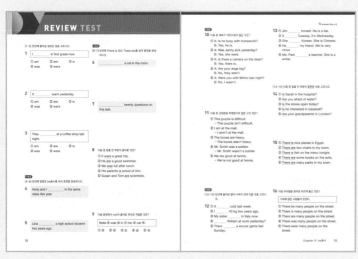

REVIEW TEST

실제 학교 시험과 가장 유사한 유형의 문제들로 구성하여 실전에 대비할 수 있습니다.
고난도 어법 문제와 서술형 문제를 대폭 수록하여 학교 내신 시험의 서술형 주관식 문항에 완벽 대비할 수 있도록 하였습니다.

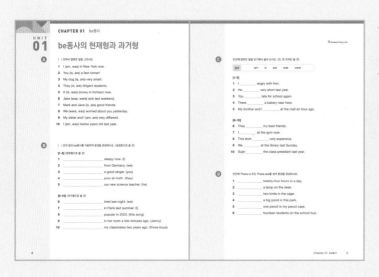

WORKBOOK

각 Unit별 연습문제와 쓰기 문제, Chapter별 Review Test를 수록하였습니다.
더 많은 문제를 풀어봄으로써 문법을 보다 완벽하게 익힐 수 있도록 하였습니다.

CONTENTS

GRAMMAR BASICS   6

CHAPTER 01   be동사

Unit 01   be동사의 현재형과 과거형   12
Unit 02   be동사의 부정문과 의문문   14

CHAPTER 02   일반동사

Unit 01   일반동사의 현재형   24
Unit 02   일반동사의 과거형   26
Unit 03   일반동사의 부정문   28
Unit 04   일반동사의 의문문   30

CHAPTER 03   조동사

Unit 01   can, may   40
Unit 02   must, have to, should   42

CHAPTER 04   진행형과 미래시제

Unit 01   진행형   52
Unit 02   will, be going to   54

CHAPTER 05   동사의 종류

Unit 01   감각동사 + 형용사   64
Unit 02   목적어가 두 개 필요한 동사   66
Unit 03   목적격 보어가 필요한 동사   68

CHAPTER 06   명사와 관사

Unit 01   셀 수 있는 명사 vs. 셀 수 없는 명사   78
Unit 02   관사   80

CHAPTER 07 대명사

Unit 01	인칭대명사, 재귀대명사	90
Unit 02	this, that, it	92
Unit 03	one, some, any	94

CHAPTER 08 형용사와 부사

Unit 01	형용사	104
Unit 02	부사	106
Unit 03	원급, 비교급, 최상급	108

CHAPTER 09 to부정사와 동명사

Unit 01	to부정사의 명사적 용법	118
Unit 02	to부정사의 형용사적, 부사적 용법	120
Unit 03	동명사의 역할	122

CHAPTER 10 전치사

Unit 01	장소를 나타내는 전치사	132
Unit 02	시간을 나타내는 전치사	134
Unit 03	기타 전치사	136

CHAPTER 11 접속사

Unit 01	and, but, or, so	146
Unit 02	when, before, after, until	148
Unit 03	because, if, that	150

CHAPTER 12 의문문, 명령문, 감탄문

Unit 01	의문사 who, what, which	160
Unit 02	의문사 when, where, why, how	162
Unit 03	부가의문문	164
Unit 04	부정의문문, 선택의문문	166
Unit 05	명령문, 감탄문	168

GRAMMAR BASICS

01 품사

- Wow, this tastes really good!
  감탄사 대명사 동사   부사   형용사

- The sweet and sour sauce on the steak is great.
  관사 형용사 접속사 형용사 명사 전치사 관사 명사 동사 형용사

명사 **1** 사람, 동물, 사물, 장소 등의 이름을 나타내는 말이다.

Tom, man, dog, bag, school, Korea, love …

2 문장에서 주어, 목적어, 보어로 쓰인다.

Seoul is a big city.
I saw a **movie**.
He is a **doctor**.

cf. 관사: 명사 앞에 쓰여 명사의 의미와 성질을 나타내는 말로, 막연한 하나를 나타내는 a, an과 특정한 대상을 가리키는 the가 있다.
a book, **an** apple, **the** boy …

대명사 **1** 명사를 대신하는 말로 주로 명사의 반복을 피하기 위해 쓰인다.

I, you, we, he, she, it, this, that …

2 문장에서 주어, 목적어, 보어로 쓰인다.

This is my camera.
I know **him** well.
The book is **mine**.

동사 **1** 사람, 동물, 사물 등의 상태나 행동을 나타내는 말이다.

am, are, is, feel, have, go, ask, can, may, must …

2 동사에는 be동사, 일반동사, 조동사가 있다.

We **are** tired.
Kate **lives** in Korea.
I **will** play tennis tomorrow.

형용사

1 명사, 대명사의 성질, 상태 등을 나타내는 말이다.

good, smart, friendly, hungry, lonely, lucky …

2 문장에서 명사나 대명사를 꾸며주는 수식어 또는 보어로 쓰인다.

You did a **good** *job*.
The game is **interesting**.

부사

1 시간, 장소, 방법, 정도, 빈도 등을 나타내는 말이다.

today, here, quietly, happily, very, always, never …

2 문장에서 동사나 형용사, 다른 부사, 문장 전체를 꾸며주는 수식어로 쓰인다.

I *know* this town **well**.
I am **very** *hungry*.
I got up **too** *early*.
Luckily, *I found the key*.

전치사

명사나 대명사의 앞에 쓰여 시간, 장소, 목적 등을 나타내는 말이다.

in, at, on, over, under, about, by, for, to, with …

I had lunch **at** *noon*.
We'll meet **in** *the library*.
I have a present **for** *you*.

접속사

단어와 단어, 구와 구, 절과 절을 이어주는 말이다.

and, but, or, so, when, before, after, until, because, if, that …

We'll *sing* **and** *dance* together.
I'll leave *on Saturday* **or** *on Sunday*.
The exam was easy, **but** *I failed*.

감탄사

기쁨, 슬픔, 놀람 등의 감정을 나타내는 말이다.

Oh, Wow, Hooray, Oops, Bravo …

Wow, you look amazing!
Oops, I made a mistake.

02 문장의 성분

- He is an English teacher.
  주어 동사   보어

- He teaches English at a middle school.
  주어   동사   목적어   수식어

주어 1 행동의 주체가 되는 말로, 문장에서 '누가'에 해당한다. 주로 문장의 맨 앞에 온다.

2 주로 명사(구), 대명사가 주어로 쓰인다.

Bob is a pianist.
She works hard.

동사 주어의 상태나 행동을 나타내는 말로, 문장에서 '~이다, ~하다'에 해당한다. 주로 주어 뒤에 온다.

Your answer **is** correct.
She **runs** fast.

목적어 1 동사의 대상이 되는 말로, 문장에서 '무엇을'에 해당한다. 주로 동사 뒤에 온다.

2 주로 명사(구), 대명사가 목적어로 쓰인다.

I need **a computer**.
Jenny likes **you**.

보어 1 동사를 도와 주어나 목적어를 설명해 주는 말이다. 주격 보어는 동사 뒤에 오고 목적격 보어는 목적어 뒤에 온다.

2 주로 명사(구), 대명사, 형용사(구)가 보어로 쓰인다.

She became **a doctor**.
The winner is **him**.
My dog makes me **happy**.

수식어 문장의 필수 요소는 아니지만, 문장에 더 자세한 의미를 더해주는 말이다.

Peter is a **smart** student.
I did my homework **quickly**.
They study **in the library**.

03 구와 절

- Jim sings <u>a beautiful song</u>.
  명사구

- I think that <u>Jim sings</u> well.
  주어 동사
  명사절

구

1 두 개 이상의 단어가 모여 문장 내에서 명사, 형용사, 부사처럼 쓰이는 것으로, '주어 + 동사'를 포함하지 않는다.

at home, in the morning, to be a pianist …

2 문장에서의 역할에 따라 명사구, 형용사구, 부사구로 나뉜다.

❶ 명사구: 명사처럼 문장에서 주어, 목적어, 보어로 쓰인다.

He bought **a big black bag**.

❷ 형용사구: 형용사처럼 문장에서 명사를 꾸며주는 수식어 또는 보어로 쓰인다.

I have some water **to drink**.
Reading a lot of books is **very helpful**.

❸ 부사구: 부사처럼 문장에서 동사나 형용사, 다른 부사, 문장 전체를 꾸며주는 수식어로 쓰인다.

Sandra goes to school **by bus**.

절

1 '주어 + 동사'를 포함한 여러 단어가 모여 문장 내에서 명사, 형용사, 부사처럼 쓰이는 것이다.

that I know you, when I was young, if he comes early …

2 문장에서의 역할에 따라 명사절, 형용사절, 부사절로 나뉜다.

❶ 명사절: 명사처럼 문장에서 주어, 목적어, 보어로 쓰인다.

I know **that you're honest**.

❷ 형용사절: 형용사처럼 문장에서 명사를 꾸며주는 수식어로 쓰인다.

This is the book **which I told you about**.

❸ 부사절: 부사처럼 문장에서 동사나 형용사, 다른 부사를 꾸며주는 수식어로 쓰인다.

You should wash your hands **before you eat**.

ESSENTIAL RULES OF ENGLISH GRAMMAR

CHAPTER

01

be동사

be동사는 '~이다', '(~에) 있다'의 뜻으로
주어의 상태를 나타낸다.

UNIT 01　be동사의 현재형과 과거형

UNIT 02　be동사의 부정문과 의문문

be동사의 현재형과 과거형

Ⓐ **be동사의 쓰임**

be동사는 주어 뒤에 쓰여 '~이다', '(~에) 있다'의 의미를 나타낸다.

I **am** a new student here.
My bag **is** on the desk.

Ⓑ **be동사의 형태**

be동사는 주어의 수와 인칭에 따라 형태가 달라지며, 일상 대화에서는 줄임말을 주로 사용한다.

1 be동사의 현재형

주어		be동사 현재형	줄임말
단수	1인칭 I	am	I'm
	2인칭 You	are	You're
	3인칭 He/She/It	is	He's/She's/It's
복수	1인칭 We		We're
	2인칭 You	are	You're
	3인칭 They		They're

We are in the kitchen. / **We're** in the kitchen.

2 be동사의 과거형

am, is의 과거형은 was, are의 과거형은 were이다.

I *am* fourteen years old. I **was** thirteen last year.

Ⓒ **There is/are**

1 「There is/are + 주어」는 '~가 있다'의 의미를 나타내며, 뒤에 나오는 주어에 따라 is 또는 are를 쓴다.

There is	단수명사, 셀 수 없는 명사
There are	복수명사

There is *a bank* near here.
There are *thirty students* in my class.

2 There is/are의 과거형: There was/were + 주어

There was *a math test* yesterday.

CHECK UP 빈칸에 알맞은 말을 고르시오.

1 Mark _____ in the museum now.
ⓐ are ⓑ is ⓒ was

PRACTICE

🔍 Answer Key p.2

STEP 1

밑줄 친 부분을 줄여 쓰시오.

1 It <u>is</u> rainy outside. _____

2 <u>I am</u> in second grade. _____

3 <u>You are</u> very kind. _____

4 <u>He is</u> a police officer. _____

5 <u>They are</u> good at sports. _____

STEP 2

빈칸에 알맞은 말을 보기에서 골라 쓰시오. (단, 한 번씩만 쓸 것)

보기	is	am	are	was	were

1 I _____ on the mountain now.

2 Dave _____ from Canada.

3 They _____ in Berlin in 2020.

4 Andrew and Joan _____ cousins.

5 He _____ my neighbor two years ago.

STEP 3

빈칸에 There is 또는 There are를 넣어 문장을 완성하시오.

1 _____ a tiger in the cage.

2 _____ seven days in a week.

3 _____ a man at the door.

4 _____ old trees in her garden.

5 _____ lots of cars in the parking lot.

STEP 4

우리말과 일치하도록 (   ) 안의 말을 이용하여 문장을 완성하시오.

1 내가 가장 좋아하는 과목은 영어다. (my favorite subject)

→ _____ _____ _____ _____ English.

2 지난 주말에는 날씨가 좋았다. (the weather)

→ _____ _____ _____ nice last weekend.

3 Teddy와 나는 친한 친구이다. (Teddy and I)

→ _____ _____ _____ _____ close friends.

4 내 우편함에 이메일 한 통이 있었다. (an email)

→ _____ _____ _____ _____ in my mailbox.

02 be동사의 부정문과 의문문

A

be동사의 부정문

1 be동사 현재형의 부정문(~가 아니다, (~에) 없다): am/are/is + not

주어	be동사 + not	줄임말	
I	am not	I'm not	
You	are not	You're not	You aren't
He/She/It	is not	He's/She's/It's not	He/She/It isn't
We/You/They	are not	We're/You're/They're not	We/You/They aren't

He's not in the office. / **He isn't** in the office.

2 be동사 과거형의 부정문: was/were + not

It **wasn't[was not]** cold yesterday.
We **weren't[were not]** at home last week.

B

be동사의 의문문

1 be동사 현재형의 의문문(~입니까?, (~에) 있습니까?): Am/Are/Is + 주어 ~?

be동사 + 주어 ~?	긍정의 대답	부정의 대답
Am I ~?	Yes, you are.	No, you aren't.
Are you ~?	Yes, I am.	No, I'm not.
Is he/she/it ~?	Yes, he/she/it is.	No, he/she/it isn't.
Are we/you/they ~?	Yes, you/we/they are.	No, you/we/they aren't.

A: **Is he** American?
B: **Yes, he is. / No, he isn't.**

cf. 긍정의 대답을 할 때는 주어와 be동사를 줄여 쓰지 않는다.
~~Yes, I'm.~~   ~~Yes, he's.~~

2 be동사 과거형의 의문문: Was/Were + 주어 ~?

A: **Was she** at the party yesterday?
B: **Yes, she was. / No, she wasn't.**

┃CHECK UP┃ 빈칸에 알맞은 말을 고르시오.

1 She _____ my sister.
ⓐ am not　　ⓑ aren't　　ⓒ isn't

2 _____ they in the room?
ⓐ Be　　ⓑ Are　　ⓒ Is

✚ PLUS : There is/are의 부정문과 의문문

부정문: There is/are + not ~
의문문: Is/Are there ~?

There aren't many stars in the sky.
Is there a bank near here?

PRACTICE

🔍 Answer Key p-2

STEP 1

밑줄 친 부분을 줄여 쓰시오.

1 <u>I am not</u> a liar.   _____

2 <u>You are not</u> a kid.   _____

3 <u>He is not</u> on vacation.   _____

4 <u>She was not</u> in the cafeteria.   _____

5 <u>They are not</u> interested in science.   _____

STEP 2

빈칸에 be동사의 부정형을 써서 문장을 완성하시오. (줄임말로 쓸 것)

1 China is a big country. It _____ small.

2 We are in Seoul now. We _____ in Busan.

3 The dogs were in the yard. They _____ in the house.

4 Tom and I are baseball fans. We _____ soccer fans.

5 Bob was a member of a book club. He _____ a member of a movie club.

STEP 3

( ) 안의 말과 be동사를 이용하여 의문문을 완성하시오.

1 A: _____ a cook? (you)
  B: No, I'm not.

2 A: _____ too loud? (I)
  B: No, you aren't.

3 A: _____ with you? (Peter)
  B: No, he isn't.

4 A: _____ nice to you? (they)
  B: Yes, they were.

STEP 4

우리말과 일치하도록 ( ) 안의 말을 이용하여 문장을 완성하시오. (부정문은 줄임말로 쓸 것)

1 식사는 맛있지 않다. (the meal)
  → _____ _____ _____ delicious.

2 우리는 지금 바쁘지 않다. (busy)
  → We _____ _____ now.

3 A: 그 영화 무서웠니? B: 응, 무서웠어. (the movie)
  → A: _____ _____ _____ scary?
    B: Yes, it _____.

GRAMMAR FOR WRITING

A 우리말과 일치하도록 (   ) 안의 말을 이용하여 문장을 완성하시오.

1 이 샐러드는 신선하다. (fresh)

→ This salad _____.

2 길모퉁이에 버스가 한 대 있다. (there, a bus)

→ _____ on the corner.

3 너 지금 춥니? (you, cold)

→ _____ now?

4 그들은 5분 전에 거기에 없었다. (they, there)

→ _____ five minutes ago.

5 Mary는 키가 크지 않다. (tall)

→ _____.

6 한 해에는 사계절이 있다. (there, four seasons)

→ _____ in a year.

7 내 남동생은 작년에 6살이었다. (six years old)

→ My little brother _____ last year.

B 우리말과 일치하도록 (   ) 안에 주어진 말을 바르게 배열하시오.

1 우리는 중학생이다. (are, middle school students, we)

→ _____.

2 너는 수줍음이 많은 아이였다. (were, a shy kid, you)

→ _____.

3 그 거리는 밤에 위험하니? (dangerous, that street, is)

→ _____ at night?

4 공원에 세 명의 아이들이 있었다. (there, three children, were)

→ _____ in the park.

5 그 책은 재미있지 않았다. (interesting, not, the book, was)

→ _____.

6 너는 어젯밤에 콘서트에 있었니? (you, at the concert, were)

→ _____ last night?

C 표에 주어진 말과 be동사를 이용하여 문장을 완성하시오.

	yesterday	now
I	tired	not/tired
Emily	at school	not/at school
my parents	at home	not/at home
Lisa and I	not/in the library	in the library

1 a. I _____ yesterday.

b. I _____ now.

2 a. Emily _____ yesterday.

b. Emily _____ now.

3 a. My parents _____ yesterday.

b. My parents _____ now.

4 a. Lisa and I _____ yesterday.

b. Lisa and I _____ now.

D 그림을 보고 There is 또는 There are와 ( ) 안의 말을 함께 써서 문장을 완성하시오.

[1-2]  [3-4]

1 _____ in the garden. (a tree)

2 _____ in the tree. (two birds)

3 _____ on the shelf. (three hats)

4 _____ next to the hats. (a bag)

REVIEW TEST

[1–3] 빈칸에 들어갈 알맞은 말을 고르시오.

1

I _____ in first grade now.

① am ② are ③ is
④ was ⑤ were

2

It _____ warm yesterday.

① am ② are ③ is
④ was ⑤ were

3

They _____ at a coffee shop last night.

① am ② are ③ is
④ was ⑤ were

서술형

[4–5] 빈칸에 알맞은 be동사를 써서 문장을 완성하시오.

4

Andy and I _____ in the same class this year.

5

Lina _____ a high school student two years ago.

서술형

[6–7] 빈칸에 There is 또는 There are를 넣어 문장을 완성하시오.

6

_____ a cat in the room.

7

_____ twenty questions on this test.

8 다음 중 밑줄 친 부분이 올바른 것은?

① It <u>were</u> a great trip.
② He <u>are</u> a good swimmer.
③ We <u>was</u> full after lunch.
④ His parents <u>is</u> proud of him.
⑤ Susan and Tom <u>are</u> scientists.

9 다음 문장에서 not이 들어갈 위치로 적절한 것은?

Bella ⓐ was ⓑ in ⓒ her ⓓ car ⓔ.

① ⓐ ② ⓑ ③ ⓒ ④ ⓓ ⑤ ⓔ

빈출

10 다음 중 대화가 자연스럽지 <u>않은</u> 것은?

① A: Is he busy with homework?
B: Yes, he is.
② A: Was Jenny sick yesterday?
B: Yes, she were.
③ A: Is there a camera on the desk?
B: Yes, there is.
④ A: Are your dogs big?
B: No, they aren't.
⑤ A: Were you with Minho last night?
B: No, I wasn't.

11 다음 중 긍정문을 부정문으로 <u>잘못</u> 고친 것은?

① This puzzle is difficult.
→ This puzzle isn't difficult.
② I am at the mall.
→ I amn't at the mall.
③ The boxes are heavy.
→ The boxes aren't heavy.
④ Mr. Smith was a soldier.
→ Mr. Smith wasn't a soldier.
⑤ We are good at tennis.
→ We're not good at tennis.

빈출

[12-13] 빈칸에 들어갈 말이 나머지 넷과 <u>다른</u> 것을 고르시오.

12 ① It _____ cold last week.
② I _____ 40 kg two years ago.
③ My sister _____ in Italy now.
④ _____ William at work yesterday?
⑤ There _____ a soccer game last
Sunday.

13 ① Jim _____ honest. He is a liar.
② It _____ Tuesday. It's Wednesday.
③ She _____ Korean. She is Chinese.
④ He _____ my friend. We're very
close.
⑤ Ms. Park _____ a teacher. She is a
writer.

[14-15] 다음 중 밑줄 친 부분이 잘못된 것을 고르시오.

14 ① <u>Is</u> Sarah in the hospital?
② <u>Are</u> you afraid of water?
③ <u>Is</u> the stores open today?
④ <u>Is</u> he interested in baseball?
⑤ <u>Are</u> your grandparents in London?

15 ① <u>There is</u> nice places in Egypt.
② <u>There are</u> two chairs in my room.
③ <u>There is</u> fish on the menu tonight.
④ <u>There are</u> some books on the sofa.
⑤ <u>There are</u> many parks in my town.

16 다음 우리말을 영어로 바르게 옮긴 것은?

거리에 많은 사람들이 있었다.

① There be many people on the street.
② There is many people on the street.
③ There are many people on the street.
④ There was many people on the street.
⑤ There were many people on the
street.

[17-18] 빈칸에 알맞은 be동사를 써서 대화를 완성하시오.

17
A: _____ this jacket yours?
B: Yes, it _____.

18
A: _____ we late for the train?
B: No, we _____. We have enough time.

[19-20] 다음 문장을 ( ) 안의 지시대로 바꿔 쓰시오.

19 This movie is funny. (의문문으로)

→ _____?

20 Jack and Bill are twins. (부정문으로)

→ _____.

[21-23] 우리말과 일치하도록 ( ) 안의 말을 이용하여 문장을 완성하시오.

21 무대 위에 마이크가 하나 있다. (there, a microphone)

→ _____ on the stage.

22 이 책은 두껍지만 지루하지 않다. (thick, boring)

→ This book _____, but it _____.

23 그들은 어제 수영장에 있었다. (in the swimming pool)

→ They _____ yesterday.

24 우리말과 일치하도록 주어진 조건에 맞게 문장을 완성하시오.

그 티켓은 비싸지 않았다.

〈조건〉 1. the ticket, expensive를 이용할 것
2. 줄임말을 쓸 것

→ _____.

고난도

25 다음 중 어법상 옳은 것을 모두 고르면?

① He were a great dancer.
② Are they honest people?
③ Tokyo aren't a small city.
④ Mom was a nurse ten years ago.
⑤ There is five people in my family.

26 다음 중 어법상 옳은 것으로 바르게 짝지어진 것은?

> a. The firefighter was brave.
> b. The baby is three months old.
> c. The smartphone were not cheap.
> d. There are honey in the jar.
> e. Is she your aunt?

① a, b, c   ② a, b, d   ③ a, b, e
④ b, c, d   ⑤ b, c, e

고난도

27 다음 중 어법상 옳은 것의 개수는?

> · Jenny were hungry this morning.
> · The girls was noisy on the subway.
> · Were they happy at the party?
> · There was a fire last night.
> · My hometown is not far from Seoul.

① 1개   ② 2개   ③ 3개
④ 4개   ⑤ 5개

서술형

[28-30] 밑줄 친 부분이 어법상 옳은지 판단하고, 틀리면 바르게 고치시오.

28 Claire and I <u>are</u> members of the band last year.

(O / X) _____

29 The dog <u>is</u> smart and cute.

(O / X) _____

30 There <u>is</u> a lot of books in my bag.

(O / X) _____

서술형   고난도

[31-33] 어법상 틀린 부분을 찾아 바르게 고치시오.

31 There was a great comedy show last night. Two comedians was on the show. They were very funny. (1개)

32 My English teacher are nice, and his class is interesting. (1개)

33 Busan is a nice city. There is beautiful beaches there. I were at the beach last summer. I had a great time there. (2개)

LET'S REVIEW

주요 예문을 다시 한번 확인하고, 우리말과 일치하도록 빈칸을 채우시오.

- I **am** a new student here. 나는 이곳에 새로 온 학생이다. Unit 01 - A
- My bag ¹_____ on the desk. 나의 가방은 책상 위에 있다. Unit 01 - A

- We **are** in the kitchen. 우리는 부엌에 있다. Unit 01 - B
- I **am** fourteen years old. 나는 열네 살이다.
  I ²_____ thirteen last year. 나는 작년에 열세 살이었다. Unit 01 - B

- **There is** a bank near here. 여기 근처에 은행이 하나 있다. Unit 01 - C
- There ³_____ thirty students in my class. 나의 반에는 30명의 학생들이 있다. Unit 01 - C
- There ⁴_____ a math test yesterday. 어제 수학 시험이 있었다. Unit 01 - C

- **He's** ⁵_____ in the office. 그는 사무실에 있지 않다. Unit 02 - A
- It **wasn't** cold yesterday. 어제는 춥지 않았다. Unit 02 - A
- We ⁶_____ at home last week. 우리는 지난주에 집에 없었다. Unit 02 - A

- A: **Is he** American? 그는 미국인이니?
  B: **Yes, he** ⁷_____. 응, 맞아. Unit 02 - B
- A: ⁸_____ she at the party yesterday? 그녀는 어제 파티에 있었니?
  B: **No, she wasn't.** 아니, 그렇지 않았어. Unit 02 - B

- **There aren't** many stars in the sky. 하늘에 별이 많이 있지 않다. Unit 02 - PLUS
- ⁹_____ a bank near here? 이 근처에 은행이 있나요? Unit 02 - PLUS

🔍 **Answers**

¹ is   ² was   ³ are   ⁴ was   ⁵ not   ⁶ weren't[were not]   ⁷ is   ⁸ Was   ⁹ Is there

ESSENTIAL RULES OF

ENGLISH GRAMMAR

CHAPTER
02

일반동사

일반동사는 be동사와 조동사를 제외한
모든 동사로, 주어의 동작이나 상태를
나타낸다.

UNIT 01 일반동사의 현재형

UNIT 02 일반동사의 과거형

UNIT 03 일반동사의 부정문

UNIT 04 일반동사의 의문문

01 일반동사의 현재형

일반동사의 현재형은 현재 사실이나 반복되는 습관을 나타낸다.

A 일반동사의 현재형

1 주어가 1인칭, 2인칭, 복수일 때는 동사원형을 쓰고, 3인칭 단수인 경우에는 「동사원형 + -(e)s」 형태로 쓴다.

I **like** Chinese food.
You **speak** Korean very well.
They **know** my phone number.
He **plays** baseball on Saturdays.

> *cf.* 과학적 사실이나 변함없는 진리를 나타낼 때에도 현재형을 쓴다.
> The earth **moves** around the sun.

2 일반동사의 3인칭 단수 현재형 만드는 법

규칙 변화	대부분의 동사	동사원형 + -s	comes eats sleeps plays sees speaks knows learns reads likes loves buys
	-o, -s, -ch, -sh, -x로 끝나는 동사	동사원형 + -es	does goes passes misses watches teaches washes brushes fixes mixes
	〈자음 + y〉로 끝나는 동사	y를 i로 고치고 + -es	cry → cries study → studies fly → flies try → tries
불규칙 변화	have → **has**		

He **reads** a lot of books.
Kevin **studies** English every day.
My sister **has** brown eyes.

CHECK UP 빈칸에 알맞은 말을 고르시오.

1 I often _____ my hands.
ⓐ wash   ⓑ washs   ⓒ washes

2 Jessica _____ her homework after school.
ⓐ do   ⓑ dos   ⓒ does

3 Daniel _____ bread in the morning.
ⓐ buy   ⓑ buys   ⓒ buies

PRACTICE

🔍 Answer Key p-3

STEP 1

( ) 안에서 알맞은 말을 고르시오.

1 We (eat, eats) cereal for breakfast.

2 The baby (cry, cries) every night.

3 You (have, has) a beautiful smile.

4 Emily (sleep, sleeps) on the bed.

5 My mom (work, works) for a bank.

6 They (go, goes) to church on Sundays.

STEP 2

( ) 안에 주어진 동사의 현재형을 써서 문장을 완성하시오.

1 I _____ my email every morning. (check)

2 Sandra _____ in the evening. (study)

3 He _____ his dog after dinner. (wash)

4 Eric and I _____ hip-hop music. (love)

5 Mr. Jones _____ science in a middle school. (teach)

6 My sister _____ mystery novels at night. (read)

STEP 3

빈칸에 알맞은 동사를 보기에서 골라 현재형으로 써서 문장을 완성하시오.

보기	speak	have	try	watch

1 Jane _____ lots of friends.

2 He _____ his best all the time.

3 My father _____ the news at nine o'clock.

4 Those students _____ English well.

STEP 4

우리말과 일치하도록 ( ) 안의 말을 이용하여 문장을 완성하시오.

1 나는 저 여자아이를 안다. (know, that girl)

→ I _____ _____ _____.

2 그들은 런던에 산다. (live, in London)

→ They _____ _____ _____.

3 Julie는 아침 8시에 학교에 간다. (go to school)

→ Julie _____ _____ _____ at eight in the morning.

UNIT

02 일반동사의 과거형

일반동사의 과거형은 과거에 일어난 일을 나타낸다.

A 일반동사의 과거형

1 주어의 수와 인칭에 관계없이 「동사원형 + -(e)d」 형태로 쓴다. 주로 yesterday, last night/week/ month/year, ~ ago 등의 과거를 나타내는 표현과 함께 쓴다.

We **watched** a movie *yesterday*.
Paul **lived** in New York *two years ago*.

2 일반동사의 과거형 만드는 법

<table>
<tr><td rowspan="4">규칙
변화</td><td>대부분의 동사</td><td>동사원형 + -ed</td><td>watched talked listened walked
wanted started ended rained</td></tr>
<tr><td>〈자음 + e〉로
끝나는 동사</td><td>동사원형 + -d</td><td>lived moved liked loved smiled
danced invited changed saved</td></tr>
<tr><td>〈자음 + y〉로
끝나는 동사</td><td>y를 i로 고치고
+ -ed</td><td>cry → cried   study → studied
try → tried   worry → worried</td></tr>
<tr><td>〈단모음 + 단자음〉
으로 끝나는 동사</td><td>자음을 한 번 더
쓰고 + -ed</td><td>stop → stopped   plan → planned
chat → chatted   drop → dropped</td></tr>
<tr><td rowspan="2">불규칙
변화</td><td>현재형과 과거형이
같은 동사</td><td colspan="2">put → put   cut → cut   hit → hit   read → read</td></tr>
<tr><td>현재형과 과거형이
다른 동사</td><td colspan="2">do → did   have → had   come → came
go → went   tell → told   sleep → slept
eat → ate   get → got   speak → spoke
run → ran   see → saw   make → made
meet → met   drink → drank   take → took
write → wrote give → gave   hear → heard
bring → brought teach → taught buy → bought</td></tr>
</table>

Mary **studied** for the test last night.
He **cut** the paper with scissors.
I **bought** some flowers for Kate.

 CHECK UP   빈칸에 알맞은 말을 고르시오.

1 I _____ here last month.
ⓐ move   ⓑ moves   ⓒ moved

2 Nancy _____ to school this morning.
ⓐ walk   ⓑ walking   ⓒ walked

3 They _____ to Brazil a year ago.
ⓐ go   ⓑ went   ⓒ goed

PRACTICE

🔍 Answer Key p-3

STEP 1

( ) 안에서 알맞은 말을 고르시오.

1 Andrew (speaks, spoke) to her yesterday.

2 She (put, putted) sugar in her coffee.

3 Mia (make, made) a sandwich for me.

4 He (sleeps, slept) on the sofa last night.

5 Kelly (wash, washed) her hair this morning.

STEP 2

( ) 안에 주어진 동사의 과거형을 써서 문장을 완성하시오.

1 Ted _____ a trip to Seoul last month. (plan)

2 I _____ lunch thirty minutes ago. (have)

3 She _____ home yesterday. (come)

4 Jenny _____ cookies last weekend. (bake)

5 My father _____ a new car last year. (buy)

6 He _____ Korean food for the first time. (try)

STEP 3

빈칸에 알맞은 동사를 보기에서 골라 과거형으로 써서 문장을 완성하시오.

보기	go	finish	invite	worry

1 The doctor _____ about my health.

2 I _____ my homework before dinner.

3 Dongho _____ me to his birthday party.

4 We _____ to the mountains last Saturday.

STEP 4

우리말과 일치하도록 ( ) 안의 말을 이용하여 문장을 완성하시오.

1 나는 어제 Ann을 만났다. (meet, Ann)

→ I _____ _____ yesterday.

2 그는 2년 전에 학교에서 영어를 가르쳤다. (teach, English)

→ He _____ _____ at a school two years ago.

3 Mike는 오늘 아침에 이메일 한 통을 받았다. (get, an email)

→ Mike _____ _____ _____ this morning.

4 우리는 어젯밤에 축구 경기를 봤다. (watch, the soccer game)

→ We _____ _____ _____ _____ last night.

일반동사의 부정문

일반동사의 부정문은 일반동사 앞에 do/does/did + not을 써서 나타낸다.

A 일반동사 현재형의 부정문

주어	부정문
1인칭, 2인칭, 복수	don't[do not] + 동사원형
3인칭 단수	doesn't[does not] + 동사원형

I **don't drink** coffee.
We **don't know** his address.
They **do not use** bad words.

Dan **doesn't speak** French.
She **does not keep** her promises.

B 일반동사 과거형의 부정문

주어	부정문
모든 인칭	didn't[did not] + 동사원형

We **didn't eat** breakfast this morning.
Steve **did not play** games last night.

cf. 일상 대화에서는 줄임말인 don't, doesn't, didn't를 많이 사용한다.
James **doesn't** exercise.
I **didn't** visit Tony's office yesterday.

CHECK UP 빈칸에 알맞은 말을 고르시오.

1 I _____ watch TV.
ⓐ am not　　ⓑ don't　　ⓒ doesn't

2 Donna _____ like cats.
ⓐ isn't　　ⓑ don't　　ⓒ doesn't

3 They didn't _____ me the truth.
ⓐ tell　　ⓑ tells　　ⓒ told

4 We _____ go to the concert yesterday.
ⓐ don't　　ⓑ doesn't　　ⓒ didn't

PRACTICE

Answer Key p.4

STEP 1

빈칸에 don't와 doesn't 중 알맞은 것을 쓰시오.

1 I _____ eat carrots.

2 She _____ understand Korean.

3 They _____ believe in ghosts.

4 Mark _____ have a class today.

5 The post office _____ open on Sundays.

6 Ms. Green _____ work here.

STEP 2

( ) 안의 말을 이용하여 과거형 부정문을 완성하시오.

1 It _____ yesterday. (rain)
It was sunny.

2 I _____ Michelle. (call)
I sent her a text message.

3 Jake _____ the math test. (pass)
He failed it.

STEP 3

빈칸에 알맞은 말을 보기에서 골라 ( ) 안의 동사와 함께 써서 부정문을 완성하시오.

보기	don't doesn't didn't

1 We waited for him, but he _____. (come)

2 I _____ big cities. They are too crowded. (like)

3 That store is a bakery. It _____ vegetables. (sell)

STEP 4

우리말과 일치하도록 ( ) 안의 말을 이용하여 문장을 완성하시오.

1 이 컴퓨터는 작동하지 않는다. (work)

→ This computer _____ _____.

2 나는 시끄러운 음악을 듣지 않는다. (listen)

→ I _____ _____ to loud music.

3 Lisa는 오늘 아침에 버스를 타지 않았다. (take)

→ Lisa _____ _____ a bus this morning.

4 그들은 교복을 입지 않는다. (wear)

→ They _____ _____ school uniforms.

UNIT 04 일반동사의 의문문

일반동사의 의문문은 주어 앞에 Do/Does/Did를 써서 나타낸다.

A 일반동사 현재형의 의문문

주어	의문문	긍정의 대답	부정의 대답
1인칭, 2인칭, 복수	Do + 주어 + 동사원형?	Yes, 주어 + do.	No, 주어 + don't.
3인칭 단수	Does + 주어 + 동사원형?	Yes, 주어 + does.	No, 주어 + doesn't.

A: **Do you wear** glasses?
B: **Yes, I do. / No, I don't.**

A: **Do his parents live** in Sydney?
B: **Yes, they do. / No, they don't.**

A: **Does Lucy go** to middle school?
B: **Yes, she does. / No, she doesn't.**

B 일반동사 과거형의 의문문

주어	의문문	긍정의 대답	부정의 대답
모든 인칭	Did + 주어 + 동사원형?	Yes, 주어 + did.	No, 주어 + didn't.

A: **Did we make** a mistake?
B: **Yes, we did. / No, we didn't.**

A: **Did he go** to the hospital?
B: **Yes, he did. / No, he didn't.**

CHECK UP　빈칸에 알맞은 말을 고르시오.

1 Does Betty _____ soccer?
　ⓐ like　　　ⓑ likes　　　ⓒ liked

2 _____ you need help?
　ⓐ Are　　　ⓑ Do　　　ⓒ Does

3 _____ they meet Alex yesterday?
　ⓐ Do　　　ⓑ Does　　　ⓒ Did

4 _____ he work at a hotel?
　ⓐ Is　　　ⓑ Do　　　ⓒ Does

PRACTICE

🔍 Answer Key p.4

STEP 1

빈칸에 Do와 Does 중 알맞은 것을 쓰시오.

1 _____ Sarah have a daughter?

2 _____ you listen to the radio?

3 _____ this bus go to city hall?

4 _____ they study in the same class?

5 _____ your brother come home late?

STEP 2

( ) 안의 말을 이용하여 대화를 완성하시오.

1 A: _____ you _____ the party last night? (enjoy)
B: Yes, I did. It was really fun.

2 A: _____ Ally _____ to New York last summer? (go)
B: No, she didn't. She was busy.

3 A: _____ they _____ baseball last Saturday? (play)
B: No, they didn't. It rained.

STEP 3

다음 질문에 대한 대답을 완성하시오.

1 A: Do I speak too fast?　　　　　　　　B: No, _____ _____.

2 A: Does she drive a car?　　　　　　　　B: Yes, _____ _____.

3 A: Did you have a good weekend?　　　　B: Yes, _____ _____.

4 A: Did they visit the museum yesterday?　B: No, _____ _____.

STEP 4

우리말과 일치하도록 보기에서 알맞은 동사를 골라 의문문을 완성하시오.

보기	buy	like	sing	plant

1 Susan은 노래를 잘 하니?

→ _____ _____ _____ well?

2 너는 멕시코 음식을 좋아하니?

→ _____ _____ _____ Mexican food?

3 그는 그 책을 샀니?

→ _____ _____ _____ the book?

4 그들은 작년에 나무를 심었니?

→ _____ _____ _____ a tree last year?

GRAMMAR FOR WRITING

A 우리말과 일치하도록 ( ) 안의 말을 이용하여 문장을 완성하시오.

1 그는 카메라를 가지고 있지 않다. (have a camera)

→ He _____.

2 그 가게는 9시에 문을 연다. (open at nine)

→ The store _____.

3 그들은 어젯밤에 일찍 잠자리에 들지 않았다. (go to bed)

→ They _____ early last night.

4 나는 의자에 발을 부딪쳤다. (hit my foot)

→ I _____ on the chair.

5 Jack은 스페인어를 말하니? (speak)

→ _____ Spanish?

6 나는 그의 이름이 기억나지 않는다. (remember his name)

→ I _____.

7 너는 콘서트 표를 샀니? (you, buy)

→ _____ the concert tickets?

B 우리말과 일치하도록 ( ) 안에 주어진 말을 바르게 배열하시오.

1 그녀는 돈을 저축하지 않는다. (money, save, doesn't)

→ She _____.

2 우리는 저 TV 프로그램을 보지 않는다. (not, watch, do, that TV show)

→ We _____.

3 Jane은 Brian이랑 싸웠니? (Jane, did, fight with)

→ _____ Brian?

4 나는 화요일마다 피아노 레슨을 받는다. (piano lessons, I, take)

→ _____ on Tuesdays.

5 그들은 집에 애완동물이 있니? (pets, they, do, have)

→ _____ at home?

6 Emily는 지난 금요일에 할머니를 방문했다. (her grandmother, visited, Emily)

→ _____ last Friday.

C 다음은 지원이가 매일 하는 일들을 나타낸 표이다. 주어진 말을 이용하여 문장을 완성하시오.

7:00 a.m.	8:00 a.m.	12:00 p.m.	4:30 p.m.	5:00 p.m.	6:00 p.m.	9:00 p.m.

get up		have lunch		watch TV		study English

| | go to school | | come home | | have dinner | |

1 Jiwon _____ at seven in the morning.

2 Jiwon _____ at eight o'clock.

3 Jiwon _____ at noon.

4 Jiwon _____ at 4:30 p.m. in the afternoon.

5 Jiwon _____ at 5:00 p.m.

6 Jiwon _____ at nine o'clock.

D 그림을 보고 ( ) 안의 말을 이용하여 대화를 완성하시오.

1	2	3	4

1 A: Is Kevin good at tennis?
   B: No, he isn't. He _____ sports. (not/like)

2 A: _____ brothers or sisters? (have)
   B: No, she doesn't. She is an only child.

3 A: You look tired.
   B: Yes. I _____ well last night. (not/sleep)

4 A: _____ the novel yesterday? (read)
   B: Yes, I did. It was interesting.

1 다음 중 동사의 3인칭 단수 현재형이 <u>잘못</u> 연결된 것은?

① see – sees   ② have – has

③ pass – passes   ④ learn – learns

⑤ fly – flys

2 다음 중 두 단어의 관계가 나머지 넷과 <u>다른</u> 하나는?

① chat – chatted   ② see – saw

③ run – runs   ④ cry – cried

⑤ cut – cut

[3-5] 빈칸에 들어갈 알맞은 말을 고르시오.

3

| _____ likes chocolate. |

① I   ② We   ③ Sarah

④ They   ⑤ Joe and Jane

4

| _____ Tim exercise every day? |

① Is   ② Was   ③ Were

④ Do   ⑤ Does

5

| I _____ in the game yesterday. |

① am not play   ② wasn't play

③ don't play   ④ doesn't play

⑤ didn't play

[6-8] 빈칸에 들어갈 말이 바르게 짝지어진 것을 고르시오.

6

| • Karen _____(A)_____ to school by bus. |
| • We _____(B)_____ a walk after dinner. |

    (A)   (B)

① go   ……   take

② go   ……   takes

③ go   ……   took

④ goes   ……   take

⑤ goes   ……   takes

7

| • He _____(A)_____ eat vegetables. |
| • _____(B)_____ you like animals? |

    (A)   (B)

① don't   ……   Do

② don't   ……   Does

③ doesn't   ……   Do

④ doesn't   ……   Does

⑤ didn't   ……   Does

8

| • I _____(A)_____ my hands ten minutes ago. |
| • They _____(B)_____ to the airport by taxi last night. |

    (A)   (B)

① wash   ……   go

② washes   ……   goes

③ washes   ……   went

④ washed   ……   go

⑤ washed   ……   went

[9-10] 다음 밑줄 친 부분을 바르게 고치시오.

9
Every night, Mina ⓐ take a shower. She also ⓑ brush her teeth.

ⓐ _____ ⓑ _____

13
① I don't know his favorite movie.
② Does Kevin go to the gym often?
③ Jane didn't turn off the computer.
④ Did you came to Korea last year?
⑤ We painted the door two weeks ago.

10
We ⓐ have a soccer game last Friday. Our team did our best, but we ⓑ don't win.

ⓐ _____ ⓑ _____

[14-15] 빈칸에 알맞은 말을 써서 대화를 완성하시오.

14
A: Alice, did you get my text message?
B: No, _____ _____.

15
A: Do they live near your house?
B: No, _____ _____. They moved to another city.

11 빈칸에 들어갈 말을 각각 쓰시오.

• I ___ⓐ___ drink coffee, but I drink green tea.
• Colin ___ⓑ___ live in Seoul. He lives in New York.

ⓐ _____ ⓑ _____

16 대화를 읽고 ( ) 안의 말을 이용하여 글을 완성하시오.

Emma: Did you bring a pen?
Tom: Oh, I forgot. Do you have one for me?
Emma: Yes. Here you are.

↓

Tom ___ⓐ___ (bring) a pen yesterday. Emma ___ⓑ___ (give) a pen to him.

ⓐ _____ ⓑ _____

[12-13] 다음 중 밑줄 친 부분이 잘못된 것을 고르시오.

12
① Amy has long hair.
② Do you keep a diary?
③ I had a hamburger for lunch.
④ Did you finish your homework?
⑤ Danny swims in the sea last week.

17

Nicole은 새 원피스를 샀니?

① Do Nicole buy a new dress?
② Does Nicole buy a new dress?
③ Does Nicole buys a new dress?
④ Did Nicole buy a new dress?
⑤ Did Nicole bought a new dress?

18

그는 수학을 좋아하지 않는다.

① He don't like math.
② He didn't like math.
③ He doesn't like math.
④ Doesn't he like math.
⑤ He doesn't likes math.

19 다음 질문에 대한 대답으로 알맞지 <u>않은</u> 것은?

Did you put the key on the table?

① Yes, I do.
② Yes, I did.
③ No, I didn't.
④ No, I put it in my bag.
⑤ Yes, I put it on the table.

서술형

[20-21] (   ) 안의 말을 이용하여 문장을 완성하시오.

20

My father smoked last year, but he _____ now. (smoke)

21

It _____ heavily last night, but it _____ this morning. (rain, stop)

서술형

[22-24] 우리말과 일치하도록 (   ) 안의 말을 이용하여 문장을 완성하시오.

22

Jeremy는 매일 그의 방을 청소한다. (clean his room)

→ Jeremy _____ every day.

23

나는 지난주에 책을 한 권 읽었다. (read a book)

→ I _____ last week.

24

그녀는 오늘 학교에 오지 않았다. (come to school)

→ She _____ today.

고난도

25 다음 중 어법상 옳은 것을 모두 고르면?

① My smartphone doesn't work.
② Did Alice met Nick last night?
③ My grandmother cook very well.
④ We have a good time last Friday.
⑤ Kelly bought a new schoolbag last week.

26 다음 중 어법상 옳은 것으로 바르게 짝지어진 것은?

> a. Mr. Finch don't teach English.
> b. Do we need eggs for the salad?
> c. I put some milk in my coffee.
> d. Harry not played tennis yesterday.
> e. Did they go to the beach together?

① a, e   ② b, c   ③ b, c, d
④ b, c, e   ⑤ c, d, e

27 다음 중 어법상 옳은 것의 개수는?

> • This shirt does not has pockets.
> • Did Carry like your present?
> • I visited Singapore last month.
> • Do you learn Chinese now?
> • Santa Claus comes to town every Christmas Eve.

① 1개   ② 2개   ③ 3개
④ 4개   ⑤ 5개

[28-30] 밑줄 친 부분이 어법상 옳은지 판단하고, 틀리면 바르게 고치시오.

28 Does he <u>walks</u> fast?

(O / X) _____

29 I didn't <u>took</u> my medicine this morning.

(O / X) _____

30 My mom <u>fixs</u> everything in our house.

(O / X) _____

[31-33] 어법상 틀린 부분을 찾아 바르게 고치시오.

31 My sister and I went to a nice restaurant last weekend. We eat lots of delicious food there. (1개)

32 I doesn't get letters often. But yesterday, I find a letter in my mailbox. It was from my friend Jessica. (2개)

33 A: Do you have a blog, Dave?
B: Yes, I do. I writes my blog every day. Yesterday I spent five hours on it.
A: Five hours?
B: Yes. I go to bed very late. And I didn't do my homework. (2개)

LET'S REVIEW

주요 예문을 다시 한번 확인하고, 우리말과 일치하도록 빈칸을 채우시오.

- I **like** Chinese food. 나는 중화요리를 좋아한다. `Unit 01 - A`
- They [1]_____ my phone number. 그들은 내 전화번호를 안다. `Unit 01 - A`
- He **plays** baseball on Saturdays. 그는 토요일마다 야구를 한다. `Unit 01 - A`
- My sister [2]_____ brown eyes. 내 여동생은 갈색 눈을 가지고 있다. `Unit 01 - A`

- We **watched** a movie yesterday. 우리는 어제 영화를 보았다. `Unit 02 - A`
- Mary [3]_____ for the test last night. Mary는 어젯밤에 시험공부를 했다. `Unit 02 - A`
- He [4]_____ the paper with scissors. 그는 가위로 종이를 잘랐다. `Unit 02 - A`
- I **bought** some flowers for Kate. 나는 Kate를 위해 꽃을 조금 샀다. `Unit 02 - A`

- I **don't drink** coffee. 나는 커피를 마시지 않는다. `Unit 03 - A`
- She [5]_____ **keep** her promises. 그녀는 약속을 지키지 않는다. `Unit 03 - A`

- We [6]_____ **eat** breakfast this morning. 우리는 오늘 아침에 아침을 먹지 않았다. `Unit 03 - B`
- Steve **did not play** games last night. Steve는 어젯밤에 게임을 하지 않았다. `Unit 03 - B`

- A: **Do you wear** glasses? 너는 안경을 끼니?
  B: **No, I don't.** 아니, 그렇지 않아. `Unit 04 - A`
- A: [7]_____ **Lucy go** to middle school? Lucy는 중학교에 다니니?
  B: **Yes, she** [8]_____. 응, 맞아. `Unit 04 - A`

- A: [9]_____ **we make** a mistake? 우리가 실수했니?
  B: **No, we didn't.** 아니, 안 했어. `Unit 04 - B`

🔍 **Answers**

[1] know [2] has [3] studied [4] cut [5] doesn't[does not] [6] didn't[did not] [7] Does [8] does
[9] Did

38

ESSENTIAL RULES OF
ENGLISH GRAMMAR

CHAPTER
03

조동사

조동사는 동사에 능력, 허가, 추측, 의무 등의
의미를 더해주는 말이다.

UNIT 01 can, may

UNIT 02 must, have to, should

UNIT 01 can, may

조동사는 주어의 인칭이나 수에 따라 형태가 변하지 않으며 뒤에 항상 동사원형을 쓴다.

A can

1 ~할 수 있다(능력, 가능)

Daniel **can** swim.
I **can't[cannot]** write Chinese characters.
Can you cook spaghetti?

① can의 과거형은 could이고, 과거 부정형은 couldn't[could not]이다.
Lisa **could** read at the age of three.
We **couldn't** fix the car.

① be able to는 can(~할 수 있다)과 같은 의미를 나타내며, 부정형은 be not able to이다.
Steve **is able to** speak five languages.
　　　= can
I**'m not able to** open this file.
　　= can't

2 ~해도 좋다(허가)

You **can** come in.
A: **Can** I use your pen?
B: Of course. / Sorry, you can't.

B may

1 ~일지도 모른다(추측)

The rumor **may** be true.
He **may not** know the password.

2 ~해도 좋다(허가, can보다 정중한 표현)

You **may** sit here.
A: **May** I speak to Lily now?
B: Sure. / I'm sorry, but you may not.

CHECK UP　빈칸에 알맞은 말을 고르시오.

1 _____ you play the piano well?
ⓐ Are　　　　ⓑ Can　　　ⓒ May

2 I _____ be late. The traffic is bad.
ⓐ can't　　　ⓑ may　　　ⓒ am able to

PRACTICE

🔍 Answer Key p-5

STEP 1

밑줄 친 부분에 해당하는 의미를 보기에서 고르시오.

보기	ⓐ ~할 수 있다	ⓑ ~해도 좋다	ⓒ ~일지도 모른다

1 Ryan can run very fast. _____

2 She may be in the kitchen. _____

3 Can I borrow your notebook? _____

4 May I use the bathroom? _____

5 Can you go to the concert tonight? _____

6 Alice may live in San Francisco. _____

STEP 2

can 또는 can't와 ( ) 안의 말을 이용하여 문장을 완성하시오.

1 It's too noisy outside. I _____. (sleep)

2 I'm thirsty. _____ I _____ some water? (have)

3 Brian is smart. He _____ difficult math problems. (solve)

4 Sue is a great painter. She _____ beautiful pictures. (draw)

STEP 3

may 또는 may not과 보기의 말을 이용하여 문장을 완성하시오.

보기	be	see	come

1 I can't find my umbrella. It _____ in the car.

2 Christine is sick. She _____ to school today.

3 A: _____ I _____ your ticket?

   B: Sure. Here you are.

STEP 4

우리말과 일치하도록 ( ) 안의 말을 이용하여 문장을 완성하시오.

1 나는 토요일에 너를 방문할 수 없다. (visit)

   → I _____ _____ you on Saturday.

2 제가 이 컴퓨터를 사용해도 될까요? (I, use)

   → _____ _____ _____ this computer?

3 Tom은 맨 위 선반에 닿을 수 없었다. (reach)

   → Tom _____ _____ the top shelf.

4 나는 그 무거운 상자들을 들 수 있다. (lift)

   → I _____ _____ _____ _____ the heavy boxes.

UNIT 02

must, have to, should

A must

1 '~해야 한다(의무)'의 의미이다. 부정형인 must not은 '~해서는 안 된다(강한 금지)'라는 의미이다.

I **must** go to the dentist now.
You **must not** drive fast in the school zone.

2 ~임에 틀림없다(강한 추측)

Jack didn't have lunch. He **must** be hungry now.
Kate reads books all the time. She **must** love books.

> *cf.* '~일 리가 없다(강한 부정의 추측)'의 의미를 나타낼 때는 must not이 아니라 can't[cannot]를 쓴다.
> It *must* be true. (그것은 사실임에 틀림없다.)
> ↔ It **can't** be true. (그것은 사실일 리가 없다.)

B have to

must(~해야 한다)와 같은 의미이다. 주어가 3인칭 단수일 때는 has to를 쓴다. 부정형인 don't/doesn't have to는 '~할 필요가 없다'라는 의미이다.

You **have to** stay here.
Nancy **has to** clean the classroom.
I **don't have to** wear glasses.

C should

'~해야 한다'의 의미로 의무, 충고, 제안 등을 나타낸다. must보다는 강제성이 약하다.

You **should** turn off your cell phone in class.
You **shouldn't[should not]** believe him.

 빈칸에 알맞은 말을 고르시오.

1 My computer doesn't work. I _____ to fix it.

ⓐ must   ⓑ have   ⓒ should

2 You _____ eat fast food. It's bad for you.

ⓐ must   ⓑ have to   ⓒ shouldn't

3 This book _____ be Jane's. It has her name on it.

ⓐ must   ⓑ must not   ⓒ shouldn't

4 She has enough time. She _____ run.

ⓐ has to   ⓑ don't have to   ⓒ doesn't have to

PRACTICE

Answer Key p-5

STEP 1

( ) 안에서 알맞은 말을 고르시오.

1 They should (follow, followed) the rules.

2 You must (not be, be not) late again.

3 Susan (have to, has to) come home by 7:00 p.m.

4 You (don't have to, have not to) wait for me.

5 He (must, cannot) be at the mall. I just saw him at school!

6 You (must not, don't have to) tell this to anyone. It's a secret.

STEP 2

빈칸에 have to 또는 has to를 써서 문장을 완성하시오.

1 We _____ take vitamins every day.

2 Dad _____ work this weekend.

3 You _____ be careful with scissors.

4 She _____ leave early tomorrow.

5 Kevin _____ buy a new T-shirt.

STEP 3

must not 또는 don't have to와 ( ) 안의 말을 이용하여 문장을 완성하시오. (필요하면 형태를 바꿀 것)

1 The floor is slippery. You _____. (run)

2 You can delete that email. You _____ it. (keep)

3 The light is red. You _____ the street. (cross)

4 Emily doesn't have a class tomorrow. She _____ early. (get up)

STEP 4

우리말과 일치하도록 보기에서 알맞은 말을 골라 ( ) 안의 말과 함께 써서 문장을 완성하시오.

보기	should	doesn't have to	should not

1 Tim은 그녀에게 미안하다고 말해야 한다. (say)

→ Tim _____ sorry to her.

2 너는 시간을 낭비해서는 안 된다. (waste)

→ You _____ your time.

3 그는 나를 도와줄 필요가 없다. (help)

→ He _____ me.

GRAMMAR FOR WRITING

A 우리말과 일치하도록 ( ) 안의 말을 이용하여 문장을 완성하시오.

1 Paul은 행복한 것이 틀림없다. (be, happy)

→ Paul _____ .

2 제가 당신의 우산을 빌려도 될까요? (I, borrow)

→ _____ your umbrella?

3 너는 그 질문에 대답할 수 있니? (you, answer)

→ _____ the question?

4 그녀는 회의에 늦을지도 모른다. (be late)

→ She _____ for the meeting.

5 너는 밤에 소음을 내서는 안 된다. (make noise)

→ You _____ at night.

6 너는 안전벨트를 매야 한다. (wear a seat belt)

→ You _____ .

7 우리는 팁을 남길 필요가 없다. (leave a tip)

→ We _____ .

B 우리말과 일치하도록 ( ) 안에 주어진 말을 바르게 배열하시오.

1 너는 첼로를 연주할 수 있니? (you, play, can, the cello)

→ _____ ?

2 Jessica가 거짓말쟁이일 리가 없다. (can't, a liar, be)

→ Jessica _____ .

3 제가 이 신발을 신어봐도 되나요? (I, try on, may, these shoes)

→ _____ ?

4 Nancy는 수화를 사용할 수 있다. (able, to, is, use)

→ Nancy _____ sign language.

5 너는 남동생과 싸워서는 안 된다. (fight with, should, your brother, not)

→ You _____ .

6 나는 오늘 Gary에게 전화해야 한다. (have, I, Gary, call, to)

→ _____ today.

C 보기에서 알맞은 조동사를 골라 ( ) 안의 말과 함께 써서 대화를 완성하시오. (단, 한 번씩만 쓸 것)

보기	must	can	have to	may

1 A: I don't have enough money for that book!
B: It's okay. I _____ it for you. (buy)

2 A: _____ the window? (I, open)
B: Yes, of course.

3 A: Do you know that boy?
B: He _____ Helen's brother. He looks like her. (be)

4 A: The air is bad these days.
B: Yes. _____ a mask. (you, wear)

D 그림을 보고 보기에서 알맞은 말을 골라 ( ) 안의 조동사와 함께 써서 문장을 완성하시오.

보기	ride a bike	put trash in the bin
	bring your pets	pick the flowers

Park Rules

1 You _____. (can)

2 You _____. (must)

3 You _____. (have to)

4 You _____. (should)

REVIEW TEST

[1-3] 다음 밑줄 친 부분과 의미가 같은 것을 고르시오.

1

You <u>may</u> go home now.

① are   ② do   ③ can
④ must   ⑤ should

2

You <u>must</u> come to class on time.

① can   ② could   ③ may
④ have to   ⑤ are able to

3

Andrew <u>can</u> do magic tricks.

① may   ② must   ③ should
④ has to   ⑤ is able to

[4-5] 빈칸에 들어갈 알맞은 말을 고르시오.

4

A: _____ I use the bathroom?
B: Sure. It's over there.

① Am   ② Do   ③ Can
④ Must   ⑤ Should

5

This computer doesn't work now. It _____ have a problem.

① can't   ② has to   ③ may
④ is able to   ⑤ shouldn't

6 빈칸에 공통으로 들어갈 말은?

· We _____ protect the earth.
· Joe always talks about baseball. He _____ like baseball.

① can   ② may   ③ must
④ have to   ⑤ is able to

서술형

[7-9] 우리말과 일치하도록 빈칸에 알맞은 조동사를 쓰시오.

7

Jason의 팀이 경기를 이겼다. 그는 행복할 것이 틀림없다.

→ Jason's team won the game. He _____ be happy.

8

Jenna는 다리를 다쳤다. 그녀는 잘 걸을 수 없다.

→ Jenna hurt her leg. She _____ walk very well.

9

너는 그 개를 조심해야 한다. 널 물지도 모른다.

→ You should be careful of the dog. He _____ bite you.

[10-12] 밑줄 친 부분의 의미가 나머지 넷과 다른 것을 고르시오.

10 ① <u>Can</u> you make Korean food?
② <u>Can</u> I stay in your house?
③ <u>Can</u> they get here by 2:00 p.m.?
④ He <u>can</u> play tennis very well.
⑤ I <u>can</u> find the information on the internet.

11 ① He <u>must</u> listen to his father.
② I <u>must</u> clean my room. It's a mess.
③ You <u>must</u> go to bed now. It's late.
④ This book <u>must</u> be interesting. Everybody likes it.
⑤ You <u>must</u> bring your passport.

12 ① They <u>may</u> be busy.
② He <u>may</u> call you tonight.
③ Tony <u>may</u> have the key.
④ You <u>may</u> take a break.
⑤ Judy <u>may</u> be with her friends.

13 다음 중 밑줄 친 부분이 잘못된 것은?

① You <u>can watch</u> TV after dinner.
② Peter <u>may join</u> our tennis club.
③ Sam <u>have to read</u> the report again.
④ I <u>must save</u> money for the future.
⑤ You <u>should wait</u> in line here.

14 다음 중 대화가 자연스럽지 <u>않은</u> 것은?

① A: May I see your picture?
B: Yes. You may see it.
② A: Do we have to pay now?
B: No, you can pay later.
③ A: Can I borrow your bike?
B: Sorry, you can't.
④ A: Should I watch that movie?
B: Yes, you should. It's great.
⑤ A: Must I wear a suit today?
B: No, you must not. You can wear jeans.

[15-17] 빈칸에 알맞은 말을 보기에서 골라 문장을 완성하시오. (단, 한 번씩만 쓸 것)

보기	must not	can't	don't have to

15 You _____ throw trash on the street.

16 You _____ buy a ticket. The concert is free.

17 Mr. Smith _____ see you now. He is in a meeting.

18 빈칸에 들어갈 말로 알맞지 <u>않은</u> 것은?

A: I didn't eat anything today.
B: Oh, really? _____.

① You must be very hungry.
② You can't be very hungry.
③ You should eat some food.
④ You have to eat some food.
⑤ I can cook some food for you.

19 다음 우리말을 영어로 바르게 옮긴 것은?

나는 시험을 통과하지 못할지도 모른다.

① I can't pass the exam.
② I may not pass the exam.
③ I must not pass the exam.
④ I shouldn't pass the exam.
⑤ I don't have to pass the exam.

서술형
[20-22] 우리말과 일치하도록 밑줄 친 부분을 바르게 고치
시오.

20 그는 그의 어머니를 돌봐드려야 한다.
→ He <u>have to take care of</u> his mother.

_____

21 우리는 달걀을 살 필요가 없다.
→ We <u>must not buy</u> eggs.

_____

22 나는 10월에 유럽에 갈지도 모른다.
→ I <u>should go</u> to Europe in October.

_____

서술형
[23-24] 우리말과 일치하도록 ( ) 안의 말을 이용하여 문장
을 완성하시오.

23 우리는 우리의 개를 찾을 수 없었다. (can, find)

→ We _____ our
dog.

24 그 식당은 훌륭한 것이 틀림없다. 그곳은 항상 붐빈다.
(must, great)

→ The restaurant _____.
It's always busy.

서술형
25 우리말과 일치하도록 주어진 조건에 맞게 문장을 완성하
시오.

우리는 물을 낭비해서는 안 된다.

〈조건〉 1. should, waste, water를 이용할 것
2. 4단어로 쓸 것

→ _____.

26 다음 중 어법상 옳은 것을 모두 고르면?

① May I leave early today?
② You should not enter the room.
③ You may cooks dinner tonight.
④ She can able to pass the test.
⑤ You must don't be late for the class.

27 다음 중 어법상 옳은 것으로 바르게 짝지어진 것은?

> a. You should take a taxi.
> b. He doesn't able to move the table.
> c. My wallet must be in my bag.
> d. Mr. Reese may be angry with us.
> e. She doesn't have to cleaning her room.

① a, b, c   ② a, c, d   ③ a, c, e
④ b, d, e   ⑤ c, d, e

고난도

28 다음 중 어법상 옳은 것의 개수는?

> • I can arrive on time.
> • Claire and Sue has to study all night.
> • This dress may not be comfortable.
> • The birthday cake don't have to be big.
> • Can your brother drive a car?

① 1개   ② 2개   ③ 3개
④ 4개   ⑤ 5개

서술형

[29-31] 밑줄 친 부분이 어법상 옳은지 판단하고, 틀리면 바르게 고치시오.

29 You <u>can</u> take a seat.

(O / X) _____

30 Sam may <u>come not</u> to the party.

(O / X) _____

31 She <u>doesn't has to</u> explain the rule.

(O / X) _____

서술형 고난도

[32-34] 어법상 틀린 부분을 찾아 바르게 고치시오.

32 In the library, you must are quiet. And you cannot use your phone. (1개)

33 You should say not bad things about Jamie. It may hurt his feelings. You have to say sorry to him. (1개)

34 A: Amy didn't come to school today. She may is sick.
B: Oh, I should call her. Do you know her phone number?
A: No, I don't. But Sarah must knows it. They are best friends. (2개)

LET'S REVIEW

주요 예문을 다시 한번 확인하고, 우리말과 일치하도록 빈칸을 채우시오.

- Daniel **can** swim. Daniel은 수영할 수 있다. Unit 01 - A
- [1]_____ you cook spaghetti? 너는 스파게티를 요리할 수 있니? Unit 01 - A
- We **couldn't** fix the car. 우리는 그 차를 수리할 수 없었다. Unit 01 - A
- Steve **is** [2]_____ **to** speak five languages. Steve는 5개 국어를 말할 수 있다. Unit 01 - A
- You **can** come in. 너는 들어와도 좋다. Unit 01 - A
- **Can** I use your pen? 내가 당신의 펜을 써도 될까요? Unit 01 - A

- The rumor [3]_____ be true. 그 소문은 사실일지도 모른다. Unit 01 - B
- You [4]_____ sit here. 너는 여기 앉아도 좋다. Unit 01 - B

- I **must** go to the dentist now. 나는 지금 치과에 가야 한다. Unit 02 - A
- You [5]_____ drive fast in the school zone. 너는 스쿨존에서 빨리 운전하면 안 된다. Unit 02 - A
- Kate reads books all the time. She [6]_____ love books.
  Kate는 항상 책을 읽는다. 그녀는 책을 매우 좋아하는 것임에 틀림없다. Unit 02 - A
- It **can't** be true. 그것은 사실일 리가 없다. Unit 02 - A

- You **have to** stay here. 너는 여기 머물러야 한다. Unit 02 - B
- Nancy [7]_____ clean the classroom. Nancy는 교실을 청소해야 한다. Unit 02 - B
- I [8]_____ wear glasses. 나는 안경을 쓸 필요가 없다. Unit 02 - B

- You [9]_____ turn off your cell phone in class.
  너는 수업 시간에 핸드폰을 꺼야 한다. Unit 02 - C
- You **shouldn't** believe him. 너는 그를 믿지 말아야 한다. Unit 02 - C

Answers

[1] Can [2] able [3] may [4] may[can] [5] must[should] not [6] must [7] has to[must, should]
[8] don't have to [9] should[must, have to]

ESSENTIAL RULES OF
ENGLISH GRAMMAR

CHAPTER
04

진행형과
미래시제

UNIT 01 진행형

UNIT 02 will, be going to

진행형은 특정한 시점에서 진행 중인 일을
나타내고, 미래시제는 앞으로 일어날 일을
나타낸다.

UNIT 01 진행형

A 현재진행형과 과거진행형

1 현재진행형: 지금 진행 중인 일을 나타내며 「be동사의 현재형(am, are, is) + v-ing」 형태로 쓴다.

※ v-ing 만드는 법

대부분의 동사	동사원형 + -ing	doing going eating playing watching talking speaking reading walking learning asking helping waiting
-e로 끝나는 동사	e를 빼고 + -ing	come → coming live → living make → making write → writing take → taking smile → smiling (예외: see → seeing)
-ie로 끝나는 동사	ie를 y로 고치고 + -ing	lie → lying die → dying tie → tying
〈단모음 + 단자음〉으로 끝나는 동사	자음을 한 번 더 쓰고 + -ing	sit → sitting cut → cutting run → running get → getting swim → swimming begin → beginning

They **are talking** on the phone.
Joan **is writing** an essay.

2 과거진행형: 과거의 한 시점에 진행 중이던 일을 나타내며 「be동사의 과거형(was, were) + v-ing」 형태로 쓴다.

The baby **was smiling** at me.
We **were shopping** at the mall.

B 진행형의 부정문과 의문문

1 진행형의 부정문: be동사 + not + v-ing

He**'s not studying**. He is playing computer games.
I **was not sleeping**. I was reading a book in bed.

2 진행형의 의문문: be동사 + 주어 + v-ing?

A: **Are you listening** to me?
B: Yes, I am. / No, I'm not.

CHECK UP   빈칸에 알맞은 말을 고르시오.

1 Tommy _____ to school now.
   ⓐ went   ⓑ going   ⓒ is going

2 We _____ the computer now.
   ⓐ not using   ⓑ are not using   ⓒ are using not

➕ PLUS : 진행형을 쓰지 않는 동사

have, like, hate, want, know, remember처럼 소유나 감정, 상태를 나타내는 동사는 진행형으로 쓰지 않는다. 단, have가 '먹다'의 의미일 경우 진행형으로 쓸 수 있다.

I **like** math. (~~am liking~~)
I **am having** pizza.

52

PRACTICE

🔍 Answer Key p-6

STEP 1

( ) 안에서 알맞은 말을 고르시오.

1 I (eating, am eating) ice cream.

2 We're (wait, waiting) for Stephanie.

3 They're (not working, working not) now.

4 Are you (learn, learning) taekwondo?

5 Kevin is (dances, dancing) on the stage.

6 My sister (is staying, was staying) in Paris now.

STEP 2

( ) 안의 말을 이용하여 현재진행형 문장을 완성하시오. (부정문은 줄임말을 쓸 것)

1 You _____ on my chair. (sit)

2 You don't have to be so serious. I _____. (joke)

3 The baby _____. He must be hungry. (cry)

4 Let's go out. It _____ now. (not/rain)

5 Those flowers _____. They are fresh. (not/die)

STEP 3

보기에서 알맞은 말을 골라 과거진행형 문장을 완성하시오. (부정문은 줄임말을 쓸 것)

보기	run	not/lie	study	watch

1 We _____ the Olympic Games last night.

2 I _____ in the park this morning.

3 They _____ in the library yesterday.

4 Matt _____. He was telling the truth.

STEP 4

우리말과 일치하도록 ( ) 안의 말을 이용하여 문장을 완성하시오.

1 그들은 점심을 먹고 있다. (have)

→ They _____ _____ lunch.

2 Nick은 재킷을 입고 있지 않다. (wear)

→ Nick _____ _____ a jacket.

3 너는 케이크를 자르고 있었니? (cut)

→ _____ _____ _____ the cake?

4 나는 내 여동생을 찾고 있었어. (look for)

→ I _____ _____ _____ my sister.

will, be going to

will

1 will + 동사원형: ~할 것이다(미래에 대한 예측), ~하겠다(의지)

They **will arrive** next week.
I **will call** you later.

① 「대명사 주어 + will」은 줄임말로 쓸 수 있다.
I'll be there by eight o'clock.

2 will의 부정문: won't[will not] + 동사원형

I **won't[will not] talk** to him again.

3 will의 의문문: Will + 주어 + 동사원형?

A: **Will you wash** your clothes?
B: Yes, I will. / No, I won't.

B be going to

1 be going to + 동사원형: ~할 예정이다(예정), ~할 것이다(미래에 대한 예측)

We**'re going to play** tennis on Saturday.
It **is going to snow** this afternoon.

2 be going to의 부정문: be not going to + 동사원형

They**'re not going to join** our club.

3 be going to의 의문문: be동사 + 주어 + going to + 동사원형?

A: **Are you going to fix** the computer?
B: Yes, I am. / No, I'm not.

CHECK UP 빈칸에 알맞은 말을 고르시오.

1 I _____ write a book someday.
  ⓐ be   ⓑ will   ⓒ be going to

2 I _____ wear this shirt. I don't like it.
  ⓐ will   ⓑ won't   ⓒ isn't going to

3 Chris _____ to New York next month.
  ⓐ will going   ⓑ be going to go   ⓒ is going to go

PRACTICE

🔍 Answer Key p.6

( ) 안에서 알맞은 말을 고르시오.

1 I'll (be, am) in Europe next year.

2 Are you going (take, to take) a bus?

3 We will (not forget, forget not) him.

4 Will Betty (change, changes) her mind?

5 They (be going to, are going to) visit us next week.

will 또는 won't와 ( ) 안의 말을 이용하여 대화를 완성하시오.

1 A: This bag is heavy.
   B: Oh, I _____ you. (help)

2 A: You are late!
   B: I'm sorry. I _____ late again. (be)

3 A: I'm so cold.
   B: I _____ hot cocoa for you. (make)

be going to와 ( ) 안의 말을 이용하여 문장을 완성하시오. (주어와 be동사는 줄임말을 쓸 것)

1 Next week is our vacation.
   _____ to Hawaii. (we, go)

2 I'm not hungry.
   _____ lunch. (I, not/eat)

3 Ben's shoes are dirty.
   _____ them. (he, clean)

STEP 4

우리말과 일치하도록 ( ) 안의 말을 이용하여 문장을 완성하시오.

1 나는 햄버거를 하나 먹겠다. (will, have)

   → I _____ _____ a hamburger.

2 그는 약속을 깨지 않을 것이다. (will, break)

   → He _____ _____ his promise.

3 Tom은 내일 이사 갈 것이다. (be going to, move)

   → Tom _____ _____ _____ _____ tomorrow.

4 너는 오늘 밤에 수학을 공부할 거니? (be going to, study)

   → _____ you _____ _____ _____ math tonight?

GRAMMAR FOR WRITING

A 우리말과 일치하도록 (   ) 안의 말을 이용하여 문장을 완성하시오.

1 우리는 마스크를 쓰고 있다. (wear)

→ We _____ masks.

2 메시지를 남기시겠어요? (you, will, leave)

→ _____ a message?

3 내 고양이는 바닥에 누워 있었다. (lie)

→ My cat _____ on the floor.

4 나는 내일 집에 없을 것이다. (will, be, at home)

→ I _____ tomorrow.

5 너는 새 스마트폰을 살 거니? (you, be going to, buy)

→ _____ a new smartphone?

6 나는 음악을 듣고 있지 않았다. (listen to)

→ I _____ music.

7 나는 그 영화를 보지 않을 것이다. (be going to, watch)

→ I _____ that movie.

B 우리말과 일치하도록 (   ) 안에 주어진 말을 바르게 배열하시오.

1 기차가 지금 도착하고 있다. (arriving, the train, is)

→ _____ now.

2 나와 함께 체스를 둘래? (you, play, will, chess)

→ _____ with me?

3 Nancy는 파티에 케이크를 가져올 것이다. (is, Nancy, bring, going to)

→ _____ a cake to the party.

4 뮤지컬은 오후 6시에 시작할 예정이니? (the musical, is, start, going to)

→ _____ at 6:00 p.m.?

5 그는 그녀에게 편지를 쓰고 있었니? (writing, he, was, a letter)

→ _____ to her?

6 우리는 서로에게 말을 하지 않고 있다. (are, speaking, not, we)

→ _____ to each other.

C 보기에서 알맞은 말을 골라 진행형으로 바꾸어 대화를 완성하시오. (단, 한 번씩만 쓸 것)

보기	cook	stand	take	shine	not/sleep

1 A: Look! The rain stopped.
B: Oh, great. The sun _____ now.

2 A: Are they awake?
B: Yes. They _____.

3 A: Is Alex in the kitchen?
B: Yes. He _____ dinner.

4 A: Excuse me. You _____ on my foot.
B: Oh, I'm sorry.

5 A: _____ you _____ a bath?
B: No, I wasn't. I was cleaning the bathroom.

D 그림을 보고 ( ) 안의 말을 이용하여 대화를 완성하시오.

1 **2** **3** **4**

1 A: Are you taking pictures for your blog?
B: Yes. I _____ them tonight. (be going to, post)

2 A: The TV is too loud!
B: Okay. I _____ the volume. (will, turn down)

3 A: Julie, hurry up. We must arrive at the airport on time.
B: We have enough time. We _____ late. (will, be)

4 A: _____ you _____ this magazine? (be going to, read)
B: No, I already read it.

REVIEW TEST

1 다음 중 동사의 v-ing형이 잘못 연결된 것은?

① live – living　　② play – playing
③ sit – sitting　　④ see – seing
⑤ read – reading

[2-4] 빈칸에 들어갈 알맞은 말을 고르시오.

2

| Linda _____ her hair now. |

① tie　　　　　② tied
③ is tying　　　④ will tying
⑤ going to tie

3

| I _____ you tomorrow. |

① sees　　　　② saw
③ will see　　④ going to see
⑤ will going to see

4

| We _____ to Bali next month. |

① went　　　　② will goes
③ going to go　④ are going to go
⑤ will going to go

[5-6] 빈칸에 공통으로 들어갈 말을 고르시오.

5

| · Jack _____ visit his friend in Beijing soon.
· _____ you help me with my English homework tomorrow? |

① be[Be]　　　　② is[Is]
③ do[Do]　　　　④ does[Does]
⑤ will[Will]

6

| · I _____ chatting online last night.
· _____ it raining that morning? |

① be[Be]　　② am[Am]　　③ is[Is]
④ was[Was]　⑤ will[Will]

빈출

[7-8] 빈칸에 들어갈 말로 알맞지 <u>않은</u> 것을 고르시오.

7

| Andrew _____ soccer. |

① plays　　　　② played
③ is playing　　④ will play
⑤ are going to play

8

| The kids _____ snowmen on the street. |

① made　　　　② are making
③ was making　④ will make
⑤ are going to make

[9-10] ( ) 안의 동사를 진행형으로 바꾸어 대화를 완성하시오.

9

A: Is Jenny writing in her diary?
B: No, she isn't. She _____ cartoons. (draw)

10

A: Did you see Sean in the park?
B: Yes. He _____ on the track there. (run)

서술형

[11-12] 다음은 Ian의 내일 계획이다. be going to와 표에 주어진 말을 이용하여 문장을 완성하시오.

| 오전 | water the plants in the house |
| 오후 | go to the movies with Jenny |

11

Ian _____ _____ _____ _____ the plants in the house tomorrow morning.

12

Ian and Jenny _____ _____ _____ _____ to the movies tomorrow afternoon.

[13-14] 다음 중 밑줄 친 부분이 잘못된 것을 고르시오.

13 ① Your phone is ringing.
② I'm not going home now.
③ Is Daniel writing a book report?
④ Jim doesn't wearing a coat.
⑤ She is growing flowers in her garden.

14 ① It will be cold tomorrow.
② Will he buys a new camera?
③ I won't make a mistake again.
④ Will you tell me about the secret?
⑤ Cindy and I will go to the concert tonight.

서술형

15 우리말과 일치하도록 주어진 조건에 맞게 문장을 완성하시오.

그들은 새 집을 지을 예정이니?

〈조건〉 1. build를 이용할 것
2. be동사로 시작할 것

→ _____ a new house?

16 다음 우리말을 영어로 바르게 옮긴 것은?

나는 Tom에게 문자 메시지를 보내고 있었다.

① I send a text message to Tom.
② I sent a text message to Tom.
③ I will send a text message to Tom.
④ I am sending a text message to Tom.
⑤ I was sending a text message to Tom.

17 다음 중 대화가 자연스럽지 <u>않은</u> 것은?

① A: Will you help me?
　B: Yes, I will.
② A: Is he going to the mall?
　B: No, he isn't.
③ A: Are you reading my letter?
　B: No, I won't.
④ A: Are you going to buy that book?
　B: Yes, I am.
⑤ A: Were they holding hands?
　B: Yes, they were.

서술형

[18-19] 다음 밑줄 친 부분을 바르게 고치시오.

18 Mike and I ⓐ <u>are travel</u> in Mexico now. We ⓑ <u>going to visit</u> the National Museum tomorrow. We are excited.

ⓐ _____　ⓑ _____

19 I ⓐ <u>will am</u> a famous singer in the future. I am practicing hard. I ⓑ <u>not will give up</u> my dream.

ⓐ _____　ⓑ _____

서술형

[20-22] 우리말과 일치하도록 ( ) 안의 말을 이용하여 문장을 완성하시오.

20 Danny는 신발을 신고 있는 중이다.
(put on his shoes)

→ Danny _____.

21 그들은 오늘 아침에 산책을 하고 있었다.
(take a walk)

→ They _____ this morning.

22 나는 지금 만화책을 읽고 있지 않다. 나는 소설을 읽고 있다. (read a comic book)

→ I _____ now. I'm reading a novel.

서술형

[23-24] 우리말과 일치하도록 ( ) 안에 주어진 말을 바르게 배열하시오.

23 너는 그 시계를 살 거니?
(you, will, the watch, buy)

→ _____?

24 우리는 이번 주에 만나지 않을 것이다.
(we, not, are, meet, going to)

→ _____ this week.

고난도

25 다음 중 어법상 옳은 것을 모두 고르면?

① Andy won't change his opinion.
② Are you going to the bank?
③ Will Jina likes your plan?
④ It is going not to be sunny soon.
⑤ We're going to miss you.

26 다음 문장이 어법상 옳으면 O, 틀리면 X의 철자를 선택할 때, 순서대로 만들어지는 단어는?

	O	X
They'll take care of their baby.	b	h
I'm not call Peter now.	o	e
The movie is going to end soon.	s	a
My sister and I was talking.	r	t

① host ② hear
③ boat ④ best
⑤ bear

고난도

27 다음 중 어법상 옳은 것의 개수는?

- I was knowing the answer.
- Will you explain your idea to Philip?
- They were dancing on the stage.
- She won't cries in front of people.
- Is Ben and Lily going to play the game?

① 1개 ② 2개 ③ 3개
④ 4개 ⑤ 5개

서술형

[28-30] 밑줄 친 부분이 어법상 옳은지 판단하고, 틀리면 바르게 고치시오.

28 <u>Will</u> you going to stay in Korea?

(O / X) _____

29 Tony and Mickey <u>was having</u> dinner at that time.

(O / X) _____

30 I'm <u>going not to</u> invite Jack to my party.

(O / X) _____

서술형 고난도

[31-33] 어법상 틀린 부분을 찾아 바르게 고치시오.

31 Jenna is sleep now. She will gets up in an hour. (2개)

32 A: Did you watch *K-pop Idol* last night?
B: No, I didn't. I am studying for an exam.
A: It was really interesting. I will show you the video. (1개)

33 A: Are you going to go to the airport?
B: Yes, I met Eric there this afternoon. His plane are going to arrive at 3:00 p.m.
A: Is he going to travel in Korea?
B: No, he is going not to travel. He will study Korean at a university. (3개)

LET'S REVIEW

주요 예문을 다시 한번 확인하고, 우리말과 일치하도록 빈칸을 채우시오.

- They **are talking** on the phone. 그들은 전화로 이야기하고 있다. <u>Unit 01 - A</u>
- Joan ¹_____ an essay. Joan은 에세이를 쓰는 중이다. <u>Unit 01 - A</u>
- The baby **was smiling** at me. 그 아기는 나를 보며 웃고 있었다. <u>Unit 01 - A</u>
- We ²_____ at the mall. 우리는 쇼핑몰에서 쇼핑하고 있었다. <u>Unit 01 - A</u>

- He's **not studying**. He is playing computer games.
  그는 공부하고 있지 않다. 그는 컴퓨터 게임을 하고 있다. <u>Unit 01 - B</u>
- I ³_____. I was reading a book in bed.
  나는 자고 있지 않았다. 나는 침대에서 책을 읽고 있었다. <u>Unit 01 - B</u>
- ⁴_____ **listening** to me? 너 내 말을 듣고 있니? <u>Unit 01 - B</u>

- They ⁵_____ **arrive** next week. 그들은 다음 주에 도착할 것이다. <u>Unit 02 - A</u>
- I **will call** you later. 내가 나중에 너에게 전화할게. <u>Unit 02 - A</u>
- I **won't talk** to him again. 나는 그에게 다시 말하지 않을 것이다. <u>Unit 02 - A</u>
- ⁶_____ **you wash** your clothes? 너는 너의 옷을 세탁할 거니? <u>Unit 02 - A</u>

- We're **going to play** tennis on Saturday. 우리는 토요일에 테니스를 칠 것이다. <u>Unit 02 - B</u>
- It **is** ⁷_____ this afternoon. 오늘 오후에 눈이 올 것이다. <u>Unit 02 - B</u>
- They're ⁸_____ **join** our club. 그들은 우리 동아리에 가입하지 않을 것이다. <u>Unit 02 - B</u>
- ⁹_____ **fix** the computer? 너는 그 컴퓨터를 고칠 거니? <u>Unit 02 - B</u>

Answers

¹ is writing   ² were shopping   ³ wasn't[was not] sleeping   ⁴ Are you   ⁵ will[are going to]

⁶ Will   ⁷ going to snow   ⁸ not going to   ⁹ Are you going to / Will you

ESSENTIAL RULES OF
ENGLISH GRAMMAR

CHAPTER
05

동사의 종류

동사는 문장의 핵심 요소로
그 종류에 따라 뒤에 오는 말들이 달라진다.

UNIT 01 감각동사 + 형용사

UNIT 02 목적어가 두 개 필요한 동사

UNIT 03 목적격 보어가 필요한 동사

감각동사 + 형용사

look, feel, sound, smell, taste와 같이 감각을 표현하는 동사를 감각동사라고 하고, 이 동사들 뒤에는 형용사를 쓴다.

look, feel, sound, smell, taste	형용사

A **look + 형용사: ~해 보이다**

She **looks** *busy* today.
That sofa **looks** *comfortable*.

cf. 감각동사 뒤에 명사가 올 때는 전치사 like와 함께 쓴다.
The girl **looks like** *a doll*.

B **feel + 형용사: ~하게 느끼다[느껴지다]**

I **feel** *tired*. I didn't sleep well last night.
Cotton candy **feels** *soft*.

C **sound + 형용사: ~하게 들리다**

Your idea **sounds** *wonderful*.
That **sounds** *strange*. Is it true?

D **smell + 형용사: ~한 냄새가 나다**

This shampoo **smells** *nice*.
The milk **smells** *bad*. You shouldn't drink it.

E **taste + 형용사: ~한 맛이 나다**

This egg salad **tastes** *great*.
These oranges **taste** *sweet*.

CHECK UP 빈칸에 알맞지 <u>않은</u> 말을 고르시오.

1 I feel _____.
ⓐ cold ⓑ hungry ⓒ sadly

2 The pizza _____ delicious.
ⓐ looks ⓑ sees ⓒ tastes

PRACTICE

🔍 Answer Key p.8

STEP 1

( ) 안에서 알맞은 말을 고르시오.

1 I felt (warm, warmly) by the fire.

2 The flowers smell (nice, nicely).

3 Sally looks (love, lovely) in that dress.

4 Her accent (smells, sounds) strange.

5 The chocolate cookies taste (good, well).

STEP 2

밑줄 친 부분이 올바르면 ○표, 틀리면 바르게 고치시오.

1 That chair looks <u>strongly</u>.　　　　　　　_____

2 The story <u>sounds</u> interesting to me.　　　_____

3 I feel <u>sleep</u>. I should go to bed now.　　_____

4 Your new perfume smells <u>wonderful</u>.　　_____

5 The soup tastes <u>salt</u>. I need some water.　_____

STEP 3

빈칸에 알맞은 동사를 보기에서 골라 현재형으로 써서 문장을 완성하시오. (단, 한 번씩만 쓸 것)

보기	look　　feel　　sound　　smell

1 A: How are you today?
　B: I _____ good. And you?

2 A: Do you know this song?
　B: No, I don't. But it _____ nice.

3 A: You _____ sad today. What's wrong?
　B: My cat is sick.

4 A: What are you cooking? It _____ delicious.
　B: I'm cooking pasta.

STEP 4

우리말과 일치하도록 ( ) 안의 말을 이용하여 문장을 완성하시오.

1 아기의 피부는 부드럽게 느껴졌다. (soft)
　→ The baby's skin _____ _____.

2 너의 계획은 신나게 들린다. (exciting)
　→ Your plan _____ _____.

3 이 사진에서 너는 아름다워 보인다. (beautiful)
　→ You _____ _____ in this picture.

UNIT 02 목적어가 두 개 필요한 동사

A 수여동사 + 간접목적어 + 직접목적어

'~에게 …을 (해)주다'라는 의미의 동사를 수여동사라고 한다. 수여동사는 간접목적어(~에게)와 직접목적어 (…을)에 해당하는 두 개의 목적어를 필요로 한다.

give, send, pass, lend, bring, show, tell, write, teach, make, cook, buy, get, ask 등	간접목적어(~에게)	직접목적어(…을)

I **gave** *Tim chocolate* on Valentine's Day.
Can you **show** *me your car*?

B 수여동사 + 직접목적어 + to/for/of + 간접목적어

「수여동사 + 간접목적어 + 직접목적어」는 「수여동사 + 직접목적어 + to/for/of + 간접목적어」의 형태로 바꿔 쓸 수 있다. 이때 대부분의 동사는 간접목적어 앞에 전치사 to를 쓰지만 동사에 따라 for나 of를 쓰기도 한다.

give, send, pass, lend, show, tell, write, teach 등	직접목적어	to	간접목적어
make, cook, buy, get 등		for	
ask	favor	of	

My father **sent** me a text message.
→ My father **sent** a text message **to** me.

Susie **bought** me a book.
→ Susie **bought** a book **for** me.

Jake **asked** me a favor.
→ Jake **asked** a favor **of** me.

CHECK UP 빈칸에 알맞은 말을 고르시오.

1 He always _____ us interesting stories.
ⓐ sounds ⓑ wants ⓒ tells

2 Susan _____ some tea for us.
ⓐ gave ⓑ made ⓒ asked

3 I lent my bike _____ Paul.
ⓐ to ⓑ for ⓒ of

PRACTICE

🔍 Answer Key p.8

STEP 1

( ) 안에서 알맞은 말을 고르시오.

1 I bought some flowers (to, for) Mom.

2 Nancy showed her house (to, of) me.

3 She cooked dinner (for, of) me last night.

4 I made a gift (to, for) Liam yesterday.

5 I will ask a favor (for, of) him.

STEP 2

빈칸에 알맞은 동사를 보기에서 골라 과거형으로 써서 문장을 완성하시오. (단, 한 번씩만 쓸 것)

보기	buy cook send pass

1 Diana _____ me the ball in the soccer game.

2 I got a new camera. My dad _____ it for me.

3 We were hungry, so Peter _____ ramen for us.

4 Paul is in Paris now. He _____ me a postcard from there.

STEP 3

두 문장의 의미가 같도록 빈칸에 알맞은 말을 쓰시오.

1 I wrote an email to him.

→ I wrote _____ _____ _____.

2 Julia made some sandwiches for me.

→ Julia made _____ _____ _____.

3 Kevin lent me his cell phone.

→ Kevin lent _____ _____ _____ _____ _____.

STEP 4

우리말과 일치하도록 ( ) 안의 말을 이용하여 문장을 완성하시오.

1 Tim은 그들에게 수학을 가르쳐 주었다. (teach, them, math)

→ Tim _____ _____ _____.

2 나의 개가 나에게 신문을 가져다주었다. (bring, me, a newspaper)

→ My dog _____ _____ _____ _____.

3 그녀는 남동생에게 장갑을 만들어 주었다. (make, gloves, her brother)

→ She _____ _____ _____ _____.

4 나는 David에게 생일 카드를 보냈다. (send, a birthday card, David)

→ I _____ _____ _____ _____ _____.

UNIT 03 목적격 보어가 필요한 동사

일부 동사들은 목적어 뒤에 목적어의 성질, 상태 등을 설명하는 목적격 보어를 필요로 한다. 목적격 보어로는 주로 명사, 형용사, to부정사 등을 쓴다.

make, call, name, keep, find, want, expect, tell, order, ask, advise, allow 등	목적어	목적격 보어

A 목적격 보어로 명사를 쓰는 동사

make, call, name 등의 동사는 목적격 보어로 명사를 쓴다.

The video **made** her *a star*.
My friends **call** me *Eddie*.

B 목적격 보어로 형용사를 쓰는 동사

keep, make, find 등의 동사는 목적격 보어로 형용사를 쓴다.

He always **keeps** his room *clean*.
I **found** the book *difficult*.

C 목적격 보어로 to부정사를 쓰는 동사

want, expect, tell, order, ask, advise, allow 등의 동사는 목적격 보어로 to부정사를 쓴다.

I **want** you *to come* with me.
We **expected** John *to win* the game.

cf. have, make, let(~가 …하도록 하다/시키다)과 see, watch, hear, feel(~가 …하는 것을 보다/듣다/느끼다) 등의 동사들은 목적격 보어로 동사원형을 쓴다.
My mom **made** me *study*.
I **saw** Tom *sing* at the festival.

CHECK UP 빈칸에 알맞은 말을 고르시오.

1 The news made us _____.
　ⓐ happy　　ⓑ happily　　ⓒ to be happy

2 We _____ our cat Sophie.
　ⓐ called　　ⓑ made　　ⓒ told

3 Sarah _____ me to wait for her.
　ⓐ kept　　ⓑ found　　ⓒ told

4 I asked Jimmy _____.
　ⓐ quiet　　ⓑ be quiet　　ⓒ to be quiet

68

PRACTICE

🔍 Answer Key p-8

STEP 1

( ) 안에서 알맞은 말을 고르시오.

1 The business made her (rich, to be rich).

2 I want you (helpful, to help) me tomorrow.

3 These boots will keep your feet (warm, warmly).

4 She asked me (answer, to answer) the phone.

STEP 2

빈칸에 알맞은 말을 보기에서 골라 쓰시오. (단, 한 번씩만 쓸 것)

보기	easy sad fresh an angel

1 The movie made me _____. I cried a lot.

2 I found the test _____. I finished it quickly.

3 Annie helps others all the time. People call her _____.

4 Trees keep the air _____. I will plant more trees.

STEP 3

빈칸에 알맞은 말을 보기에서 골라 적절한 형태로 바꾸어 문장을 완성하시오. (단, 한 번씩만 쓸 것)

보기	be give read stop

1 My dad wants me _____ polite.

2 The police ordered him _____ the car.

3 I expected Lily _____ me a birthday gift.

4 Tom advised me _____ lots of books.

STEP 4

우리말과 일치하도록 ( ) 안의 말을 이용하여 문장을 완성하시오.

1 얼음이 내 주스를 차갑게 유지시킨다. (keep, my juice, cold)

→ The ice _____ _____ _____ _____.

2 이 발명품은 그를 백만장자로 만들어 주었다. (make, him, a millionaire)

→ This invention _____ _____ _____ _____.

3 나는 그녀에게 크게 말해달라고 부탁했다. (ask, her, speak up)

→ I _____ _____ _____ _____.

4 엄마는 나에게 숙제를 먼저 끝내라고 말씀하셨다. (tell, me, finish)

→ Mom _____ _____ _____ _____ my homework first.

GRAMMAR FOR WRITING

A 우리말과 일치하도록 (   ) 안의 말을 이용하여 문장을 완성하시오.

1 이 시계는 비싸 보인다. (look, expensive)

→ This watch _____.

2 아버지는 나에게 연을 만들어 주셨다. (make, I, a kite)

→ My dad _____.

3 선수들은 경기 후에 목이 마름을 느꼈다. (feel, thirsty)

→ The players _____ after the game.

4 Yoko는 나에게 일본어를 가르쳐 주었다. (teach, I, Japanese)

→ Yoko _____.

5 그 경험은 그를 훌륭한 작가로 만들었다. (make, he, a great writer)

→ That experience _____.

6 의사는 나에게 채소를 더 많이 먹으라고 충고했다. (advise, I, eat)

→ The doctor _____ more vegetables.

7 Tony는 그녀에게 그의 카메라를 빌려 주었다. (lend, she, his camera)

→ Tony _____.

B 우리말과 일치하도록 (   ) 안에 주어진 말을 바르게 배열하시오.

1 나는 부모님께 성적표를 보여드렸다. (my parents, showed, to, my report card)

→ I _____.

2 이 비누는 냄새가 좋지 않다. (this soap, smell, doesn't, good)

→ _____.

3 나는 창문이 열려 있는 것을 발견했다. (open, found, the window)

→ I _____.

4 우리는 세상을 더 나은 곳으로 만들 수 있다. (the world, make, a better place)

→ We can _____.

5 인터넷은 우리에게 유용한 정보를 준다. (gives, useful information, us)

→ The internet _____.

6 Nora는 나에게 그 단어를 설명해달라고 부탁했다. (me, asked, to, the word, explain)

→ Nora _____.

C 보기에서 알맞은 동사를 골라 ( ) 안의 말과 함께 써서 대화를 완성하시오. (단, 한 번씩만 쓸 것)

보기	feel	pass	call	keep

1 A: Should I put the macaron in the refrigerator?
　 B: Yes. You should _____. (it, cool)

2 A: Can you _____? (me, the salt)
　 B: Sure. Here you are.

3 A: What's your name?
　 B: My name is Kimberly, but people _____. (me, Kim)

4 A: I _____. I have a bad cold. (terrible)
　 B: You should see a doctor.

D 그림을 보고 보기에서 알맞은 동사를 골라 ( ) 안의 말과 함께 써서 문장을 완성하시오. (과거형으로 쓸 것)

보기	ask	taste	make	feel	smell

1 In the afternoon, I _____. (hungry)

2 I _____ a snack for me. (my brother, make)

3 He _____, (me, pancakes)
　 and they _____. (great)

4 Yuck! They _____. (strange)

REVIEW TEST

[1-2] 빈칸에 들어갈 알맞은 말을 고르시오.

1

> She _____ this chocolate for me.

① gave   ② passed   ③ showed
④ bought   ⑤ asked

2

> A: The onion soup _____.
> B: Yes, it will be very delicious.

① tastes salt   ② tastes greatly
③ smells amazing   ④ smells bad
⑤ feels wonderfully

[3-5] 빈칸에 들어갈 말로 알맞지 <u>않은</u> 것을 고르시오.

3

> Your coat looks _____.

① warm   ② good   ③ soft
④ nicely   ⑤ terrible

4

> They keep the room _____.

① cold   ② fresh   ③ clean
④ dark   ⑤ quietly

5

> My mom _____ me to go to bed early.

① told   ② wanted   ③ made
④ ordered   ⑤ advised

서술형

[6-7] 두 문장의 의미가 같도록 빈칸에 알맞은 말을 쓰시오.

6

> Susan sent him a fan letter.

→ Susan sent _____ _____
     _____ _____ _____.

7

> I'll get you some napkins.

→ I'll get _____ _____
     _____ _____.

빈출

8 밑줄 친 부분의 쓰임이 나머지 넷과 <u>다른</u> 것은?

① The news <u>made</u> him sad.
② Mike <u>made</u> his dream real.
③ My uncle <u>made</u> us a bookshelf.
④ His joke <u>made</u> people laugh.
⑤ The game <u>made</u> him a national hero.

9 다음 중 빈칸에 to를 쓸 수 <u>없는</u> 것은?

① I passed the ball _____ Sam.

② Dad told me _____ come early.

③ I want you _____ visit my blog.

④ Peter lent an umbrella _____ me.

⑤ Linda cooked chicken soup _____ me.

빈출

10 빈칸에 공통으로 들어갈 말은?

> • Matt showed his book _____ me.
> • My teacher advised me _____ keep a diary every day.

① to   ② for   ③ of

④ about   ⑤ with

11 빈칸에 들어갈 말이 바르게 짝지어진 것은?

> • Mary's voice ____(A)____ nice.
> • I ____(B)____ a Christmas card to him.
> • He ____(C)____ us to be honest.

	(A)		(B)		(C)
①	hears	……	made	……	let
②	hears	……	sent	……	told
③	sounds	……	sent	……	told
④	sounds	……	sent	……	let
⑤	sounds	……	made	……	told

서술형

[12-13] ( ) 안의 말을 이용하여 대화를 완성하시오.

12
A: Your shirt looks nice.
B: Thanks. My sister _____ me. (give, it)

13
A: The boys are talking too loudly.
B: Yeah. I _____ quiet. (want, them, be)

[14-15] 다음 중 밑줄 친 부분이 <u>잘못된</u> 것을 고르시오.

14 ① You look <u>tired</u> today.

② Computers make work <u>easy</u>.

③ I found the song <u>beautifully</u>.

④ He always keeps his desk <u>clean</u>.

⑤ Everybody felt <u>happy</u> at the party.

15 ① I bought <u>a watch for him</u>.

② Jay asked <u>her a question</u>.

③ Kevin gave <u>me his game CDs</u>.

④ My friend sent <u>a package to me</u>.

⑤ Mom made <u>hot chocolate to me</u>.

16 다음 중 대화가 자연스럽지 <u>않은</u> 것은?

① A: Did they name their baby?
   B: Yes. They named him Jamie.

② A: Is your dad a teacher?
   B: Yes. He teaches students math.

③ A: Did you buy this scarf?
   B: No. Mom made it for me.

④ A: This cake tastes good. Can I have some more?
   B: Of course.

⑤ A: I'm going to travel around Europe this summer.
   B: Your plan sounds interestingly.

[17-18] 다음 우리말을 영어로 바르게 옮긴 것을 고르시오.

17 나는 Jack에게 내 비밀을 이야기했다.

① I told my secret Jack.
② I told Jack my secret.
③ I told my secret for Jack.
④ I told to Jack my secret.
⑤ I told Jack to my secret.

18 우리는 Tony가 늦을 것이라고 예상했다.

① We expected Tony late.
② We expected Tony be late.
③ We expected Tony to be late.
④ We expected Tony being late.
⑤ We expected Tony to being late.

서술형

[19-20] 우리말과 일치하도록 ( ) 안의 말을 이용하여
문장을 완성하시오.

19 이 약은 쓴 맛이 난다. (bitter)

→ This medicine _____.

20 그 마을은 평화로워 보인다. (peaceful)

→ The village _____.

서술형

[21-23] 우리말과 일치하도록 ( ) 안에 주어진 말을 바르게
배열하시오.

21 그녀는 나에게 책들을 옮겨달라고 부탁했다.
(me, asked, to, her books, carry)

→ She _____.

22 Matt는 우편함이 빈 것을 발견했다.
(the mailbox, found, empty)

→ Matt _____.

23 내가 너희에게 쿠키를 좀 만들어 줄게.
(for, make, you, some cookies)

→ I'll _____.

서술형

24 우리말과 일치하도록 주어진 조건에 맞게 문장을 완성하
시오.

그는 내가 그의 전화기를 쓰는 걸 허락했다.

〈조건〉 1. allow, use, his phone을 이용할 것
       2. 7단어로 쓸 것

→ _____.

고난도

25 다음 중 어법상 옳은 것을 모두 고르면?

① Mom told me eat breakfast.
② I want him to fix my bike.
③ His plan sounds very nicely.
④ My best friend called me a liar.
⑤ Someone sent Julia flowers.

26 다음 중 어법상 옳은 것으로 바르게 짝지어진 것은?

> a. My hands feel dry in the winter.
> b. The TV show made him popular.
> c. He teaches Hangeul for Emma.
> d. Jane saw Mom cook noodles.
> e. My boss ordered me finish the work today.

① b, e ② a, b, c ③ a, b, d
④ b, d, e ⑤ a, b, c, e

고난도
27 다음 중 어법상 옳은 것의 개수는?

> • I didn't expect my brother to help me.
> • My fashion blog made me famous.
> • I showed to my grandmother the painting.
> • The baby looks like an angel.
> • Neil bought a ring for his girlfriend.

① 1개 ② 2개 ③ 3개
④ 4개 ⑤ 5개

서술형
[28-30] 밑줄 친 부분이 어법상 옳은지 판단하고, 틀리면 바르게 고치시오.

28 The sausage tasted too <u>salty</u>.

(O / X) _____

29 She found my advice very <u>usefully</u>.

(O / X) _____

30 Eric lent some money <u>for his brother</u>.

(O / X) _____

서술형 고난도
[31-33] 어법상 틀린 부분을 찾아 바르게 고치시오.

31 Mike's room smelled strangely. I told him to clean his room. (1개)

32 On the street, I found a homeless puppy. I felt sorry for him, so I brought him home. I named Tori him. Now Tori looks happily with my family. (2개)

33 A: Melany asked me come to her birthday party.
B: Did you buy a present to her?
A: No. Do you have any ideas?
B: How about a hairpin?
A: That sounds great. (2개)

LET'S REVIEW

주요 예문을 다시 한번 확인하고, 우리말과 일치하도록 빈칸을 채우시오.

- That sofa [1]_____ comfortable. 저 소파는 편안해 보인다. **Unit 01 - A**

- Cotton candy [2]_____ soft. 솜사탕은 부드럽게 느껴진다. **Unit 01 - B**

- Your idea [3]_____ wonderful. 네 생각은 정말 멋지게 들린다. **Unit 01 - C**

- This shampoo [4]_____ nice. 이 샴푸는 좋은 냄새가 난다. **Unit 01 - D**

- These oranges [5]_____ sweet. 이 오렌지는 달콤한 맛이 난다. **Unit 01 - E**

- I [6]_____ Tim chocolate on Valentine's Day.
  나는 밸런타인데이에 Tim에게 초콜릿을 주었다. **Unit 02 - A**

- Can you **show** me your car? 나에게 네 차를 보여줄 수 있니? **Unit 02 - A**

- My father **sent** me a text message.
  → My father **sent** a text message [7]_____ me.
    우리 아버지께서는 나에게 문자 메시지를 보내셨다. **Unit 02 - B**

- The video [8]_____ her a star. 그 동영상은 그녀를 스타로 만들었다. **Unit 03 - A**
- My friends [9]_____ me Eddie. 내 친구들은 나를 Eddie라고 부른다. **Unit 03 - A**

- He always **keeps** his room clean. 그는 항상 그의 방을 깨끗하게 유지한다. **Unit 03 - B**
- I **found** the book difficult. 나는 그 책이 어렵다고 생각했다. **Unit 03 - B**

- We **expected** John to win the game. 우리는 John이 그 경기를 이길 거라고 예상했다. **Unit 03 - C**

🔍 **Answers**

[1] looks   [2] feels   [3] sounds   [4] smells   [5] taste   [6] gave   [7] to   [8] made   [9] call

76

ESSENTIAL RULES OF ENGLISH GRAMMAR

CHAPTER
06

명사와 관사

명사는 사람, 사물, 장소 등의 이름을
나타내는 말이고, 관사는 명사 앞에서
명사의 성격에 대한 정보를 주는 말이다.

UNIT 01   셀 수 있는 명사 vs. 셀 수 없는 명사

UNIT 02   관사

셀 수 있는 명사 vs. 셀 수 없는 명사

A 셀 수 있는 명사

1 '하나, 둘 …'의 형태로 셀 수 있는 명사로, 단수는 「a/an + 명사」, 복수는 주로 「명사 + -(e)s」 형태로 쓴다.

I have **a brother**. / I have two **brothers**.

2 셀 수 있는 명사의 복수형 만드는 법

대부분의 명사	명사 + -s	dogs maps books computers houses
-s, -x, -ch, -sh, -o로 끝나는 명사	명사 + -es	buses classes boxes watches dishes potatoes tomatoes (예외: pianos, photos)
〈자음 + y〉로 끝나는 명사	y를 i로 고치고 + -es	baby → bab**ies** city → cit**ies** lady → lad**ies** fly → fl**ies**
-f, -fe로 끝나는 명사	f, fe를 v로 고치고 + -es	leaf → lea**ves** knife → kni**ves** thief → thie**ves** (예외: roofs)
불규칙 변화		man → **men** woman → **women** foot → **feet** tooth → **teeth** child → **children** person → **people** mouse → **mice**
형태가 같은 경우		fish → **fish** deer → **deer** sheep → **sheep**

B 셀 수 없는 명사

1 '하나, 둘…'의 형태로 셀 수 없는 명사로, 항상 단수형으로 쓰고 앞에 a/an을 쓰지 않는다.

Can I have **water**? (~~a water~~)

2 셀 수 없는 명사의 종류

1) 셀 수 없는 물질을 나타내는 명사(물질명사): water, coffee, bread, salt, paper, money 등
2) 추상적인 개념을 나타내는 명사(추상명사): happiness, luck, love, friendship, health, help 등
3) 사람, 장소 등의 고유한 이름을 나타내는 명사(고유명사): Tom, New York, Korea 등

3 물질명사의 수량은 단위를 나타내는 표현을 써서 나타낸다.

- a glass of water/milk/juice
- a piece of paper/furniture
- a bottle of water/cola
- a cup of coffee/tea
- a slice[piece] of bread/cheese/pizza/cake
- a bowl of soup/cereal/rice

I'll drink **a cup of tea**.
I need **two pieces of paper**.

CHECK UP 빈칸에 알맞지 <u>않은</u> 말을 고르시오.

1 I ate _____ this morning.
ⓐ an apple   ⓑ a bread   ⓒ a piece of cake

2 Jane brought me a _____ of water.
ⓐ glass   ⓑ bottle   ⓒ piece

✚ PLUS : 항상 복수형으로 쓰는 명사

pants(바지), jeans(청바지), shoes(신발), socks(양말), glasses(안경), scissors(가위)처럼 두 개가 한 쌍을 이루는 명사는 항상 복수형으로 쓰며 a pair of, two pairs of...의 형태로 수를 나타낸다.

I bought **a pair of jeans**.

PRACTICE

🔍 Answer Key p-9

STEP 1

주어진 명사의 복수형을 쓰시오.

1	watch	– _____	**2**	song	– _____
3	knife	– _____	**4**	woman	– _____
5	mouse	– _____	**6**	photo	– _____
7	bus	– _____	**8**	sheep	– _____
9	tomato	– _____	**10**	toy	– _____
11	baby	– _____	**12**	foot	– _____

STEP 2

밑줄 친 부분이 올바르면 ○표, 틀리면 바르게 고치시오.

1 I have two <u>cat</u>. _____

2 Dave doesn't like big <u>citys</u>. _____

3 <u>A health</u> is important. _____

4 We need three <u>boxes</u>. _____

5 My little sister has four <u>tooths</u>. _____

6 I had two slices of <u>breads</u> for breakfast. _____

STEP 3

빈칸에 알맞은 말을 보기에서 골라 ( ) 안의 말과 함께 써서 문장을 완성하시오.

보기	slice	cup	bowl	piece

1 Dad made _____ for Mom. (a, coffee)

2 I'm not hungry. I just had _____. (a, soup)

3 This burger has _____ on it. (two, cheese)

4 There were _____ in the living room. (three, furniture)

STEP 4

우리말과 일치하도록 ( ) 안의 말을 이용하여 문장을 완성하시오.

1 나는 오늘 수업이 다섯 개 있다. (class)

→ I have _____ today.

2 그는 수프에 소금을 넣었다. (salt)

→ He put _____ in the soup.

3 나는 신발 한 켤레를 신어 보았다. (shoes)

→ I tried on _____.

부정관사 a/an

셀 수 있는 명사의 단수형 앞에는 a/an을 쓴다. 발음이 자음으로 시작하는 단어 앞에는 a, 발음이 모음으로 시작하는 단어 앞에는 an을 쓴다.

a house, **a** week, **an** egg, **an** hour, **an** old man ...

1 특정하지 않은 하나를 나타낼 때
   I'm going to buy **a** shirt.

2 하나의(= one)
   Alice picked **a** card.

3 ~마다(= per)
   I go to the dentist once **a** year.

정관사 the

1 앞에 언급되었거나 정황상 무엇인지 알 수 있는 특정한 것을 나타낼 때
   I watched *a* movie last night. **The** movie was great.
   Can I use **the** computer?

2 명사 뒤에 수식어구가 있어 가리키는 대상이 분명할 때
   The flowers *in my garden* are roses.

3 the + 세상에 하나밖에 없는 것: **the** sun, **the** moon, **the** sky, **the** earth, **the** world ...

4 the + 일부 매체: **the** internet, **the** radio, (go to) **the** movies ...   *cf.* (watch) TV

5 play the + 악기 이름: play **the** piano, play **the** violin ...

관사를 쓰지 않는 경우

1 식사 이름 앞: (have) breakfast/lunch/dinner

2 운동 경기 이름 앞: (play) baseball/soccer/tennis ...

3 by + 교통/통신 수단(~로): by bus/taxi/train/email ...

4 장소가 본래의 목적으로 쓰일 때: go to bed(잠자리에 들다), go to school(등교하다),
   go to church(예배 보러 가다) ...

CHECK UP   빈칸에 알맞은 말을 고르시오.

1 I can play _____ violin.
   ⓐ a   ⓑ an   ⓒ the

2 I usually have _____ lunch with Steve.
   ⓐ a   ⓑ the   ⓒ 필요 없음

PRACTICE

🔍 Answer Key p-9

STEP 1

( ) 안에서 알맞은 말을 고르시오.

1 You should bring (a, an) umbrella today.

2 I go to school (by bus, by a bus).

3 Nora plays (a, the) piano very well.

4 My family goes out for dinner twice (a, the) month.

5 (An, The) earth goes around (a, the) sun.

6 There is a store on the corner. (A, The) store sells nice shoes.

STEP 2

밑줄 친 부분이 올바르면 ○표, 틀리면 바르게 고치시오.

1 I eat three meals the day. _____

2 There is a orange on the table. _____

3 Mary is listening to the radio. _____

4 My family went to Busan by train. _____

5 We bought a new camera. A camera works well. _____

STEP 3

빈칸에 알맞은 말을 보기에서 골라 쓰시오. (X는 필요 없음을 뜻함)

보기	a	an	the	X

1 We had chicken for _____ dinner last night.

2 I have _____ idea for Joe's birthday party.

3 I went to _____ movies last Saturday.

4 Dad works five days _____ week.

5 You can send me the file by _____ email.

6 I know _____ man on the bench.

STEP 4

우리말과 일치하도록 ( ) 안의 말을 이용하여 문장을 완성하시오.

1 창문을 좀 열어도 될까요? (window)

→ Can I open _____?

2 Kevin은 일찍 잠자리에 든다. (bed)

→ Kevin goes to _____ early.

3 Peter는 주말마다 테니스를 친다. (play, tennis)

→ Peter _____ every weekend.

GRAMMAR FOR WRITING

A 우리말과 일치하도록 ( ) 안의 말을 이용하여 문장을 완성하시오. (필요하면 알맞은 관사를 넣을 것)

1 Jake는 시계를 두 개 가지고 있다. (have, watch)

→ Jake _____.

2 그 방에는 4명의 여자들이 있었다. (woman)

→ There were _____ in the room.

3 에어컨을 켜도 될까요? (turn on, air conditioner)

→ Can I _____?

4 나는 가게에서 물 한 병을 샀다. (water)

→ I bought _____ at the store.

5 Terry는 자전거로 공원에 갔다. (go to the park, bike)

→ Terry _____.

6 나는 동물원에서 코끼리 한 마리를 보았다. (see, elephant)

→ I _____ at the zoo.

7 Sarah는 점심으로 피자 두 조각을 먹었다. (pizza)

→ Sarah ate _____ for lunch.

B 우리말과 일치하도록 ( ) 안에 주어진 말을 바르게 배열하시오.

1 그녀는 7시에 아침을 먹는다. (at, breakfast, seven o'clock, has)

→ She _____.

2 세상은 빠르게 변하고 있다. (world, changing, is, the)

→ _____ fast.

3 탁자 위에 놓인 그림은 아름답다. (picture, is, the, on the table)

→ _____ beautiful.

4 Asher는 일 년에 세 번 치과에 간다. (a, goes to the dentist, three times, year)

→ Asher _____.

5 내 여동생은 신발 열 켤레를 가지고 있다. (has, of, shoes, pairs, ten)

→ My sister _____.

6 그는 인터넷으로 책을 샀다. (bought, on, books, internet, the)

→ He _____.

C ( ) 안의 말을 이용하여 대화를 완성하시오. (필요하면 알맞은 관사를 넣을 것)

1 A: Did you buy a plane ticket to Gwangju?

B: No, I didn't. I'll _____. (travel, train)

2 A: Did you see my key?

B: Yes. I _____ on your desk. (see, key)

3 A: Do you exercise?

B: Yes. I _____ on Sundays. (play, soccer)

4 A: Do you go to the movies often?

B: I go to the movies _____. (once, month)

5 A: Is it going to rain today?

B: I think so. There are dark clouds _____. (in, sky)

6 A: Do you like music?

B: Yes. I often sing and _____. (play, drums)

D 다음은 네 사람이 먹은 아침 식사이다. 그림을 보고 보기에서 알맞은 말을 골라 ( ) 안의 말과 함께 써서 문장을 완성하시오.

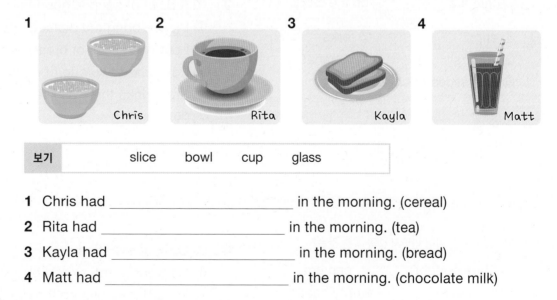

| 보기 | slice | bowl | cup | glass |

1 Chris had _____ in the morning. (cereal)

2 Rita had _____ in the morning. (tea)

3 Kayla had _____ in the morning. (bread)

4 Matt had _____ in the morning. (chocolate milk)

REVIEW TEST

[1-2] 다음 중 명사의 복수형이 잘못 연결된 것을 고르시오.

1 ① day – days ② fish – fish
   ③ map – maps ④ roof – roofs
   ⑤ piano – pianoes

2 ① box – boxes ② lady – ladies
   ③ knife – knifes ④ tooth – teeth
   ⑤ potato – potatoes

3 빈칸에 들어갈 말로 알맞지 않은 것은?

There are _____ on the table.

① cups ② forks
③ sugars ④ bananas
⑤ four slices of cheese

4 빈칸에 들어갈 말이 나머지 넷과 다른 것은?
   ① Mary bought _____ camera.
   ② We found _____ empty seat.
   ③ I want _____ new school bag.
   ④ There is _____ book on the desk.
   ⑤ He is _____ university student.

[5-8] 다음 중 밑줄 친 부분이 잘못된 것을 고르시오.

5 ① I need hot <u>water</u>.
   ② Ms. Brown has <u>four children</u>.
   ③ We don't have much <u>moneys</u>.
   ④ There are <u>buses</u> on the road.
   ⑤ I bought <u>a cell phone</u> yesterday.

6 ① I wish you <u>luck</u>.
   ② We took <u>an elevator</u>.
   ③ The <u>babies</u> are crying.
   ④ He is from <u>an Australia</u>.
   ⑤ Ally always listens to <u>music</u>.

7 ① <u>A bowl of soup</u> is good for a cold.
   ② Please bring me <u>a piece of paper</u>.
   ③ I put <u>two slices of bread</u> on the plate.
   ④ Edwin had <u>two cup of coffees</u> today.
   ⑤ She drinks <u>three glasses of water</u> a day.

8 ① Look at the stars in <u>the sky</u>.
   ② He went to the airport <u>by a bus</u>.
   ③ I heard the song on <u>the radio</u>.
   ④ She <u>goes to bed</u> after 10:00 p.m.
   ⑤ I watched a TV show last night. <u>The show</u> was interesting.

84

서술형
[9-10] ( ) 안의 단어를 적절한 형태로 써서 문장을 완성하시오.

9 There were many _____ on the street. (leaf)

10 In China, most people drink _____. (tea)

빈출

11 다음 중 보기의 밑줄 친 부분과 쓰임이 같은 것은?

> 보기   She works five days a week.

① They live in a city.
② I got an email from Paul.
③ I bought a new bike last week.
④ There is a bakery on the corner.
⑤ Mark drove his car 60 km an hour.

빈출

12 빈칸에 들어갈 말이 바르게 짝지어진 것은?

> Kim bought ____(A)____ jacket yesterday. ____(B)____ jacket looks good on her.

	(A)		(B)
①	a	……	A
②	a	……	The
③	an	……	A
④	an	……	The
⑤	the	……	A

13 다음 중 밑줄 친 부분을 잘못 고친 것은?

① This is a interesting story. → an
② We took some photoes at the beach.
   → photos
③ Will you send me the information by a fax? → by the fax
④ I always carry two waters in my backpack. → two bottles of water
⑤ We had the dinner at the new restaurant. → dinner

서술형

[14-16] 빈칸에 알맞은 관사를 보기에서 골라 한 번씩만 써서 문장을 완성하시오. (X는 필요 없음을 뜻함)

> 보기   an   the   X

14 Do you have _____ email address?

15 Students don't go to _____ school on Saturdays.

16 I'll travel around _____ world someday.

서술형

17 빈칸에 공통으로 들어갈 관사를 쓰시오.

- Turn off _____ TV. It's too loud.
- _____ moon is full tonight.

서술형

18 우리말과 일치하도록 주어진 조건에 맞게 문장을 완성하시오.

뉴질랜드에는 많은 양들이 있다.

〈조건〉 1. many, sheep, New Zealand를 이용할 것
2. There로 시작할 것

→ _____ in _____.

19 다음 우리말을 영어로 바르게 옮긴 것은?

James는 피아노를 매일 친다.

① James plays piano every day.
② James plays a piano every day.
③ James plays an piano every day.
④ James plays the piano every day.
⑤ James plays pianos every day.

서술형

[20-21] 우리말과 일치하도록 ( ) 안의 말을 이용하여 문장을 완성하시오.

20 토마토는 건강에 좋다. (health)

→ Tomatoes are good for _____.

21 탁자 위에 있는 신문은 어제 것이다. (newspaper)

→ _____ on the table is from yesterday.

22 주어진 단어를 바르게 배열할 때 네 번째에 오는 단어는?

slices, I, of, need, cheese, two

① slices ② of ③ need
④ cheese ⑤ two

서술형

[23-24] ( ) 안의 말을 이용하여 대화를 완성하시오.

23 A: How did you get here?
B: I came here _____. (taxi)

24 A: Do you want some dessert?
B: Yes, I will have _____.
(a piece, cake)

고난도

25 다음 중 어법상 옳은 것을 모두 고르면?

① I saw three mans at the door.
② Matt had two bowls of rice.
③ Do you need my helps?
④ Mom bought a pair of jeans for me.
⑤ She wrote down her phone number on a piece of paper.

26 다음 중 어법상 옳은 것으로 바르게 짝지어진 것은?

> a. I play basketball in my free time.
> b. Keith went to Chicago by plane.
> c. A sun is behind the clouds.
> d. I take swimming lessons three times a week.
> e. I didn't have the breakfast this morning.

① a, b   ② a, c   ③ a, b, d
④ b, c, d   ⑤ c, d, e

고난도

27 다음 중 어법상 옳은 것의 개수는?

> · Minho sent me pictures by the email.
> · Debbie works forty hours a week.
> · I usually go to school at 8:30 a.m.
> · I read the book for a hour.
> · My foot are too cold in winter.

① 1개   ② 2개   ③ 3개
④ 4개   ⑤ 5개

서술형

[28-30] 밑줄 친 부분이 어법상 옳은지 판단하고, 틀리면 바르게 고치시오.

28 Two <u>thiefs</u> came into Kevin's house.

(O / X) _____

29 <u>A pencil</u> on the desk is Susie's.

(O / X) _____

30 I ordered a sweater on <u>internet</u>.

(O / X) _____

서술형   고난도

[31-33] 어법상 틀린 부분을 찾아 바르게 고치시오.

31 There is a big supermarket near my house. A supermarket sells a lot of things. I bought a orange yesterday. (2개)

32 I went to movies with Jenna last night. We watched an action movie. We enjoyed a movie a lot. (2개)

33 I went to a café with Sean. We had two cups of teas and two pieces of cheesecakes. We had a great time. (2개)

LET'S REVIEW

주요 예문을 다시 한번 확인하고, 우리말과 일치하도록 빈칸을 채우시오.

- I have **a brother.** 나는 남자 형제 한 명이 있다. `Unit 01 - A`

- I have two [1]_____. 나는 남자 형제 두 명이 있다. `Unit 01 - A`

- Can I have [2]_____? 제가 물을 마셔도 될까요? `Unit 01 - B`

- I'll drink [3]_____ **tea.** 나는 차 한 잔을 마실 것이다. `Unit 01 - B`

- I need [4]_____ **paper.** 나는 종이 두 장이 필요하다. `Unit 01 - B`

- I bought [5]_____ **jeans.** 나는 청바지 한 벌을 샀다. `Unit 01 - PLUS`

- I'm going to buy **a** shirt. 나는 셔츠 한 장을 살 것이다. `Unit 02 - A`

- Alice picked **a** card. Alice는 카드 한 장을 골랐다. `Unit 02 - A`

- I go to the dentist once [6]_____ **year.** 나는 일 년마다 한 번씩 치과에 간다. `Unit 02 - A`

- I watched a movie last night. [7]_____ movie was great.
  나는 어젯밤에 영화를 한 편 보았다. 그 영화는 훌륭했다. `Unit 02 - B`

- Can I use **the** computer? 내가 그 컴퓨터를 써도 되니? `Unit 02 - B`

- [8]_____ flowers in my garden are roses. 나의 정원에 있는 꽃들은 장미다. `Unit 02 - B`

🔍 **Answers**

[1] brothers   [2] water   [3] a cup of   [4] two pieces of   [5] a pair of   [6] a   [7] The   [8] The

ESSENTIAL RULES OF ENGLISH GRAMMAR

CHAPTER
07

대명사

대명사는 명사를 대신해서 쓰는 말로,
주로 명사의 반복을 피하기 위해 쓴다.

UNIT 01 인칭대명사, 재귀대명사

UNIT 02 this, that, it

UNIT 03 one, some, any

01 인칭대명사, 재귀대명사

A 인칭대명사와 재귀대명사

수	인칭	주격	소유격	목적격	소유대명사	재귀대명사
단수	1인칭	I	my	me	mine	myself
	2인칭	you	your	you	yours	yourself
	3인칭	he	his	him	his	himself
		she	her	her	hers	herself
		it	its	it	-	itself
복수	1인칭	we	our	us	ours	ourselves
	2인칭	you	your	you	yours	yourselves
	3인칭	they	their	them	theirs	themselves

Joan looks like **her** mother.
A: Is this bag **yours**?   B: Yes, it's **mine**.
                                        = my bag

① 고유명사의 소유격과 소유대명사는 뒤에 's를 붙여 나타낸다.
I know **Sarah's** email address.
The cell phone is **Kevin's**.
                        = Kevin's cell phone

B 재귀대명사의 쓰임

1 목적어가 주어와 같을 때 목적어 자리에 재귀대명사를 쓴다. 이 경우 '~ 자신'의 의미이며 생략할 수 없다.

You should take care of **yourself**.
She looked at **herself** in the mirror.

2 주어의 행동을 강조하고자 할 때 재귀대명사를 쓴다. 이 경우 '직접', '스스로'의 의미이며 생략이 가능하다.

I fixed the bike **myself**.

3 재귀대명사를 이용한 관용 표현

• by oneself: 혼자(다른 사람 없이), 혼자 힘으로   • for oneself: 혼자 힘으로, 스스로를 위해서
• help oneself (to): (~을) 마음껏 먹다   • make oneself at home: 편히 쉬다

Help yourself to the food!

CHECK UP 빈칸에 알맞은 말을 고르시오.

1 I bought a new dress. _____ color is red.
   ⓐ It   ⓑ Its   ⓒ It's

2 Did he draw this picture _____?
   ⓐ he   ⓑ him   ⓒ himself

PRACTICE

🔍 Answer Key p.11

( ) 안에서 알맞은 말을 고르시오.

1 The red scarf is (her, hers).

2 They visit (their, them) grandparents once a month.

3 He took lots of photos of (he, himself).

4 Were you sleeping? I called (you, yours) three times.

5 Sandra made the clothes (itself, herself).

6 Ted moved to (our, ourselves) neighborhood last weekend.

밑줄 친 부분을 대신하는 알맞은 대명사를 빈칸에 쓰시오.

1 <u>Mary</u> is funny and kind. I like _____.

2 Did you see <u>the strawberries</u>? _____ looked very fresh.

3 <u>Mr. Kim</u> is my English teacher. _____ is nice.

4 I'll buy <u>this camera</u>. _____ size is good for me.

5 <u>Tim and Julia</u> are my best friends. I see _____ every day.

빈칸에 알맞은 말을 보기에서 골라 적절한 형태로 바꿔 쓰시오. (단, 한 번씩만 쓸 것)

보기	by oneself	enjoy oneself	introduce oneself	help oneself to

1 I will _____ to you. My name is Jason.

2 Please _____ the cookies. I'll bring some tea.

3 A: Did she go to the concert with Billy?
   B: No. She went there _____.

4 A: Did you _____ at the party?
   B: Yes. I had a lot of fun.

우리말과 일치하도록 ( ) 안의 말을 이용하여 문장을 완성하시오.

1 너는 Daniel의 전화번호를 아니? (phone number)

→ Do you know _____ _____ _____?

2 그녀는 가끔씩 혼잣말을 한다. (talk to)

→ She sometimes _____ _____ _____.

3 내 컴퓨터가 작동하지 않아. 네 것을 쓸 수 있을까? (use)

→ My computer doesn't work. Can I _____ _____?

this, that, it

A

A 지시대명사

1 this는 가까운 대상을 가리킬 때 쓰며, '이것', '이 사람', '이 (~)'의 의미를 나타낸다.

> **This** is my room.
> **This** is my teacher Mrs. Parker.
> I'll buy **this** *jacket*.

2 this의 복수형은 these이다.

> **These** are my new jeans.
> **These** *questions* are very difficult.

3 that은 멀리 있는 대상을 가리킬 때 쓰며, '저것', '저 사람', '저 (~)'의 의미를 나타낸다.

> Is **that** your house?
> **That** is my little brother, Charlie.
> I know **that** *girl*.

4 that의 복수형은 those이다.

> **Those** are great movies.
> I like **those** *puppies*.

B 비인칭 주어 it

시간, 날짜, 요일, 날씨, 계절, 거리, 명암 등을 나타낼 때 비인칭 주어 it을 쓴다. 이때 it은 '그것'이라고 해석하지 않는다.

> **It** is 2:20 p.m.
> **It** is October 5.
> **It** is Monday today.
> **It** is cloudy and windy outside.
> **It** is spring in May.
> **It** is fifteen kilometers to the airport.
> **It** is dark at night.

CHECK UP 빈칸에 알맞은 말을 고르시오.

1 _____ is sunny today.

   ⓐ This   ⓑ That   ⓒ It

2 Can I borrow _____ CDs?

   ⓐ this   ⓑ these   ⓒ it

3 I went to _____ restaurant last night.

   ⓐ that   ⓑ those   ⓒ it

PRACTICE

Answer Key p.11

STEP 1

( ) 안에서 알맞은 말을 고르시오.

1 (This, Her) is my friend Donna.

2 (This, It) is 500 meters to the bus stop.

3 I like (this, these) pictures.

4 (That, It) is winter in Australia.

5 (That, Those) are Nick's socks.

6 Can you see (that, those) castle on the hill?

STEP 2

빈칸에 알맞은 말을 보기에서 골라 쓰시오. (단, 한 번씩만 쓸 것)

보기	this	that	those

1 You look great in _____ pants.

2 Can you read _____ sign over there?

3 I'll introduce my cousin to you. _____ is Tom.

STEP 3

( ) 안의 말을 이용하여 질문에 대한 대답을 쓰시오.

1 A: What day is it today?
B: _____. (Tuesday)

2 A: What's the weather like?
B: _____. (windy)

3 A: What time is it?
B: _____. (9:30 p.m.)

4 A: What's the date today?
B: _____. (November 15)

STEP 4

우리말과 일치하도록 ( ) 안의 말을 이용하여 문장을 완성하시오.

1 우리는 이 사진들을 2019년에 찍었다. (pictures)

→ We took _____ _____ in 2019.

2 저 노래는 내가 가장 좋아하는 것이다. (song)

→ _____ _____ is my favorite.

3 그 방 안은 밝다. (bright)

→ _____ _____ _____ in the room.

one, some, any

one

1 앞에 나온 명사와 같은 종류의 불특정한 사물이나 사람을 가리킨다.

I don't have a camera. I'll buy **one** soon.
<u>= a camera</u>

I like this T-shirt, but do you have a blue **one**?
<u>= a blue T-shirt</u>

cf. it은 앞에 나온 명사와 동일한 것을 가리킨다.
I lost my key, and I couldn't find **it**.
<u>= the key</u>

2 one의 복수형은 ones이다.

These towels are dirty. I need clean **ones**.
<u>= clean towels</u>

B

some, any

1 some은 주로 긍정문과 권유를 나타내는 의문문에 쓰여 '조금(의)', '몇 개(의)'의 의미를 나타낸다.

I need **some** money for lunch.
These apples look nice. I'll buy **some**.
Will you have **some** dessert?

2 any는 주로 부정문과 의문문에 쓰여 '조금(도)', '어떤', '아무'의 의미를 나타낸다.

We don't have **any** homework today.
A: Do you have **any** ideas?
B: No, I don't have **any**.

① some과 any는 셀 수 있는 명사와 셀 수 없는 명사 둘 다에 쓸 수 있다.

CHECK UP 빈칸에 알맞은 말을 고르시오.

1 My cell phone doesn't work. I'll buy a new _____.
ⓐ one   ⓑ ones   ⓒ it

2 I borrowed _____ books from the library.
ⓐ one   ⓑ some   ⓒ any

3 I don't have _____ plans for this weekend.
ⓐ one   ⓑ some   ⓒ any

4 A: Did you see that movie?   B: Yes, I saw _____.
ⓐ one   ⓑ ones   ⓒ it

PRACTICE

Answer Key p.11

STEP 1

( ) 안에서 알맞은 말을 고르시오.

1 Will you have (some, any) coffee?

2 Lewis doesn't have (some, any) pets.

3 I need a hairbrush. Do you have (it, one)?

4 I sent you an email yesterday. Did you get (it, one)?

5 I want (some, any) bread, but I don't want (some, any) butter on it.

STEP 2

빈칸에 알맞은 말을 보기에서 골라 쓰시오.

보기	one ones it

1 I need new glasses. I lost my old _____.

2 I don't have my wallet. I left _____ at home.

3 This bowl is too big. Can you bring me a small _____?

4 A: Can I borrow a pen?
B: Sorry, I don't have _____.

STEP 3

빈칸에 some 또는 any를 넣어 대화를 완성하시오.

1 A: Will you buy this bag?
B: No. I don't have _____ money for it.

2 A: Will you have _____ pizza?
B: No, thank you. I'm full.

3 A: I brought _____ photos of my family.
B: Can I see them?

4 A: Do you have _____ brothers or sisters?
B: No. I'm an only child.

STEP 4

우리말과 일치하도록 ( ) 안의 말을 이용하여 문장을 완성하시오.

1 Ian은 꽃을 조금도 사지 않았다. (flowers)

→ Ian didn't buy _____ _____.

2 나는 자전거가 없지만 한 대 필요하다. (need)

→ I don't have a bicycle, but I _____ _____.

3 나는 오늘 잡지를 몇 권 읽었다. (magazines)

→ I read _____ _____ today.

GRAMMAR FOR WRITING

A 우리말과 일치하도록 ( ) 안의 말을 이용하여 문장을 완성하시오.

1 오늘은 비가 내리고 바람이 분다. (rainy and windy)

→ _____ today.

2 이 거리는 깨끗하다. (street)

→ _____ is clean.

3 너는 너 자신을 사랑해야 한다. (should, love)

→ _____.

4 나는 그에게서 어떤 소식도 듣지 못했다. (news)

→ I didn't hear _____ from him.

5 우리는 Cindy의 생일 파티를 위한 약간의 계획을 짰다. (make, plans)

→ _____ for Cindy's birthday party.

6 나는 포크를 떨어뜨렸다. 나는 새것이 필요하다. (new)

→ I dropped my fork. I need a _____.

7 선생님은 우리에게 편지를 써 주셨다. (write)

→ The teacher _____ a letter.

B 우리말과 일치하도록 ( ) 안에 주어진 말을 바르게 배열하시오.

1 저 사람들은 내 사촌들이다. (cousins, those, my, are)

→ _____.

2 나는 이 장난감들을 Ronda에게 줄 것이다. (give, toys, I, to Ronda, will, these)

→ _____.

3 이곳은 어둡다. (is, it, here, dark)

→ _____.

4 케이크를 좀 드시겠어요? (have, will, cake, you, some)

→ _____?

5 우리는 우리 자신의 사진을 찍었다. (took, we, of, ourselves, a picture)

→ _____.

6 이것이 내 이메일 주소야. 내가 네 것을 알 수 있을까? (get, can, yours, I)

→ This is my email address. _____?

C 주어진 문장의 밑줄 친 부분을 it, one, ones 중 알맞은 것으로 바꿔 써서 대화를 완성하시오.

> **1** I didn't bring <u>my ID card</u> today.
> **2** My old <u>shoes</u> don't fit anymore.
> **3** I should borrow <u>an umbrella</u>.

1 A: Can I see your ID card?
　 B: I'm sorry. I _____ today.

2 A: Did you buy new shoes?
　 B: Yes, my _____ anymore.

3 A: Did you take your umbrella?
　 B: No. I should _____.

D 그림을 보고 보기에서 알맞은 말을 골라 적절한 형태로 바꿔 써서 문장을 완성하시오. (과거형으로 쓸 것)

1　　　　**2**　　　　**3**　　　　**4**

보기	hurt oneself	help oneself	make oneself at home	by oneself

1 Dan walked along the beach _____.

2 The little girl fell down the stairs and _____.

3 Philip and Karen _____ to the food at the buffet.

4 The hotel was wonderful. We _____.

REVIEW TEST

[1–4] 빈칸에 들어갈 알맞은 말을 고르시오.

1

A: Do you know Jane?
B: No, I don't know _____.

① she   ② her   ③ hers
④ it   ⑤ them

2

_____ cookies taste good.

① It   ② This   ③ These
④ That   ⑤ They

3

A: Do you have a laptop?
B: Yes, I have a good _____.

① it   ② one   ③ ones
④ some   ⑤ any

4

I don't have _____ time today.

① it   ② one   ③ ones
④ some   ⑤ any

[5–7] 다음 중 밑줄 친 부분이 올바른 것을 고르시오.

5

① These tomato looks good.
② The children washed their hands.
③ I know hers email address.
④ Tom went for a walk by itself.
⑤ The boy is playing with its dog.

6

① It is Friday today.
② He left him wallet on the bus.
③ That is 50 km from here to Busan.
④ That woman is ours English teacher.
⑤ We enjoyed themselves on the beach.

7

① My sister looks like I.
② I have Jack's phone number.
③ I saw your at the shopping mall.
④ The hairpin on the desk is her.
⑤ I looked at oneself in the lake.

8 빈칸에 들어갈 말이 바르게 짝지어진 것은?

_____ (A) _____ bike is new, but _____ (B) _____ is very old.

	(A)		(B)
①	Peter	……	I
②	Peter	……	my
③	Peter	……	mine
④	Peter's	……	my
⑤	Peter's	……	mine

[9-10] 다음 중 대화가 자연스럽지 <u>않은</u> 것을 고르시오.

9 ① A: This is my friend Natalie.
　　B: Nice to meet you, Natalie.
② A: Will you have some water?
　　B: Yes, please.
③ A: What's the date today?
　　B: This is April 9.
④ A: Do you have any coins?
　　B: No, I don't have any.
⑤ A: What's the weather like outside?
　　B: It's sunny.

10 ① A: Is your school far from here?
　　B: No. It's only fifty meters away.
② A: Is this Emily's book?
　　B: Yes, it's hers.
③ A: What day is it?
　　B: It is Wednesday.
④ A: Is this coat yours?
　　B: Yes, they're mine.
⑤ A: Do you know that song?
　　B: No, I don't know it.

서술형
[11-12] 우리말과 일치하도록 빈칸에 알맞은 말을 쓰시오.

11 이 가방은 그의 것이다.

→ This bag is _____.

12 엄마는 우리를 위해 점심을 만들고 계신다.

→ Mom is making lunch for _____.

빈출
[13-14] 다음 중 밑줄 친 부분이 <u>잘못된</u> 것을 고르시오.

13 ① I will buy <u>some clothes</u>.
② Do you have <u>any hobbies</u>?
③ There are <u>some cups</u> on the table.
④ Diana didn't have <u>some pets</u>.
⑤ We had <u>some biscuits</u> together.

14 ① Alex is nice. <u>He</u> always helps me.
② This is Jina's notebook. Give <u>it</u> back to her.
③ He has a car. He drives <u>one</u> to work every day.
④ They live in this neighborhood. That's <u>their</u> house.
⑤ Dan has a grandmother. He visits <u>her</u> every weekend.

15 다음 중 어느 빈칸에도 들어갈 수 <u>없는</u> 것은?

___ⓐ___ was very hot yesterday. I saw an old man with ___ⓑ___ heavy boxes. I carried ___ⓒ___ for him. I was tired, but I was proud of ___ⓓ___.

① some[Some]　　② ones[Ones]
③ myself[Myself]　　④ them[Them]
⑤ it[It]

16 다음 중 밑줄 친 부분이 <u>잘못된</u> 것은?

A: Do you have ① <u>any pens</u>?
B: I have ② <u>two black ones</u> and ③ <u>a red one</u>.
A: Can I use ④ <u>a black it</u>?
B: Sure, ⑤ <u>here you are</u>.
A: Thank you.

서술형

17 빈칸에 알맞은 재귀대명사를 쓰시오.

> I don't need any help. I can do it
> _____.

서술형

18 빈칸에 공통으로 들어갈 말을 쓰시오.

> A: _____ is very cold today. Can
> you turn on the heater?
> B: Sorry. _____ doesn't work now.

서술형

19 대화가 성립되도록 (   ) 안에서 알맞은 말을 골라 쓰시오.

> A: Is there a bank near here?
> B: Yes, there is ⓐ (it, one) on Queen
> Street.
> A: Is ⓑ (it, one) far from here to the
> bank?
> B: Not really.

ⓐ _____   ⓑ _____

서술형

[20-24] 우리말과 일치하도록 (   ) 안의 말을 이용하여
문장을 완성하시오.

20 이 선물은 너를 위한 거야. (gift)

→ _____ is for you.

21 차를 좀 드시겠어요? (tea)

→ Will you have _____?

22 지금은 2시다. (two o'clock)

→ _____ now.

23 거리에는 눈이 조금도 없었다. (snow)

→ There wasn't _____ on the
street.

24 너는 너 자신을 믿어야 한다. (trust, oneself)

→ You should _____.

고난도

25 다음 중 어법상 옳은 것을 모두 고르면?

① This is very bright outside.
② There is any water in the bottle.
③ My brother made dinner for himself.
④ These pants are too tight for me.
⑤ This is she computer, not mine.

26 다음 중 어법상 옳은 것으로 바르게 짝지어진 것은?

> a. That is January 24.
> b. These teddy bears are cute.
> c. I met his at the station.
> d. Jason finished the work by himself.
> e. I bought my watch last year. But now I want a new one.

① a, d ② b, e ③ a, b, e
④ b, d, e ⑤ c, d, e

고난도

27 다음 중 어법상 옳은 것의 개수는?

> • This gloves protect my hands.
> • He burned himself on the stove.
> • Those are mine new toys.
> • I have to leave now. It's 8:00 a.m.
> • He brought some letters to me.

① 1개 ② 2개 ③ 3개
④ 4개 ⑤ 5개

서술형

[28-30] 밑줄 친 부분이 어법상 옳은지 판단하고, 틀리면 바르게 고치시오.

28 Do you speak <u>any</u> foreign languages?

(O / X) _____

29 I think of <u>me</u> as a nice person.

(O / X) _____

30 Anna is a popular blogger. This fashion blog is <u>she's</u>.

(O / X) _____

서술형 고난도

[31-33] 어법상 틀린 부분을 찾아 바르게 고치시오.

31 My sister bought a pair of black boots. She bought purple one, too. She must be rich! (1개)

32 It was Christmas Day yesterday. My parents gave mine a gift. It was a scarf. I liked its. (2개)

33 A: Do you want some pasta and salad?
B: Yes, please. I didn't eat some food this morning.
A: You must be hungry. Help oneself.
B: Thank you. (2개)

LET'S REVIEW

주요 예문을 다시 한번 확인하고, 우리말과 일치하도록 빈칸을 채우시오.

- Joan looks like **her** mother. Joan은 그녀의 어머니를 닮았다. `Unit 01 - A`
- A: Is this bag **yours**? 이 가방은 네 것이니?
  B: Yes, it's ¹_____. 응, 그것은 내 거야. `Unit 01 - A`

- She looked at **herself** in the mirror. 그녀는 거울 속 자신을 바라보았다. `Unit 01 - B`
- I fixed the bike ²_____. 나는 자전거를 내가 직접 고쳤다. `Unit 01 - B`
- ³_____ the food! 음식을 마음껏 드세요! `Unit 01 - B`

- I'll buy ⁴_____ jacket. 나는 이 재킷을 살 것이다. `Unit 02 - A`
- **These** questions are very difficult. 이 질문들은 매우 어렵다. `Unit 02 - A`
- Is **that** your house? 저것이 너의 집이니? `Unit 02 - A`
- ⁵_____ are great movies. 저것들은 훌륭한 영화이다. `Unit 02 - A`

- **It** is 2:20 p.m. 오후 2시 20분이다. `Unit 02 - B`
- ⁶_____ is October 5. 10월 5일이다. `Unit 02 - B`
- **It** is Monday today. 오늘은 월요일이다. `Unit 02 - B`
- **It** is cloudy and windy outside. 밖은 흐리고 바람이 분다. `Unit 02 - B`

- I don't have a camera. I'll buy ⁷_____ soon.
  나는 카메라가 없다. 나는 조만간 하나를 살 것이다. `Unit 03 - A`
- These towels are dirty. I need clean ⁸_____.
  이 수건들은 더럽다. 나는 깨끗한 것들이 필요하다. `Unit 03 - A`

- I need ⁹_____ money for lunch. 나는 점심을 위한 돈이 좀 필요하다. `Unit 03 - B`
- Will you have **some** dessert? 너 디저트를 좀 먹을래? `Unit 03 - B`
- We don't have ¹⁰_____ homework today. 우리는 오늘 숙제가 조금도 없다. `Unit 03 - B`
- Do you have **any** ideas? 너는 아이디어가 좀 있니? `Unit 03 - B`

Answers

¹ mine   ² myself   ³ Help yourself to   ⁴ this   ⁵ Those   ⁶ It   ⁷ one   ⁸ ones   ⁹ some   ¹⁰ any

CHAPTER

08

형용사와 부사

형용사는 명사, 대명사를 꾸며주거나
주어, 목적어를 설명해 주는 보어 역할을
하고, 부사는 주로 동사, 형용사를 꾸며준다.

UNIT 01 형용사

UNIT 02 부사

UNIT 03 원급, 비교급, 최상급

형용사

형용사의 쓰임

1 명사, 대명사의 앞이나 뒤에서 명사, 대명사를 꾸며준다. -thing, -body, -one으로 끝나는 대명사는
형용사가 뒤에서 꾸며준다.

We climbed a **high** *mountain*.
I want *something* **cold**.

2 동사 또는 목적어의 뒤에서 주어나 목적어를 보충 설명하는 보어 역할을 한다.

This bag is **heavy**.
The news made *him* **happy**.

수와 양을 나타내는 형용사

1 many, much, a lot of, lots of

many(많은)	셀 수 있는 명사의 복수형
much(많은)	셀 수 없는 명사
a lot of, lots of(많은)	셀 수 있는 명사의 복수형, 셀 수 없는 명사

Bill has **many** *friends*.
There isn't **much** *water* in the bottle.
I meet **a lot of**[lots of] *people* online.

2 a few, few, a little, little

a few(조금 있는, 약간의) / few(거의 없는)	셀 수 있는 명사의 복수형
a little(조금 있는, 약간의) / little(거의 없는)	셀 수 없는 명사

I read **a few** *books* last month.
Few *animals* can live in the desert.

She poured **a little** *milk* into her tea.
We had **little** *snow* last winter.

CHECK UP 빈칸에 알맞지 <u>않은</u> 말을 고르시오.

1 Joan is a _____ girl.
  ⓐ smart   ⓑ polite   ⓒ love

2 We have _____ time now.
  ⓐ a few   ⓑ a little   ⓒ a lot of

PRACTICE

🔍 Answer Key p.12

( ) 안에서 알맞은 말을 고르시오.

1 They were (friend, friendly) to me.

2 Seven is a (luck, lucky) number.

3 I invited (a few, a little) people for dinner.

4 She doesn't have (many, much) experience.

5 There's (wrong something, something wrong) with my computer.

STEP 2

( ) 안의 형용사가 들어갈 알맞은 곳을 고르시오.

1 I ⓐ need ⓑ a ⓒ bicycle. (new)

2 These ⓐ cakes ⓑ look ⓒ. (delicious)

3 That's ⓐ a ⓑ problem ⓒ. (serious)

4 That song ⓐ makes ⓑ me ⓒ. (sad)

STEP 3

빈칸에 알맞은 말을 보기에서 골라 쓰시오. (단, 한 번씩만 쓸 것)

보기	few	little	a lot of	much

1 I have _____ money. I can't buy that jacket.

2 She reads _____ books. She is a bookworm.

3 There were _____ people on the train. It wasn't crowded.

4 Tony doesn't have _____ work this week. He's not busy.

우리말과 일치하도록 ( ) 안의 말을 이용하여 문장을 완성하시오.

1 Nora는 어제 아팠다. (sick)

   → Nora _____ _____ yesterday.

2 나는 커피를 거의 마시지 않는다. (coffee)

   → I drink _____ _____ .

3 이 잼에는 많은 설탕이 들어있다. (sugar)

   → This jam has _____ _____ _____ in it.

4 그는 너를 어떤 좋은 사람에게 소개해 줄 것이다. (nice, someone)

   → He'll introduce you to _____ _____ .

UNIT
02 부사

A 부사의 쓰임

1 부사는 주로 동사, 형용사를 꾸며준다.

Sarah *sings* **beautifully**.
This math question is **very** *difficult*.

2 다른 부사나 문장 전체를 꾸며주기도 한다.

He came home **quite** *early*.
Luckily, *I got free tickets*.

B 부사의 형태

대부분의 부사	형용사 + -ly	sad**ly** slow**ly** loud**ly** kind**ly** real**ly** beautiful**ly**	
-y로 끝나는 형용사로 만드는 부사	y를 i로 고치고 + -ly	happy → happ**ily** lucky → luck**ily**	easy → eas**ily** heavy → heav**ily**
형용사와 형태가 같은 부사	fast(빠른) → **fast**(빠르게) early(이른) → **early**(일찍) late(늦은) → **late**(늦게) high(높은) → **high**(높게) hard(어려운, 열심히 하는) → **hard**(열심히)		
〈부사 + ly〉가 다른 뜻을 가지는 부사	**hard**(열심히) – **hardly**(거의 ~않는) **late**(늦게) – **lately**(최근에)	**high**(높게) – **highly**(매우) **near**(가까이) – **nearly**(거의)	

Cars move **slowly** in rush hour.
I got up **late** this morning.

cf. Susan was *late* for class again.

Mike is working **hard**. / I **hardly** know her.

C 빈도부사

빈도부사는 어떤 일이 얼마나 자주 일어나는지를 나타내는 말로, be동사나 조동사의 뒤, 일반동사의 앞에 쓴다.

(0%) never → seldom, rarely → sometimes → often → usually → always (100%)
(결코 ~ 않다)   (거의 ~ 않다)   (가끔)   (자주)   (보통, 대개)   (항상)

Laura *is* **always** busy on weekends.
Tom **sometimes** *plays* the guitar.

CHECK UP 빈칸에 알맞지 <u>않은</u> 말을 고르시오.

1 She talked _____.
ⓐ easy   ⓑ quietly   ⓒ seriously

2 Kevin drives _____.
ⓐ fast   ⓑ slowly   ⓒ careful

➕ PLUS : -ly로 끝나는 형용사

lovely(사랑스러운), friendly(상냥한),
lonely(외로운), lively(활기찬) 등은 -ly로
끝나지만 부사가 아니라 형용사이다.

He is a **friendly** boy.

PRACTICE

Answer Key p.12

STEP 1

( ) 안에서 알맞은 말을 고르시오.

1 My father eats (fast, fastly).

2 It is raining (heavy, heavily).

3 (Sad, Sadly), my best friend moved to another city.

4 He came (late, lately) to the meeting again.

5 I (always eat, eat always) healthy meals.

STEP 2

밑줄 친 부사가 꾸며주는 말에 동그라미 하시오.

1 I studied <u>hard</u> for the test.

2 <u>Surprisingly</u>, this tree is 500 years old.

3 She spent her money <u>wisely</u>.

4 The movie was <u>really</u> long.

5 Emily speaks <u>very</u> loudly.

6 <u>Honestly</u>, I don't remember his name.

STEP 3

( ) 안의 말을 알맞은 곳에 넣어 문장을 완성하시오.

1 You should lock the door. (always)

→ You _____.

2 He is absent from work. (rarely)

→ He _____.

3 I will tell your secret to others. (never)

→ I _____.

4 Jane has strawberry ice cream for dessert. (usually)

→ Jane _____.

STEP 4

우리말과 일치하도록 ( ) 안의 말을 이용하여 문장을 완성하시오.

1 그는 일찍 잠자리에 든다. (go to bed, early)

→ He _____ _____ _____ _____.

2 우리는 그 건물을 쉽게 찾았다. (find, easy)

→ We _____ the building _____.

3 Oliver는 거의 밤을 새지 않는다. (stay up, seldom)

→ Oliver _____ _____ _____ all night.

원급, 비교급, 최상급

A 원급

as + 형용사/부사의 원급 + as: ~만큼 …한/하게

I am **as old as** you.

B 비교급

형용사/부사의 비교급 + than: ~보다 더 …한/하게

Today is **warmer than** yesterday.

ⓘ 비교급 앞에 much, far, a lot, even 등을 써서 비교급을 강조할 수 있다.
My cell phone is **much** *smaller* than yours.

C 최상급

the + 형용사/부사의 최상급: 가장 ~한/하게

This is **the fastest** way to the airport.

ⓘ 최상급 뒤에 「in + 장소, 단체를 나타내는 단수명사」, 「of + 복수명사」를 써서 비교의 범위를 나타낼 수 있다.
This is *the tallest* building **in the city**.

D 비교급, 최상급 만드는 법

<table>
<tr><td colspan="3"></td><td>원급</td><td>비교급</td><td>최상급</td></tr>
<tr><td rowspan="5">규칙변화</td><td>대부분의 형용사/부사</td><td>+ -er/-est</td><td>small</td><td>smaller</td><td>smallest</td></tr>
<tr><td>-e로 끝나는
형용사/부사</td><td>+ -r/-st</td><td>nice</td><td>nicer</td><td>nicest</td></tr>
<tr><td>〈단모음 + 단자음〉으로
끝나는 형용사/부사</td><td>자음을 한 번 더 쓰고
+ -er/-est</td><td>big</td><td>bigger</td><td>biggest</td></tr>
<tr><td>-y로 끝나는
형용사/부사</td><td>y를 i로 고치고
+ -er/-est</td><td>easy</td><td>easier</td><td>easiest</td></tr>
<tr><td>3음절 이상의 형용사/부사와
-ous, -ful 등으로 끝나는 2음절어</td><td>more/most +</td><td>interesting</td><td>**more**
interesting</td><td>**most**
interesting</td></tr>
<tr><td colspan="2" rowspan="4">불규칙 변화</td><td>good/well</td><td>**better**</td><td>**best**</td></tr>
<tr><td>bad</td><td>**worse**</td><td>**worst**</td></tr>
<tr><td>many/much</td><td>**more**</td><td>**most**</td></tr>
<tr><td>little</td><td>**less**</td><td>**least**</td></tr>
</table>

This is a *good* camera. It's **better** than that one. It's the **best** camera in this shop.

CHECK UP 빈칸에 알맞은 말을 고르시오.

1 Jessica is the _____ person in her family.
ⓐ young　　ⓑ younger　　ⓒ youngest

PRACTICE

🔍 Answer Key p.13

 STEP 1

( ) 안에서 알맞은 말을 고르시오.

1 The shirt is as (new, newer) as the sweater.

2 Next week will be (hot, hotter) than this week.

3 She speaks English (well, better) than me.

4 That man has the (longer, longest) name in the world.

5 The sofa is (more comfortable, most comfortable) than the chair.

STEP 2

( ) 안의 말을 적절한 형태로 바꿔 비교급 문장을 완성하시오.

1 Daniel is _____ me. (tall)

2 China is _____ India. (large)

3 This laptop is _____ that one. (thin)

4 My sister's room is _____ mine. (big)

5 My father came home _____ me today. (early)

6 This test is _____ the last one. (difficult)

STEP 3

빈칸에 알맞은 말을 보기에서 골라 적절한 형태로 바꿔 최상급 문장을 완성하시오. (단, 한 번씩만 쓸 것)

보기	bad smart strong crowded

1 Max is _____ student in the class. He always gets As.

2 That team is _____ of all. They will win the championship.

3 Yesterday was _____ day of my life. I made a terrible mistake.

4 This is _____ restaurant in the city. It serves excellent food.

STEP 4

우리말과 일치하도록 ( ) 안의 말을 이용하여 문장을 완성하시오.

1 Joan은 나보다 더 빨리 수영한다. (fast)

→ Joan swims _____ _____ me.

2 이곳은 시내에서 가장 좋은 호텔이다. (good, hotel)

→ This is _____ _____ _____ in town.

3 이 신발은 저 신발만큼 멋지다. (nice)

→ These shoes are _____ _____ _____ those ones.

4 그 영화는 책보다 더 인기 있었다. (popular)

→ The movie was _____ _____ _____ the book.

GRAMMAR FOR WRITING

A 우리말과 일치하도록 ( ) 안의 말을 이용하여 문장을 완성하시오.

1 Maria는 정직하다. (honest)

→ Maria _____.

2 벽에 아름다운 그림 하나가 있었다. (beautiful, picture)

→ There was a _____ on the wall.

3 그는 문을 조용히 닫았다. (the door, quiet)

→ He closed _____.

4 교실에 몇몇 학생들이 있다. (students)

→ There are _____ in the classroom.

5 목성은 금성보다 훨씬 더 크다. (much, big, Venus)

→ Jupiter is _____.

6 이것은 그 영화에서 가장 유명한 장면이다. (famous, scene)

→ This is _____ in the movie.

7 그 배우는 거의 인터뷰를 하지 않는다. (rarely, have interviews)

→ The actor _____.

B 우리말과 일치하도록 ( ) 안에 주어진 말을 바르게 배열하시오.

1 그녀는 그 소식에 슬펐다. (felt, about the news, sad, she)

→ _____.

2 그는 빵 위에 약간의 버터를 발랐다. (little, spread, he, a, butter)

→ _____ on the bread.

3 John은 그의 팀에서 가장 훌륭한 선수이다. (the, player, is, best, on his team)

→ John _____.

4 나는 Amy만큼 열심히 공부했다. (as, studied, as, hard, Amy)

→ I _____.

5 내게는 수학이 과학보다 훨씬 더 재미있다. (more, science, interesting, than, much)

→ Math is _____ for me.

6 Kevin은 자주 두통을 앓는다. (often, a headache, Kevin, has)

→ _____.

C 주어진 내용을 읽고 ( ) 안의 말을 이용하여 비교급 또는 최상급 문장을 완성하시오.

1
> Emily and Ann are my cousins.
> Emily is ten years old. Ann is eight years old.

→ Emily is _____ Ann. (old)

2
> I bought a novel and a comic book at the bookstore.
> The novel cost $8. The comic book cost $4.

→ The novel was _____ the comic book. (expensive)

3
> We have three runners in our class: Judy, Steve, and Lucy.
> Judy runs 100 meters in 16 seconds.
> Steve runs 100 meters in 15 seconds.
> Lucy runs 100 meters in 17 seconds.

→ Steve is _____ runner in our class. (fast)

D 그림을 보고 보기에서 알맞은 말을 골라 ( ) 안의 말과 함께 써서 문장을 완성하시오.

1   **2**   **3**   **4**

보기	little	few	many	much

1 Sharks have _____. (tooth)

2 There are _____ in the parking lot. (car)

3 I don't have _____. I should hurry up. (time)

4 We had _____ last year. It was too dry. (rain)

REVIEW TEST

[1-2] 빈칸에 들어갈 말로 알맞지 <u>않은</u> 것을 고르시오.

1

| A _____ baby is sleeping in the bed. |

① cute   ② pretty   ③ little

④ lovely   ⑤ happily

2

| The train is _____ faster than the bus. |

① very   ② much   ③ even

④ far   ⑤ a lot

[3-4] 다음 중 밑줄 친 부분이 올바른 것을 고르시오.

3   ① Andrew walks <u>fastly</u>.

② The people were <u>quietly</u>.

③ This bicycle is <u>expensively</u>.

④ They live in a <u>largely</u> house.

⑤ This sweater feels <u>good</u>.

4   ① This room has a <u>nicely</u> view.

② He listened to me <u>carefully</u>.

③ Jisu speaks English <u>perfect</u>.

④ Sue looked <u>well</u> in a red dress.

⑤ She finished her homework <u>quick</u>.

서술형

[5-7] ( ) 안의 말을 이용하여 문장을 완성하시오.

5

Susan is _____ her mother. They're both 160 cm tall. (tall)

6

My bag is _____ Eric's bag. I have more books in it. (heavy)

7

Tokyo is _____ city in Japan. It is also the capital of the country. (big)

빈출

[8-9] ( ) 안의 말이 들어갈 위치를 고르시오.

8

| (usually)
I ① go ② to ③ school ④ by ⑤ bus. |

9

| (never)
I ① will ② tell ③ a lie ④ to ⑤ you. |

[10-11] 다음 중 밑줄 친 부분이 잘못된 것을 고르시오.

10 ① He is an <u>honest</u> boy.
② The glass is <u>nearly</u> empty.
③ She <u>kindly</u> helped us.
④ This is my <u>newly</u> address.
⑤ Baseball is an <u>exciting</u> sport.

11 ① My suitcase is <u>lighter than</u> yours.
② He plays the piano <u>better than</u> me.
③ The skirt costs <u>more than</u> the shorts.
④ This book is <u>as useful as</u> that book.
⑤ Today was <u>the most cold</u> day of the year.

[12-13] 다음 우리말을 영어로 바르게 옮긴 것을 고르시오.

12 우리 언니는 나보다 더 빠르게 타자를 친다.

① I type more quick than my sister.
② I type more quickly than my sister.
③ My sister types as quick as me.
④ My sister types more quicker than me.
⑤ My sister types more quickly than me.

13 그녀는 학교에서 가장 어린 학생이다.

① She is young student in school.
② She is younger student in school.
③ She is the most young student in school.
④ She is the youngest student in school.
⑤ She is the most youngest student in school.

서술형 빈출

[14-16] 빈칸에 알맞은 말을 보기에서 골라 문장을 완성하시오. (단, 한 번씩만 쓸 것)

| 보기 | a few | much | little |

14 I don't have _____ furniture in my room.

15 I bought _____ magazines at the bookstore.

16 There is _____ air in the balloon. It is almost empty.

[17-18] 빈칸에 들어갈 말이 바르게 짝지어진 것을 고르시오.

17

> • A turtle is ____(A)____ .
> • You should eat your food ____(B)____ .

	(A)		(B)
①	slow	......	slow
②	slowly	......	slow
③	slow	......	slowly
④	slowly	......	slowly
⑤	slower	......	slow

18

> • It was a ____(A)____ question.
>   I couldn't answer it.
> • The two women ____(B)____ know
>   each other.

	(A)		(B)
①	hard	......	hard
②	hard	......	hardly
③	hardly	......	hardly
④	hardly	......	hard
⑤	hardest	......	hard

서술형

[19-20] 우리말과 일치하도록 ( ) 안의 말을 이용하여 문장
을 완성하시오.

19 내 새로운 휴대 전화는 예전 것보다 더 좋다. (good)

→ My new cell phone is _____
my old one.

20 아인슈타인은 역사상 가장 똑똑한 사람이다.
(intelligent, person)

→ Einstein is _____ in
history.

서술형

[21-22] 우리말과 일치하도록 ( ) 안에 주어진 말을 바르게
배열하시오.

21 이번 봄은 작년 봄만큼 따뜻하다.
(as, is, warm, last spring, as)

→ This spring _____.

22 우리는 인터넷에서 흥미로운 것을 발견했다.
(found, we, interesting, something)

→ _____
on the internet.

23 주어진 단어를 바르게 배열할 때 세 번째에 오는 단어는?

> their, visit, they, grandparents, often,
> will

① their   ② visit   ③ they
④ often   ⑤ will

서술형

24 다음 표를 보고 주어진 조건에 맞게 비교급 문장을 완성
하시오.

Movie	Running Time
Soul	1 hour 47 minutes
Toy Story 4	1 hour 40 minutes

〈조건〉 1. be동사, short를 이용할 것
       2. 현재시제로 쓸 것

→ *Toy Story 4* _____.

25 다음 중 어법상 옳은 것을 모두 고르면?

① Kelly saw a cute dog today.
② Sumi buys sometimes things online.
③ The show was quite boring.
④ I'll tell you something funny.
⑤ I have a little problems with my sister.

26 다음 중 어법상 옳은 것으로 바르게 짝지어진 것은?

> a. I spent a few money in the market.
> b. Canada is as cold as Russia.
> c. My hair is longer than yours.
> d. I go rarely to the park for jogging.
> e. Colin's hat is more nice than mine.

① b, c   ② c, e   ③ a, b, c
④ b, c, d   ⑤ b, c, e

27 다음 중 어법상 옳은 것의 개수는?

> · Suddenly, he fell down the stairs.
> · Kate often feels tired these days.
> · Jill is much kinder than Tracy.
> · Andy didn't put many salt in his soup.
> · Did you hear new anything?

① 1개   ② 2개   ③ 3개
④ 4개   ⑤ 5개

[28-29] 밑줄 친 부분이 어법상 옳은지 판단하고, 틀리면 바르게 고치시오.

28 This cake has <u>few</u> sugar, so it's not very sweet.

(O / X) _____

29 My cat can jump <u>highly</u> in the air.

(O / X) _____

[30-32] 어법상 틀린 부분을 찾아 바르게 고치시오.

30 Dad drives usually the car slowly. But today he was very lately. He had to drive fast! (2개)

31 A: I had a greatly vacation. I traveled through Europe.
B: That sounds amazing! Where did you like the most?
A: Switzerland. It was the more beautiful country of all. (2개)

32 My friend Joan is the most smart girl in the class. She is also the funnyest. She tells us much funny stories. (3개)

LET'S REVIEW

주요 예문을 다시 한번 확인하고, 우리말과 일치하도록 빈칸을 채우시오.

- I want something [1]_____. 나는 차가운 것을 원한다. Unit 01 - A
- The news made him **happy**. 그 소식은 그를 행복하게 만들었다. Unit 01 - A

- Bill has **many** friends. Bill은 친구들이 많다. Unit 01 - B
- There isn't [2]_____ water in the bottle. 병에 물이 많지 않다. Unit 01 - B
- I meet **a lot of[lots of]** people online. 나는 온라인에서 많은 사람들을 만난다. Unit 01 - B
- I read **a few** books last month. 나는 지난달에 몇 권의 책을 읽었다. Unit 01 - B
- [3]_____ animals can live in the desert. 사막에서는 동물들이 거의 살 수 없다. Unit 01 - B
- She poured **a little** milk into her tea. 그녀는 그녀의 차에 약간의 우유를 부었다. Unit 01 - B
- We had [4]_____ snow last winter. 우리는 지난 겨울에 눈이 거의 없었다. Unit 01 - B

- Sarah sings **beautifully**. Sarah는 아름답게 노래를 부른다. Unit 02 - A
- **Luckily**, I got free tickets. 다행히도 나는 무료 티켓을 받았다. Unit 02 - A

- Mike is working [5]_____. Mike는 열심히 일하고 있다. Unit 02 - B
- I **hardly** know her. 나는 그녀를 거의 알지 못한다. Unit 02 - B

- Laura is [6]_____ busy on weekends. Laura는 주말에 항상 바쁘다. Unit 02 - C
- Tom **sometimes** plays the guitar. Tom은 가끔 기타를 친다. Unit 02 - C

- I am [7]_____ old _____ you. 나는 너랑 나이가 같다. Unit 03 - A

- Today is warmer [8]_____ yesterday. 오늘은 어제보다 더 따뜻하다. Unit 03 - B

- This is [9]_____ way to the airport. 이것이 공항으로 가는 가장 빠른 길이다. Unit 03 - C

- It's the [10]_____ camera in this shop. 이것이 이 가게에서 가장 좋은 카메라이다. Unit 03 - D

🔍 **Answers**

[1] cold   [2] much[a lot of, lots of]   [3] Few   [4] little   [5] hard   [6] always   [7] as, as   [8] than
[9] the fastest   [10] best

116

ESSENTIAL RULES OF
ENGLISH GRAMMAR

CHAPTER
09

to부정사와
동명사

UNIT 01 to부정사의 명사적 용법

UNIT 02 to부정사의 형용사적, 부사적 용법

UNIT 03 동명사의 역할

to부정사는 「to + 동사원형」 형태로 문장에서
명사, 형용사, 부사처럼 쓰이고, 동명사는
「동사원형 + ing」 형태로 문장에서 명사처럼
쓰여 주어, 목적어, 보어 역할을 한다.

to부정사의 명사적 용법

to부정사의 형태: to + 동사원형

to부정사의 명사적 용법: to부정사는 명사처럼 문장 안에서 주어, 목적어, 보어 역할을 한다.

A 주어 역할: ~하는 것은

to부정사가 주어로 쓰일 경우 보통 주어 자리에 가주어 It을 사용하여 「It ~ to-v」 형태로 쓴다.

It is exciting **to play** tennis.
(= **To play** tennis is exciting.)
It isn't easy **to learn** a foreign language.

B 목적어 역할: ~하는 것을

to부정사가 동사 want, need, hope, plan, promise, decide, like, start 등의 목적어 역할을 한다.

Cindy *wants* **to be** a doctor.
He *started* **to date** Julie.

C 보어 역할: ~하는 것(이다)

to부정사가 주격 보어로 쓰여 주어의 성질, 상태 등을 나타낸다.

Ted's dream is **to become** a pilot.
My plan is **to finish** this book today.

D 의문사 + to-v

- what to-v: 무엇을 ~할지
- when to-v: 언제 ~할지
- who(m) to-v: 누구를 ~할지
- how to-v: 어떻게 ~할지
- where to-v: 어디서[어디로] ~할지
- whether to-v or not: ~할지 말지

I don't know **what to wear** today.
We decided **where to go** for our holidays.

CHECK UP 빈칸에 알맞은 말을 고르시오.

1 _____ is important to learn history.
　ⓐ It 　　　　ⓑ That 　　　　ⓒ This

2 Colin and his family plan _____ soon.
　ⓐ move 　　　ⓑ moves 　　　ⓒ to move

3 I don't know _____ to solve the problem.
　ⓐ what 　　　ⓑ how 　　　ⓒ whom

⊕ PLUS

to부정사의 부정형은 to 앞에 not/never를 붙여 나타낸다.

He promised **not to lie** again.

PRACTICE

🔍 Answer Key p.14

STEP 1

밑줄 친 to부정사가 문장에서 주어, 목적어, 보어 중 어떤 역할을 하는지 쓰시오.

1 I hope <u>to see</u> you again. _____

2 It is fun <u>to learn</u> new things. _____

3 Jake's job is <u>to fix</u> computers. _____

4 We plan <u>to go</u> on a trip this summer. _____

5 My hope is <u>to travel</u> all over the world. _____

STEP 2

주어진 동사를 동사원형 또는 to부정사 중 적절한 형태로 써서 문장을 완성하시오.

1 go a. Where did Jason _____ yesterday?

b. Where do you want _____ on vacation?

2 walk a. It is good for your health _____.

b. They _____ around the park every morning.

3 win a. Our soccer team will _____ the game.

b. Her goal is _____ a gold medal at the Olympics.

STEP 3

빈칸에 알맞은 말을 보기에서 골라 적절한 형태로 바꿔 문장을 완성하시오.

보기	when/take	whom/ask	where/stay	whether/believe

1 I don't know _____ for help.

2 The doctor told me _____ the medicine.

3 Eric is not sure _____ her or not.

4 We can't decide _____ in London.

STEP 4

우리말과 일치하도록 ( ) 안의 말을 이용하여 문장을 완성하시오.

1 그 건물을 찾는 것은 어려웠다. (find)

→ _____ was hard _____ _____ the building.

2 나는 그에게 뭐라고 말해야 할지 모르겠다. (what, say)

→ I don't know _____ _____ _____ to him.

3 나의 목표는 올해 책 100권을 읽는 것이다. (read)

→ My goal _____ _____ _____ a hundred books this year.

4 Karen은 휴식을 좀 취할 필요가 있다. (need, get)

→ Karen _____ _____ _____ some rest.

to부정사의 형용사적, 부사적 용법

A **to부정사의 형용사적 용법: ~하는, ~할**

to부정사가 형용사처럼 명사, 대명사를 꾸며준다. 이때 to부정사는 반드시 꾸며주는 말 뒤에 위치한다.

I have *a question* **to ask**.
Rome is *a good place* **to visit**.

ⓘ -thing, -one, -body로 끝나는 대명사를 형용사와 to부정사가 같이 꾸며주는 경우, 어순은 「-thing/-one/
-body + 형용사 + to-v」이다.
I want **something cold to drink**.

B **to부정사의 부사적 용법**

to부정사가 부사처럼 동사, 형용사 등을 꾸며주며, 목적, 감정의 원인, 결과 등을 나타낸다.

1 목적: ~하기 위해서

I boiled water **to make** tea.
David raised his hand **to get** a taxi.

cf. 목적의 의미를 확실히 하기 위하여 in order to를 쓰기도 한다. (to부정사보다 격식을 갖춘 표현)
He studied hard **in order to become** a doctor.

2 감정의 원인: ~해서

to부정사가 happy, glad, sad, sorry 등 감정을 나타내는 형용사 뒤에 쓰인다.

I'm *glad* **to see** you again.
We were *surprised* **to hear** the news.

3 결과: (…해서) ~하다

She grew up **to be** a famous writer.

CHECK UP 빈칸에 알맞은 말을 고르시오.

1 I have lots of work _____ .
ⓐ do   ⓑ to do   ⓒ will do

2 Jane was happy _____ a high score.
ⓐ get   ⓑ got   ⓒ to get

3 Mike called me _____ about homework.
ⓐ ask   ⓑ asked   ⓒ to ask

4 He grew up _____ a movie star.
ⓐ be   ⓑ to be   ⓒ will be

✚ PLUS : enough to-v, too ~ to-v

• 형용사/부사 + enough to-v:
~할 만큼 충분히 …하다
Paul was kind **enough to help** me.

• too + 형용사/부사 + to-v:
너무 ~해서 …할 수 없다
The table was **too** heavy **to move**.

PRACTICE

🔍 **Answer Key p.14**

STEP 1

밑줄 친 to부정사가 꾸며주는 말에 동그라미 하시오.

1 It's time to go to bed.

2 Bangkok is an interesting city to visit.

3 Brian has something important to say.

4 I don't have enough money to buy the shoes.

STEP 2

자연스러운 문장이 되도록 알맞게 연결하시오.

1 I woke up •
2 I listen to music •
3 James was upset •
4 Alice needs somebody •

• ⓐ to help her.
• ⓑ to lose his smartphone.
• ⓒ to feel comfortable.
• ⓓ to find myself in a hospital.

STEP 3

to부정사를 이용하여 두 문장을 연결하시오.

1 I have a lot of books. I should read them.

→ I have a lot of books _____ _____.

2 We came early. We wanted to get good seats.

→ We came early _____ _____ _____ _____.

3 John went to Italy. He studied music there.

→ John went to Italy _____ _____ _____.

4 Diana was happy. She won the prize.

→ Diana was happy _____ _____ _____ _____.

STEP 4

우리말과 일치하도록 ( ) 안의 말을 이용하여 문장을 완성하시오.

1 너에게 줄 게 있어. (something, give)

→ I have _____ _____ _____ you.

2 나는 옛 친구들을 만나서 기뻤다. (glad, meet)

→ I was _____ _____ _____ my old friends.

3 그들은 식당을 열 계획이 있다. (plans, open)

→ They have _____ _____ _____ a restaurant.

4 Tony는 옷을 사기 위해 자주 인터넷을 이용한다. (buy, clothes)

→ Tony often uses the internet _____ _____ _____.

동명사의 역할

동명사의 형태: 동사원형 + ing

동명사의 역할: 동명사는 명사처럼 문장 안에서 주어, 목적어, 보어 역할을 한다.

A 주어 역할: ~하는 것은

동명사가 주어로 쓰일 경우 3인칭 단수 취급한다.

Recycling *is* good for the environment.
Listening to others *is* important.

B 목적어 역할: ~하는 것을

1 동명사가 동사 enjoy, finish, keep, mind, avoid, stop, quit, give up 등의 목적어 역할을 한다.

Mia *enjoys* **taking** pictures.

① 동사 like, love, start, begin 등은 to부정사와 동명사를 모두 목적어로 쓸 수 있다.

We *began* **crying[to cry]**.

2 동명사가 전치사의 목적어 역할을 한다.

We are excited *about* **going** to Hawaii.

C 보어 역할: ~하는 것(이다)

동명사가 주격 보어로 쓰여 주어의 성질, 상태 등을 나타낸다.

His favorite activity is **drawing** cartoons.
My good habit is **drinking** lots of water.

D 자주 쓰이는 동명사 표현

- go v-ing: ~하러 가다
- be worth v-ing: ~할 가치가 있다
- be busy v-ing: ~하느라 바쁘다
- feel like v-ing: ~하고 싶다

They **are busy cleaning** the house.
This movie **is worth watching** twice.

CHECK UP 빈칸에 알맞은 말을 고르시오.

1 _____ summer vacation is exciting.
   ⓐ Plan   ⓑ Planning   ⓒ To planning

2 Would you mind _____ the door?
   ⓐ close   ⓑ to close   ⓒ closing

3 We went _____ last weekend.
   ⓐ hike   ⓑ hiking   ⓒ to hiking

➕ PLUS

동명사의 부정형은 동명사 앞에 not/never를 붙여 나타낸다.

I'm sorry for **not answering** your message.

PRACTICE

🔍 Answer Key p.14

STEP 1

밑줄 친 동명사가 문장에서 주어, 목적어, 보어 중 어떤 역할을 하는지 쓰시오.

1 He quit <u>working</u> in the bank. _____

2 My dream is <u>being</u> a singer-songwriter. _____

3 The boys kept <u>running</u> to arrive on time. _____

4 Grandpa's new hobby is <u>baking</u> cookies. _____

5 <u>Eating</u> delicious food makes me happy. _____

STEP 2

( ) 안의 말을 적절한 형태로 바꿔 문장을 완성하시오.

1 He finished _____ the files to the site. (upload)

2 Thank you for _____ me the gift. (give)

3 Sandra gave up _____ chocolate. (not/eat)

4 My family will go _____ during the winter vacation. (ski)

STEP 3

빈칸에 알맞은 말을 보기에서 골라 적절한 형태로 바꿔 문장을 완성하시오. (단, 한 번씩만 쓸 것)

보기	travel	write	make	spend	buy

1 _____ abroad is expensive.

2 I feel like _____ a snack.

3 His job is _____ stories for kids.

4 She enjoyed _____ time with her friends.

5 You don't have to be afraid of _____ mistakes.

STEP 4

우리말과 일치하도록 ( ) 안의 말을 이용하여 문장을 완성하시오.

1 학생들은 시험을 준비하느라 바쁘다. (busy, prepare)

→ Students _____ _____ _____ for the exam.

2 이집트에서는 돼지고기를 먹는 것을 피해야 한다. (avoid, eat)

→ You should _____ _____ pork in Egypt.

3 너의 아이디어는 시도할 가치가 있다. (worth, try)

→ Your idea _____ _____ _____.

4 Fred는 바이올린 연주하는 것을 잘한다. (play, the violin)

→ Fred is good at _____ _____ _____.

GRAMMAR FOR WRITING

A 우리말과 일치하도록 ( ) 안의 말을 이용하여 문장을 완성하시오.

1 나는 내 방을 갖기를 바란다. (hope, have)

→ I _____ my own room.

2 우리는 그 차를 살 돈이 없다. (money, buy)

→ We don't have _____ the car.

3 저는 창문을 열어도 상관 없어요. (open, the window)

→ I don't mind _____.

4 그 야구 경기를 보는 것은 재미있었다. (exciting, watch)

→ It was _____ the baseball game.

5 Tina는 우유를 좀 사기 위해 밖에 나갔다. (go out, get)

→ Tina _____ some milk.

6 나는 롤러코스터를 타는 것이 무섭다. (ride, the rollercoaster)

→ I'm afraid of _____.

7 Cindy는 내게 카메라를 어떻게 사용하는지 가르쳐 주었다. (how, use)

→ Cindy taught me _____ the camera.

B 우리말과 일치하도록 ( ) 안에 주어진 말을 바르게 배열하시오.

1 나의 꿈은 해변가에 집을 갖는 것이다. (a house, to, is, have, on the beach)

→ My dream _____.

2 안전벨트를 매지 않는 것은 위험하다. (a seat belt, wearing, not)

→ _____ is dangerous.

3 나는 너에게 보여줄 특별한 게 있어. (special, something, to, you, show)

→ I have _____.

4 그 문제를 해결하는 것은 불가능하다. (solving, impossible, is, the problem)

→ _____.

5 Chloe는 뉴스를 보기 위해 TV를 켰다. (the TV, the news, watch, to, turned on)

→ Chloe _____.

6 나는 이번 주말에 무엇을 할지 생각 중이다. (do, what, to)

→ I'm thinking about _____ this weekend.

C ( ) 안의 말을 이용하여 대화를 완성하시오.

1 A: Did you do well in the exam yesterday?

B: No. It was _____ the questions. (difficult, answer)

2 A: How was the movie?

B: It was very sad. I _____. (keep, cry)

3 A: Will you _____ with me this afternoon? (go, shop)

B: I'm sorry, but I have many things to do.

4 A: What will Jenny do after graduation?

B: She will study in New York _____. (be a designer)

5 A: I really liked the festival!

B: Me too. The best part was _____. (watch, the parade)

6 A: Jake broke his leg in a car accident.

B: Oh, I'm _____ the bad news. (sorry, hear)

D 그림을 보고 ( ) 안의 말을 이용하여 문장을 완성하시오.

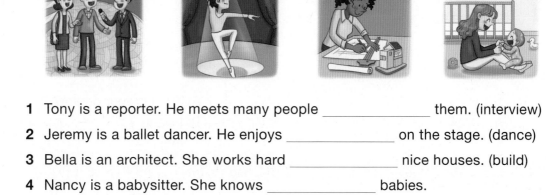

1 Tony is a reporter. He meets many people _____ them. (interview)

2 Jeremy is a ballet dancer. He enjoys _____ on the stage. (dance)

3 Bella is an architect. She works hard _____ nice houses. (build)

4 Nancy is a babysitter. She knows _____ babies.
(how, take care of)

REVIEW TEST

[1–4] 빈칸에 들어갈 알맞은 말을 고르시오.

1

| _____ is great to have a good friend. |

① I   ② It   ③ This
④ That   ⑤ What

2

| We enjoy _____ the quiz show at night. |

① watch   ② watches   ③ watched
④ watching   ⑤ to watch

3

| Bill is not a person _____ a lie. |

① tell   ② tells   ③ told
④ to tell   ⑤ to telling

4

| We have to decide _____ to go or not. |

① what   ② whom   ③ where
④ when   ⑤ whether

빈출

5 다음 중 보기의 밑줄 친 부분과 쓰임이 같은 것은?

| 보기   I like to read comic books. |

① It's time to say goodbye.
② I'm sorry to bother you.
③ It is difficult to get up early.
④ She promised to keep the secret.
⑤ Mom went to the store to buy some fruit.

서술형

6 빈칸에 공통으로 들어갈 말을 쓰시오.

- I was surprised _____ see the crowd.
- I turned on the computer _____ check my email.

서술형

[7–8] ( ) 안의 말을 이용하여 대화를 완성하시오.

7
A: What is your dream?
B: I want _____ a famous singer.
   (be)

8
A: Did you finish _____ the wall?
   (paint)
B: No, I'm going to finish it tomorrow.

빈출

[9-11] 밑줄 친 부분의 쓰임이 나머지 넷과 다른 것을 고르시오.

9 ① I want to know the truth.
② Jessica started to sing a song.
③ We planned to go to the beach.
④ I decided to invite Mike to my house.
⑤ I bought some vegetables to make a salad.

10 ① I bought a newspaper to read.
② Do you have anything to tell me?
③ The woman lived to be ninety years old.
④ I need something to eat on the train.
⑤ Jane doesn't have a dress to wear to the party.

11 ① He quit drinking coffee.
② Her job was drawing cartoons.
③ He gave up fixing the machine.
④ You should stop wasting water.
⑤ Do you mind turning off the heater?

12 다음 중 밑줄 친 부분이 잘못된 것은?

① He grew up to be a great artist.
② I don't have enough time to read.
③ I planned to not attend the meeting.
④ They asked where to take a bus to city hall.
⑤ He rides a bike to work in order to save money.

서술형

[13-15] 빈칸에 알맞은 말을 보기에서 골라 적절한 형태로 바꿔 쓰시오. (단, 한 번씩만 쓸 것)

보기	pick up his friend
	leave her hometown
	take acting lessons

13 Jenny was sad _____
_____ .

14 Paul went to the airport _____
_____ .

15 Amanda was interested in _____
_____ .

16 다음 우리말을 영어로 바르게 옮긴 것은?

나는 해야 할 중요한 일이 있어.

① I have to do important something.
② I have important something to do.
③ I have something to do important.
④ I have something important to do.
⑤ I have important to do something.

17

· It is fun   (A)   pictures.
· I don't have a key   (B)   the door.

	(A)		(B)
①	draw	······	lock
②	draw	······	to lock
③	to draw	······	lock
④	to draw	······	to lock
⑤	drawing	······	lock

18

· He will tell you   (A)   the work.
· This video is about   (B)   pizza.

	(A)		(B)
①	what to start	······	what to make
②	what to start	······	how to make
③	when to start	······	who to make
④	when to start	······	what to make
⑤	when to start	······	how to make

서술형

[19-20] ( ) 안의 지시대로 두 문장을 연결하시오.

19 Eric is busy. He is talking to the guests.
(동명사 이용)

→ Eric is _____.

20 They went to a park. They wanted to rest on the grass. (to부정사 이용)

→ They went to a park _____
_____.

서술형

[21-22] 우리말과 일치하도록 ( ) 안의 말을 이용하여 문장을 완성하시오.

21 큰 소리로 음악을 듣는 것은 귀에 나쁘다. (listen)

→ _____ to music loudly is bad for your ears.

22 규칙적으로 운동하는 것은 건강에 좋다. (exercise)

→ _____ is good for your health _____ _____ regularly.

서술형

[23-24] 우리말과 일치하도록 ( ) 안에 주어진 말을 바르게 배열하시오.

23 우리는 경기를 이기기를 바란다.
(we, to, the game, hope, win)

→ _____.

24 우리는 선수들을 응원하는 것을 중단했다.
(stopped, the players, we, cheering for)

→ _____.

25 다음 중 어법상 옳은 것을 모두 고르면?

① Ben kept talking about his plans.
② Teaching Korean to foreigners are hard.
③ This coffee is too hot to drink.
④ The man needed some water to drink.
⑤ We visited Germany enjoy the festival.

26 다음 중 어법상 옳은 것으로 바르게 짝지어진 것은?

> a. I don't mind waiting a few days.
> b. Can you give me to wear something?
> c. My plan for Sunday is not doing anything.
> d. It's impossible lose so much weight in a month.
> e. I ran fast enough to catch the bus.

① a, c ② c, e ③ a, c, d
④ a, c, e ⑤ b, c, d

고난도

27 다음 중 어법상 옳은 것의 개수는?

> • He promised sending me presents.
> • I decided not to buy a new dress.
> • Robert went fish with his dad.
> • Lucy avoids driving on rainy days.
> • I need someone to take care of my dog.

① 1개 ② 2개 ③ 3개
④ 4개 ⑤ 5개

서술형

[28-30] 밑줄 친 부분이 어법상 옳은지 판단하고, 틀리면 바르게 고치시오.

28 The water is too cold <u>take</u> a shower.

(O / X) _____

29 Fred gave up <u>to study</u> Chinese. It was too difficult.

(O / X) _____

30 We were happy <u>to see</u> him there.

(O / X) _____

서술형 고난도

[31-33] 어법상 틀린 부분을 찾아 바르게 고치시오.

31 I want to be an animal trainer. It is fun learn about animals. (1개)

32 I decided stay at home today because I was sick. I felt like to have some chicken soup, so I asked Mom. Eating hot soup made me better. (2개)

33 A: I'm going abroad this summer.
B: That sounds great. Did you decide where go to?
A: Yes. My plan is to go to Singapore. There are lots of places visit in the city.
B: Right. It is worth travel. (3개)

LET'S REVIEW

주요 예문을 다시 한번 확인하고, 우리말과 일치하도록 빈칸을 채우시오.

- It is exciting ¹_____ tennis. 테니스를 치는 것은 재미있다. **Unit 01 - A**

- ²_____ isn't easy **to learn** a foreign language.
  외국어를 배우는 것은 쉽지 않다. **Unit 01 - A**

- Cindy wants ³_____ a doctor. Cindy는 의사가 되기를 원한다. **Unit 01 - B**

- My plan is ⁴_____ this book today. 내 계획은 오늘 이 책을 끝내는 것이다. **Unit 01 - C**

- I don't know **what to wear** today. 나는 오늘 무엇을 입을지 모르겠다. **Unit 01 - D**

- We decided ⁵_____ for our holidays. 우리는 휴가로 어디를 갈지 결정했다. **Unit 01 - D**

- I have a question **to ask**. 나는 물어 볼 질문이 하나 있다. **Unit 02 - A**

- I boiled water ⁶_____ **make** tea. 나는 차를 만들기 위해 물을 끓였다. **Unit 02 - B**

- We were surprised ⁷_____ the news. 우리는 그 소식을 듣고 놀랐다. **Unit 02 - B**

- She grew up **to be** a famous writer. 그녀는 자라서 유명한 작가가 되었다. **Unit 02 - B**

- **Recycling** is good for the environment. 재활용하는 것은 환경에 좋다. **Unit 03 - A**

- Mia enjoys **taking** pictures. Mia는 사진 찍는 것을 즐긴다. **Unit 03 - B**

- We are excited about ⁸_____ to Hawaii. 우리는 하와이에 가는 것에 신이 나 있다. **Unit 03 - B**

- His favorite activity is **drawing** cartoons. 그가 가장 좋아하는 활동은 만화 그리기이다. **Unit 03 - C**

- They **are busy** ⁹_____ the house. 그들은 집을 청소하느라 바쁘다. **Unit 03 - D**

- This movie **is worth watching** twice. 이 영화는 두 번 볼 가치가 있다. **Unit 03 - D**

Q Answers

¹ to play   ² It   ³ to be[become]   ⁴ to finish / finishing   ⁵ where to go   ⁶ to[in order to]

⁷ to hear   ⁸ going   ⁹ cleaning

CHAPTER

10

전치사

전치사는 명사, 대명사 앞에 쓰여
장소나 시간 등을 나타내는 말이다.

UNIT 01   장소를 나타내는 전치사

UNIT 02   시간을 나타내는 전치사

UNIT 03   기타 전치사

장소를 나타내는 전치사

A

in, at, on

in + 공간의 내부, 도시, 국가 (~ 안에, ~에)	at + 장소의 한 지점 (~에)	on + 접촉해 있는 장소 (~ 위에, ~에)
in a box **in** a house **in** New York **in** Korea	**at** home **at** school **at** the party **at** the airport	**on** the table **on** the sofa **on** the wall **on** the floor

There are apples **in** the box.
I left my umbrella **at** school.
Kevin put his pen **on** the desk.

B

장소를 나타내는 기타 전치사

1 over(~ 위에 [접촉해 있지 않은 상태]), under(~ 아래에)

He threw the ball **over** my head.
The dog was hiding **under** the table.

2 in front of(~ 앞에), behind(~ 뒤에)

I'll wait for you **in front of** the gate.
The parking lot is **behind** the building.

3 near(~ 근처에), next to(~ 옆에), across from(~ 맞은편에)

Is there a post office **near** this building?
Can I sit **next to** the window?
The bakery is **across from** the hospital.

4 between A and B(A와 B 사이에), from A to B(A부터 B까지)

City hall is **between** the park **and** the library.
I walked **from** school **to** my home.

CHECK UP 빈칸에 알맞은 말을 고르시오.

1 We are _____ London now.
  ⓐ in   ⓑ at   ⓒ on

2 I met Tom _____ the party.
  ⓐ in   ⓑ at   ⓒ on

PRACTICE

🔍 Answer Key p.15

STEP 1

( ) 안에서 알맞은 말을 고르시오.

1 David lives (in, at) Canada.

2 Emily spilled water (in, on) the carpet.

3 The boys are lying (at, on) the grass.

4 Joe is studying (at, on) school now.

5 You should be quiet (in, on) the library.

6 Tony and I will meet (at, on) the subway station.

STEP 2

빈칸에 알맞은 말을 보기에서 골라 쓰시오. (단, 한 번씩만 쓸 것)

보기	in	at	on

1 There is sugar _____ the jar.

2 His apartment is _____ the ninth floor.

3 I saw Picasso's paintings _____ the museum.

STEP 3

그림을 보고 빈칸에 알맞은 말을 보기에서 골라 쓰시오.

보기	over	behind	in front of

1 A dog is playing _____ a house.

2 There is a mountain _____ the house.

3 There is a rainbow _____ the mountain.

STEP 4

우리말과 일치하도록 ( ) 안의 말을 이용하여 문장을 완성하시오.

1 우리는 나무 아래에 앉아 있었다. (a tree)

→ We were sitting _____ _____ _____.

2 Bill은 우리 집 옆에 산다. (my house)

→ Bill lives _____ _____ _____ _____.

3 우리 학교 맞은편에 서점이 하나 있다. (my school)

→ There is a bookstore _____ _____ _____ _____.

4 우리는 호텔에서부터 시내까지 택시를 탔다. (the hotel, downtown)

→ We took a taxi _____ _____ _____ _____ _____.

시간을 나타내는 전치사

A in, at, on

in + 오전, 오후, 월, 계절, 연도	at + 구체적인 시각, 하루의 때	on + 날짜, 요일, 특정한 날
in the morning	**at** 2:30 p.m.	**on** February 24
in September	**at** noon	**on** Saturday
in spring	**at** night	**on** Monday morning
in 2018	**at** lunchtime	**on** Christmas Day

I graduated from elementary school **in** 2020.
I get up **at** six o'clock every day.
The museum doesn't open **on** Mondays.

B 시간을 나타내는 기타 전치사

1 before(~ 전에), after(~ 후에)

I washed my hands **before** dinner.
We will play baseball **after** school.

2 for, during(~ 동안)

for 뒤에는 숫자를 포함한 구체적인 기간을 쓰고, during 뒤에는 특정한 때를 나타내는 명사를 쓴다.

for *a week*, for *three months*, for *two years* ...
during *the game*, during *the vacation*, during *the winter* ...

Tim played smartphone games **for** an hour.
I will visit my cousin **during** summer vacation.

3 around(~경에, ~ 무렵에)

I will call you **around** noon.

4 between A and B(A와 B 사이에), from A to B(A부터 B까지)

You can come to my office **between** 2:00 **and** 4:00 p.m.
I play online games **from** morning **to** night.

 CHECK UP 빈칸에 알맞은 말을 고르시오.

1 I went to the movies _____ Sunday.
ⓐ in   ⓑ at   ⓒ on

2 We plan to travel to New York _____ May.
ⓐ in   ⓑ at   ⓒ on

PRACTICE

🔍 Answer Key p.15

STEP 1

( ) 안에서 알맞은 말을 고르시오.

1 The store opens (in, at) 9:00 a.m.

2 We have a lot of snow here (in, on) winter.

3 Lucy likes to read books (in, at) night.

4 I have piano lessons (in, on) Wednesdays.

5 The World Cup will be (in, on) June.

6 Winter vacation starts (in, on) December 22.

STEP 2

Tony의 일과표를 보고 빈칸에 알맞은 전치사를 쓰시오.

7:30 a.m.	have breakfast
8:00 a.m.	go to school
5:00 p.m.	come home
5:00 – 6:00 p.m.	do homework
6:00 p.m.	have dinner
7:00 – 8:00 p.m.	watch TV

1 Tony has breakfast _____ 7:30 a.m.

2 Tony goes to school _____ breakfast.

3 Tony does his homework _____ dinner.

4 Tony watches TV _____ an hour _____ the evening.

STEP 3

for 또는 during과 ( ) 안의 말을 함께 써서 문장을 완성하시오.

1 It rained a lot _____. (the summer)

2 Tim stayed at his uncle's house _____. (two weeks)

3 We had a great time _____. (our vacation)

4 You may not use your cell phone _____. (class)

5 I waited for the bus _____ this morning. (thirty minutes)

STEP 4

우리말과 일치하도록 ( ) 안의 말을 이용하여 문장을 완성하시오.

1 Bryce는 자정 무렵에 집에 올 것이다. (midnight)

→ Bryce will come home _____ _____.

2 우리 아빠는 월요일부터 금요일까지 일하신다. (Monday, Friday)

→ My dad works _____ _____ _____ _____.

3 나는 오늘 3시와 5시 사이에 한가하다. (three, five o'clock)

→ I'm free _____ _____ _____ _____ today.

기타 전치사

전치사 뒤에 대명사가 올 때는 목적격을 쓴다.

I'm worried **about her**. (~~about she~~)

A 기타 전치사

1 about(~에 관하여/관한)

This book is **about** animals.

2 by(~로)

We traveled the island **by** bike.
I'll send you the photos **by** email.

① by + 교통/통신 수단
by bus, by car, by taxi, by subway, by train, by plane ...
by email, by mail, by fax, by telephone, by text message ...

3 for(~을 위해)

I want to do something nice **for** Mom.

4 to(~로, ~에게)

We went **to** Spain last year.
Sandra told a funny story **to** me.

5 with(~와 함께, ~을 가지고)

I live **with** my grandparents.
Jane cut the cake **with** a knife.

CHECK UP 빈칸에 알맞은 말을 고르시오.

1 The story is _____ friendship.
ⓐ about ⓑ by ⓒ to

2 Jenny baked these cupcakes _____ us.
ⓐ by ⓑ for ⓒ to

3 I went shopping _____ my sister yesterday.
ⓐ by ⓑ to ⓒ with

4 Paul sent me a Christmas card _____ mail.
ⓐ by ⓑ for ⓒ to

PRACTICE

Answer Key p.16

STEP 1

( ) 안에서 알맞은 말을 고르시오.

1 Brenda lent her umbrella to (I, me).

2 I bought some flowers (to, for) Laura.

3 We will keep in touch (by, with) email.

4 We went (about, to) the zoo yesterday.

5 Can you tell me (about, to) the accident?

STEP 2

자연스러운 문장이 되도록 알맞게 연결하시오.

1 I have a few questions •   • ⓐ by train.

2 He is exercising •   • ⓑ for his health.

3 I wrote my name in the book •   • ⓒ with a pencil.

4 Danny traveled across the country •   • ⓓ about today's class.

STEP 3

빈칸에 공통으로 들어갈 말을 보기에서 골라 쓰시오.

보기	by	to	with

1 Jane gave a movie ticket _____ me.

Peter will go _____ Beijing next Monday.

2 You can send me the report _____ email.

We decided to go to Busan _____ plane.

3 Mandy tied her hair _____ a ribbon.

I played tennis _____ Jacob this afternoon.

STEP 4

우리말과 일치하도록 ( ) 안의 말을 이용하여 문장을 완성하시오.

1 Jake는 배트를 가지고 공을 쳤다. (a bat)

→ Jake hit the ball _____.

2 나는 2차 세계 대전에 관한 책을 읽었다. (the Second World War)

→ I read a book _____.

3 Vanessa는 친구들을 위해 스파게티를 요리했다. (her friends)

→ Vanessa cooked spaghetti _____.

4 Daniel은 주말마다 서점에 간다. (the bookstore)

→ Daniel goes _____ every weekend.

GRAMMAR FOR WRITING

A 우리말과 일치하도록 (   ) 안의 말을 이용하여 문장을 완성하시오.

1 병 안에 물이 조금 있다. (the bottle)

→ There is some water _____ .

2 그들은 경기 전에 긴장했다. (the game)

→ They were nervous _____ .

3 나는 친구들과 함께 콘서트에 갔다. (my friends)

→ I went to the concert _____ .

4 우체국은 오후 5시에 문을 닫는다. (5:00 p.m.)

→ The post office closes _____ .

5 나는 좌석 아래에서 내 지갑을 찾았다. (the seat)

→ I found my wallet _____ .

6 Jack은 훈련 중에 왼발을 다쳤다. (training)

→ Jack hurt his left foot _____ .

7 그의 사무실은 2층에 있다. (the second floor)

→ His office is _____ .

B 우리말과 일치하도록 (   ) 안에 주어진 말을 바르게 배열하시오.

1 그는 내 옆에 섰다. (stood, to, me, next)

→ He _____ .

2 우리는 TV 앞에 앉았다. (in, of, sat, front, the TV)

→ We _____ .

3 우리 가게는 화요일부터 금요일까지 세일을 할 것이다. (from, have, Friday, will, a sale, Tuesday, to)

→ Our store _____ .

4 한국은 중국과 일본 사이에 있다. (between, is, and, Japan, China)

→ Korea _____ .

5 우리는 Amy를 위해 깜짝 파티를 계획했다. (planned, for, a surprise party, Amy)

→ We _____ .

6 그는 식당 맞은편에 주차했다. (parked, from, the restaurant, across)

→ He _____ .

C 그림을 보고 보기에서 알맞은 말을 골라 (　) 안의 말과 함께 써서 문장을 완성하시오. (단, 한 번씩만 쓸 것)

보기

under
around
with
in

1 There is a clock _____ . (the park)

2 It's _____ . (2:00 p.m.)

3 There is a man _____ . (a tree)

4 He is painting _____ . (a brush)

D 간판을 보고 보기에서 알맞은 말을 골라 (　) 안의 말과 함께 써서 문장을 완성하시오. (단, 한 번씩만 쓸 것)

Sunny Restaurant
Open: 8:00 a.m. — 6:00 p.m.
Closed: Mondays
Breakfast Buffet: 8:00 a.m. — 10:00 a.m.
(two hours)
Reservation: call 202-346-7328

보기	on	for	by	to	in

1 The restaurant is open from 8:00 a.m. _____ . (6:00 p.m.)

2 It is closed _____ . (Mondays)

3 The breakfast buffet is open _____ .
(two hours, the morning)

4 You can make a reservation _____ . (telephone)

REVIEW TEST

[1-3] 빈칸에 들어갈 알맞은 말을 고르시오.

1

> I will go to the dentist _____ Monday.

① in   ② at   ③ on
④ for   ⑤ during

2

> The school festival is _____ September.

① in   ② at   ③ on
④ for   ⑤ between

3

> We stayed _____ home last weekend.

① in   ② at   ③ on
④ under   ⑤ between

서술형

[4-5] 빈칸에 들어갈 알맞은 말을 쓰시오.

4

> We had dinner at six o'clock. We watched a movie at seven o'clock.

→ We watched a movie _____ dinner.

5

> We have a break after science class.
> We have music class after the break.

→ We have a break _____ science _____ music class.

[6-8] 빈칸에 공통으로 들어갈 말을 고르시오.

6

> · Sally gave her pen _____ me.
> · His family moved _____ Jeju Island last month.

① about   ② by   ③ for
④ to   ⑤ with

7

> · You should study hard _____ your future.
> · Nick broke his leg. He stayed in the hospital _____ two weeks.

① about   ② by   ③ for
④ to   ⑤ during

8

> · Julie is talking _____ Andy.
> · A cat was playing _____ a ball.

① at   ② by   ③ for
④ to   ⑤ with

서술형 **빈출**

[9-11] 다음은 Jim의 내일 계획이다. 빈칸에 알맞은 전치사를 써서 문장을 완성하시오.

9:00 – 11:00 a.m.	ride a bike (Seoul Station – the Han River)
12:00 p.m.	meet Sujin
12:00 – 1:00 p.m.	have lunch with Sujin
3:00 – 4:00 p.m.	take a guitar lesson

9 Jim will ride a bike _____ Seoul Station to the Han River.

10 Jim will meet Sujin _____ noon.

11 Jim will take a guitar lesson _____ an hour.

빈출

[12-13] 빈칸에 들어갈 말이 나머지 넷과 <u>다른</u> 것을 고르시오.

12 ① Brian is lying _____ the bed.
② There is somebody _____ the door.
③ I said goodbye to Jeff _____ the airport.
④ We had a good time _____ the party.
⑤ John is waiting for a train _____ the station.

13 ① Ben is _____ France now.
② We met _____ the bus stop.
③ I put my cell phone _____ the bag.
④ Six people are _____ the elevator.
⑤ There are lots of tall buildings _____ Chicago.

서술형

[14-16] 다음 지도를 보고 빈칸에 알맞은 말을 쓰시오.

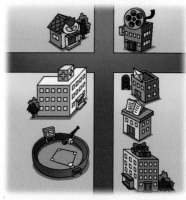

14 The flower shop is _____ _____ the movie theater.

15 The bookstore is _____ the post office _____ the department store.

16 The hospital is _____ _____ the baseball stadium.

[17-19] 다음 중 밑줄 친 부분이 잘못된 것을 고르시오.

17 ① Parents' Day is in May.
② The news begins at nine o'clock.
③ Sandra is always busy on weekends.
④ The actor will visit Seoul in March 26.
⑤ They eat turkey on Thanksgiving Day.

18 ① The dog jumped over the fence.
② Kevin put his coat at the closet.
③ Cindy studied fashion in New York.
④ There is a vase on the table.
⑤ We had a picnic lunch under a tree.

19 ① His office is near city hall.
② Kate went to the park with us.
③ I bought a small gift to James.
④ The boy is hiding behind the door.
⑤ We read an article about global warming.

20 다음 우리말을 영어로 바르게 옮긴 것은?

> 나는 오전 10시부터 11시 30분까지 회의가 있다.

① I have a meeting at 10:00 to 11:30 a.m.
② I have a meeting to 10:00 from 11:30 a.m.
③ I have a meeting after 10:00 to 11:30 a.m.
④ I have a meeting from 10:00 to 11:30 a.m.
⑤ I have a meeting from 10:00 and 11:30 a.m.

서술형 빈출
[21-23] 빈칸에 들어갈 알맞은 말을 쓰시오.

21 Ava는 그 이슈에 관한 그녀의 기사를 이메일로 보냈다.

→ Ava sent her article _____ the issue _____ email.

22 나는 점심 식사 후에 2시간 동안 낮잠을 잤다.

→ I took a nap _____ two hours _____ lunch.

23 그 가족은 전쟁 동안 미국으로 이주했다.

→ The family moved _____ America _____ the war.

서술형
[24-25] 우리말과 일치하도록 ( ) 안에 주어진 말을 바르게 배열하시오.

24 Bill은 Kelly와 Tim 사이에 앉아 있었다.
(Kelly, between, Tim, and)

→ Bill was sitting _____.

25 우리는 은행 앞에 있다.
(in, the bank, are, of, front)

→ We _____.

142

26 다음 중 어법상 옳은 것을 모두 고르면?

① Someone screamed in midnight.
② She often feels sleepy on the afternoon.
③ I take a shower around 7:00 a.m.
④ Cathy is writing about her childhood.
⑤ Ken studied math with Maria.

27 다음 중 어법상 옳은 것으로 바르게 짝지어진 것은?

> a. They played tennis in the evening.
> b. Dad hid the gift under the pillow.
> c. I will stay in Taiwan during six days.
> d. You need to check the weather before your trip.
> e. There is a tower between the river to the buildings.

① a, d   ② c, d   ③ a, b, d
④ a, b, e   ⑤ c, d, e

28 다음 중 어법상 옳은 것의 개수는?

> • It is sunny and warm on spring.
> • The café opens from 2:00 to 10:00 p.m.
> • I ate soup with a spoon.
> • Maggie cooked dinner for Mom.
> • I fell asleep during Mr. White's science class.

① 1개   ② 2개   ③ 3개
④ 4개   ⑤ 5개

[29-31] 밑줄 친 부분이 어법상 옳은지 판단하고, **틀리면** 바르게 고치시오.

29 We will get our grades <u>in</u> Friday.

(O / X) _____

30 I don't know much about <u>he</u>.

(O / X) _____

31 Is there a supermarket <u>near</u> your house?

(O / X) _____

[32-34] 어법상 **틀린** 부분을 찾아 바르게 고치시오.

32 Joe Brooks will have a concert in May 14. It will be at the City Concert Hall, and it will begin on 7:00 p.m. (2개)

33 Yesterday, I went to a famous Japanese restaurant with Eric. It was next the beach. We went there with taxi. (2개)

34 My class went camping last weekend. We hiked at the morning. After lunch, we swam at the sea. In night, we had a campfire. (3개)

LET'S REVIEW

주요 예문을 다시 한번 확인하고, 우리말과 일치하도록 빈칸을 채우시오.

- There are apples **in** the box. 상자 안에 사과가 있다. Unit 01 - A

- I left my umbrella **at** school. 나는 우산을 학교에 두고 왔다. Unit 01 - A

- Kevin put his pen ¹_____ the desk. Kevin은 그의 펜을 책상 위에 놓았다. Unit 01 - A

- He threw the ball **over** my head. 그는 내 머리 위로 공을 던졌다. Unit 01 - B

- The dog was hiding **under** the table. 그 개는 탁자 아래 숨어 있었다. Unit 01 - B

- I'll wait for you **in front of** the gate. 나는 정문 앞에서 너를 기다릴 거야. Unit 01 - B

- The parking lot is ²_____ the building. 주차장은 건물 뒤에 있다. Unit 01 - B

- I graduated from elementary school **in** 2020. 나는 2020년에 초등학교를 졸업했다. Unit 02 - A

- I get up ³_____ six o'clock every day. 나는 매일 6시에 일어난다. Unit 02 - A

- The museum doesn't open ⁴_____ Mondays. 그 박물관은 월요일마다 열지 않는다. Unit 02 - A

- I washed my hands **before** dinner. 나는 저녁 식사 전에 손을 씻었다. Unit 02 - B

- We will play baseball ⁵_____ school. 우리는 방과 후에 야구를 할 것이다. Unit 02 - B

- Tim played smartphone games **for** an hour. Tim은 한 시간 동안 스마트폰 게임을 했다. Unit 02 - B

- I will visit my cousin **during** summer vacation.
  나는 여름 방학 동안 나의 사촌을 방문할 것이다. Unit 02 - B

- This book is ⁶_____ animals. 이 책은 동물에 관한 것이다. Unit 03 - A

- We traveled the island **by** bike. 우리는 자전거로 그 섬을 여행했다. Unit 03 - A

- I want to do something nice ⁷_____ Mom.
  나는 엄마를 위해 뭔가 좋은 일을 하고 싶다. Unit 03 - A

- Sandra told a funny story ⁸_____ me.
  Sandra는 나에게 재미있는 이야기를 해 주었다. Unit 03 - A

- I live **with** my grandparents. 나는 조부모님과 함께 산다. Unit 03 - A

- Jane cut the cake ⁹_____ a knife. Jane은 칼로 케이크를 잘랐다. Unit 03 - A

Q Answers

¹ on ² behind ³ at ⁴ on ⁵ after ⁶ about ⁷ for ⁸ to ⁹ with

ESSENTIAL RULES OF

ENGLISH GRAMMAR

CHAPTER

11

접속사

접속사는 단어와 단어, 구와 구,
절과 절을 연결해 주는 말이다.

UNIT 01   and, but, or, so

UNIT 02   when, before, after, until

UNIT 03   because, if, that

and, but, or, so

and, but, or는 문법적으로 대등한 단어와 단어, 구와 구, 절과 절을 연결해 준다.

A

and: 그리고

I ate soup **and** salad for lunch.
He built a dog house **and** painted it.

ⓘ both A and B: A와 B 둘 다
Both the book **and** the movie were great.

B

but: 그러나

This story is short **but** fun.
The machine is old, **but** it works well.

C

or: 또는

Mike may leave today **or** tomorrow.
You can take a bus **or** walk to the museum.

ⓘ either A or B: A 또는 B 둘 중 하나
You can have **either** fish **or** chicken.

D

so: 그래서

so는 원인과 결과의 관계를 나타내며 절과 절을 연결해준다.

I was really tired, **so** I took a break.

CHECK UP 빈칸에 알맞은 말을 고르시오.

1 Do you want coffee _____ tea?

ⓐ but ⓑ or ⓒ so

2 I have two brothers _____ one sister.

ⓐ and ⓑ but ⓒ or

3 The camera is nice, _____ it's too expensive.

ⓐ and ⓑ but ⓒ or

4 I can't swim, _____ I won't go to the pool with you.

ⓐ but ⓑ or ⓒ so

PRACTICE

🔍 Answer Key p.17

STEP 1

( ) 안에서 알맞은 말을 고르시오.

1 She invited Tommy (and, but) his friends for dinner.

2 The lecture was long but (interest, interesting).

3 We'll go either to the beach (and, or) to the mountains.

4 Jessica missed the bus, (but, so) she was late for work.

5 You can put your coat on the sofa (or, so) in the closet.

STEP 2

빈칸에 알맞은 말을 보기에서 골라 두 문장을 연결하시오. (단, 한 번씩만 쓸 것)

보기	and	but	or	so

1 Jisu speaks Korean. She speaks Japanese.

→ Jisu speaks Korean _____ Japanese.

2 You can fix the computer. You can buy a new one.

→ You can fix the computer _____ buy a new one.

3 I called Nick. He didn't answer.

→ I called Nick, _____ he didn't answer.

4 I ate a lot of snacks. I'm full now.

→ I ate a lot of snacks, _____ I'm full now.

STEP 3

빈칸에 알맞은 말을 보기에서 골라 쓰시오.

보기	he weighs 70 kg	he went to the doctor
	he lost the game	he will go to the movies

1 Daniel was sick, so _____.

2 Alex did his best, but _____.

3 Henry is 175 cm tall, and _____.

4 Chris will go shopping, or _____.

STEP 4

우리말과 일치하도록 ( ) 안의 말을 이용하여 문장을 완성하시오.

1 Bill은 저녁으로 피자와 파스타 둘 다 먹었다. (pizza, pasta)

→ Bill had _____ _____ _____ _____ for dinner.

2 나는 머무르고 싶지만 가야 한다. (should, leave)

→ I want to stay, _____ _____ _____ _____.

02 when, before, after, until

when, before, after, until은 시간을 나타내는 접속사로, 절과 절을 연결해 준다.

A

when: ~할 때

I use chopsticks **when** I eat.
When the telephone rang, I was in the bathroom.

B

before: ~하기 전에

Kate makes a list **before** she goes to the market.
Before you leave, you should finish the work.

C

after: ~한 후에

I feel great **after** I exercise.
After I read the book, I lent it to John.

D

until: ~할 때까지

I read the page **until** I understood it.
Until I was two, I couldn't walk.

① 시간을 나타내는 접속사가 이끄는 절에서는 미래를 나타내더라도 현재시제를 쓴다.
　I'll wait *until* you **come**. (~~will come~~)

CHECK UP 빈칸에 알맞은 말을 고르시오.

1 My family had a dog _____ I was little.
　ⓐ when　　ⓑ before　　ⓒ after

2 _____ I woke up, I had a glass of water.
　ⓐ Until　　ⓑ Before　　ⓒ After

3 You should turn off the lights _____ you go out.
　ⓐ after　　ⓑ before　　ⓒ until

4 You should take this medicine _____ you feel better.
　ⓐ until　　ⓑ when　　ⓒ after

PRACTICE

🔍 Answer Key p-17

STEP 1

( ) 안에서 알맞은 말을 고르시오.

1 (Before, When) I'm alone, I feel lonely.

2 I will call you when I (get, will get) home.

3 (Until, After) he graduated, he became a doctor.

4 I won't talk to Sue (when, until) she apologizes to me.

5 Mary wrote down his number (before, after) she forgot it.

STEP 2

자연스러운 문장이 되도록 알맞게 연결하시오.

1 I take a shower   •

2 I stayed with my aunt   •

3 You must stop and wait •

4 Give me the laptop   •

• ⓐ after you use it.

• ⓑ before I go to bed.

• ⓒ until the light turns green.

• ⓓ when I was in Los Angeles.

STEP 3

( ) 안의 말을 이용하여 두 문장을 연결하시오.

1 She saw me. She smiled at me. (when)

→ _____, she smiled at me.

2 We must stay inside. The storm is over. (until)

→ We must stay inside _____.

3 I want to see him. He leaves Korea. (before)

→ I want to see him _____.

4 The party was over. We cleaned our house. (after)

→ _____, we cleaned our house.

STEP 4

우리말과 일치하도록 ( ) 안의 말을 이용하여 문장을 완성하시오.

1 우리는 버스가 올 때까지 기다렸다. (the bus, come)

→ We waited _____ _____ _____ _____.

2 우리는 저녁을 먹은 후에 산책을 했다. (have dinner)

→ _____ _____ _____ _____, we took a walk.

3 내가 어렸을 때, 나는 선생님이 되고 싶었다. (young)

→ _____ _____ _____ _____, I wanted to be a teacher.

4 영화가 시작하기 전에 휴대 전화를 끄세요. (the movie, start)

→ Turn off your cell phone _____ _____ _____ _____.

because, if, that

A

because: ~하기 때문에(이유, 원인)

I like this house **because** it has a nice garden.
Because it's raining, you should take your umbrella.

B

if: 만약 ~하다면(조건)

If you need money, I'll lend you some.
You can eat this pizza **if** you're hungry.

① 조건을 나타내는 if절에서는 미래를 나타내더라도 현재시제를 쓴다.
  We'll be happy *if* we **win** the game tonight. (~~will win~~)

C

that

「that + 주어 + 동사」 형태의 that절은 문장에서 주어, 목적어, 보어 역할을 한다.

1 that절이 문장에서 주어로 쓰여, '~하는 것은'의 의미를 나타낸다. 이 경우에는 보통 주어 자리에
   가주어 It을 사용하여 「It ~ that + 주어 + 동사」 형태로 쓴다.
   It is true **that** Andy likes Lisa.

2 that절이 문장에서 목적어로 쓰여, '~하는 것을'의 의미를 나타낸다. 이때의 that은 생략 가능하다.
   I think (**that**) Andrew is funny.

   cf. that절을 목적어로 쓰는 동사: think, know, believe, hope, tell, say 등
     She *said* (**that**) she could help me.

3 that절이 문장에서 보어로 쓰여, '~하는 것(이다)'의 의미를 나타낸다.
   The problem is **that** I don't know the answer.

┇ CHECK UP ┇ 빈칸에 알맞은 말을 고르시오.

1 I was late _____ the traffic was heavy.
   ⓐ because   ⓑ if   ⓒ that

2 I know _____ you have a talent for music.
   ⓐ because   ⓑ if   ⓒ that

3 We will go on a picnic _____ it's sunny tomorrow.
   ⓐ because   ⓑ if   ⓒ that

PRACTICE

🔍 Answer Key p.17

STEP 1

( ) 안에서 알맞은 말을 고르시오.

1 It's sad (to, that) you have to go.

2 (If, That) you are busy, I'll call you later.

3 I hope (because, that) you will get better soon.

4 They were tired (because, that) they woke up early this morning.

5 If he (doesn't come, won't come) here soon, we'll leave without him.

STEP 2

빈칸에 알맞은 말을 보기에서 골라 쓰시오.

보기	because	if	that

1 The bad news is _____ we are out of money.

2 _____ you have any questions, you can email me.

3 Junho said _____ he wanted to go to Europe.

4 Dana didn't go to school _____ she was sick.

STEP 3

빈칸에 알맞은 말을 보기에서 골라 쓰시오.

보기	if you need my help
	that he is brilliant
	because she was too busy

1 I think _____.

2 _____, you can ask me anytime.

3 Janet didn't come to the party _____.

STEP 4

우리말과 일치하도록 ( ) 안의 말을 이용하여 문장을 완성하시오.

1 John은 그가 옳다고 믿는다. (right)

→ John believes _____ _____ _____ _____.

2 나는 열심히 공부했기 때문에 시험에 합격했다. (study hard)

→ I passed the exam _____ _____ _____ _____.

3 네가 그를 기억하지 못하는 것은 이상하다. (strange)

→ _____ _____ _____ _____ you don't remember him.

4 네가 택시를 타면 제시간에 도착할 것이다. (take a taxi)

→ _____ _____ _____ _____ _____, you will be on time.

GRAMMAR FOR WRITING

A 우리말과 일치하도록 ( ) 안의 말을 이용하여 문장을 완성하시오.

1 나는 결승선을 통과할 때까지 달렸다. (cross the finish line)

→ I ran _____.

2 나는 이 표가 비싸다고 생각한다. (this ticket, expensive)

→ I think _____.

3 그가 자주 거짓말을 하기 때문에 나는 그를 믿지 않는다. (often, tell lies)

→ I don't trust him _____.

4 Luna는 자기 전에 일기를 쓴다. (go to bed)

→ Luna writes in her diary _____.

5 이 카메라는 낡았지만 유용하다. (old, useful)

→ This camera _____.

6 Eric은 지갑을 잃어버려서 새것을 샀다. (buy a new one)

→ Eric lost his wallet, _____.

7 우리는 버스가 떠난 후에 버스 터미널에 도착했다. (the bus, leave)

→ We arrived at the bus terminal _____.

B 우리말과 일치하도록 ( ) 안에 주어진 말을 바르게 배열하시오.

1 그녀는 시장에서 고기와 채소를 샀다. (and, bought, meat, she, vegetables)

→ _____ at the market.

2 Brian은 그 소식을 들었을 때 기뻤다. (heard, when, the news, he)

→ Brian was happy _____.

3 너를 돕고 싶지만, 나는 매우 바쁘다. (I'm, but, busy, very)

→ I want to help you, _____.

4 그가 패스트푸드를 좋아하는 것은 사실이다. (true, it, that, is)

→ _____ he likes fast food.

5 질문이 있으면 손을 들어 주세요. (any, if, questions, have, you)

→ Please raise your hand _____.

6 우리는 정상에 도달할 때까지 멈추지 않을 것이다. (reach, until, the top, we)

→ We won't stop _____.

C A와 B에서 각각 어울리는 말을 찾아 연결하여 문장을 완성하시오.

A	B
and	I made a reservation.
but	He bought some clothes.
or	She lost the contest.
so	I will give you a hint.

1 Amy practiced hard, _____.

2 You can keep trying, _____.

3 John went shopping, _____.

4 The restaurant is very popular, _____.

D 그림을 보고 보기에서 알맞은 말을 골라 (   ) 안의 말과 함께 써서 문장을 완성하시오. (단, 한 번씩만 쓸 것)

1   **2**   **3**   **4**

보기	when because after before

1 Ben went to the supermarket _____. (he left the office)

2 He cooked dinner _____. (his wife got home)

3 _____, she was pleased. (his wife arrived)

4 _____, they ate too much. They were very full.
(the food was delicious)

REVIEW TEST

[1-3] 빈칸에 들어갈 알맞은 말을 고르시오.

1

> The city was very clean _____ beautiful.

① and   ② but   ③ or
④ when   ⑤ until

2

> We can drive a car _____ take the subway to the zoo.

① but   ② or   ③ so
④ because   ⑤ that

3

> I want to buy some fruit, _____ I can't find a supermarket.

① and   ② but   ③ or
④ so   ⑤ if

4 다음 중 밑줄 친 부분이 올바른 것은?

① It is cold <u>but</u> snowy in winter.
② I want to visit both London <u>or</u> Paris.
③ These shoes are nice <u>or</u> expensive.
④ Ava was sick, <u>so</u> she took some medicine.
⑤ You may add either water <u>and</u> milk.

[5-7] 다음 중 밑줄 친 부분이 잘못된 것을 고르시오.

5

① The students <u>joked and laughed</u>.
② He ate the pizza <u>quickly and quiet</u>.
③ She may be <u>in the park or at home</u>.
④ He was <u>young but very brave</u>.
⑤ Isabel was tired, <u>but she couldn't sleep</u>.

6

① I will be there <u>before you arrive</u>.
② I can't rest <u>until I finish this work</u>.
③ <u>If we will hurry</u>, we will catch the bus.
④ <u>After we have lunch</u>, we will go to the beach.
⑤ <u>If you tell me your secret</u>, I will tell you mine.

7

① <u>If you visit them</u>, they will be happy.
② He wasn't at the office <u>if I called him</u>.
③ I have to clean my room <u>before</u> Mom gets home.
④ <u>After</u> we moved to a bigger house, I had my own room.
⑤ We won't start the meeting <u>until</u> everyone is here.

154

12 The best thing is _____ this product is good for the environment.

[8-9] 빈칸에 들어갈 말이 나머지 넷과 <u>다른</u> 것을 고르시오.

8 ① I missed the bus, _____ I wasn't late.

② I was tired, _____ I took a nap.

③ The room was too hot, _____ I opened the window.

④ Andrew didn't study a lot for the test, _____ he was worried.

⑤ It was cold, _____ I turned off the air conditioner.

[13-15] 빈칸에 공통으로 들어갈 말을 고르시오.

13
- I stayed in bed _____ I was sick.
- I love this song _____ the singer's voice is lovely.

① but ② so ③ that
④ before ⑤ because

9 ① The book is very long _____ fun to read.

② Eric and I sometimes fight, _____ we are best friends.

③ We looked for the key _____ couldn't find it.

④ The phone rang again, _____ she didn't answer it.

⑤ She's probably in the garden _____ the kitchen.

14
- The water in the pool wasn't clean, _____ I didn't swim.
- We didn't have enough time, _____ we took a taxi.

① so ② but ③ or
④ when ⑤ because

[10-12] 빈칸에 알맞은 접속사를 써서 대화를 완성하시오.

10 A: Do you want pork _____ beef?
B: Beef, please.

15
- It got dark quickly _____ the sun set.
- I dried my hair _____ I washed it.

11 He isn't tall, _____ he's a good basketball player.

① so ② before ③ after
④ that ⑤ until

[16-17] 대화를 읽고 물음에 답하시오.

A: I want to buy this shirt.
B: Do you like the blue one _____(A)_____ the white one?
A: I like the blue one 파란색은 내가 가장 좋아하는 색이기 때문에. (blue, my favorite color)
B: I think _____(B)_____ it's a good choice.

16 빈칸 (A)와 (B)에 들어갈 말이 바르게 짝지어진 것은?

	(A)		(B)
①	and	……	if
②	and	……	that
③	or	……	that
④	or	……	because
⑤	but	……	because

서술형

17 우리말과 일치하도록 (   ) 안의 말을 이용하여 대화를 완성하시오.

_____

서술형

[18-19] 우리말과 일치하도록 (   ) 안의 말을 이용하여 문장을 완성하시오.

18 초인종이 울렸을 때 나는 자고 있었다.
(the doorbell, ring)

→ I was sleeping _____.

19 네가 한가하다면, 여기에 더 오래 머물러도 좋다.
(free)

→ _____, you can stay here longer.

서술형

[20-21] 우리말과 일치하도록 (   ) 안의 말을 이용하여 대화를 완성하시오.

20
A: I don't have an umbrella.
B: You can stay here 비가 그칠 때까지.
(the rain, stop)

→ _____

21
A: What did you do yesterday?
B: I took care of my little sister 부모님이 외출하셨기 때문에. (my parents, go out)

→ _____

서술형

[22-23] 우리말과 일치하도록 (   ) 안에 주어진 말을 바르게 배열하시오.

22 그가 프랑스어를 할 수 있다는 것은 놀랍다.
(surprising, he, it, that, is)

→ _____ can speak French.

23 그녀는 테니스를 친 뒤 샤워를 한다.
(plays, after, tennis, she)

→ She takes a shower _____
_____.

24 다음 중 어법상 옳은 것을 모두 고르면?

① Will you wear pants and a skirt today?
② I know that she has three sisters.
③ Susan will help you if has time.
④ I felt cold, so I put on a jacket.
⑤ Carl gave me flowers, but I didn't take them.

25 다음 중 어법상 옳은 것으로 바르게 짝지어진 것은?

> a. That he loves me, I'll be happy.
> b. I'll buy either a camera or a tablet.
> c. Look both ways before you cross the street.
> d. I ate a lot because I was hungry.
> e. It is strange if he didn't call you.

① a, b, c   ② a, d, e   ③ b, c, d
④ b, c, e   ⑤ c, d, e

26 다음 중 어법상 옳은 것의 개수는?

> • If you are busy, I'll just go alone.
> • I'll be an engineer after I finish school.
> • Both Ian or Mickey are great artists.
> • I'll wait until the bus will come.
> • It's important that we reduce waste.

① 1개   ② 2개   ③ 3개
④ 4개   ⑤ 5개

[27-29] 밑줄 친 부분이 어법상 옳은지 판단하고, 틀리면 바르게 고치시오.

27 The problem is <u>if</u> I don't have enough money.

(O / X) _____

28 She will keep taking selfies until she <u>will get</u> a good one.

(O / X) _____

29 If you want to succeed, you have to use your time wisely.

(O / X) _____

[30-32] 어법상 틀린 부분을 찾아 바르게 고치시오.

30 I think it Julia should be class president. If she will become class president, she'll make our class the best in the school. (2개)

31 Yesterday was a holiday, but I didn't go to school. I went to the amusement park with Peter or Pam. We were tired or happy. (3개)

32 A: Do you know a lot about Jeju Island?
B: Yes. If I was a child, I lived there.
A: I think that it's popular with tourists.
B: Right. They like it before it's beautiful. (2개)

LET'S REVIEW

주요 예문을 다시 한번 확인하고, 우리말과 일치하도록 빈칸을 채우시오.

- I ate soup [1]_____ salad for lunch. 나는 점심으로 수프와 샐러드를 먹었다. Unit 01 - A

- The machine is old, [2]_____ it works well. 그 기계는 오래되었지만 잘 작동한다. Unit 01 - B

- You can take a bus [3]_____ walk to the museum.
  너는 박물관까지 버스를 타거나 걸어갈 수 있다. Unit 01 - C

- I was really tired, [4]_____ I took a break. 나는 정말 피곤해서 휴식을 취했다. Unit 01 - D

- I use chopsticks **when** I eat. 나는 먹을 때 젓가락을 사용한다. Unit 02 - A

- [5]_____ you leave, you should finish the work.
  너는 떠나기 전에 그 일을 끝내야 한다. Unit 02 - B

- I feel great **after** I exercise. 나는 운동한 후에 기분이 정말 좋다. Unit 02 - C

- I read the page [6]_____ I understood it.
  나는 그 페이지를 이해할 때까지 그것을 읽었다. Unit 02 - D

- I like this house **because** it has a nice garden. 나는 이 집이 멋진 정원을 가지고 있어서 좋다. Unit 03 - A

- [7]_____ you need money, I'll lend you some.
  만약 네가 돈이 필요하다면 내가 너에게 좀 빌려줄게. Unit 03 - B

- It is true [8]_____ Andy likes Lisa. Andy가 Lisa를 좋아하는 것은 사실이다. Unit 03 - C

- I think **(that)** Andrew is funny. 나는 Andrew가 웃기다고 생각한다. Unit 03 - C

- The problem is [9]_____ I don't know the answer.
  문제는 내가 답을 알지 못한다는 것이다. Unit 03 - C

🔍 **Answers**

[1] and   [2] but   [3] or   [4] so   [5] Before   [6] until   [7] If   [8] that   [9] that

ESSENTIAL RULES OF

ENGLISH GRAMMAR

CHAPTER
12

의문문, 명령문, 감탄문

영어 문장은 내용에 따라 평서문, 의문문,
명령문, 감탄문으로 나뉜다.

UNIT 01 의문사 who, what, which

UNIT 02 의문사 when, where, why, how

UNIT 03 부가의문문

UNIT 04 부정의문문, 선택의문문

UNIT 05 명령문, 감탄문

의문사 who, what, which

A

who: 누구

Who is that man?
Who closed the door?
Who did you meet at the party?

cf. whom: 누구를(일상 대화에서는 whom 대신 who를 더 많이 쓴다.)
Who(m) do you look like?

cf. whose: 누구의
Whose *cell phone* is ringing?

B

what: 무엇, 무슨 (~)

What is your blood type?
What does he do for a living?
What *day* is it today?
What *kind of music* do you listen to?

C

which: 어느 것, 어떤 (~)

Which is better, this one or that one?
Which do you prefer, coffee or tea?
Which *color* do you want, red or blue?

cf. what은 정해진 범위 없이 물을 때 쓰고, which는 정해진 범위 안에서 선택을 물을 때 쓴다.
What is your favorite fruit?
Which do you like better, apples or peaches?

CHECK UP 빈칸에 알맞은 말을 고르시오.

1 _____ is your name?
ⓐ Who   ⓑ Whom   ⓒ What

2 _____ bag is this?
ⓐ Who   ⓑ Whom   ⓒ Whose

3 _____ is your favorite singer?
ⓐ Who   ⓑ Whom   ⓒ Whose

4 _____ do you prefer, English or math?
ⓐ Who   ⓑ Whom   ⓒ Which

⊕ PLUS

의문사가 주어일 때는 3인칭 단수 취급한다.

Who **knows** the answer?
What **makes** you happy?
Which **is** faster, the bus or the subway?

PRACTICE

🔍 Answer Key p.18

STEP 1

( ) 안에서 알맞은 말을 고르시오.

1 A: (Who, What) is the girl in this photo?
B: She's my cousin Ally.

2 A: (Whom, Whose) are you calling?
B: I'm calling John.

3 A: (Who, Which) do you want to have, chicken or beef?
B: Chicken, please.

STEP 2

자연스러운 대화가 되도록 알맞게 연결하시오.

1 Whose coat is on the sofa? •　　　• ⓐ I like both.

2 Who sits next to you in class? •　　　• ⓑ It's my father's.

3 What are you going to do tomorrow? •　　　• ⓒ Steve sits next to me.

4 Which do you prefer, books or movies? •　　　• ⓓ I'm going to go shopping.

STEP 3

빈칸에 알맞은 말을 보기에서 골라 대화를 완성하시오. (단, 한 번씩만 쓸 것)

보기	who　　whose　　what　　which

1 A: _____ key is on the table?
B: It's mine.

2 A: _____ do you do after you have dinner?
B: I usually watch TV.

3 A: _____ turned on the lights?
B: I did.

4 A: _____ do you like better, baseball or soccer?
B: I like soccer better.

STEP 4

우리말과 일치하도록 ( ) 안의 말을 이용하여 문장을 완성하시오.

1 이것과 저것 중 어느 것이 더 싸니? (cheaper)

→ _____ _____ _____, this one or that one?

2 너는 누구를 가장 존경하니? (respect)

→ _____ _____ _____ _____ the most?

3 그는 대학에서 무엇을 공부했니? (study)

→ _____ _____ _____ _____ in university?

의문사 when, where, why, how

A   **when: 언제**

When is Valentine's Day?
When do you usually eat dinner?

B   **where: 어디에, 어디서**

Where is the post office?
Where did you get the information?

C   **why: 왜**

why에 대한 대답에는 주로 because(왜냐하면)가 사용된다.

A: **Why** are you so upset?
B: **Because** we lost the game.

cf. Why don't you ~?는 '(너) ~하는 것이 어때?', Why don't we ~?는 '우리 ~하지 않을래?'의 의미이다.
   Why don't you start doing yoga?
   Why don't we go hiking? (= Let's go hiking.)

D   **how: 어떤, 어떻게, 얼마나 ~한/하게**

1   어떤, 어떻게

   How are you doing?
   How do you spend your free time?

2   how + 형용사/부사: 얼마나 ~한/하게

- how old: 몇 살의
- how tall: 얼마나 키가 큰/높은
- how long: 얼마나 긴/오래
- how far: 얼마나 먼
- how often: 얼마나 자주
- how much: 얼마(의)
- how many + 셀 수 있는 명사: 얼마나 많은 수의 ~
- how much + 셀 수 없는 명사: 얼마나 많은 양의 ~

   How old is your dog?
   How long will you stay here?
   How much *water* do you drink a day?

CHECK UP   빈칸에 알맞은 말을 고르시오.

1   A: _____ is your birthday? B: It's February 8.
    ⓐ When   ⓑ Where   ⓒ How

2   A: _____ often do you call your grandparents? B: Once a month.
    ⓐ When   ⓑ Why   ⓒ How

PRACTICE

🔍 Answer Key p.18

STEP 1

( ) 안에서 알맞은 말을 고르시오.

1 A: (When, Where) is my sweater?
B: It's in the closet.

2 A: (Why, How) do you feel now?
B: I feel better.

3 A: (When, How) did you take this picture?
B: Two months ago.

STEP 2

자연스러운 대화가 되도록 알맞게 연결하시오.

1 When does the movie start? •   • ⓐ By bus.

2 Where does your mother work? •   • ⓑ At the bank.

3 Why do you study in the library? •   • ⓒ At seven o'clock.

4 How did you get to the museum? •   • ⓓ Because it's quiet there.

STEP 3

빈칸에 알맞은 말을 보기에서 골라 대화를 완성하시오.

보기	how old	how long	how far	how much

1 A: _____ is your little sister?
B: She is eleven years old.

2 A: _____ is the ticket?
B: It's $50.

3 A: _____ did the concert last?
B: About two hours.

4 A: _____ is it from here to Seoul Station?
B: About one kilometer.

STEP 4

우리말과 일치하도록 빈칸에 알맞은 말을 써서 문장을 완성하시오.

1 Erica는 어디에 사니?

→ _____ _____ _____ live?

2 그들은 언제 만났니?

→ _____ _____ _____ meet?

3 너는 왜 액션 영화를 좋아하니?

→ _____ _____ _____ like action movies?

UNIT 03 부가의문문

A 부가의문문

1 부가의문문은 사실을 확인하거나 상대방에게 동의를 구하기 위해 평서문 뒤에 붙이는 간단한 의문문으로, '그렇지?', '그렇지 않니?'의 의미를 나타낸다.

Marvin is a doctor, **isn't he**?

2 부가의문문 만드는 법

1) 긍정문 뒤에는 부정의 부가의문문을 쓰고, 부정문 뒤에는 긍정의 부가의문문을 쓴다.
2) 부가의문문의 시제는 앞의 평서문의 동사와 같은 시제를 쓴다.

주어	주어 → 대명사	*Tom* is a student, isn't **he**? *Your sister* isn't at home, is **she**?
동사	be동사 → be동사 조동사 → 조동사 일반동사 → do/does/did	You *are* Korean, **aren't** you? He *can't* dance well, **can** he? They *live* here, **don't** they?

Your mother was a cook, **wasn't she**?
Ted and Ray won't come to the party, **will they**?
Kevin studied late last night, **didn't he**?

B 부가의문문에 대한 대답

질문의 긍정, 부정과 상관없이 대답하는 내용이 긍정이면 Yes, 부정이면 No를 쓴다.

A: They won't join our club, will they?
B: **Yes, they will.** (They will join our club.) /
　 No, they won't. (They won't join our club.)

A: Jason has his own blog, doesn't he?
B: **Yes, he does.** (He has his own blog.) /
　 No, he doesn't. (He doesn't have his own blog.)

 CHECK UP　빈칸에 알맞은 말을 고르시오.

1 She was playing tennis, _____?
　ⓐ is she　　ⓑ was she　　ⓒ wasn't she

2 Kevin can't ride a bicycle, _____?
　ⓐ can Kevin　ⓑ can he　　ⓒ can't he

3 These cookies smell good, _____?
　ⓐ aren't they　ⓑ don't they　ⓒ didn't they

4 They don't speak English, _____?
　ⓐ do they　　ⓑ did they　　ⓒ don't they

➕ PLUS : 명령문과 권유문의 부가의문문

명령이나 권유의 긍정, 부정과 상관없이 명령문의 부가의문문은 「~, will you?(그래 줄래?)」, 권유문의 부가의문문은 「~, shall we?(그럴래?)」를 쓴다.

Turn down the music, **will you**?
Don't be late, **will you**?
Let's go for a walk, **shall we**?

PRACTICE

🔍 Answer Key p-19

( ) 안에서 알맞은 말을 고르시오.

1 Scott is a great actor, isn't (Scott, he)?

2 Your house is not far from here, (is, isn't) it?

3 He will be at home tomorrow, (will, won't) he?

4 You didn't forget our promise, (did, were) you?

5 They went to Hong Kong on vacation, (don't, didn't) they?

빈칸에 알맞은 말을 써서 부가의문문을 완성하시오.

1 The party starts at 7:00 p.m., _____ _____?

2 You brought lunch, _____ _____?

3 We shouldn't sit here, _____ _____?

4 Bill was the best player in the game, _____ _____?

5 The students weren't in the classroom, _____ _____?

빈칸에 알맞은 말을 써서 대화를 완성하시오.

1 A: John can't swim, _____ _____?
　　B: Yes, _____ _____.

2 A: Ann and Mary are twins, _____ _____?
　　B: Yes, _____ _____.

3 A: You came from Australia, _____ _____?
　　B: No, _____ _____. I came from New Zealand.

4 A: This café doesn't sell milk tea, _____ _____?
　　B: No, _____ _____.

우리말과 일치하도록 빈칸에 알맞은 말을 써서 부가의문문을 완성하시오.

1 문을 닫아줘, 그래 줄래?

　→ Close the door, _____ _____?

2 너는 내년에 졸업할 거야, 그렇지 않니?

　→ You will graduate next year, _____ _____?

3 우리 내일 수영 가자, 그럴래?

　→ Let's go swimming tomorrow, _____ _____?

부정의문문, 선택의문문

A 부정의문문

1 부정의문문은 동사의 부정형으로 시작하는 의문문으로, '~이지/하지 않니?'의 의미를 나타낸다.

※ 부정의문문 만드는 법

동사		부정의문문	
be동사	현재형	Isn't/Aren't	
	과거형	Wasn't/Weren't	
일반동사	현재형	Don't/Doesn't	주어 ~?
	과거형	Didn't	
조동사	〈조동사 + not〉의 줄임말	Can't/Won't ...	

Aren't you tired?
Didn't you go to the beach with him?
Can't we leave now?

2 대답: 질문의 긍정, 부정과 상관없이 대답하는 내용이 긍정이면 Yes, 부정이면 No를 쓴다.

A: **Don't** Mexicans speak Spanish?
B: **Yes**, they **do**. (They speak Spanish.)

B 선택의문문

1 선택의문문은 or를 써서 어느 한 쪽을 선택할 것을 요구하는 의문문이다.

Will you go there *by bus* **or** *by taxi*?
Which do you like better, *math* **or** *science*?

2 대답할 때는 Yes/No로 답할 수 없음에 유의한다.

A: Do you want to *go out* **or** *stay* at home?
B: **I want to stay at home.**

CHECK UP   빈칸에 알맞은 말을 고르시오.

1 _____ Mina in your class?
   ⓐ Isn't   ⓑ Doesn't   ⓒ Can't

2 Which do you like better, dogs _____ cats?
   ⓐ and   ⓑ but   ⓒ or

PRACTICE

🔍 Answer Key p.19

STEP 1

( ) 안에서 알맞은 말을 고르시오.

1 (Aren't, Don't) you know my name?

2 Do you study at home (but, or) in the library?

3 (Which, How) do you prefer, vanilla or chocolate ice cream?

4 A: Can't you help me with my report?
　 B: (Yes, No), I can't. I'm busy now.

5 A: Are they American or French?
　 B: (No, they aren't., They are French.)

STEP 2

( ) 안의 말을 이용하여 부정의문문을 완성하시오.

1 A: _____ _____ _____ outside? (cold)
　 B: No, it isn't. It's warm today.

2 A: _____ _____ _____ to the party? (come)
　 B: Yes, she did. She enjoyed the party.

3 A: _____ _____ _____ us for dinner? (join)
　 B: Yes, I will. I'm hungry.

STEP 3

다음 두 문장을 연결하여 선택의문문을 완성하시오.

1 Did you read a book? Did you read a newspaper?

→ _____ ?

2 Do you walk home? Do you take the subway?

→ _____ ?

3 Will he come this Saturday? Will he come next Saturday?

→ _____ ?

STEP 4

우리말과 일치하도록 ( ) 안의 말을 이용하여 문장을 완성하시오.

1 그녀는 아침에 일찍 일어나지 않니? (get up)

→ _____ _____ _____ _____ early in the morning?

2 너는 여름과 겨울 중 어느 것을 더 좋아하니? (summer, winter)

→ _____ do you like better, _____ _____ _____ ?

명령문, 감탄문

명령문

명령문은 명령, 부탁, 권유 등을 나타내는 문장이다.

1 보통 주어(you)를 생략하고 동사원형으로 시작한다.

동사원형 ~	~해라
Don't[Do not] + 동사원형 ~	~하지 마라

Finish your meal.
Do not smoke.

> *cf.* 명령문의 앞이나 뒤에 please를 붙이면 공손한 표현이 된다.
> Stand up, **please**. / **Please** stand up.

2 Let's + 동사원형: ~하자 (권유, 제안)

Let's + 동사원형 ~	(우리) ~하자
Let's not + 동사원형 ~	(우리) ~하지 말자

Let's play soccer after school.
Let's not go to the movies tonight.

감탄문

감탄문은 기쁨, 슬픔, 놀라움 등의 감정을 표현하는 문장으로, '매우 ~하구나!'의 의미를 나타낸다.

what으로 시작하는 감탄문	What + a(n) + 형용사 + 명사 (+ 주어 + 동사)!
how로 시작하는 감탄문	How + 형용사/부사 (+ 주어 + 동사)!

What an exciting game (it is)!
How smart that boy is!

> *cf.* what으로 시작하는 감탄문에서 명사가 복수형이거나 셀 수 없는 명사일 때는 a(n)를 쓰지 않는다.
> **What beautiful *eyes*** she has! (~~What a beautiful eyes~~)
> **What cold *water*** it is! (~~What a cold water~~)

CHECK UP 빈칸에 알맞은 말을 고르시오.

1 _____ meet at the coffee shop.
ⓐ Be ⓑ Does ⓒ Let's

2 _____ a small world it is!
ⓐ Let's ⓑ What ⓒ How

➕ PLUS : 명령문 + and/or ~

명령문, and ~	~해라, 그러면 …할 것이다
명령문, or ~	~해라, 그러지 않으면 …할 것이다

Hurry up, and you'll catch the train.
Hurry up, or you'll miss the train.

PRACTICE

🔍 Answer Key p·19

STEP 1

( ) 안에서 알맞은 말을 고르시오.

1 (What, How) a great idea it is!

2 (Clean, Cleans) your room right now.

3 (Don't leave, Not leave) your wallet in the car.

4 (What, How) beautiful this beach is!

5 (Let's not, Don't let's) worry about that.

6 (Don't please, Please don't) turn off the light.

STEP 2

( ) 안의 말을 이용하여 명령문을 완성하시오. (Let's는 사용하지 말 것)

1 _____. The baby is sleeping. (be, quiet)

2 _____ the pot. It's really hot. (not/touch)

3 _____ afraid. I'll be with you. (not/be)

4 _____ your mask. There is a lot of fine dust today. (wear)

5 You're driving too fast. _____.
(please, slow down)

STEP 3

다음 문장을 감탄문으로 바꿔 쓰시오.

1 Susan is very lazy.

→ How _____!

2 It was a really great movie.

→ What _____!

3 The man is very handsome.

→ How _____!

4 These are very expensive shoes.

→ What _____!

STEP 4

우리말과 일치하도록 ( ) 안의 말을 이용하여 문장을 완성하시오.

1 수업 중에 떠들지 마라. (make noise)

→ _____ _____ _____ during class.

2 매우 귀여운 강아지구나! (cute, puppy)

→ _____ _____ _____ _____!

3 저녁 식사 후에 아이스크림을 먹자. (eat ice cream)

→ _____ _____ _____ _____ after dinner.

GRAMMAR FOR WRITING

A 우리말과 일치하도록 ( ) 안의 말을 이용하여 문장을 완성하시오.

1 축제는 언제였니? (the festival)

→ _____?

2 제가 수족관에 어떻게 갈 수 있나요? (can, get)

→ _____ to the aquarium?

3 누가 이 케이크를 만들었니? (make)

→ _____ this cake?

4 너는 어디에서 이 원피스를 샀니? (buy)

→ _____ this dress?

5 도움이 필요하면 내게 말해. (tell)

→ _____ if you need any help.

6 Jones 씨가 너희 음악 선생님이시지 않니? (Ms. Jones)

→ _____ your music teacher?

7 Sarah는 다음 달에 중국을 방문할 거야, 그렇지 않니? (will, visit China)

→ Sarah _____ next month, _____?

B 우리말과 일치하도록 ( ) 안에 주어진 말을 바르게 배열하시오.

1 우리 산에 가자. (go, the mountains, let's, to)

→ _____.

2 이 건물은 매우 높구나! (this, tall, building, is, how)

→ _____!

3 너는 얼마나 자주 외식을 하니? (often, eat out, do, how, you)

→ _____?

4 너 이 책을 읽어보는 게 어때? (don't, why, this book, you, read)

→ _____?

5 저 방에 들어가지 마라. (enter, that room, not, do)

→ _____.

6 너는 런던과 파리 중 어느 곳이 더 좋았니? (which, like better, you, did)

→ _____, London or Paris?

C 각 대답을 보고 알맞은 의문문을 완성하시오.

1 A: _____ city hall?

B: It's on Main Street.

2 A: _____ you the story?

B: Bill told me.

3 A: _____ for lunch?

B: I ate pizza and salad.

4 A: _____ your homework?

B: I'll do it in the evening.

5 A: _____ looking for?

B: She is looking for her mom.

6 A: _____, the novel or the movie?

B: The novel is more interesting.

D 각 인물에 대한 정보를 보고 부가의문문과 대답을 써서 대화를 완성하시오.

Eric	**Daisy**	**Melody**
• doctor	• teacher	• singer
• plays the guitar	• has a blog	• likes soccer
• came from Paris	• came from New York	• came from New York

1 A: Eric has a blog, _____?

B: _____.

2 A: Daisy isn't a singer, _____?

B: _____.

3 A: Daisy and Melody came from New York, _____?

B: _____.

4 A: Eric doesn't play the guitar, _____?

B: _____.

[1-3] 빈칸에 들어갈 알맞은 말을 고르시오.

1

A: _____ did you call me?
B: Because I wanted to invite you to dinner.

① Who   ② What   ③ When
④ Where   ⑤ Why

2

A: _____ is the boy over there?
B: That's Joe.

① Who   ② Whom   ③ Whose
④ What   ⑤ Which

3

A: _____ are you going now?
B: I'm going to the supermarket.

① How   ② What   ③ When
④ Which   ⑤ Where

빈출

[4-5] 다음 중 대화가 자연스럽지 <u>않은</u> 것을 고르시오.

4

① A: Whose camera is this?
   B: It's mine.
② A: Where is the bakery?
   B: It is on the next street.
③ A: Which do you want, juice or milk?
   B: Milk, please.
④ A: Why don't you exercise?
   B: Because I want to lose weight.
⑤ A: When will you go home?
   B: At seven o'clock.

5

① A: How old are you?
   B: I'm fourteen years old.
② A: How often do you cook?
   B: I never cook.
③ A: How many cookies did you eat?
   B: I ate five.
④ A: How long will you stay in Japan?
   B: It takes three hours by plane.
⑤ A: How far is it from your house to the post office?
   B: It's only 300 meters.

서술형

[6-7] 빈칸에 알맞은 말을 써서 대화를 완성하시오.

6

A: Don't you remember me?
B: _____, _____ _____.
   We met at the summer camp.

7

A: Isn't she a pianist?
B: _____, she _____. She's an engineer.

서술형

[8-9] 다음 문장을 감탄문으로 바꿔 쓰시오.

8

He is a very fast runner.

→ What _____!

9

This show is very boring.

→ How _____!

13 ① How nice you are!
② What a lovely day it is!
③ What a wonderful picture!
④ How beautiful the sunset is!
⑤ How good friends you have!

10 다음 중 밑줄 친 부분이 올바른 것은?

① Paul likes baseball, does Paul?
② She is a great singer, isn't she?
③ You will stay with us, don't you?
④ Amy doesn't eat meat, doesn't she?
⑤ They didn't attend the meeting, do they?

빈출
14 빈칸에 들어갈 말이 바르게 짝지어진 것은?

____(A)____ color do you like better, white ____(B)____ black?

	(A)		(B)
①	What	……	and
②	What	……	or
③	Which	……	and
④	Which	……	or
⑤	Which	……	but

[11-13] 다음 중 밑줄 친 부분이 잘못된 것을 고르시오.

11 ① Where is my cell phone?
② Who wants to go for a walk?
③ When will you go to America?
④ What do you think about this dress?
⑤ How much countries are there in the world?

[15-16] 다음 대답에 알맞은 의문문을 고르시오.

15

I bought it yesterday.

① Why did you buy the book?
② How did you buy the book?
③ When did you buy the book?
④ What did you buy yesterday?
⑤ Where did you buy the book?

12 ① Don't tell lies.
② Open your book.
③ Not let's eat here.
④ Let's go to the beach.
⑤ Please be there at 6:00 p.m.

16

I went there with Jane.

① Where is the theater?
② Why did you go to the theater?
③ How did you go to the theater?
④ When did you go to the theater?
⑤ Who did you go to the theater with?

[17-18] 빈칸에 공통으로 들어갈 말을 쓰시오.

17
· A: _____ much is this shirt?
  B: It is $50.
· A: _____ did you spend your
  weekend?
  B: I went camping with my family.

18
· _____ waste your time.
· A: _____ you know this song?
  B: No, I don't. But it sounds great.

19 다음 우리말을 영어로 바르게 옮긴 것은?

너 네 생일 파티에 Tim을 초대하는 게 어때?

① How did you invite Tim to your
   birthday party?
② How can you invite Tim to your
   birthday party?
③ Why do you invite Tim to your
   birthday party?
④ Why don't you invite Tim to your
   birthday party?
⑤ Why don't we invite Tim to your
   birthday party?

[20-21] 우리말과 일치하도록 ( ) 안의 말을 이용하여 문장
      을 완성하시오.

20 코트를 입어라, 그러지 않으면 너는 감기에 걸릴 것이
   다. (wear)

→ _____ a coat, _____ you
  will catch a cold.

21 우리 버스 정류장을 찾아보자. (find)

→ _____ a bus stop.

[22-23] 우리말과 일치하도록 ( ) 안에 주어진 말을 바르게
      배열하시오.

22 우리에게 돈이 얼마나 있습니까?
   (we, how, do, have, much, money)

→ _____?

23 당신의 차를 여기에 주차하지 마세요.
   (your car, don't, here, park)

→ _____.

24 우리말과 일치하도록 주어진 조건에 맞게 감탄문을 완성
   하시오.

그것은 정말 좋은 계획이구나!

〈조건〉 1. a nice plan, it을 이용할 것
       2. 주어, 동사를 생략하지 말 것

→ _____!

25 다음 중 어법상 옳은 것을 모두 고르면?

① Doesn't Frank wear glasses?
② When does your class start?
③ Let's don't talk about the exam.
④ How much English books do you have?
⑤ Tom doesn't like Asian food, does he?

26 다음 중 어법상 옳은 것으로 바르게 짝지어진 것은?

a. Be kind to your friends.
b. What a lucky girls we are!
c. Whose father is that man?
d. Be careful, won't you?
e. We should finish the work today, shouldn't we?

① a, c, d　　② a, c, e　　③ a, d, e
④ b, c, d　　⑤ c, d, e

27 다음 중 어법상 옳은 것의 개수는?

· How diligent are they!
· Let's have some ice cream, shall we?
· When did you learn Spanish?
· What kind of movies does she like?
· Don't turns off the air conditioner.

① 1개　　② 2개　　③ 3개
④ 4개　　⑤ 5개

[28-30] 밑줄 친 부분이 어법상 옳은지 판단하고, 틀리면 바르게 고치시오.

28 A: Doesn't Ann have a brother?
B: <u>No, she doesn't.</u> His name is Larry.

(O / X) _____

29 Danny had an appointment with you yesterday, <u>hadn't Danny</u>?

(O / X) _____

30 A: Who <u>know</u> Luke's number?
B: Kate may know it.

(O / X) _____

[31-33] 어법상 틀린 부분을 찾아 바르게 고치시오.

31 What dirty it is! Clean your room, shall you? (2개)

32 A: Which do you want to drink, coffee and tea?
B: Coffee, please.
A: What do you like coffee?
B: Because it smells great. (2개)

33 A: Looked at the sky! It's so lovely, is it?
B: Yes, it is. Why do we go on a picnic?
A: That's a good idea. (3개)

LET'S REVIEW

주요 예문을 다시 한번 확인하고, 우리말과 일치하도록 빈칸을 채우시오.

- 1_____ is that man? 저 남자는 누구니? Unit 01 - A

- **What** is your blood type? 네 혈액형은 무엇이니? Unit 01 - B

- 2_____ day is it today? 오늘은 무슨 요일이니? Unit 01 - B

- 3_____ is better, this one or that one? 이것과 저것 중에 어느 것이 더 낫니? Unit 01 - C

- **When** do you usually eat dinner? 너는 보통 언제 저녁을 먹니? Unit 02 - A

- 4_____ is the post office? 우체국은 어디에 있니? Unit 02 - B

- A: 5_____ are you so upset? 너는 왜 그렇게 화가 났니?
  B: **Because** we lost the game. 왜냐하면 우리가 경기에서 졌기 때문이야. Unit 02 - C

- 6_____ do you spend your free time? 너는 여가 시간을 어떻게 보내니? Unit 02 - D

- Your mother was a cook, 7_____ she? 네 어머니는 요리사셨어, 그렇지 않니? Unit 03 - A

- A: They won't join our club, **will they**? 그들은 우리 동아리에 가입하지 않을 거야, 그렇지?
  B: **Yes, they will.** 아냐, 그들은 가입할 거야. Unit 03 - B

- **Aren't** you tired? 너는 피곤하지 않니? Unit 04 - A

- A: Do you want to go out 8_____ stay at home? 너는 밖에 나가고 싶니 집에 있고 싶니?
  B: **I want to stay at home.** 나는 집에 있고 싶어. Unit 04 - B

- **Finish** your meal. 식사를 마쳐라. Unit 05 - A

- 9_____ **play** soccer after school. 방과 후에 축구 하자. Unit 05 - A

- 10_____ **an exciting game (it is)!** 매우 흥미진진한 경기구나! Unit 05 - B

- **How smart that boy is!** 저 소년은 매우 똑똑하구나! Unit 05 - B

Answers

1 Who   2 What   3 Which   4 Where   5 Why   6 How   7 wasn't   8 or   9 Let's   10 What

MEMO

MEMO

MEMO

MEMO

MEMO

MEMO

MEMO

지은이

NE능률 영어교육연구소

NE능률 영어교육연구소는 혁신적이며 효율적인 영어 교재를 개발하고
영어 학습의 질을 한 단계 높이고자 노력하는 NE능률의 연구조직입니다.

GRAMMAR Inside 〈Level 1〉

펴 낸 이	주민홍
펴 낸 곳	서울특별시 마포구 월드컵북로 396(상암동) 누리꿈스퀘어 비즈니스타워 10층
	㈜NE능률 (우편번호 03925)
펴 낸 날	2022년 1월 5일 개정판 제1쇄 발행
	2024년 8월 15일 제17쇄
전 화	02 2014 7114
팩 스	02 3142 0356
홈 페 이 지	www.neungyule.com
등 록 번 호	제1-68호
I S B N	979-11-253-3707-2 53740
정 가	15,500원

NE 능률

고객센터

교재 내용 문의: contact.nebooks.co.kr (별도의 가입 절차 없이 작성 가능)
제품 구매, 교환, 불량, 반품 문의: 02-2014-7114
☎ 전화문의는 본사 업무시간 중에만 가능합니다.

GRAMMAR Inside

LEVEL 1

A 4-level grammar course
with abundant writing practice

NE_ Neungyule

CONTENTS

GRAMMAR BASICS

01	품사	2
02	문장의 성분	3
03	구와 절	3

CHAPTER 01 be동사

Unit 01	be동사의 현재형과 과거형	4
Unit 02	be동사의 부정문과 의문문	7
REVIEW TEST		10

CHAPTER 02 일반동사

Unit 01	일반동사의 현재형	13
Unit 02	일반동사의 과거형	16
Unit 03	일반동사의 부정문	19
Unit 04	일반동사의 의문문	22
REVIEW TEST		25

CHAPTER 03 조동사

Unit 01	can, may	28
Unit 02	must, have to, should	31
REVIEW TEST		34

CHAPTER 04 진행형과 미래시제

Unit 01	진행형	37
Unit 02	will, be going to	40
REVIEW TEST		43

CHAPTER 05 동사의 종류

Unit 01	감각동사 + 형용사	46
Unit 02	목적어가 두 개 필요한 동사	49
Unit 03	목적격 보어가 필요한 동사	52
REVIEW TEST		55

CHAPTER 06 명사와 관사

Unit 01	셀 수 있는 명사 vs. 셀 수 없는 명사	58
Unit 02	관사	61
REVIEW TEST		64

CHAPTER 07 대명사

Unit 01	인칭대명사, 재귀대명사	67
Unit 02	this, that, it	70
Unit 03	one, some, any	73
REVIEW TEST		76

CHAPTER 08 형용사와 부사

Unit 01	형용사	79
Unit 02	부사	82
Unit 03	원급, 비교급, 최상급	85
REVIEW TEST		88

CHAPTER 09 to부정사와 동명사

Unit 01	to부정사의 명사적 용법	91
Unit 02	to부정사의 형용사적, 부사적 용법	94
Unit 03	동명사의 역할	97
REVIEW TEST		100

CHAPTER 10 전치사

Unit 01	장소를 나타내는 전치사	103
Unit 02	시간을 나타내는 전치사	106
Unit 03	기타 전치사	109
REVIEW TEST		112

CHAPTER 11 접속사

Unit 01	and, but, or, so	115
Unit 02	when, before, after, until	118
Unit 03	because, if, that	121
REVIEW TEST		124

CHAPTER 12 의문문, 명령문, 감탄문

Unit 01	의문사 who, what, which	127
Unit 02	의문사 when, where, why, how	130
Unit 03	부가의문문	133
Unit 04	부정의문문, 선택의문문	136
Unit 05	명령문, 감탄문	139
REVIEW TEST		142

GRAMMAR BASICS

01 품사

A 다음 중 품사가 <u>다른</u> 하나를 고르시오.

1 we, I, that, with, he, they, it

2 over, about, for, by, to, may, in

3 until, because, after, at, but, and, or

4 feel, go, must, learn, be, think, never

5 very, happily, quietly, friendly, well, always

6 good, useful, hungry, lucky, sad, ask, deep

7 man, bravo, school, love, Katherine, park, apple

B 다음 밑줄 친 부분의 품사를 보기에서 골라 쓰시오.

보기	명사 대명사 동사 형용사 부사 전치사 접속사 감탄사

1 <u>This</u> is my bag. _____

2 Do you have a pencil <u>or</u> a pen? _____

3 The book is <u>under</u> the desk. _____

4 <u>Wow</u>, this is amazing! _____

5 She speaks English <u>well</u>. _____

6 Paris is a <u>beautiful</u> city. _____

7 My dad loves our <u>dog</u>. _____

8 I <u>drink</u> a lot of water. _____

9 She is a <u>famous</u> singer. _____

10 The book <u>is</u> interesting. _____

11 It is a nice <u>dress</u>. _____

12 Soccer is a <u>very</u> exciting sport. _____

2

02 문장의 성분   03 구와 절

A 다음 문장의 밑줄 친 부분의 성분을 보기에서 골라 쓰시오.

보기	주어	동사	목적어	보어	수식어

1 I broke <u>the window</u>. _____

2 <u>July</u> is my favorite month. _____

3 She is <u>a science teacher</u>. _____

4 The movie made me <u>sad</u>. _____

5 He <u>became</u> a great musician. _____

6 Veronica is <u>my best friend</u>. _____

7 <u>Michael's brother</u> is handsome. _____

8 We like John's songs <u>very much</u>. _____

9 I don't remember <u>his phone number</u>. _____

10 The test <u>was</u> very difficult for me. _____

B 다음 밑줄 친 부분이 구인지 또는 절인지 쓰시오.

1 I go to school <u>by bus</u>.

2 Tim told me <u>what to do</u>.

3 I think <u>that the movie is funny</u>.

4 The baby looks <u>like an angel</u>.

5 She likes <u>her new computer</u>.

6 He will visit me <u>in the afternoon</u>.

7 There is nothing <u>to drink in the kitchen</u>.

8 You can go <u>after you finish your homework</u>.

9 I want to be her friend <u>because she is kind to me</u>.

10 I will go to an amusement park <u>when the exams are over</u>.

UNIT 01

be동사의 현재형과 과거형

Ⓐ ( ) 안에서 알맞은 말을 고르시오.

1 I (am, was) in New York now.

2 You (is, are) a fast runner!

3 My dog (is, are) very smart.

4 They (is, are) diligent students.

5 It (is, was) snowy in Incheon now.

6 Jake (was, were) sick last weekend.

7 Mark and Jane (is, are) good friends.

8 We (were, was) worried about you yesterday.

9 My sister and I (am, are) very different.

10 I (am, was) twelve years old last year.

Ⓑ ( ) 안의 말과 be동사를 이용하여 문장을 완성하시오. (긍정문으로 쓸 것)

[1-5] (현재형으로 쓸 것)

1 _____ sleepy now. (I)

2 _____ from Germany. (we)

3 _____ a good singer. (you)

4 _____ poor at math. (they)

5 _____ our new science teacher. (he)

[6-10] (과거형으로 쓸 것)

6 _____ tired last night. (we)

7 _____ in Paris last summer. (I)

8 _____ popular in 2020. (this song)

9 _____ in her room a few minutes ago. (Jenny)

10 _____ my classmates two years ago. (those boys)

C 빈칸에 알맞은 말을 보기에서 골라 쓰시오. (단, 한 번씩만 쓸 것)

보기	am	is	are	was	were

[1-5]

1 I _____ angry with him.

2 He _____ very short last year.

3 You _____ late for school again.

4 There _____ a bakery near here.

5 My brother and I _____ at the mall an hour ago.

[6-10]

6 They _____ my best friends.

7 I _____ at the gym now.

8 This shirt _____ very expensive.

9 We _____ at the library last Sunday.

10 Sujin _____ the class president last year.

D 빈칸에 There is 또는 There are를 넣어 문장을 완성하시오.

1 _____ twenty-four hours in a day.

2 _____ a lamp on the desk.

3 _____ two birds in the cage.

4 _____ a big pond in this park.

5 _____ one pencil in my pencil case.

6 _____ fourteen students on the school bus.

WRITING PRACTICE

🔍 Answer Key p.22

A 우리말과 일치하도록 ( ) 안의 말을 이용하여 문장을 완성하시오.

1 네 옷은 소파 위에 있다. (your clothes)

→ _____ on the sofa.

2 바구니 안에 오렌지가 하나 있다. (there, an orange)

→ _____ in the basket.

3 우리 아버지는 택시 운전사이다. (my father)

→ _____ a taxi driver.

4 그들은 좋은 이웃들이었다. (they)

→ _____ good neighbors.

5 어제는 날씨가 흐렸다. (it, cloudy)

→ _____ yesterday.

6 한 해에는 열두 달이 있다. (there, twelve months)

→ _____ in a year.

7 저기에 커피숍이 하나 있었다. (there, a coffee shop)

→ _____ over there.

B 우리말과 일치하도록 ( ) 안에 주어진 말을 바르게 배열하시오.

1 그는 테니스 선수이다. (he, a tennis player, is)

→ _____.

2 그것은 슬픈 영화였다. (a sad movie, it, was)

→ _____.

3 상자 안에 책 다섯 권이 있었다. (five books, were, there)

→ _____ in the box.

4 나는 2년 전에 키가 150cm였다. (was, 150 cm tall, I)

→ _____ two years ago.

5 우리는 지금 교실 안에 있다. (we, in the classroom, are)

→ _____ now.

6 그들은 오늘 아침에 직장에 늦었다. (were, late for work, they)

→ _____ this morning.

UNIT 02

be동사의 부정문과 의문문

🔍 Answer Key p.22

A ( ) 안에서 알맞은 말을 고르시오.

1 (Is, Are) you full now?

2 It (is, isn't) my coat. It's Debra's coat.

3 (Is, Are) your sister a doctor?

4 I (am not, not am) a cook. I'm a waiter.

5 (Is, Are) these letters for you?

6 These computers (isn't, aren't) on sale.

7 (Was, Were) the story interesting?

8 I (wasn't, weren't) late for the concert.

9 This suitcase (is not, are not) heavy. It is light.

10 My parents (wasn't, weren't) upset about my grade.

B 빈칸에 be동사의 부정형을 써서 문장을 완성하시오. (줄임말로 쓸 것)

1 Jeff _____ rich ten years ago. He was poor.

2 They _____ brothers. They are just friends.

3 This street _____ quiet last night. It was noisy.

4 It _____ cool in this room. It is hot.

5 The puppies _____ asleep. They are awake.

6 Her birthday _____ yesterday. It was last Friday.

7 These cups _____ dirty before lunch. They were clean.

8 Your answer _____ right. It's wrong.

9 We _____ in Paris last month. We were in Rome.

10 Mr. Peterson _____ a science teacher. He is a music teacher.

( ) 안의 말과 be동사를 이용하여 의문문을 완성하시오.

1 A: _____ thirsty? (you)

  B: No, I'm not.

2 A: _____ sunny outside? (it)

  B: No, it isn't.

3 A: _____ in the same group? (we)

  B: Yes, we are.

4 A: _____ the only girl on this team? (I)

  B: Yes, you are.

5 A: _____ yours? (this cell phone)

  B: No, it isn't.

6 A: _____ near the airport? (the hotel)

  B: No, it wasn't.

7 A: _____ alone at home? (you)

  B: Yes, I was.

8 A: _____ in the hospital? (Billy)

  B: Yes, he was.

D

밑줄 친 부분이 올바르면 ○표, 틀리면 바르게 고치시오.

1 This apple aren't fresh. _____

2 Is they famous actors? _____

3 I am not angry. I'm just sad. _____

4 Is Fred in the class yesterday? _____

5 Junho and I am not in the kitchen now. _____

6 Are your brother on the soccer team last year? _____

7 Were you in this book club now? _____

8 You are only ten years old. You are an adult. _____

WRITING PRACTICE

A 우리말과 일치하도록 (   ) 안의 말을 이용하여 문장을 완성하시오.

1 나는 외롭지 않다. (I)

→ _____ lonely.

2 너는 지금 신나니? (you)

→ _____ excited now?

3 그녀는 유명한 화가니? (she)

→ _____ a famous artist?

4 너희 부모님은 어제 집에 계셨니? (your parents)

→ _____ at home yesterday?

5 그는 농구 선수가 아니었다. (he)

→ _____ a basketball player.

6 박물관은 버스 정류장에서 멀지 않다. (the museum)

→ _____ far from the bus stop.

B 우리말과 일치하도록 (   ) 안에 주어진 말을 바르게 배열하시오.

1 그는 친절하지 않았다. (was, kind, not, he)

→ _____.

2 우리는 게으르지 않다. (are, we, lazy, not)

→ _____.

3 이 만화책들은 재미있지 않았다. (interesting, these comic books, not, were)

→ _____.

4 Susan은 공항에 있지 않다. (Susan, at the airport, isn't)

→ _____.

5 저분이 Woods 씨니? (Mr. Woods, that man, is)

→ _____?

6 그 식당은 어제 열려 있었니? (was, open, the restaurant)

→ _____ yesterday?

7 그들이 우리의 새로운 이웃들이니? (our new neighbors, they, are)

→ _____?

REVIEW TEST

1

I _____ at the bookstore now.

① am   ② are   ③ is
④ was   ⑤ were

2

Mr. and Mrs. Smith _____ on vacation now.

① am   ② are   ③ is
④ was   ⑤ were

3

Paul and Jack _____ my classmates last year.

① am   ② are   ③ is
④ was   ⑤ were

4

She _____ at home a few hours ago.

① am not   ② aren't   ③ isn't
④ wasn't   ⑤ weren't

[5-6] 빈칸에 들어갈 말이 바르게 짝지어진 것을 고르시오.

5

Mike _____(A)_____ sick last week. He _____(B)_____ fine now.

    (A)   (B)
① is   ……   is
② is   ……   was
③ was   ……   is
④ was   ……   was
⑤ were   ……   is

6

There _____(A)_____ thirty books on the bookshelf. They _____(B)_____ my brother's.

    (A)   (B)
① is   ……   is
② is   ……   are
③ are   ……   am
④ are   ……   is
⑤ are   ……   are

서술형

[7-8] 빈칸에 There is 또는 There are를 넣어 문장을 완성하시오.

7

_____ three middle schools in this town.

8

_____ a rock near the tree.

서술형

[9-10] 빈칸에 알맞은 be동사를 써서 대화를 완성하시오.

9
A: _____ you and Brandon at the station yesterday?
B: Yes, we _____.

10
A: _____ it rainy outside now?
B: No, it _____. It's just cloudy.

11 다음 중 밑줄 친 부분이 잘못된 것은?

① It <u>is</u> sunny today.
② Jason <u>is</u> funny.
③ They <u>are</u> busy last month.
④ The scissors <u>were</u> in the drawer.
⑤ Mary's birthday <u>was</u> last Friday.

12 다음 문장에서 not이 들어갈 위치로 적절한 것은?

Math ⓐ and ⓑ science ⓒ are ⓓ my ⓔ favorite subjects.

① ⓐ   ② ⓑ   ③ ⓒ   ④ ⓓ   ⑤ ⓔ

빈출

13 다음 중 대화가 자연스럽지 <u>않은</u> 것은?

① A: Is this card $5?
   B: Yes, it is.
② A: Is Chris a kind boy?
   B: Yes, he is.
③ A: Are you a writer?
   B: Yes, I'm.
④ A: Is your sister eleven years old?
   B: Yes, she is.
⑤ A: Are Amy and Sam from England?
   B: No, they aren't.

빈출

14 빈칸에 들어갈 말이 나머지 넷과 <u>다른</u> 것은?

① This _____ a gift for you.
② The song _____ very popular.
③ My wallet _____ in my pocket.
④ The vase _____ on the table.
⑤ LA and Miami _____ cities in the US.

15 다음 우리말을 영어로 바르게 옮긴 것은?

이 책들은 Jessy를 위한 선물들이니?

① Is these books presents for Jessy?
② Am these books presents for Jessy?
③ Are these books presents for Jessy?
④ Was these books presents for Jessy?
⑤ Were these books presents for Jessy?

[16-19] 다음 문장을 ( ) 안의 지시대로 바꿔 쓰시오.

16 John was a shy student. (부정문으로)

→ _____ .

17 The kids are at school. (부정문으로)

→ _____ .

18 Julia was with her family. (의문문으로)

→ _____ ?

19 Karen and Mark were doctors.
(의문문으로)

→ _____ ?

[20-23] 우리말과 일치하도록 ( ) 안의 말을 이용하여 문장을 완성하시오.

20 책상 위에 사진이 몇 장 있었다.
(there, some photos)

→ _____ on the desk.

21 저 펜들은 네 것이니? (those pens)

→ _____ yours?

22 오늘은 월요일이다. 어제는 일요일이었다.
(Monday, Sunday)

→ It _____ today. It
_____ yesterday.

23 이 도넛은 건강에 좋진 않지만 맛있다.
(healthy, tasty)

→ This donut _____ , but it
_____ .

[24-25] 어법상 틀린 부분을 찾아 바르게 고치시오.

24 A: Are Mr. Bonds American?
B: No, he aren't. He's British. (2개)

25 It is my birthday yesterday. There
was a party at my house. The party
weren't big, but it was very fun! (2개)

UNIT 01

일반동사의 현재형

🔍 Answer Key p·23

A ( ) 안에서 알맞은 말을 고르시오.

1 They (live, lives) in this apartment.

2 This restaurant (open, opens) at 11:00 a.m.

3 I (take, takes) vitamin C for my health.

4 This toy (have, has) batteries in it.

5 This plant (grow, grows) very fast.

6 Asher (trys, tries) his best every day.

7 She (watch, watches) comedy shows on weekends.

8 Chris (learn, learns) Japanese every Saturday.

9 You (make, makes) the best pizza in town!

10 My brother and I (do, does) our homework in the evening.

B ( ) 안에 주어진 동사의 현재형을 써서 문장을 완성하시오.

1 Monica _____ to the pool every Thursday. (go)

2 Lucy always _____ at people. (smile)

3 The bus _____ every ten minutes. (come)

4 Dad _____ computers well. (fix)

5 He _____ law at university. (study)

6 My mom _____ her hair every morning. (brush)

7 The team members _____ twice a week. (meet)

8 Tom usually _____ his school tests. (pass)

9 That airplane _____ very fast. (fly)

10 The man _____ hot dogs on the street. (sell)

빈칸에 알맞은 동사를 보기에서 골라 현재형으로 써서 문장을 완성하시오. (단, 한 번씩만 쓸 것)

[1-5]

보기	cry	have	wash	send	speak

1 Elephants _____ long noses.

2 She _____ text messages all the time.

3 I _____ three languages.

4 My father _____ his car on Sundays.

5 The baby _____ loudly every night.

[6-10]

보기	drink	love	run	snow	teach

6 They always _____ tea in the afternoon.

7 It _____ a lot in winter here.

8 Many foreigners _____ bulgogi.

9 Mr. Jones _____ history in my school.

10 Jack _____ 4 km every morning.

밑줄 친 부분이 올바르면 ○표, 틀리면 바르게 고치시오.

1 Spring <u>comes</u> every year. _____

2 He <u>walk</u> to his office every day. _____

3 My dog <u>catch</u> balls very well. _____

4 I <u>like</u> strawberry cake. _____

5 Roy <u>clean</u> his house once a week. _____

6 Our school <u>start</u> at nine o'clock. _____

7 John always <u>tell</u> jokes. _____

8 We <u>buy</u> our cat food in this shop. _____

WRITING PRACTICE

Answer Key p.23

A 우리말과 일치하도록 ( ) 안의 말을 이용하여 문장을 완성하시오.

1 몇몇 야생 동물들은 숲속에 산다. (some wild animals, live)

→ _____ in the woods.

2 나의 개는 어디든 나를 따라다닌다. (my dog, follow)

→ _____ me everywhere.

3 그는 항상 가방을 가지고 다닌다. (he, carry)

→ _____ his bag all the time.

4 체리는 안에 큰 씨가 있다. (cherries, have)

→ _____ big seeds in them.

5 Rachel은 패스트푸드를 너무 자주 먹는다. (eat)

→ _____ fast food too often.

6 Susan은 다른 사람들을 잘 이해한다. (understand)

→ _____ other people well.

7 요즘 많은 사람들이 이 앱을 사용한다. (a lot of people, use)

→ _____ this app these days.

B 우리말과 일치하도록 ( ) 안에 주어진 말을 바르게 배열하시오. (동사는 현재형으로 쓸 것)

1 나는 그녀의 삼촌을 안다. (know, her uncle)

→ I _____.

2 달은 지구 주위를 돈다. (the earth, goes around)

→ The moon _____.

3 우리 엄마는 식당에서 일하신다. (in a restaurant, works)

→ My mother _____.

4 민지와 유미는 자매처럼 보인다. (sisters, look like)

→ Minji and Yumi _____.

5 Owen은 저녁 식사 후에 항상 TV를 본다. (after dinner, TV, watches)

→ Owen always _____.

6 이 기차는 5시 정각에 역을 출발한다. (the station, at five o'clock, leaves)

→ This train _____.

CHAPTER 02 일반동사

일반동사의 과거형

( ) 안에서 알맞은 말을 고르시오.

1 We (stay, stayed) in London in 2020.

2 He (meet, met) the president last month.

3 James and I (talks, talked) about sports.

4 My grandparents (live, lived) with my aunt now.

5 She (buys, bought) green shoes last week.

6 They (study, studied) in the library two days ago.

7 Jeff (invites, invited) me to his birthday party last week.

8 Miho (leaves, left) a message for you a minute ago.

9 I (share, shared) my sandwich with Jiho yesterday.

10 Cathy isn't busy at work. She (comes, came) back home early these days.

( ) 안에 주어진 동사의 과거형을 써서 문장을 완성하시오.

1 The skier _____ very high. (jump)

2 Sam _____ many questions. (ask)

3 He _____ his bag on the floor. (put)

4 Jimmy _____ about his future. (worry)

5 I _____ my cell phone by mistake. (drop)

6 We _____ a good time at the beach. (have)

7 A waiter _____ our food. (bring)

8 Andy _____ a marathon last year. (run)

9 I _____ him on the street this morning. (see)

10 Ron and Annie _____ a walk in the park. (take)

C 빈칸에 알맞은 동사를 보기에서 골라 과거형으로 써서 문장을 완성하시오. (단, 한 번씩만 쓸 것)

보기	move	forget	read	stop	sit

1 The rain _____ in the afternoon.

2 They _____ on the bench.

3 Erica _____ a science fiction novel.

4 I _____ your birthday. I'm sorry.

5 His family _____ to Berlin last year.

D ( ) 안의 말을 이용하여 보기와 같이 과거형 문장을 완성하시오.

> **보기**
> I usually drink milk for breakfast.
> This morning, I <u>drank a smoothie</u> for breakfast. (a smoothie)

1 Mary usually goes to bed at 10:00 p.m.

Last night, she _____. (after midnight)

2 We usually buy some apples at the market.

Yesterday, we _____ there. (some grapes)

3 My father usually sleeps for seven hours a night.

Last night, he _____. (for four hours)

4 David and I usually meet at the bus stop.

This morning, we _____. (in front of the school)

5 The students usually play soccer after school.

Yesterday, they _____ after school. (baseball)

6 The mailman usually comes in the morning.

Yesterday, he _____. (in the afternoon)

7 Mom usually gives us cheesecake for dessert.

Last Sunday, she _____ for dessert. (chocolate cake)

WRITING PRACTICE

A 우리말과 일치하도록 ( ) 안의 말을 이용하여 문장을 완성하시오.

1 Steve는 우리에게 무서운 이야기를 해주었다. (tell)

→ _____ us a scary story.

2 그는 그의 만화에 나를 그렸다. (he, draw)

→ _____ me in his cartoon.

3 어제는 하루종일 비가 왔다. (it, rain)

→ _____ all day yesterday.

4 그들은 어젯밤 내 개를 공원에서 찾았다. (they, find)

→ _____ my dog in the park last night.

5 버스 시간표가 지난주에 바뀌었다. (the bus schedule, change)

→ _____ last week.

6 Kevin이 내게 이 인형을 주었다. (give)

→ _____ this doll to me.

7 우리는 최선을 다했고 시험에 통과했다. (we, try)

→ _____ our best and passed the exam.

B 우리말과 일치하도록 ( ) 안에 주어진 말을 바르게 배열하시오. (동사는 과거형으로 쓸 것)

1 나는 어제 감기에 걸렸다. (yesterday, a cold, have)

→ I _____.

2 그는 오전 6시에 내게 전화했다. (call, at 6:00 a.m., me)

→ He _____.

3 Larry는 지난 주말에 토론토를 떠났다. (leave, last weekend, Toronto)

→ Larry _____.

4 Roy와 나는 파티에서 노래를 불렀다. (at the party, a song, sing)

→ Roy and I _____.

5 나는 10분 전에 세수를 했다. (wash, I, my face)

→ _____ ten minutes ago.

6 Joe는 며칠 전에 내 휴대 전화를 고장 냈다. (Joe, my cell phone, break)

→ _____ a few days ago.

UNIT 03

일반동사의 부정문

🔍 Answer Key p-23

A

( ) 안에서 알맞은 말을 고르시오.

1 They (don't, doesn't) live in LA.

2 Ryan (don't, doesn't) trust anyone.

3 I (don't, didn't) take a shower last night.

4 They (don't, doesn't) accept credit cards.

5 Vicky (doesn't, didn't) send me a card last year.

6 My roommate (don't, doesn't) clean his desk.

7 We (don't, didn't) win the game yesterday.

8 The store (don't, doesn't) close on holidays.

9 She (don't, doesn't) know about the surprise party.

10 Billy (doesn't, didn't) check the weather this morning.

B

( ) 안에 주어진 동사의 부정형을 써서 문장을 완성하시오. (줄임말로 쓸 것)

1 I like apple juice now.

  I _____ it before. (like)

2 She only eats vegetables.

  She _____ meat. (eat)

3 Our team lost many games last year.

  We _____ well at that time. (play)

4 Ted and his sister ride bikes to school.

  They _____ to school. (walk)

5 The circus was terrible.

  We _____ it. (enjoy)

6 Jenny has a bad memory.

  She _____ names. (remember)

C 빈칸에 알맞은 동사를 보기에서 골라 부정형으로 써서 문장을 완성하시오. (단, 한 번씩만 쓸 것)

[1-5] (현재형으로 쓸 것)

보기	bite	need	talk	use	work

1 We _____ any help.

2 These dogs _____ people.

3 My parents _____ paper cups.

4 Harry is a quiet boy. He _____ much.

5 This printer is very old. It _____ well.

[6-10] (과거형으로 쓸 것)

보기	cry	watch	meet	stop	wash

6 I _____ the quiz show.

7 She _____ at the sad news.

8 The car _____ at the red light.

9 You _____ your hands! They are dirty.

10 I _____ Tiffany last night.

D 밑줄 친 부분이 올바르면 ○표, 틀리면 바르게 고치시오.

1 He <u>don't like</u> hip-hop music.   _____

2 I <u>don't enjoy</u> computer games.   _____

3 She <u>didn't understood</u> the question.   _____

4 The festival <u>didn't start</u> last Monday.   _____

5 My sister <u>didn't eats</u> dinner last night.   _____

6 They <u>didn't left</u> home early this morning.   _____

7 We <u>don't go</u> to school on Children's Day.   _____

8 Mike <u>doesn't call</u> his girlfriend yesterday.   _____

WRITING PRACTICE

Q Answer Key p.24

A 우리말과 일치하도록 ( ) 안의 말을 이용하여 문장을 완성하시오.

1 우리 아버지는 생선을 좋아하지 않으신다. (like)

→ My father _____ fish.

2 나는 아침에 일찍 일어나지 않는다. (get up early)

→ I _____ in the morning.

3 Robert는 많은 돈을 모으지 않았다. (save much money)

→ Robert _____.

4 이 바지는 내게 잘 맞지 않는다. (fit me)

→ These pants _____ well.

5 회의는 정오에 시작하지 않았다. (begin)

→ The meeting _____ at noon.

6 Hailey는 그녀의 여동생과 싸우지 않는다. (fight with her sister)

→ Hailey _____.

B 우리말과 일치하도록 ( ) 안에 주어진 말을 바르게 배열하시오.

1 나는 별명이 없다. (have, don't, a nickname)

→ I _____.

2 그는 내 질문에 대답하지 않았다. (didn't, my question, answer)

→ He _____.

3 우리는 극장에 가지 않았다. (go to, did, the theater, not)

→ We _____.

4 너는 오늘 행복해 보이지 않는구나. (don't, you, look happy)

→ _____ today.

5 나는 오늘 교과서를 가지고 오지 않았다. (my textbook, didn't, I, bring)

→ _____ today.

6 Becky는 액션 영화를 보지 않는다. (does, action movies, not, watch)

→ Becky _____.

7 내 남자 친구는 오른손으로 글씨를 쓰지 않는다. (doesn't, with his right hand, write)

→ My boyfriend _____.

UNIT 04

일반동사의 의문문

A ( ) 안에서 알맞은 말을 고르시오.

1 (Do, Does) you miss her?

2 (Do, Does) she travel abroad a lot?

3 (Do, Does) they like Japanese food?

4 (Do, Did) we come to this park last year?

5 (Do, Does) your brother drive?

6 (Do, Did) they build this stadium last year?

7 (Do, Does) you brush your teeth after meals?

8 (Do, Did) Ms. Adams draw this painting?

9 (Do, Does) Angela use chopsticks?

10 (Does, Did) you see Alice this morning?

B ( ) 안의 말을 이용하여 의문문을 완성하시오.

1 A: _____ you _____ Larry? (remember)
B: Yes, I do. He was my classmate.

2 A: _____ he _____ the drums? (play)
B: Yes, he does. He's a drummer.

3 A: _____ your parents _____ you? (forgive)
B: No, they didn't. They were very angry.

4 A: _____ Sarah _____ in New York? (live)
B: No, she doesn't. She lives in Chicago.

5 A: _____ you _____ to Molly? (lie)
B: No, I didn't. I told the truth!

6 A: _____ they _____ breakfast every morning? (eat)
B: No, they don't. They are too busy in the mornings.

7 A: _____ Helen _____ a good time at the party? (have)
B: Yes, she did. She enjoyed it very much.

C 보기에서 알맞은 동사를 골라 ( ) 안의 말과 함께 써서 의문문을 완성하시오. (단, 한 번씩만 쓸 것)

보기	catch	play	have	go	watch

1 A: _____ to university? (your sister)

B: Yes, she does. Her major is history.

2 A: _____ the train? (the man)

B: No, he didn't. He was too late.

3 A: _____ a good dream last night? (you)

B: Yes, I did. I became a movie star in my dream.

4 A: _____ tennis? (Amy and Dennis)

B: No, they don't. They don't like any sports.

5 A: _____ TV late at night? (your father)

B: No, he doesn't. He goes to bed early.

D 밑줄 친 부분이 올바르면 ○표, <u>틀리면</u> 바르게 고치시오.

1 <u>Are you want</u> a sandwich? _____

2 <u>Do</u> she like ice cream? _____

3 <u>Does</u> lions live in jungles? _____

4 <u>Did they forget</u> Mary's birthday? _____

5 <u>Does he come</u> to school yesterday? _____

6 Did Bobby <u>wrote</u> a letter to you? _____

7 <u>Do you get up</u> early this morning? _____

8 <u>Did you take</u> your medicine this morning? _____

9 <u>Did Sam dances</u> with Tina last night? _____

10 <u>Do you hear</u> that noise a few minutes ago? _____

WRITING PRACTICE

Q Answer Key p-24

A 우리말과 일치하도록 ( ) 안의 말을 이용하여 문장을 완성하시오.

1 그가 그 소식을 들었니? (he, hear)

→ _____ the news?

2 우리는 여권이 필요하니? (we, need)

→ _____ our passports?

3 Anna가 그의 이야기를 믿니? (believe)

→ _____ his story?

4 너희들은 인기 있는 게임 앱을 아니? (you, know)

→ _____ any popular game apps?

5 그들은 어제 Dave를 만났니? (they, meet)

→ _____ Dave yesterday?

6 너는 그의 새 소설을 읽었니? (you, read)

→ _____ his new novel?

B 우리말과 일치하도록 ( ) 안에 주어진 말을 바르게 배열하시오.

1 너는 빨간색 셔츠를 원하니? (you, do, a red shirt, want)

→ _____ ?

2 그 아이들이 이 창문을 깨뜨렸니? (this window, did, break, the kids)

→ _____ ?

3 Kate는 노트북을 가지고 있니? (Kate, does, a laptop, have)

→ _____ ?

4 Lena는 드레스를 골랐니? (Lena, her dress, pick, did)

→ _____ ?

5 우리는 시청에 버스로 가니? (we, city hall, do, go to)

→ _____ by bus?

6 네 남동생은 우비를 가지고 왔니? (his raincoat, did, bring, your brother)

→ _____ ?

7 네 삼촌은 이 학교에서 일하시니? (your uncle, work, does)

→ _____ in this school?

REVIEW TEST

Answer Key p.24

1 다음 중 동사의 3인칭 단수 현재형이 <u>잘못</u> 연결된 것은?

① do – does ② come – comes
③ fly – flies ④ teach – teachs
⑤ wash – washes

2 다음 중 동사의 과거형이 <u>잘못</u> 연결된 것은?

① hit – hat ② tell – told
③ talk – talked ④ drink – drank
⑤ stop – stopped

[3–5] 빈칸에 들어갈 알맞은 말을 고르시오.

3
> My little sister _____ a teddy bear. She always carries it with her.

① is ② was
③ have ④ has
⑤ had

4
> My parents _____ Chinese food. They don't eat it.

① like ② likes
③ don't like ④ doesn't like
⑤ didn't like

5
> Sarah _____ him at the station yesterday.

① see ② sees
③ saw ④ do see
⑤ did saw

서술형

[6–8] 빈칸에 알맞은 말을 써서 대화를 완성하시오.

6
A: Do you and your brother fight a lot?
B: No, _____ _____. We get along well.

7
A: Did King Sejong invent Hangeul?
B: Yes, _____ _____. He invented it in 1443.

8
A: Does Diana have dogs?
B: No, _____ _____. She has two cats.

[9-10] 다음 밑줄 친 부분을 바르게 고치시오.

9
Jack is a chef. He ⓐ <u>work</u> in a restaurant. Every day, he ⓑ <u>go</u> to work by subway.

ⓐ _____ ⓑ _____

10
Last week, I ⓐ <u>watch</u> a horror movie on TV. That night, I ⓑ <u>have</u> a scary dream.

ⓐ _____ ⓑ _____

[11-12] 빈칸에 들어갈 말이 바르게 짝지어진 것을 고르시오.

11
Andrew always ____(A)____ his car on Sundays. After that, he ____(B)____ to the gym.

	(A)		(B)
①	wash	......	go
②	wash	......	goes
③	washes	......	go
④	washes	......	goes
⑤	washed	......	goes

12
Yesterday, my sister and I ____(A)____ a walk in the park. We ____(B)____ our dog with us.

	(A)		(B)
①	take	......	don't bring
②	take	......	doesn't bring
③	takes	......	didn't bring
④	took	......	doesn't bring
⑤	took	......	didn't bring

13 다음 중 대화가 자연스럽지 <u>않은</u> 것은?

① A: Do you miss Robert?
  B: Yes, I do.
② A: Does your father cook?
  B: Yes, he does.
③ A: Did you clean your room?
  B: No, you didn't.
④ A: Does Charlie study in Paris?
  B: No, he doesn't.
⑤ A: Did Eric and Andy practice the guitar last night?
  B: Yes, they did.

[14-15] 다음 중 밑줄 친 부분이 잘못된 것을 고르시오.

14 ① I always <u>go to bed</u> before 10:00 p.m.
② Kate <u>stays</u> at my house yesterday.
③ Minsu <u>drinks</u> a lot of milk every day.
④ Mom <u>baked</u> some cookies yesterday.
⑤ He <u>sends</u> me a birthday card every year.

15 ① Mike <u>don't like</u> steak.
② Mr. Kim <u>doesn't teach</u> history.
③ I <u>didn't pass</u> the final exam last week.
④ We <u>didn't enjoy</u> the festival yesterday.
⑤ Susan <u>doesn't talk</u> much about her boyfriend.

[16-17] ( ) 안의 말을 이용하여 문장을 완성하시오.

16
I _____ taekwondo two years ago. It was very exciting. (learn)

26

17
My sister _____ clothes.
She always wears mine! (not/buy)

18 다음 우리말을 영어로 바르게 옮긴 것은?

> 그들은 내게 새로운 노래를 가르쳐 주지 않았다.

① They don't teach me a new song.
② They don't taught me a new song.
③ They doesn't teach me a new song.
④ They didn't teach me a new song.
⑤ They didn't taught me a new song.

서술형
[19-21] 우리말과 일치하도록 (   ) 안의 말을 이용하여 문장을 완성하시오.

19 어젯밤에 비가 왔니? (it, rain)

→ _____ last night?

20 나는 어제 자전거를 탔다. (ride a bike)

→ I _____ yesterday.

21 도서관은 일요일에 열지 않는다. (open)

→ The library _____
on Sundays.

서술형
[22-23] 우리말과 일치하도록 (   ) 안에 주어진 말을 바르게 배열하시오.

22 Billy는 체육관에서 운동하니?
(Billy, at the gym, exercise, does)

→ _____?

23 네가 어젯밤 내게 전화했니?
(you, me, call, did)

→ _____
last night?

서술형
[24-25] 밑줄 친 부분이 어법상 옳은지 판단하고, 틀리면 바르게 고치시오.

24 I didn't <u>gave</u> you that chocolate.

(O / X) _____

25 William and his brother <u>walk</u> home
from school every day.

(O / X) _____

can, may

A

( ) 안에서 알맞은 말을 고르시오.

1   He can (sleep, sleeps) late on weekends.

2   Your key may (be, is) on the table.

3   (May, Can) you understand Spanish?

4   Jeff could (answer, answered) the question.

5   Penguins are birds, but they (can't, may not) fly.

6   Take your coat. It (may, may not) be cold at night.

7   We (able to, are able to) help you, so don't worry.

8   She (not may, may not) go on the picnic today. She looks tired.

9   Maria (can't, couldn't) come home early. She was too busy.

10   It is very cloudy. It (may, may not) rain in the afternoon.

B

알맞은 조동사와 ( ) 안의 말을 이용하여 문장을 완성하시오.

[1-5] (can 또는 can't를 쓸 것)

1   Larry's father is a chef. He _____ very well. (cook)

2   We _____ this sofa. It's too expensive. (buy)

3   I'm strong. I _____ 30 kg. (lift)

4   My sister broke her arm. She _____ it. (use)

5   Mika studies art. She _____ pictures very well. (draw)

[6-10] (may 또는 may not을 쓸 것)

6   _____ I _____ your student ID? (see)

7   Jimmy is busy. He _____ us for lunch today. (join)

8   The class is over. You _____ the classroom now. (leave)

9   The kids left some food. They _____ full. (be)

10   She doesn't enjoy sweets. She _____ this chocolate. (like)

C 보기와 같이 be able to 또는 be not able to를 이용하여 문장을 바꿔 쓰시오.

보기	She can type English very fast. → She <u>is able to type</u> English very fast.

1 I can jump rope very well.

→ I _____ rope very well.

2 We can't finish the project by tomorrow.

→ We _____ the project by tomorrow.

3 Tim and Amy cannot play the piano.

→ Tim and Amy _____ the piano.

4 He can get tickets for the baseball game.

→ He _____ tickets for the baseball game.

5 You passed the driving test. You can drive now.

→ You passed the driving test. You _____ now.

6 She can't arrive on time. She took the wrong bus.

→ She _____ on time. She took the wrong bus.

D 밑줄 친 부분이 올바르면 ○표, 틀리면 바르게 고치시오.

1 You <u>may</u> eat my dessert. _____

2 Anna <u>can't</u> sleep well last night. _____

3 I'm <u>not able</u> answer the phone now. _____

4 <u>May</u> I ask your email address? _____

5 Julie ran for two hours. She <u>may is</u> thirsty. _____

6 This math problem is easy. She <u>can solves</u> it. _____

7 He <u>may not is</u> at home. The lights are off. _____

8 My TV doesn't work. I <u>can</u> watch the soccer game. _____

WRITING PRACTICE

Answer Key p.24

A 우리말과 일치하도록 ( ) 안의 말을 이용하여 문장을 완성하시오.

1 제가 그에게 메시지를 남겨도 될까요? (I, leave)

→ _____ a message for him?

2 나는 물구나무를 설 수 있다. (stand on my hands)

→ I _____.

3 내 여동생은 자전거를 타지 못한다. (ride a bike)

→ My sister _____.

4 숙제를 끝냈구나. 너는 이제 자러 가도 좋다. (go to bed)

→ You finished your homework. You _____ now.

5 그들은 뉴욕으로 이사 갈지도 모른다. (move to New York)

→ They _____.

6 오늘은 따뜻하다. 눈이 오지 않을지도 모른다. (snow)

→ It's warm today. It _____.

7 우리는 호텔 안에서 인터넷을 사용할 수 없었다. (use the internet)

→ We _____ in the hotel.

B 우리말과 일치하도록 ( ) 안에 주어진 말을 바르게 배열하시오.

1 우리는 여기서 호수를 볼 수 있다. (see, we, the lake, can)

→ _____ from here.

2 그의 사무실은 오늘 열려 있지 않을지도 모른다. (be, may, his office, open, not)

→ _____ today.

3 제가 이 잡지를 읽어도 되나요? (read, this magazine, I, may)

→ _____?

4 Anderson 씨와 통화할 수 있을까요? (I, speak to, can, Mr. Anderson)

→ _____, please?

5 Neil은 지금 도서관에 있을지도 모른다. (Neil, be, in the library, may)

→ _____ now.

6 네 고양이는 나무에 올라갈 수 있니? (climb, your cat, can, trees)

→ _____?

UNIT 02

must, have to, should

🔍 Answer Key p.25

A ( ) 안에서 알맞은 말을 고르시오.

1 Alice (have, has) to go now.

2 They must (is, be) on time for work.

3 Lisa and Tom (have to, has to) take this flight.

4 We should (meet, met) him at the subway station.

5 He (don't have to, doesn't have to) pay for dinner.

6 I hurt my leg. I (should, shouldn't) see a doctor.

7 You look tired. You (have to, don't have to) go to bed early.

8 You (must not, not must) use your cell phone in the classroom.

9 It snowed a lot last night. The road (must, can't) be slippery.

10 Students (must not, don't have to) cheat during the exam.

B must 또는 have to와 ( ) 안의 말을 이용하여 문장을 완성하시오. (둘 다 가능한 경우에는 have to를 쓸 것)

1 I _____ dinner for my friends. They're hungry. (make)

2 He is honest. His story _____ true. (be)

3 We only have five minutes. We _____. (hurry up)

4 You have an exam tomorrow. You _____ hard. (study)

5 They are flight attendants. They _____ uniforms. (wear)

6 Karl lived in Paris for seven years. He _____ the city well. (know)

7 We _____ early tomorrow. Our plane leaves at 7:00 a.m. (get up)

8 Sarah knows a lot about movies. She _____ to the movies often. (go)

C must not 또는 don't have to와 ( ) 안의 말을 이용하여 문장을 완성하시오. (필요하면 형태를 바꿀 것)

1 You _____ about Steve. He's fine. (worry)

2 You _____ with fire. It's dangerous. (play)

3 We _____ our friends. It's bad. (hit)

4 I can do it alone. You _____ me. (help)

5 Children _____ around the pool. (run)

6 They _____ at the hotel. They can stay in my house. (stay)

7 You _____ the dog. She is a guide dog. (touch)

8 I already got the tickets. We _____ in line. (stand)

9 This is not a parking lot. He _____ his car here. (park)

10 Nick _____ next week. It's his summer vacation. (work)

D 밑줄 친 부분이 올바르면 ○표, <u>틀리면</u> 바르게 고치시오.

1 You <u>not must</u> take photos in this museum. _____

2 Bill <u>should wear</u> a tie for his interview. _____

3 He <u>have to</u> finish his homework by 6:00 p.m. _____

4 We <u>have not to</u> take a taxi. We have enough time. _____

5 She <u>must has</u> a cat. She always buys cat food here. _____

6 Children <u>shouldn't drink</u> too much cola. _____

7 Mike <u>don't have to</u> buy expensive gifts. _____

8 I <u>must fix</u> my cell phone today. _____

WRITING PRACTICE

Q Answer Key p·25

A 우리말과 일치하도록 ( ) 안의 말을 이용하여 문장을 완성하시오.

1 그는 오늘 밤 늦게까지 일해야 한다. (have to, work)

→ He _____ late tonight.

2 우리는 여기서 Jake를 기다려야 한다. (should, wait for)

→ We _____ Jake here.

3 너는 그 편지를 영어로 쓸 필요가 없다. (write the letter)

→ You _____ in English.

4 아이들은 일찍 잠자리에 들어야 한다. (have to, go to bed)

→ Kids _____ early.

5 미나는 그에 대해 이야기를 많이 한다. 그녀는 그를 좋아하는 게 틀림없다. (like him)

→ Mina talks a lot about him. She _____.

6 너는 이 방에 있는 어떤 것도 만져서는 안 된다. (must, touch anything)

→ You _____ in this room.

7 초인종이 울렸다. 피자 배달원인 것이 틀림없다. (be)

→ The doorbell rang. It _____ the pizza delivery man.

B 우리말과 일치하도록 ( ) 안에 주어진 말을 바르게 배열하시오.

1 우리는 지금 떠나야 한다. (leave, should, we, now)

→ _____.

2 그는 내 충고를 들어야 한다. (my advice, has, listen to, to)

→ He _____.

3 그 환자는 더 이상 약을 먹을 필요가 없다. (to, medicine, have, take, doesn't)

→ The patient _____ anymore.

4 Naomi는 꽃을 기르는 게 틀림없다. (grow, Naomi, must, flowers)

→ _____.

5 James는 아이스크림을 너무 자주 먹어서는 안 된다. (should, ice cream, not, eat, James)

→ _____ too often.

6 너는 이 건물에 들어오면 안 된다. (not, enter, this building, must)

→ You _____.

REVIEW TEST

[1-3] 빈칸에 들어갈 알맞은 말을 고르시오.

1

> A: Can you lend me some money, please?
> B: Ask Sam. He _____ have some money.

① can't   ② may   ③ must not
④ have to   ⑤ shouldn't

2

> A: Can I borrow this book?
> B: Sure, but you _____ return it by next Monday.

① can   ② may   ③ should
④ has to   ⑤ don't have to

3

> Richard got an A on the test. He _____ take the test again.

① can   ② may   ③ should
④ has to   ⑤ doesn't have to

[4-5] 다음 중 밑줄 친 부분이 잘못된 것을 고르시오.

4   ① I can solve this puzzle.
② We should eat slowly.
③ They have to paint the wall.
④ He may comes tomorrow.
⑤ You must write your address here.

5   ① I shouldn't believe him.
② Fred can't speak Chinese.
③ We doesn't have to pay the tax.
④ You must not swim in this river.
⑤ Ms. Green may not check her email.

서술형

[6-8] 빈칸에 알맞은 말을 보기에서 골라 대화를 완성하시오.
(단, 한 번씩만 쓸 것)

보기	can	have to	may not

6

> A: _____ I sit here?
> B: I'm sorry, but you can't. It's Mike's seat.

7

> A: Does Brian feel better now?
> B: I don't think so. He _____ be able to come today.

8

> A: Let's eat at this restaurant tonight.
> B: That's a good idea. But we _____ book a table first.

34

9 빈칸에 들어갈 말이 바르게 짝지어진 것은?

> • She forgot the password, so she ____(A)____ log in.
> • This is a non-smoking area. You ____(B)____ smoke here.

	(A)		(B)
①	could	……	must
②	could	……	should not
③	couldn't	……	should
④	couldn't	……	must not
⑤	couldn't	……	don't have to

빈출

[10-11] 밑줄 친 부분의 의미가 나머지 넷과 <u>다른</u> 것을 고르시오.

10 ① <u>Can</u> Susan skate?
② We <u>can</u> win first prize.
③ You <u>can</u> use my computer.
④ <u>Can</u> you play the guitar?
⑤ Daniel <u>can</u> speak French well.

11 ① You <u>must</u> come home by 10:00 p.m.
② We <u>must</u> save energy.
③ Students <u>must</u> study hard.
④ Henry <u>must</u> be angry at me.
⑤ I <u>must</u> recycle paper.

빈출

12 다음 중 대화가 자연스럽지 <u>않은</u> 것은?

① A: May I come in?
B: Of course.
② A: Do I have to call again?
B: No, you should.
③ A: Is it rainy outside?
B: No, but it may rain in the afternoon.
④ A: Should we finish this work today?
B: Yes, we should.
⑤ A: Can you make pancakes?
B: Yes, I can make them for you.

[13-14] 다음 우리말을 영어로 바르게 옮긴 것을 고르시오.

13
> Mandy는 새 차를 살 수 없다.

① Mandy can't buy a new car.
② Mandy may not buy a new car.
③ Mandy must not buy a new car.
④ Mandy should not buy a new car.
⑤ Mandy doesn't have to buy a new car.

14
> 너는 밖에 나가 놀아도 좋다.

① You must go out and play.
② You may go out and play.
③ You should go out and play.
④ You have to go out and play.
⑤ You are able to go out and play.

서술형

[15-16] 다음 문장을 ( ) 안의 지시대로 바꿔 쓰시오.

15 He can kick the ball very well.
(be able to를 이용하여)

→ He _____ the ball very well.

16 Rick must explain the problem to us.
(have to를 이용하여)

→ Rick _____ the problem to us.

서술형

[17-18] 우리말과 일치하도록 ( ) 안의 말을 이용하여 문장을 완성하시오.

17 그녀는 뮤지컬을 좋아하지 않을지도 모른다. (like)

→ She _____ musicals.

18 그가 도둑일 리가 없다. (be)

→ He _____ the thief.

서술형

19 우리말과 일치하도록 주어진 조건에 맞게 문장을 완성하시오.

이것은 정답임에 틀림없다.

〈조건〉 1. this, the correct answer를 이용할 것
2. 6단어로 쓸 것

→ _____ .

서술형

[20-21] 우리말과 일치하도록 ( ) 안에 주어진 말을 바르게 배열하시오.

20 우리는 소리를 지르지 않아도 된다.
(don't, shout, to, have)

→ We _____ .

21 제가 뭔가 말해도 되나요?
(something, I, say, can)

→ _____ ?

서술형

[22-23] 밑줄 친 부분이 어법상 옳은지 판단하고, 틀리면 바르게 고치시오.

22 Diana <u>can be able to play</u> the flute.

(O / X) _____

23 You <u>must not bring</u> food into the art gallery.

(O / X) _____

UNIT 01

진행형

🔍 Answer Key p.25

A

( ) 안에서 알맞은 말을 고르시오.

1 The wind is (blow, blowing) hard.

2 (Does, Is) she playing the violin?

3 They are (lie, lying) on the beach.

4 I (is, was) thinking. I wasn't sleeping.

5 Angela was (sit, sitting) behind me.

6 Harry is (changes, changing) a tire on his bike.

7 Be quiet. The baby (sleeping, is sleeping).

8 This café (closes, closing) at nine every day.

9 My uncle (is, was) working as an engineer now.

10 A man (is knocking, are knocking) on the door.

B

( ) 안의 말을 이용하여 진행형 문장을 완성하시오. (부정문은 줄임말을 쓸 것)

1 I _____ my car now. (park)

2 Dad _____ on the phone now. (talk)

3 _____ Patrick _____ Korean these days? (learn)

4 They _____. They are just playing. (not/fight)

5 They _____ to the radio this morning. (listen)

6 The children _____ their shoelaces now. (tie)

7 He _____ an hour ago. (jog)

8 The man _____ a newspaper now. (buy)

9 _____ you _____ dinner at eight last night? (have)

10 Dan _____ the computer now. You can use it. (not/use)

보기에서 알맞은 동사를 골라 진행형 문장을 완성하시오. (긍정문으로 쓸 것)

[1-4] (현재진행형으로 쓸 것)

보기	kick snow plan waste

1 The boy _____ a soccer ball.

2 Stop it! You _____ my time.

3 It's very cold now. It _____ outside.

4 They _____ a big party.

[5-8] (과거진행형으로 쓸 것)

보기	wait walk bake raise

5 Mom _____ cookies an hour ago.

6 She _____ two dogs two years ago.

7 I _____ for the bus at the bus stop.

8 Mike and Jenny _____ on the street this morning.

D 밑줄 친 부분이 올바르면 ○표, 틀리면 바르게 고치시오.

1 Dad is <u>paint</u> the wall now.　　　　　　　　_____

2 He <u>doesn't</u> wearing a hat.　　　　　　　　_____

3 I <u>am shopping</u> with Alice now.　　　　　　_____

4 The baby <u>not is crying</u>.　　　　　　　　　_____

5 Jake <u>is liking</u> scary stories.　　　　　　　_____

6 <u>Were</u> you writing an email now?　　　　　_____

7 Those people <u>are looking</u> at me.　　　　　_____

8 I <u>wasn't drinking</u> juice. I was drinking milk.　_____

WRITING PRACTICE

Q Answer Key p.25

A 우리말과 일치하도록 (   ) 안의 말을 이용하여 문장을 완성하시오.

1 그는 노래를 부르고 있다. (sing)

→ He _____ a song.

2 나는 여행 가방을 싸고 있어. (pack)

→ I _____ my suitcase.

3 우리는 어떤 규칙도 어기고 있지 않았다. (break)

→ We _____ any rules.

4 너는 지금 우리 집에 오고 있니? (you, come)

→ _____ to my house now?

5 Eva는 미소 짓고 있지 않았어. 그녀는 화가 났었어. (smile)

→ Eva _____. She was upset.

6 너는 오늘 아침에 공원에서 운동하고 있었니? (you, exercise)

→ _____ in the park this morning?

7 아이들은 1부터 10까지 세고 있다. (count)

→ The children _____ from one to ten.

B 우리말과 일치하도록 (   ) 안에 주어진 말을 바르게 배열하시오.

1 우리 부모님은 벤치에 앉아 계신다. (are, my parents, sitting)

→ _____ on a bench.

2 Kevin은 이를 닦고 있지 않다. (Kevin, his teeth, not, brushing, is)

→ _____.

3 나는 요즘 외국 동전을 모으고 있다. (collecting, I, foreign coins, am)

→ _____ these days.

4 Amelia는 조언을 구하고 있지 않다. (asking, not, Amelia, is)

→ _____ for advice.

5 그 남자는 책들을 옮기고 있었다. (was, books, carrying, the man)

→ _____.

6 그들은 수영장에서 수영하고 있지 않았다. (they, swimming, not, were)

→ _____ in the pool.

CHAPTER 04 진행형과 미래시제

will, be going to

( ) 안에서 알맞은 말을 고르시오.

1 I will (am, be) back soon.

2 Annie will (take, took) yoga classes.

3 I'm (go, going) to lose some weight.

4 Will (they, do they) follow the rules?

5 He will (listen, listens) to your advice.

6 Justin (isn't, won't) going to forgive me.

7 Is he going (travel, to travel) around the world?

8 We are (going not, not going) to eat Chinese food.

9 Lisa is going (invite, to invite) her friends to her house.

B will 또는 won't와 보기의 말을 이용하여 문장을 완성하시오. (단, 한 번씩만 쓸 것)

[1-4]

보기	be	buy	like	come

1 This gift is for you. You _____ it.

2 Take this sweater. It _____ cold at night.

3 These pants are too tight. I _____ them.

4 She doesn't like parties. She _____ to your party.

[5-8]

보기	melt	lose	help	start

5 You can go to the restroom. The class _____ soon.

6 It is warm outside. The ice _____ in this weather.

7 Our school team is doing well. They _____ the game.

8 Emma is very kind. She _____ you.

C be going to와 ( ) 안의 말을 이용하여 대화를 완성하시오.

1 A: Do you have any plans this weekend?

B: Yes. _____ to Jeju Island. (we, go)

2 A: Are you angry at Chuck?

B: Yes. _____ him again. (I, not/see)

3 A: Monica knows about my secret.

B: Don't worry. _____ anybody. (she, not/tell)

4 A: _____ a new computer? (you, buy)

B: No, I'm not. My computer works well.

5 A: _____ your tent? (they, borrow)

B: No, they aren't. They don't need it.

6 A: I will pay for the dinner.

B: You don't have to. _____ for our dinner tonight.
(Mark, pay)

D 밑줄 친 부분이 올바르면 ○표, 틀리면 바르게 고치시오.

1 I <u>be going to</u> take a shower.   _____

2 Dad isn't <u>going smoke</u> from now on.   _____

3 My sister <u>will graduate</u> next year.   _____

4 Is she <u>going to order</u> a steak?   _____

5 Janet <u>wills move</u> to another city.   _____

6 Andy <u>won't is</u> late for the meeting.   _____

7 Are you going <u>print</u> this file?   _____

8 He <u>will finishes</u> the work tomorrow.   _____

9 She <u>is going to open</u> a flower shop soon.   _____

10 We <u>will not make</u> a sound anymore.   _____

WRITING **PRACTICE**

Answer Key p.26

A 우리말과 일치하도록 (   ) 안의 말을 이용하여 문장을 완성하시오.

1 우리가 그 집을 고칠 것이다. (be going to, fix)

→ We _____ the house.

2 그녀는 오늘 밤 집에 있을 것이다. (be going to, stay)

→ She _____ home tonight.

3 Scarlett과 Jack은 거짓말을 하지 않을 것이다. (will, tell)

→ _____ a lie.

4 그는 아내를 데리고 올 건가요? (he, be going to, bring)

→ _____ his wife?

5 이 프린터는 잘 작동하지 않을 것이다. (be going to, work)

→ This printer _____ well.

6 Grace는 그 소식에 행복해할까? (will, be happy)

→ _____ about the news?

7 Jim이 너에게 앨범을 보여줄 것이다. (will, show)

→ _____ the album to you.

B 우리말과 일치하도록 (   ) 안에 주어진 말을 바르게 배열하시오.

1 우리 형은 내년에 스무 살이 될 것이다. (twenty years old, be, my brother, will)

→ _____ next year.

2 그들이 그 노인을 도울까? (help, will, the old man, they)

→ _____ ?

3 Victor가 오늘 밤 저녁을 만들 것이다. (is, make dinner, Victor, going to)

→ _____ tonight.

4 너는 이 이야기를 믿지 않을 거야. (believe, not, will, you)

→ _____ this story.

5 나는 공포 영화를 보지 않을 거야. (not, watch, going to, I'm)

→ _____ horror movies.

6 당신은 이 회사에서 일할 예정인가요? (you, going to, work for, are)

→ _____ this company?

REVIEW TEST

Q Answer Key p.26

[1-2] 다음 중 동사의 v-ing형이 <u>잘못</u> 연결된 것을 고르시오.

1 ① eat – eating   ② stop – stoping
    ③ bake – baking   ④ bring – bringing
    ⑤ leave – leaving

2 ① fly – flying   ② die – dying
    ③ lose – loseing   ④ watch – watching
    ⑤ shop – shopping

[3-5] 빈칸에 들어갈 알맞은 말을 고르시오.

3
| We _____ spend our vacation in Italy. |

   ① are going   ② going to
   ③ be going to   ④ is going to
   ⑤ are going to

4
| Oscar has a map. He _____ get lost. |

   ① isn't   ② is going to
   ③ are going to   ④ will
   ⑤ won't

5
| A: Were you reading a book? |
| B: No. I _____ my homework. |

   ① do   ② am doing
   ③ was doing   ④ will do
   ⑤ am going to do

[6-7] 빈칸에 공통으로 들어갈 말을 고르시오.

6
| • The waiter _____ serve dessert. |
| • _____ they check their emails? |

   ① is[Is]   ② are[Are]
   ③ do[Do]   ④ does[Does]
   ⑤ will[Will]

7
| • _____ you watching TV last night? |
| • Ted and Lucy _____ flying kites in the park yesterday. |

   ① be[Be]   ② are[Are]
   ③ was[Was]   ④ were[Were]
   ⑤ will[Will]

서술형   빈출

[8-9] 빈칸에 알맞은 말을 써서 대화를 완성하시오.

8
| A: _____ Dave practicing the piano now? |
| B: Yes, he _____. His concert is next week. |

9

A: Will it snow on Christmas Day?
B: No, it _____. It
_____ be sunny.

10 다음 중 대화가 자연스럽지 <u>않은</u> 것은?

① A: The phone is ringing.
　 B: I'll get it.
② A: Are you sleeping this morning?
　 B: Yes, I was. I was tired.
③ A: Are you making tea?
　 B: Yes. Do you want some?
④ A: Is Eric going to buy a new car?
　 B: No, he isn't. He likes his old car.
⑤ A: Kate is angry at you.
　 B: I know. But I'm not going to say
　　 sorry to her.

서술형

[11-12] 다음 밑줄 친 부분을 바르게 고치시오.

11

I'm ⓐ <u>going give</u> this flower to Amy.
Will ⓑ <u>she likes</u> it?

ⓐ _____　ⓑ _____

12

We're ⓐ <u>going not to</u> eat out tonight.
Dad ⓑ <u>is cook</u> dinner now.

ⓐ _____　ⓑ _____

빈출

13 빈칸에 들어갈 말이 바르게 짝지어진 것은?

> The class will ____(A)____ over at 5:00
> p.m. After class, we ____(B)____ to a
> buffet.

	(A)		(B)
①	be	……	is going to go
②	be	……	are going to go
③	is	……	will going
④	is	……	are going to go
⑤	are	……	is going to go

[14-15] 다음 중 밑줄 친 부분이 잘못된 것을 고르시오.

14 ① I <u>was thinking</u> about you.
② Jenny <u>is running</u> in the field.
③ Ryan <u>is opening</u> a package.
④ <u>Is</u> our team <u>losing</u> the game?
⑤ Ellen <u>is cleaning</u> the floor a few
　 minutes ago.

15 ① <u>Will Fred pass</u> the audition?
② <u>I'm going fry</u> these eggs.
③ They <u>won't be</u> here on time.
④ It <u>is going to be</u> windy tonight.
⑤ Grace <u>will ask</u> for your phone number.

16 다음 우리말을 영어로 바르게 옮긴 것은?

> 너는 피자를 만들고 있었니?

① Are you making pizza?
② Did you make pizza?
③ Will you make pizza?
④ Were you making pizza?
⑤ Are you going to make pizza?

[17-18] 다음 문장을 ( ) 안의 지시대로 바꿔 쓰시오.

17 John is going to be fifteen next year.
(will을 이용하여)

→ _____ .

18 I won't eat this cake.
(be going to를 이용하여)

→ _____ .

[19-21] 우리말과 일치하도록 ( ) 안의 말을 이용하여 문장을 완성하시오.

19 Alice는 문을 잠그는 중이다. (lock)

→ Alice _____ the door.

20 그 가게는 다음 주 월요일에 세일을 하지 않을 것이다.
(will, have)

→ The store _____ a
sale next Monday.

21 나는 머리를 자르지 않을 것이다.
(be going to, get)

→ _____ a haircut.

[22-24] 우리말과 일치하도록 ( ) 안에 주어진 말을 바르게 배열하시오.

22 그가 골을 넣을까? (a goal, he, will, score)

→ _____ ?

23 그들은 눈을 감고 있니?
(their eyes, they, closing, are)

→ _____ ?

24 Lucy는 그녀의 개를 훈련시킬 예정이다.
(is, her dog, train, going to)

→ Lucy _____ .

[25-26] 밑줄 친 부분이 어법상 옳은지 판단하고, 틀리면 바르게 고치시오.

25 Richard was solving the puzzle in his room.

(O / X) _____

26 The president will visits our town next week.

(O / X) _____

UNIT
01

감각동사 + 형용사

A ( ) 안에서 알맞은 말을 고르시오.

1 This hand cream (smells, tastes) sweet.

2 His jokes (listen, sound) funny.

3 This tea tastes (coffee, like coffee).

4 I'm okay. I (sound, feel) comfortable now.

5 Does this hat (look, see) strange?

6 Dark chocolate tastes (bitter, bitterly).

7 Their new song sounds (great, greatly).

8 What happened? You look (angry, angrily).

9 Jane feels (happy, happiness) with her new school.

10 This sushi smells (bad, badly). It can't be fresh.

B ( ) 안의 말을 이용하여 문장을 완성하시오. (현재형으로 쓸 것)

1 Your hands _____. (feel, cold)

2 This soup _____. (taste, spicy)

3 This melody _____. (sound, sad)

4 This sauce _____. (smell, sour)

5 That movie _____. (look, scary)

6 This jazz music _____. (sound, nice)

7 These candles _____. (smell, good)

8 This sandwich _____. (taste, delicious)

9 We can _____ in this building. (feel, safe)

10 These Christmas trees _____. (look, beautiful)

C 보기에서 알맞은 말을 골라 대화를 완성하시오. (현재형으로 쓸 것)

보기	look young	feel healthy	sound serious
	smell terrible	taste strange	look expensive

1 A: These toy trains _____.

B: Not really. They are only $10.

2 A: My coffee _____.

B: Oh, I put salt in it instead of sugar! I'm sorry.

3 A: Do you exercise every morning?

B: Yes. I _____ these days.

4 A: Your socks _____!

B: I know. I'm going to wash them.

5 A: Mandy was in an accident. She went to the hospital.

B: Oh, no! That _____.

6 A: Your new teacher _____. How old is she?

B: She is twenty-five years old.

D 밑줄 친 부분이 올바르면 ○표, 틀리면 바르게 고치시오.

1 This soup smells well. _____

2 The radio show sounded boring. _____

3 These blankets feel softly. _____

4 This scarf will look love with your dress. _____

5 These apples smell freshly. _____

6 This computer game sees easy. _____

7 We felt tired after the soccer game. _____

8 George feels sickness after he eats peanuts. _____

WRITING PRACTICE

Q Answer Key p.26

A 우리말과 일치하도록 ( ) 안의 말을 이용하여 문장을 완성하시오.

1 저 장난감들은 위험해 보인다. (look, dangerous)

→ Those toys _____ .

2 이 쿠키는 달콤한 맛이 난다. (taste, sweet)

→ This cookie _____ .

3 나는 성적 때문에 기분이 나빴다. (feel, bad)

→ I _____ about my grades.

4 그의 이름은 나에게 친숙하게 들린다. (sound, familiar)

→ His name _____ to me.

5 네 새로운 헤어스타일은 멋져 보이는구나! (look, great)

→ Your new hairstyle _____ !

6 내 손수건은 이상한 냄새가 난다. (smell, strange)

→ My handkerchief _____ .

7 John은 한밤중에 배가 고프다고 느꼈다. (feel, hungry)

→ John _____ in the middle of the night.

B 우리말과 일치하도록 ( ) 안에 주어진 말을 바르게 배열하시오.

1 시간 여행은 흥미롭게 들린다. (sounds, time travel, exciting)

→ _____ .

2 네 보디로션은 냄새가 좋다. (nice, your body lotion, smells)

→ _____ .

3 이 채소들은 신선한 맛이 난다. (taste, these vegetables, fresh)

→ _____ .

4 우리 할아버지는 건강해 보이신다. (healthy, looks, my grandfather)

→ _____ .

5 오늘 아침에 그녀의 목소리는 슬프게 들렸다. (her voice, sad, sounded)

→ _____ this morning.

6 Linda는 결혼식 날 긴장이 되었다. (nervous, Linda, felt)

→ _____ on her wedding day.

UNIT 02

목적어가 두 개 필요한 동사

🔍 Answer Key p.26

A

( ) 안에서 알맞은 말을 고르시오.

1 Josh gave this T-shirt (to, for) me.

2 Mike cooked dinner (to, for) his wife.

3 Can I ask a favor (to, of) you?

4 Can you get some pepper (for, of) me?

5 I'll teach (them, to them) taekwondo.

6 My grandmother often (said, told) us scary stories.

7 We made paper planes (for, to) the children.

8 Will you show (me, to me) your ticket?

9 I'm going to send (him an email, an email him) tonight.

10 Andy bought (a new coat his sister, his sister a new coat).

B

빈칸에 알맞은 동사를 보기에서 골라 과거형으로 써서 문장을 완성하시오. (단, 한 번씩만 쓸 것)

[1-4]

보기	teach	buy	show	cook

1 My sister _____ this sweater for me.

2 Emily _____ spaghetti for her family.

3 They _____ photos of their baby to us.

4 Mr. Brown _____ music to us last year.

[5-8]

보기	get	tell	write	lend

5 I _____ my pen to Steve.

6 Isabel _____ the rumor to me.

7 He _____ gloves for me.

8 I _____ a letter to my parents last weekend.

두 문장의 의미가 같도록 빈칸에 알맞은 말을 쓰시오.

1 I'll bring some fruit to you.

→ I'll bring _____ _____ _____.

2 Can you pass the ketchup to me?

→ Can you pass _____ _____ _____?

3 Mom will buy me these sneakers.

→ Mom will buy _____ _____ _____ _____.

4 You can ask me a favor.

→ You can ask _____ _____ _____ _____.

5 Lily sends me cards on my birthday.

→ Lily sends _____ _____ _____ on my birthday.

6 The designer made her a beautiful dress.

→ The designer made _____ _____ _____ _____

_____.

( ) 안의 말을 이용하여 대화를 완성하시오.

1 A: Can you _____ _____ a fork? (bring, me)

B: Sure, just a minute.

2 A: Don't cry. I'll _____ a tissue _____ _____. (get, you)

B: Thank you.

3 A: Did you _____ a tip _____ _____ _____?

(give, the waiter)

B: Yes. His service was great.

4 A: Did you eat breakfast this morning?

B: Yes. Mom made _____ _____ _____ _____.

(a sandwich, me)

5 A: Did she have an interview after the game?

B: Yes. Reporters asked _____ _____ _____.

(many questions, her)

6 A: You won a medal in the competition. Congratulations!

B: Thank you. I will show _____ _____ _____ _____.

(it, my parents)

WRITING PRACTICE

🔍 Answer Key p.26

A 우리말과 일치하도록 ( ) 안의 말을 이용하여 문장을 완성하시오.

1 그는 우리에게 커피를 만들어 주었다. (make, we, coffee)

→ He _____.

2 내가 Brenda에게 그 소식을 이야기할 것이다. (tell, Brenda, the news)

→ I'll _____.

3 저에게 당신의 명함을 주실 수 있나요? (give, I, your business card)

→ Can you _____?

4 나는 지금 친구에게 이메일을 쓰고 있다. (write, my friend, an email)

→ I'm _____ now.

5 Jessica가 너에게 영어를 가르쳐줄 것이다. (teach, you, English)

→ Jessica is going to _____.

6 나는 내 남동생에게 아이스크림을 사 주었다. (buy, my brother, ice cream)

→ I _____.

B 우리말과 일치하도록 ( ) 안에 주어진 말을 바르게 배열하시오.

1 그는 우리에게 웃긴 동영상을 보냈다. (us, sent, he, funny videos)

→ _____.

2 나는 Cindy에게 이 표를 줄 것이다. (Cindy, give, this ticket, to)

→ I'll _____.

3 나는 너에게 50달러를 빌려줄 수 있다. (you, lend, fifty dollars)

→ I can _____.

4 그녀는 자신의 여권을 우리에게 보여주었다. (to, her passport, us, showed)

→ She _____.

5 저에게 주스를 좀 가져다줄 수 있나요? (some juice, get, me, for)

→ Can you _____?

6 Nicole은 내게 어려운 질문을 하나 했다. (a difficult question, asked, me)

→ Nicole _____.

7 Ryan은 그녀에게 아름다운 장미를 가져다주었다. (brought, her, to, beautiful roses)

→ Ryan _____.

UNIT 03

목적격 보어가 필요한 동사

A

( ) 안에서 알맞은 말을 고르시오.

1 People (call, want) him Steve.

2 Ms. Brown told the boy (be, to be) quiet.

3 They (named, wanted) their new dog Snoopy.

4 The man ordered us (stand, to stand) in line.

5 Her debut album (made, told) her a superstar.

6 I didn't expect her (win, to win) the first prize.

7 Regular exercise will keep you (health, healthy).

8 James asked me (open, to open) the door.

9 We found the summer camp (interest, interesting).

B

빈칸에 알맞은 말을 보기에서 골라 쓰시오. (단, 한 번씩만 쓸 것)

[1-4]

보기	a liar	boring	warm	strong

1 Many students found Mr. Wright's class _____.

2 I'm not lying! Don't call me _____!

3 Those hard times made him _____.

4 These gloves will keep your hands _____.

[5-8]

보기	fresh	angry	exciting	Henry

5 He named his son _____.

6 We found snowboarding _____.

7 The refrigerator keeps food _____.

8 My rude behavior made Mom _____.

C ( ) 안의 말을 이용하여 문장을 완성하시오. (과거형으로 쓸 것)

1 My brother _____. (call, me, a fool)

2 I _____ my family. (want, you, meet)

3 I _____. (find, Jenny, friendly)

4 We _____ before 6:00 p.m. (expect, him, arrive)

5 The man _____ the building. (tell, her, leave)

6 Your smile _____. (make, me, happy)

7 The air conditioner _____. (keep, the room, cool)

8 The old lady _____ her bags. (ask, us, carry)

9 They _____. (make, me, the class president)

10 The doctor _____ some rest. (advise, me, get)

D 밑줄 친 부분이 올바르면 ○표, 틀리면 바르게 고치시오.

1 I found New York <u>amazingly</u>. _____

2 I didn't expect him <u>say</u> sorry. _____

3 She is going to name <u>her dog Spot</u>. _____

4 Let's keep <u>the window open</u>. _____

5 My teacher advised us <u>study</u> hard. _____

6 Dad always tells <u>we to go</u> to bed early. _____

7 Mia asked <u>them wait</u> at the bus stop. _____

8 These songs made him <u>a famous musician</u>. _____

WRITING PRACTICE

Answer Key p.27

A 우리말과 일치하도록 ( ) 안의 말을 이용하여 문장을 완성하시오.

1 우리 엄마는 항상 우리 집을 깨끗하게 유지하신다. (keep, our house, clean)

→ My mom always _____.

2 나는 그가 우리 축구부에 가입하기를 바란다. (want, he, join)

→ I _____ our soccer club.

3 연습은 나를 훌륭한 선수로 만들었다. (make, I, a good player)

→ Practice _____.

4 선생님은 우리에게 자신을 따라오라고 말씀하셨다. (tell, we, follow him)

→ Our teacher _____.

5 내 이름은 Daniel이지만, 내 친구들은 나를 Dan이라고 부른다. (call, I, Dan)

→ My name is Daniel, but my friends _____.

6 우리는 우리 식당을 Lemon Tree라고 이름 지었다. (name, our restaurant, Lemon Tree)

→ We _____.

7 판사는 그에게 100달러를 지불하라고 명령했다. (order, he, pay $100)

→ The judge _____.

B 우리말과 일치하도록 ( ) 안에 주어진 말을 바르게 배열하시오.

1 그의 첫 소설은 그를 유명하게 만들어 주었다. (him, made, famous)

→ His first novel _____.

2 나는 그녀가 정직할 것이라고 기대한다. (her, expect, to, honest, be)

→ I _____.

3 너는 이 신발이 편하다는 것을 알게 될 것이다. (find, comfortable, these shoes)

→ You'll _____.

4 그 뮤직비디오는 그를 대스타로 만들었다. (him, a big star, made)

→ The music video _____.

5 그는 나에게 자신과 함께 저녁을 먹자고 요청했다. (he, to, asked, have dinner, me)

→ _____ with him.

6 우리 부모님은 나에게 중국어를 배우라고 조언하셨다. (learn, advised, to, me, Chinese)

→ My parents _____.

REVIEW TEST

🔍 Answer Key p.27

[1-5] 빈칸에 들어갈 알맞은 말을 고르시오.

1

| Julia's sunglasses look _____. |

① well　　② great　　③ badly
④ terribly　　⑤ wonderfully

2

| I was sick. Daniel cooked soup _____ me. |

① to　　② for　　③ of
④ at　　⑤ from

3

| My parents expect me _____ home early. |

① come　　② comes　　③ came
④ will come　⑤ to come

4

| A: Let's take a walk after lunch.
B: That _____ great. |

① looks　　② feels　　③ sounds
④ smells　　⑤ tastes

5

| A: Do you know that singer's real name?
B: No, I don't. People just _____ her Spider. |

① send　　② call　　③ say
④ tell　　⑤ give

서술형

[6-8] 두 문장의 의미가 같도록 빈칸에 알맞은 말을 쓰시오.

6

The man showed us his ID card.

→ The man showed _____
_____ _____ _____
_____.

7

My sister bought me a scarf.

→ My sister bought _____
_____ _____ _____.

8

Can you bring her that book?

→ Can you bring _____ _____
_____ _____?

9 밑줄 친 부분의 쓰임이 나머지 넷과 <u>다른</u> 것은?

① His death <u>made</u> me sad.
② He <u>made</u> his son a teacher.
③ Christine <u>made</u> us green tea.
④ The TV show <u>made</u> her popular.
⑤ His experience <u>made</u> him a great reporter.

10 다음 중 대화가 자연스럽지 <u>않은</u> 것은?

① A: Are you okay?
   B: No. I feel tired.
② A: This cake tastes delicious!
   B: Thanks. I made it.
③ A: Can you lend me ten dollars?
   B: Sure. Wait a minute.
④ A: What did the coach tell you?
   B: He told me practice hard.
⑤ A: Do you keep your room clean?
   B: Yes. I clean it every day.

[11-12] 빈칸에 공통으로 들어갈 말을 고르시오.

11

| • Harry lent his notebook _____ Fred. |
| • I asked my neighbor _____ watch my dog. |

① for   ② with   ③ of
④ at   ⑤ to

12

| • Your gift _____ me happy. |
| • His effort _____ him a winner. |

① found   ② wanted   ③ told
④ made   ⑤ called

[13-14] 다음 중 밑줄 친 부분이 잘못된 것을 고르시오.

13 ① The man looked <u>gentle</u>.
② They asked me <u>close</u> the door.
③ Did you send an email <u>to me</u>?
④ Your story made <u>me</u> <u>sad</u>.
⑤ Someone kept the door <u>open</u>.

14 ① She named her baby <u>Emily</u>.
② Eric found his new house <u>nice</u>.
③ After the exam, we felt <u>excited</u>.
④ Mary cooked pasta <u>to her boyfriend</u>.
⑤ We expected our parents <u>to come</u> to school today.

[15-16] 다음 밑줄 친 부분을 바르게 고치시오.

15

I watched this movie last Sunday. The movie poster ⓐ <u>watched</u> boring. But I found the movie very ⓑ <u>interest</u>.

ⓐ _____   ⓑ _____

16

My brother talked on the phone loudly last night. It made ⓐ <u>for me</u> upset. I went to his room and told him ⓑ <u>be</u> quiet.

ⓐ _____   ⓑ _____

[17-18] 다음 우리말을 영어로 바르게 옮긴 것을 고르시오.

17 나는 친구들에게 핫도그를 사주었다.

① I bought hot dogs my friends.
② I bought my friends hot dogs.
③ I bought hot dogs to my friends.
④ I bought for hot dogs my friends.
⑤ I bought my friends for hot dogs.

18 나는 그 식당이 훌륭하다는 걸 알게 되었다.

① I found the restaurant great.
② I found the restaurant greatly.
③ I found the restaurant to great.
④ I found the restaurant be great.
⑤ I found the restaurant to be greatly.

서술형

[19-20] 우리말과 일치하도록 ( ) 안의 말을 이용하여 문장을 완성하시오.

19 그녀의 목소리는 또렷하게 들린다. (clear)

→ Her voice _____.

20 이 종이는 거친 느낌이 든다. (rough)

→ This paper _____.

서술형

[21-23] 우리말과 일치하도록 ( ) 안에 주어진 말을 바르게 배열하시오.

21 그는 내게 그의 방을 보여주었다.
(me, to, his room, showed)

→ He _____.

22 신선한 공기는 우리를 건강하게 유지해 준다.
(us, healthy, fresh air, keeps)

→ _____.

23 교장 선생님께서 네가 교장실로 오길 원하셔.
(you, to, wants, the principal, come)

→ _____ to his office.

서술형 고난도

[24-25] 어법상 틀린 부분을 찾아 바르게 고치시오.

24 A: This cheese smells badly!
B: I know. But it tastes greatly. (2개)

25 I told my secret for Rachel. I expected her keep it. But she told everyone about it. It made me very angrily! (3개)

UNIT 01

셀 수 있는 명사 vs. 셀 수 없는 명사

A 주어진 명사의 복수형을 쓰시오.

1 computer – _____   2 shirt – _____

3 glass – _____   4 fly – _____

5 man – _____   6 bench – _____

7 boy – _____   8 hand – _____

9 dish – _____   10 lamp – _____

11 potato – _____   12 fish – _____

13 tooth – _____   14 lady – _____

15 deer – _____   16 roof – _____

B ( ) 안에서 알맞은 말을 고르시오.

1 (Air, An air) is important to us.

2 My brother is studying in (California, a California).

3 The printer needs (paper, a paper).

4 Mr. and Mrs. Jones have three (childs, children).

5 I don't put (sugar, a sugar) in my coffee.

6 Seoul and Incheon are (citys, cities) in Korea.

7 He gave me two (boxs, boxes) of chocolates.

8 We have four English (class, classes) every week.

9 In the movie, the two boys turned into (wolfs, wolves).

10 I saw a lot of (mice, mouses) in that old house.

C ( ) 안의 단어를 적절한 형태로 써서 문장을 완성하시오.

1 There are thirty-one _____ in January. (day)

2 The police caught two _____ last night. (thief)

3 She visited _____ last summer. (Korea)

4 She wrote ten short _____ for kids. (story)

5 The movie was about _____. (friendship)

6 There are two _____ in the music room. (piano)

7 _____ is not everything in life. (money)

8 _____ fall from many trees in autumn. (leaf)

9 Red roses are a symbol of _____ in many countries. (love)

10 Superman and Batman are _____ from comic books. (hero)

D 보기에서 알맞은 말을 골라 ( ) 안의 말과 함께 써서 문장을 완성하시오. (단, 한 번씩만 쓸 것)

[1-3]

보기	bottle	cup	piece

1 I'll have _____. (a, tea)

2 I bought _____. (two, cola)

3 There were _____ on the desk. (four, paper)

[4-6]

보기	bowl	glass	slice

4 Laura ate _____. (three, pizza)

5 Can I have _____? (a, orange juice)

6 Mom made me _____. (a, chicken soup)

WRITING PRACTICE

🔍 **Answer Key p.27**

A   우리말과 일치하도록 (   ) 안의 말을 이용하여 문장을 완성하시오.

1   Mia는 아침에 토마토 두 개를 먹었다. (eat, tomato)

→ Mia _____ in the morning.

2   칼들은 아이들에게 위험하다. (knife, dangerous)

→ _____ for kids.

3   그는 들판에서 양들을 돌본다. (look after, sheep)

→ He _____ in the field.

4   이 게스트 하우스는 여성들만을 위한 것이다. (for, woman)

→ This guesthouse is only _____.

5   그녀는 식사 후에 커피 한 잔을 마신다. (coffee)

→ She drinks _____ after meals.

6   아이들은 운동장에서 모래를 가지고 놀았다. (play, with, sand)

→ The kids _____ in the playground.

7   나는 내 볶음밥에 치즈 두 장을 올렸다. (slice, cheese)

→ I put _____ on my fried rice.

B   우리말과 일치하도록 (   ) 안에 주어진 말을 바르게 배열하시오.

1   Edward는 지금 오사카에 산다. (lives, Osaka, Edward, in)

→ _____ now.

2   우리는 집에 선풍기를 세 대 가지고 있다. (fans, we, three, have)

→ _____ in our house.

3   나는 양말 여섯 켤레를 샀다. (socks, of, I, pairs, six, bought)

→ _____.

4   여름 방학 때 찍은 네 사진들을 봐도 되니? (your photos, I, see, can)

→ _____ from summer vacation?

5   너는 매일 여덟 잔의 물을 마셔야 한다. (water, glasses, eight, drink, of)

→ You should _____ every day.

6   그 방에는 가구가 두 채 있었다. (pieces, two, furniture, of)

→ There were _____ in the room.

60

관사

🔍 Answer Key p.27

A

( ) 안에서 알맞은 말을 고르시오.

1 Do you have (a, an) pen?

2 Tom is (a, an) honest boy.

3 Can I open (an, the) window?

4 Kelly studies at (a, an) university.

5 Do you listen to (a, the) radio?

6 A lot of animals live under (a, the) sea.

7 She visits her grandparents twice (a, the) month.

8 I went to a café. (A, The) café was very nice.

9 I was busy all day. I didn't have (lunch, a lunch).

10 Turn off (a, the) computer. We are not using it.

B

빈칸에 알맞은 말을 보기에서 골라 쓰시오. (X는 필요 없음을 뜻함)

보기	a an the X

1 I had _____ dinner thirty minutes ago.

2 We went to _____ movies last weekend.

3 There is _____ big tree in her garden.

4 Robin is driving over 100 km _____ hour.

5 Did you come here by _____ bus?

6 I have _____ question about the contest.

7 _____ sandwich on the table is for Greg.

8 I put a map of _____ world on the wall.

( ) 안의 말을 이용하여 대화를 완성하시오. (필요하면 알맞은 관사를 넣을 것)

1 A: Do you often update your blog?

B: Well, I update it _____. (twice, week)

2 A: Did you walk here?

B: No, I came here _____. (by, subway)

3 A: Did you _____ on the chair? (put, box)

B: No, I put it on the floor.

4 A: It's raining. Did you _____? (bring, umbrella)

B: Yes, I did.

5 A: Do we have any fruit?

B: There are some apples _____. (in, refrigerator)

6 A: Are you tired?

B: Yes, I _____ after midnight yesterday. (go to, bed)

밑줄 친 부분이 올바르면 ○표, 틀리면 바르게 고치시오.

1 My uncle is a engineer.   _____

2 We go to school on weekdays.   _____

3 Emily has a old bike.   _____

4 I can see the ocean from here.   _____

5 We need a onion for a salad.   _____

6 Tim plays the basketball very well.   _____

7 Please turn down the volume.   _____

8 We have a film festival once the year.   _____

9 I bought a book. A book was interesting.   _____

10 Can you send me the photo by the email?   _____

WRITING PRACTICE

🔍 Answer Key p.28

A 우리말과 일치하도록 ( ) 안의 말을 이용하여 문장을 완성하시오.

1 Lena는 어제 책 한 권을 읽었다. (read, book)

→ Lena _____ yesterday.

2 너는 Sam과 점심을 먹었니? (have, lunch)

→ Did you _____ with Sam?

3 이 동영상은 인터넷에서 인기 있다. (on, internet)

→ This video is popular _____.

4 내가 Jacob에게 문자 메시지로 그것에 대해 이야기할게. (by, text message)

→ I'll tell Jacob about it _____.

5 너는 이 비타민을 하루에 세 번 먹어야 한다. (three times, day)

→ You have to take this vitamin _____.

6 그들은 방과 후에 배드민턴을 쳤다. (play, badminton)

→ They _____ after school.

7 나는 어젯밤에 영화를 한 편 봤다. 그 영화는 유령에 관한 것이었다. (movie)

→ I saw a movie last night. _____ was about ghosts.

B 우리말과 일치하도록 ( ) 안에 주어진 말을 바르게 배열하시오.

1 Tom은 은행에서 일한다. (a, works for, Tom, bank)

→ _____.

2 나는 사과 하나와 샌드위치 하나를 가져왔어. (apple, a, and, sandwich, an)

→ I brought _____.

3 하늘에 새가 한 마리 있다. (bird, in, a, sky, the)

→ There is _____.

4 너는 클라리넷을 연주할 수 있니? (clarinet, play, can, the, you)

→ _____?

5 태양은 우리에게 빛을 준다. (gives, sun, light, the, us)

→ _____.

6 Mike는 오전 8시에 학교에 간다. (school, Mike, goes to)

→ _____ at 8:00 a.m.

REVIEW TEST

[1-2] 다음 중 명사의 복수형이 잘못 연결된 것을 고르시오.

1
① man – men ② bus – buses
③ leaf – leaves ④ deer – deers
⑤ banana – bananas

2
① toy – toies ② fox – foxes
③ phone – phones ④ baby – babies
⑤ monkey – monkeys

빈출

[3-4] 빈칸에 들어갈 말이 바르게 짝지어진 것을 고르시오.
(X는 필요 없음을 뜻함)

3
- I saw ____(A)____ of glasses in the restroom.
- My sister is ____(B)____ elementary school student.

	(A)		(B)
①	piece	······	a
②	pair	······	an
③	a piece	······	a
④	a pair	······	an
⑤	two pair	······	the

4
- Did you have ____(A)____ this morning?
- Michael is from ____(B)____ Sydney.

	(A)		(B)
①	breakfast	······	a
②	breakfast	······	X
③	a breakfast	······	a
④	a breakfast	······	X
⑤	the breakfast	······	the

서술형

[5-7] ( ) 안의 단어를 적절한 형태로 써서 문장을 완성하시오.

5
Many _____ watch this show. (person)

6
There are lots of _____ in the park. (tree)

7
My _____ were dirty, so I washed them. (foot)

빈출

8 다음 중 보기의 밑줄 친 부분과 쓰임이 같은 것은?

보기 | I meet Jeremy twice a month.

① Betty has a cute cat.
② My father is a pilot.
③ I ate an orange after lunch.
④ Pick a number from one to ten.
⑤ Jenny goes to the gym once a week.

9 밑줄 친 명사의 성격이 나머지 넷과 다른 것은?

① <u>Dave</u> is my best friend.
② People waste a lot of <u>water</u>.
③ I wish you <u>happiness</u>.
④ I broke a <u>vase</u> this morning.
⑤ He went to <u>China</u> last summer.

[10-12] 다음 중 밑줄 친 부분이 잘못된 것을 고르시오.

10 ① This is <u>an</u> old building.
② <u>Love</u> is a wonderful thing.
③ There are ten <u>boys</u> on the street.
④ Do you want <u>a</u> salt in your soup?
⑤ You have to brush your <u>teeth</u> after meals.

11 ① I'll have <u>a cup of</u> hot cocoa.
② Dad ate <u>two bowls of</u> cereal.
③ Can I get <u>a pieces of</u> paper?
④ Bring them <u>two glasses of</u> water.
⑤ He spread butter on <u>a slice of</u> bread.

12 ① <u>The earth</u> is round.
② I listen to <u>radio</u> at night.
③ Jim and I played <u>table tennis</u>.
④ There's a <u>bookstore</u> near here.
⑤ Mina went to <u>bed</u> late yesterday.

서술형

[13-15] 빈칸에 알맞은 관사를 보기에서 골라 한 번씩만 써서 문장을 완성하시오. (X는 필요 없음을 뜻함)

보기	a	the	X

13 Can you close _____ door?

14 Minsu bought _____ new cell phone last week.

15 Austin traveled through European countries by _____ train.

서술형

[16-17] ( ) 안의 말을 이용하여 대화를 완성하시오.

16 A: Will you _____ with me? (go to, movies)
B: Sorry, but I have to study.

17 A: Can I have _____?
(a, green tea)
B: Sure. Give me a moment.

18 다음 우리말을 영어로 바르게 옮긴 것은?

내가 이 파일을 이메일로 보낼게.

① I will send this file by email.
② I will send this file by a email.
③ I will send this file by an email.
④ I will send this file by the email.
⑤ I will send this file by emails.

19 주어진 단어를 바르게 배열할 때 네 번째에 오는 단어는?

study, scientists, the, those, moon

① study   ② scientists   ③ the
④ those   ⑤ moon

서술형
[20-21] 우리말과 일치하도록 ( ) 안의 말을 이용하여 문장을 완성하시오.

20 너 그 도둑들에 대한 이야기를 들었니? (thief)

→ Did you hear the story about the
_____?

21 너는 배로 강을 건널 수 있다. (boat)

→ You can cross the river _____.

서술형
[22-23] 우리말과 일치하도록 ( ) 안에 주어진 말을 바르게 배열하시오.

22 나는 내 생일에 케이크 세 조각을 먹었다.
(pieces, three, cake, of)

→ I had _____ on
my birthday.

23 Cathy는 일주일에 두 번 수영장에 간다.
(swimming pool, a, twice, week, a)

→ Cathy goes to _____
_____.

서술형 고난도
[24-25] 어법상 틀린 부분을 찾아 바르게 고치시오.

24 A: Mom, this soup is too salty.
B: I'm sorry. I'll add a water. (1개)

25 I watch a talk show at night. A show
is on TV once an week—Tuesdays
at 11:00 p.m. So I go to bed late
on Tuesdays. I feel tired the next
morning, but the show is really good!
(2개)

UNIT 01 인칭대명사, 재귀대명사

🔍 Answer Key p.28

A ( ) 안에서 알맞은 말을 고르시오.

1 Welcome to (my, me) house!

2 Alice is proud of (myself, herself).

3 I will introduce (me, myself) to you.

4 I bought a new cell phone case. I love (its, it) color.

5 Baby ducks are following (its, their) mother.

6 Susan is not honest. I don't trust (her, hers).

7 Can you see those puppies? (It, They) are cute!

8 This is not our key. (Our, Ours) is in that bag.

9 This is your toothbrush, and that is (my, mine).

10 Mike and I are not close. (We, They) don't know each other well.

B 밑줄 친 부분을 대신하는 알맞은 대명사를 빈칸에 쓰시오.

1 Hi, I'm Peter. Do you remember _____?

2 Tom should take care of _____ family.

3 We lost _____ passports at the airport.

4 You don't have to wash the cup. I'll wash _____ later.

5 Julie didn't lend me _____ notebook.

6 David and Ellen are going to have _____ baby soon.

7 Where is Andy? Did you see _____ this morning?

8 I bought this hat yesterday. _____ was $30.

9 I have to fix my bike. _____ wheels don't work well.

10 Tina and Bill are waiting for a bus. _____ are late for school.

C

빈칸에 알맞은 말을 보기에서 골라 적절한 형태로 써서 대화를 완성하시오. (단, 한 번씩만 쓸 것)

보기	by oneself	burn oneself
	enjoy oneself	introduce oneself
	help oneself to	make oneself at home

1 A: Does Sarah know you?

B: No. I have to _____ to her.

2 A: Please _____ some dessert, Dave.

B: Thank you. This cake is my favorite.

3 A: Are you okay? That looks bad.

B: I _____ on the oven. It hurts a lot.

4 A: Did you _____ at Jim's birthday party?

B: Yes, I did. It was a great party.

5 A: I'll help Paula with her homework.

B: Don't help her! She should do it _____.

6 A: Welcome to my house. Please _____.

B: Thank you. You're very kind.

D

밑줄 친 부분이 올바르면 ○표, 틀리면 바르게 고치시오.

1 Don't worry. I'm not angry with <u>you</u>. _____

2 We finished <u>ours</u> project last month. _____

3 George told <u>I</u> a secret. _____

4 I like Emily. <u>It</u> is my best friend. _____

5 They fixed the roof <u>themselves</u>. _____

6 Are your shoes okay? <u>Mine</u> are wet. _____

7 He cooked this spaghetti <u>yourself</u>. _____

8 Sam likes <u>him</u> uncle very much. _____

WRITING PRACTICE

🔍 Answer Key p.28

A 우리말과 일치하도록 ( ) 안의 말을 이용하여 문장을 완성하시오.

1 안녕하세요, 저는 John Brown입니다. (be)

→ Hello, _____ John Brown.

2 그는 우리에게 샌드위치를 만들어 주었다. (make)

→ _____ sandwiches.

3 그녀는 모든 그림들을 직접 그렸다. (oneself)

→ She drew all the paintings _____.

4 이것은 그의 필통이다. (pencil case)

→ This is _____.

5 Chuck은 축구 경기 중에 다쳤다. (hurt oneself)

→ Chuck _____ during the soccer game.

6 나는 혼자 카페에 갔다. (by oneself)

→ I went to a café _____.

B 우리말과 일치하도록 ( ) 안에 주어진 말을 바르게 배열하시오.

1 이것이 당신의 여행 가방인가요? (your, this, suitcase, is)

→ _____?

2 나는 그것을 책상 위에 두었다. (it, put, on the desk, I)

→ _____.

3 그녀는 우리의 과학 선생님이시다. (science teacher, is, she, our)

→ _____.

4 Jennifer는 그녀의 귀걸이를 잃어버렸다. (earring, lost, her, Jennifer)

→ _____.

5 그 남자는 혼잣말을 하고 있다. (the man, himself, talking to, is)

→ _____.

6 나는 그들에게 내 표를 보여주었다. (them, ticket, showed, I, my)

→ _____.

7 나는 내 펜을 가지고 오지 않았다. Molly가 내게 그녀의 것을 빌려줬다. (me, Molly, hers, lent)

→ I didn't bring my pen. _____.

CHAPTER 07 대명사

this, that, it

( ) 안에서 알맞은 말을 고르시오.

1 (This, These) is the list of the guests.

2 Are (this, these) your pencils?

3 I saw (it, that) man on TV last night.

4 (This, These) seats are only for kids.

5 A zookeeper is feeding (that, those) lions in the cage.

6 (This, It) is 10:00 p.m. We should go home now.

7 (That, Those) is the new elementary school.

8 Is (it, this) going to be rainy this afternoon?

빈칸에 알맞은 말을 보기에서 골라 쓰시오. (단, 한 번씩만 쓸 것)

[1-4]

보기	this	that	these	it

1 Did you make _____ model airplanes yourself?

2 _____ is the Statue of Liberty over there.

3 _____ is my room. Please come in.

4 _____ is very warm today. You don't have to wear a coat.

[5-8]

보기	this	that	those	it

5 Look at _____ people on the beach.

6 Today is Children's Day. _____ is May 5.

7 Did you see _____ bird on the roof?

8 A: Hi, John. _____ is my brother Jeff.
   B: Nice to meet you, Jeff.

C ( ) 안의 말을 이용하여 질문에 대한 대답을 쓰시오.

1 A: What time is it now?

B: _____ . (2:30 p.m.)

2 A: What day is it today?

B: _____ . (Thursday)

3 A: What is the weather like?

B: _____ . (very hot)

4 A: Do you have the time?

B: _____ . (eight o'clock)

5 A: How far is it from Seoul to Busan?

B: _____ . (about 400 km)

6 A: How is the weather in Daejeon now?

B: _____ . (snowy)

7 A: What is the date today?

B: _____ . (December 2)

D 밑줄 친 부분이 올바르면 ○표, 틀리면 바르게 고치시오.

1 This is Monday today. _____

2 Are this your shoes? _____

3 These is my phone number. _____

4 It's May 15 tomorrow. _____

5 Can you see those tall building over there? _____

6 We should fix this bikes. _____

7 That is 9:00 p.m. I'm going to watch the news. _____

8 Robin will give those shirt to the children. _____

WRITING PRACTICE

Q Answer Key p.28

A   우리말과 일치하도록 ( ) 안의 말을 이용하여 문장을 완성하시오.

1   지금은 12시 정각이다. (twelve o'clock)

→ _____ now.

2   이 오렌지들은 달다. (oranges)

→ _____ are sweet.

3   나는 저 사진들을 하와이에서 찍었다. (photos)

→ I took _____ in Hawaii.

4   이 옷들은 네 거니? (clothes)

→ Are _____ yours?

5   선반에 있는 저 책을 볼 수 있을까요? (book)

→ Can I see _____ on the shelf?

6   그 역에서부터 우리 집까지는 겨우 100m이다. (only a hundred meters)

→ _____ from the station to my house.

7   이 포스터는 굉장하다. (poster)

→ _____ is amazing.

B   우리말과 일치하도록 ( ) 안에 주어진 말을 바르게 배열하시오.

1   이 애는 내 여동생이야. (my, this, little sister, is)

→ _____.

2   오늘이 토요일이니? (today, is, Saturday, it)

→ _____?

3   저것들은 내 장갑이 아니다. (gloves, are, my, not, those)

→ _____.

4   내일은 날씨가 흐릴 것이다. (tomorrow, be, it, cloudy, will)

→ _____.

5   저것이 Pam의 성적표니? (Pam's, is, that, report card)

→ _____?

6   이 사람들이 그 아이들을 구했다. (the children, people, saved, these)

→ _____.

UNIT
03

A

one, some, any

🔍 Answer Key p.28

( ) 안에서 알맞은 말을 고르시오.

1 We don't have (any, some) water.

2 Do you want (any, some) french fries?

3 This is Emma's doll. She bought (one, it) in China.

4 I looked for coins, but I didn't find (any, some).

5 Is there (any, some) cheese in the refrigerator?

6 Where is my English textbook? I need (it, one) now.

7 Susan bought a blue bag. I bought a red (one, ones).

8 Will you have (any, some) orange juice?

9 My brother lost his watch. He needs a new (it, one).

10 Do you need bread? I'll get you (any, some) from the bakery.

B

빈칸에 알맞은 말을 보기에서 골라 대화를 완성하시오.

보기	one	ones	it

1 A: Did you watch *Superstar A* last night?
   B: No, I didn't see _____.

2 A: Did you buy red roses?
   B: No, I bought white _____.

3 A: Is this your suitcase?
   B: No, mine is the brown _____ over there.

4 A: I made this pie for my father.
   B: _____ looks delicious.

5 A: Andy doesn't wear short pants.
   B: Right. He always wears long _____.

6 A: We missed our bus to London.
   B: Don't worry. We can take the next _____ at 12:15 p.m.

빈칸에 some 또는 any를 넣어 대화를 완성하시오.

1 A: I don't have _____ money now.
   B: Don't worry. I'll lend you some.

2 A: Did you go to the mall yesterday?
   B: Yes. I bought _____ socks there.

3 A: Do you have any questions for me?
   B: No, I don't have _____.

4 A: Please help yourself to more chicken.
   B: No, thanks. I'll just have _____ water.

5 A: I made cookies. Will you have _____?
   B: Yes, please.

6 A: Do you have _____ information about the hotel?
   B: No, I don't.

밑줄 친 부분이 올바르면 ○표, 틀리면 바르게 고치시오.

1 He didn't give me some help.   _____

2 Will you have some green tea?   _____

3 Are there some clothing stores near here?   _____

4 You should eat some vegetables.   _____

5 Did you move my book? I can't find one.   _____

6 My boots look so old. I should buy new one.   _____

7 There weren't some cars on the road.   _____

8 Tom recommended this movie. I enjoyed one.   _____

9 Fred's bike is the red ones over there.   _____

WRITING PRACTICE

Answer Key p.28

A 우리말과 일치하도록 ( ) 안의 말을 이용하여 문장을 완성하시오.

1 우리는 동물원에서 어떤 원숭이도 못 봤다. (monkeys)

→ We didn't see _____ at the zoo.

2 너 아이스크림 좀 먹을래? (ice cream)

→ Will you have _____?

3 나는 내 스마트폰을 잃어버렸다. 나는 새것을 사야 한다. (new)

→ I lost my smartphone. I should buy a _____.

4 저 포도들은 신선해 보여. 나는 조금 먹어볼래. (try)

→ Those grapes look fresh. I'll _____.

5 이 신발들은 Edward의 것이다. 검은 것들이 내 것이다. (black)

→ These shoes are Edward's. The _____ are mine.

6 여기서 지갑을 봤니? 우리 누나가 그것을 찾는 중이야. (look for)

→ Did you see a purse here? My sister _____.

B 우리말과 일치하도록 ( ) 안에 주어진 말을 바르게 배열하시오.

1 내 우산은 저 파란 것이다. (one, umbrella, that, is, my, blue)

→ _____.

2 초콜릿을 좀 먹겠니? (you, chocolate, will, have, some)

→ _____?

3 수영장에 아이들이 몇 명 있었다. (there, children, some, were)

→ _____ in the pool.

4 나는 오늘 아침에 책을 한 권 빌렸다. 나는 그것을 읽고 있다. (reading, I, it, am)

→ I borrowed a book this morning. _____.

5 그릇에 수프가 조금도 없다. (isn't, soup, any, there)

→ _____ in the bowl.

6 컵이 필요하니? 싱크대 안에 하나가 있어. (is, in the sink, one, there)

→ Do you need a cup? _____.

7 너는 여름 휴가에 대해 어떤 아이디어라도 있니? (ideas, have, any, you, do)

→ _____ for summer vacation?

REVIEW TEST

[1-4] 빈칸에 들어갈 알맞은 말을 고르시오.

1

Jimin and Yumi will be late. I have to wait for _____.

① me　　② him　　③ her
④ us　　⑤ them

2

Is this toothbrush _____?

① you　　② your　　③ yours
④ yourself　⑤ yourselves

3

_____ cars in the parking lot are nice.

① This　　② That　　③ Those
④ It　　⑤ They

4

_____ is 8:50 a.m. The class will begin soon.

① I　　② It　　③ This
④ That　⑤ They

[5-6] 빈칸에 들어갈 말이 바르게 짝지어진 것을 고르시오.

5

• Do you want ____(A)____ hot cocoa?
• I found ____(B)____ socks under the sofa.

	(A)		(B)
①	any	……	this
②	any	……	that
③	some	……	this
④	some	……	these
⑤	some	……	it

6

• Sorry, I didn't bring ____(A)____ gifts.
• I liked the white shirt, but Mom bought me a black ____(B)____.

	(A)		(B)
①	some	……	one
②	some	……	it
③	any	……	one
④	any	……	ones
⑤	any	……	it

빈출

7 밑줄 친 it의 쓰임이 나머지 넷과 <u>다른</u> 것은?

① Where did you find <u>it</u>?
② I like this toy. <u>It</u> is cute.
③ <u>It</u>'s my father's trophy.
④ <u>It</u> is cloudy and windy today.
⑤ That is my wallet. Give <u>it</u> to me.

[8-10] 빈칸에 알맞은 말을 보기에서 골라 대화를 완성하시오.
(단, 한 번씩만 쓸 것)

보기	one ones it

8
A: Where is your cell phone?
B: I put _____ in my pocket.

9
A: Do you need this eraser?
B: No, thanks. I already have
_____.

10
A: Can you show me other shoes?
B: Okay. These are the best-selling
_____ in our store.

11 다음 중 대화가 자연스럽지 <u>않은</u> 것은?

① A: Can I get you a towel?
   B: Thanks, but I have one.
② A: Did you get my package?
   B: Yes, I got it this morning.
③ A: Did you do well on the test?
   B: No, I made some mistakes.
④ A: We need bananas.
   B: I'll get some from the market.
⑤ A: Do you have any problems?
   B: No, I don't have some.

[12-13] 다음 중 밑줄 친 부분이 잘못된 것을 고르시오.

12 ① I bought <u>some</u> magazines.
② They didn't sing <u>some</u> songs.
③ There isn't <u>any</u> paper on the desk.
④ Did you have <u>any</u> fruit today?
⑤ Do you want <u>some</u> sugar in your coffee?

13 ① Did you tell <u>them</u> the truth?
② <u>It's</u> 6:15 p.m. We'll take a break now.
③ The children are riding <u>theirs</u> bikes.
④ What's the answer? I don't know <u>it</u>.
⑤ These letters are for me, and those <u>ones</u> are for you.

14 다음 중 밑줄 친 부분을 <u>잘못</u> 고친 것은?

① Can you help <u>we</u>? → us
② <u>That</u> is July 10 today. → It
③ I didn't bring <u>some</u> food today. → any
④ Look at <u>this</u> beautiful roses. → that
⑤ Kevin enjoyed <u>him</u> on the trip.
   → himself

15 다음 우리말을 영어로 바르게 옮긴 것은?

Henry는 자기 자신을 잘 안다.

① Henry knows him well.
② Henry knows his well.
③ Henry knows himself well.
④ Henry knows oneself well.
⑤ Henry knows itself well.

서술형

[16-17] 밑줄 친 부분을 대신하는 알맞은 대명사를 빈칸에 쓰시오.

16 I like <u>this restaurant</u> because _____ food is great.

17 Take these keys to <u>Jonathan</u>. They are _____.

서술형

[18-19] 대화가 성립되도록 ( ) 안에서 알맞은 말을 골라 쓰시오.

18 A: Hello, I'm looking for a camera. I want a cheap ⓐ (one, ones).
B: This black model is good.
A: All right. How much is ⓑ (one, it)?

ⓐ _____ ⓑ _____

19 A: What are you doing?
B: I'm baking ⓐ (any, some) cookies. ⓑ (It, They) are for Peter.

ⓐ _____ ⓑ _____

서술형

[20-21] 우리말과 일치하도록 ( ) 안의 말을 이용하여 문장을 완성하시오.

20 3월 25일이지만, 밖은 여전히 춥다. (March 25)

→ _____, but it is still cold outside.

21 도넛을 마음껏 드세요.
(help oneself to, the donuts)

→ Please _____.

서술형

[22-23] 우리말과 일치하도록 ( ) 안에 주어진 말을 바르게 배열하시오.

22 이곳에서부터 공원까지는 300m이다.
(300 meters, is, from here, it)

→ _____ to the park.

23 이 빌딩들은 매우 높다.
(buildings, very, are, these, tall)

→ _____.

서술형 고난도

[24-25] 어법상 <u>틀린</u> 부분을 찾아 바르게 고치시오.

24 A: Did you write this poem yourself?
B: Yes. I wrote them in the English class. (1개)

25 A: Excuse me. Is there a bakery near here?
B: Yes, there is it on Oxford Road.
A: Thanks. Is it far?
B: No. It's right around the corner. You can't miss one. (2개)

UNIT 01

형용사

🔍 Answer Key p.29

A

( ) 안에서 알맞은 말을 고르시오.

1   The lake looks (peace, peaceful).

2   I don't have (many, much) time.

3   This is a (wonder, wonderful) house.

4   I bought (a few, a little) tomatoes.

5   Good food keeps you (health, healthy).

6   There is (few, little) juice in the bottle.

7   (Lot of, Lots of) tourists visit Rome every year.

8   Is there (anything new, new anything) about Peter?

9   There were not (many, much) people in the movie theater.

10   (Strange someone, Someone strange) is following me.

B

빈칸에 알맞은 말을 보기에서 골라 쓰시오. (단, 한 번씩만 쓸 것)

[1-4]

보기	easy	long	soft	thirsty

1   My pillow feels _____.

2   That snake has a _____ tail.

3   The test was _____. I got an A.

4   Can I have some water? I am _____.

[5-8]

보기	cloudy	heavy	perfect	scary

5   That horror movie was _____.

6   It's going to be _____ this afternoon.

7   This book will be a _____ gift for Max.

8   Can you help me? These bags are _____.

( ) 안의 말 중 알맞은 것을 골라 문장을 완성하시오.

1 (many, much)

a. I don't have _____ money now.

b. We didn't take _____ photos at the beach.

2 (a few, a little)

a. Jane puts _____ syrup in her coffee.

b. I put _____ coins in the machine.

3 (few, little)

a. We have _____ choices.

b. There is _____ food in the refrigerator.

4 (many, much)

a. There are not _____ taxis on the street.

b. I didn't find _____ information on the internet.

5 (a few, a little)

a. I'll give _____ water to these plants.

b. We saw Henry _____ minutes ago.

6 (few, little)

a. _____ people know about his novels.

b. Tom has _____ experience in the field.

밑줄 친 부분이 올바르면 ○표, 틀리면 바르게 고치시오.

1 Mandy has a <u>puppy cute</u>.   _____

2 We have <u>a few</u> questions about it.   _____

3 I have to tell you <u>important something</u>.   _____

4 We saw <u>a lot of</u> animals at the zoo.   _____

5 I heard an <u>interestingly</u> story about him.   _____

6 This soup tastes <u>salt and spicy</u>.   _____

WRITING PRACTICE

🔍 Answer Key p-29

A 우리말과 일치하도록 ( ) 안의 말을 이용하여 문장을 완성하시오.

1 곰은 위험한 동물이다. (dangerous, animals)

→ Bears are _____ .

2 이 스카프는 너를 따뜻하게 유지해 줄 거야. (keep, warm)

→ This scarf will _____ .

3 지난 겨울에는 많은 눈이 오지 않았다. (snow)

→ We didn't have _____ last winter.

4 어제는 건조한 날이었다. (dry, day)

→ It was a _____ yesterday.

5 Dan은 요즘 행복해 보인다. (look, happy)

→ Dan _____ these days.

6 이 박물관에는 많은 그림들이 있다. (paintings)

→ There are _____ in this museum.

7 그들의 신상품은 특별한 것이 없다. (special, nothing)

→ Their latest product is _____ .

B 우리말과 일치하도록 ( ) 안에 주어진 말을 바르게 배열하시오.

1 그녀는 갈색 눈을 가지고 있다. (has, eyes, brown, she)

→ _____ .

2 차가운 뭔가를 마실 수 있을까요? (I, have, cold, can, something)

→ _____ ?

3 나는 Nancy로부터 몇 개의 이메일을 받았다. (got, I, a, emails, few)

→ _____ from Nancy.

4 그들은 큰 다리를 짓고 있다. (big, a, building, are, bridge)

→ They _____ .

5 그의 농담은 나를 화나게 만들었다. (angry, jokes, his, me, made)

→ _____

6 저 식당은 훌륭했다. (was, restaurant, that, excellent)

→ _____ .

UNIT
02

부사

A

( ) 안에서 알맞은 말을 고르시오.

1 The water was (very cold, cold very).

2 I understand English (good, well).

3 Nora answered the phone (quick, quickly).

4 Steve fixed the computer (easy, easily).

5 We arrived at the airport (late, lately).

6 He spoke (confident, confidently) at the meeting.

7 My mother (never drinks, drinks never) coffee.

8 I (always am, am always) sleepy after lunch.

9 Sandra practiced (hard, hardly) for the school play.

10 Mary danced (beautiful, beautifully) on the stage.

B

밑줄 친 부사가 꾸며주는 말에 동그라미 하시오.

1 Helen acted strangely.

2 He takes pictures well.

3 I read the directions carefully.

4 The weather is so hot today.

5 Sadly, the old man died alone.

6 Mary studied very hard last night.

7 She touched the baby's head gently.

8 Chris climbed really high mountains.

9 My father came home early from work.

10 This medicine is quite dangerous for kids.

C ( ) 안의 말을 알맞은 곳에 넣어 문장을 완성하시오.

1 She drinks milk in the morning. (usually)

→ She _____.

2 You should wash your hands before meals. (always)

→ You _____.

3 Naomi talks about herself. (seldom)

→ Naomi _____.

4 John wears jeans to work. (never)

→ _____ to work.

5 Jessie is polite to her neighbors. (always)

→ Jessie _____.

6 Sam visits his grandparents. (often)

→ _____ his grandparents.

D 밑줄 친 부분이 올바르면 ○표, 틀리면 바르게 고치시오.

1 I wasn't driving <u>fastly</u>. _____

2 It is raining <u>heavy</u> outside. _____

3 We <u>hardly</u> see each other. _____

4 I <u>play sometimes</u> tennis with Fred. _____

5 The accident happened <u>sudden</u>. _____

6 He felt <u>lonely</u> among the strangers. _____

7 I <u>take often</u> a nap after lunch. _____

8 We <u>highly</u> appreciate your help. _____

9 Michael <u>happy</u> opened our presents. _____

10 You should not speak <u>loudly</u> in the library. _____

WRITING PRACTICE

Answer Key p.29

A 우리말과 일치하도록 (   ) 안의 말을 이용하여 문장을 완성하시오.

1 해가 밝게 빛나고 있다. (bright)

→ The sun is shining _____ .

2 이 공원은 아침에 매우 활기차다. (very, lively)

→ This park is _____ in the morning.

3 Robert는 스포츠를 거의 보지 않는다. (rarely, watch)

→ Robert _____ sports.

4 Jamie는 전쟁에서 용감하게 싸웠다. (brave)

→ Jamie fought _____ in the war.

5 Kevin은 공을 공중으로 높이 쳤다. (hit the ball, high)

→ Kevin _____ into the air.

6 놀랍게도, 그녀는 복권에 당첨됐다. (surprising)

→ _____ , she won the lottery.

7 Steve는 자주 그의 비밀번호를 잊어버린다. (often, forget)

→ Steve _____ his password.

B 우리말과 일치하도록 (   ) 안에 주어진 말을 바르게 배열하시오.

1 오늘은 꽤 춥다. (quite, it, cold, is)

→ _____ today.

2 Karen은 항상 동물들에게 친절하다. (kind, always, Karen, is)

→ _____ to animals.

3 수영 강습은 정말 일찍 시작한다. (starts, early, the swimming lesson, really)

→ _____ .

4 그녀는 좀처럼 학교에 늦지 않는다. (late for, is, hardly, school)

→ She _____ .

5 나는 절대로 그를 용서하지 않을 거야. (will, him, I, forgive, never)

→ _____ .

6 그는 일 년에 거의 10kg이 늘었다. (gained, nearly, he, 10 kg)

→ _____ in a year.

UNIT 03

원급, 비교급, 최상급

Answer Key p.29

A ( ) 안에서 알맞은 말을 고르시오.

1 This metal is as (hard, harder) as a diamond.

2 I got a (more good, better) grade than James.

3 Can you speak (slow, more slowly)?

4 This is the (older, oldest) castle in Europe.

5 This comic book is (much, more) funnier than that one.

6 Susan came to school as early (as, than) Michael.

7 They made the (faster, fastest) cars in the world.

8 This watermelon is (bigger, more big) than that one.

9 They arrived at the meeting room (later, latest) than us.

10 Tony is the (more intelligent, most intelligent) man in his company.

B ( ) 안의 말을 이용하여 다음 두 문장을 보기와 같이 한 문장으로 만드시오.

> **보기** Mandy is fourteen years old. Sophia is fourteen years old too. (old)
> → Mandy is as old as Sophia.

1 Peter is 160 cm tall. Jack is 160 cm tall too. (tall)

→ Peter is _____ Jack.

2 My cat weighs 5 kg. My dog weighs 5 kg too. (heavy)

→ My cat is _____ my dog.

3 The fence is 4 ft. The wall is 4 ft too. (high)

→ The fence is _____ the wall.

4 I got an A on the math test. Dan got an A on the math test too. (well)

→ I did _____ Dan on the math test.

5 Jack studies two hours a day. Vicky studies two hours a day too. (much)

→ Jack studies _____ Vicky.

C ( ) 안의 말을 적절한 형태로 바꿔 비교급 문장을 완성하시오.

1 My cat is _____ yours. (fat)

2 Jason can jump _____ me. (high)

3 His handwriting is _____ mine. (bad)

4 Martin's room was _____ Jacob's. (dirty)

5 Alexander eats _____ me. (little)

6 She learns _____ other students. (fast)

7 These boxes are _____ those ones. (strong)

8 This computer game is _____ that one. (exciting)

9 A tumbler is _____ a paper cup. (useful)

10 The original novel is _____ the movie. (interesting)

D 빈칸에 알맞은 말을 보기에서 골라 적절한 형태로 바꿔 최상급 문장을 완성하시오. (단, 한 번씩만 쓸 것)

[1-3]

보기	expensive hot old

1 This is _____ building in the town. It's 800 years old.

2 Yesterday was _____ day in August. It was over 36°C.

3 Charles bought _____ camera in the shop. It was over $500.

[4-6]

보기	little diligent short

4 Jina is _____ worker in the company. She works very hard.

5 This is _____ way to the subway. We're only thirty meters away.

6 This hotel costs _____ money. I'll book a room.

WRITING PRACTICE

Answer Key p·30

A 우리말과 일치하도록 ( ) 안의 말을 이용하여 문장을 완성하시오.

1 이것은 세계에서 가장 깊은 호수이다. (deep)

→ This is _____ lake in the world.

2 Joe는 나보다 훨씬 더 용감하다. (much, brave)

→ Joe is _____ me.

3 이것은 올해 최악의 태풍이다. (bad, typhoon)

→ This is _____ of the year.

4 좋은 음식은 운동만큼 건강에 중요하다. (important)

→ Good food is _____ exercise for health.

5 그 서커스는 축제에서 가장 신나는 이벤트였다. (exciting)

→ The circus was _____ event at the festival.

6 그들의 새 집은 예전 집보다 더 클 것이다. (big)

→ Their new house will be _____ their old one.

7 Tommy는 다른 아이들보다 더 크게 소리 질렀다. (loudly)

→ Tommy screamed _____ the other kids.

B 우리말과 일치하도록 ( ) 안에 주어진 말을 바르게 배열하시오.

1 서울은 뉴욕만큼 붐빈다. (as, New York, is, crowded, as)

→ Seoul _____.

2 Lily는 너보다 춤을 더 못 춘다. (than, dances, you, worse)

→ Lily _____.

3 너의 아이디어가 Nick의 것보다 더 낫다. (is, your idea, than, better)

→ _____ Nick's.

4 이 케이크가 이 가게에서 최고의 디저트이다. (best, this cake, dessert, the, is)

→ _____ in this shop.

5 Andy의 목소리는 Mike의 것보다 훨씬 더 낮다. (a lot, is, than, lower, Mike's)

→ Andy's voice _____.

6 내 남동생은 나보다 더 빨리 자전거를 탄다. (rides, than, a bike, faster, me)

→ My brother _____.

REVIEW TEST

1 다음 중 형용사와 부사가 잘못 연결된 것은?

① sad – sadly   ② slow – slowly

③ easy – easily   ④ early – earlily

⑤ lucky – luckily

2 다음 중 형용사의 비교급이 잘못 연결된 것은?

① big – bigger   ② many – more

③ good – better   ④ happy – happier

⑤ wonderful – wonderfuler

[3-5] 빈칸에 들어갈 말로 알맞지 <u>않은</u> 것을 고르시오.

3

> Roger is _____ to his neighbors.

① kind   ② gentle   ③ rude

④ nicely   ⑤ friendly

4

> She invited _____ people to her house.

① a few   ② a little   ③ many

④ a lot of   ⑤ few

5

> This perfume smells _____ sweeter than that one.

① very   ② far   ③ much

④ even   ⑤ a lot

서술형   빈출

[6-8] 빈칸에 알맞은 말을 보기에서 골라 대화를 완성하시오. (단, 한 번씩만 쓸 것)

보기	many	a few	a little

6

> A: I feel tired.
> B: You should get _____ rest.

7

> A: Do I have any messages?
> B: Yes, Mr. Smith left _____ messages for you.

8

> A: Was the movie theater crowded?
> B: No, there were not _____ people in the theater.

9 밑줄 친 부분의 쓰임이 나머지 넷과 <u>다른</u> 것은?

① Fred took an <u>early</u> train.

② The bus arrived very <u>early</u>.

③ I went to bed <u>early</u> last night.

④ We have to book the hotel <u>early</u>.

⑤ Jane came home <u>early</u> yesterday.

빈출

[10-11] 빈칸에 들어갈 말이 바르게 짝지어진 것을 고르시오.

10
> • Her lie made me _____(A)_____.
> • A small bird is flying _____(B)_____ in the sky.

	(A)		(B)
①	anger	⋯⋯	high
②	angry	⋯⋯	high
③	angry	⋯⋯	highly
④	angrily	⋯⋯	high
⑤	angrily	⋯⋯	highly

11
> • I can't get up early _____(A)_____.
> • Today's weather is as _____(B)_____ as yesterday's.

	(A)		(B)
①	late	⋯⋯	nice
②	late	⋯⋯	nicely
③	lately	⋯⋯	nicer
④	lately	⋯⋯	nice
⑤	lately	⋯⋯	nicely

[12-13] 다음 중 밑줄 친 부분이 잘못된 것을 고르시오.

12 ① Mia <u>never wears</u> hats.

② The final exam was <u>quite difficult</u>.

③ Cathy's sister is <u>as tall as</u> Cathy.

④ My grandfather is <u>near ninety years old</u>.

⑤ There isn't <u>anything wrong</u> with my camera.

13 ① Cats can hear very <u>well</u>.

② I put <u>a little</u> butter in the pot.

③ James runs <u>as fast as</u> his brother.

④ My uncle is <u>richest</u> man in his town.

⑤ Dad <u>sometimes plays</u> chess with me.

서술형

[14-15] 대화가 성립되도록 ( ) 안에서 알맞은 말을 골라 쓰시오.

14 A: Today's music class was ⓐ (more, most) interesting than other days.

B: Yes. We listened to ⓑ (many, much) songs from the opera.

ⓐ _____ ⓑ _____

15 A: This summer is ⓐ (hotter, more hot) than last summer.

B: Right. And we have ⓑ (less, least) rain than last year too.

ⓐ _____ ⓑ _____

[16-17] 다음 우리말을 영어로 바르게 옮긴 것을 고르시오.

16 내게는 축구가 야구보다 더 신난다.

① Soccer is exciting than baseball to me.
② Soccer is very exciting than baseball to me.
③ Soccer is much exciting than baseball to me.
④ Soccer is a lot exciting than baseball to me.
⑤ Soccer is more exciting than baseball to me.

17 그는 세계에서 제일 성공한 남자이다.

① He is a successful man in the world.
② He is successfully man in the world.
③ He is most successful man in the world.
④ He is the most successful man in the world.
⑤ He is the most successfully man in the world.

서술형

[18-20] 우리말과 일치하도록 (   ) 안의 말을 이용하여 문장을 완성하시오.

18 그녀는 첼로보다 피아노를 더 잘 연주한다. (well)

→ She plays the piano _____ the cello.

19 한라산은 제주도에서 가장 높은 산이다.
(high, mountain)

→ Mt. Halla is _____ on Jeju Island.

20 주어진 단어를 바르게 배열할 때 두 번째에 오는 단어는?

for, late, are, they, meetings, rarely

① for   ② late   ③ are
④ meetings   ⑤ rarely

서술형

[21-22] 우리말과 일치하도록 (   ) 안에 주어진 말을 바르게 배열하시오.

21 우리는 학교에서 항상 교복을 입는다.
(always, we, wear, school uniforms)

→ _____
at school.

22 Amy는 한국어를 매우 잘 말한다.
(very, speaks, Korean, Amy, well)

→ _____ .

서술형

[23-24] 밑줄 친 부분이 어법상 옳은지 판단하고, 틀리면 바르게 고치시오.

23 Laura learns everything <u>quick</u>.

(O / X) _____

24 I said <u>stupid something</u> to Nicole.

(O / X) _____

90

UNIT 01

to부정사의 명사적 용법

Q Answer Key p.30

A 밑줄 친 to부정사가 문장에서 주어, 목적어, 보어 중 어떤 역할을 하는지 쓰시오.

1 Mr. Jones decided <u>to sell</u> his house. _____

2 It is interesting <u>to travel</u> with friends. _____

3 His dream is <u>to open</u> a bakery. _____

4 It is always fun <u>to talk</u> with Jay. _____

5 Kelly wants <u>to meet</u> her favorite singer. _____

6 It is dangerous <u>to play</u> with knives. _____

7 Paul hopes <u>to finish</u> his report on time. _____

8 My plan is <u>to stay</u> in Italy for three days. _____

9 I need <u>to leave</u> before 10:00 a.m. tomorrow. _____

10 It is bad <u>to steal</u> other people's things. _____

B 주어진 동사를 동사원형 또는 to부정사 중 적절한 형태로 써서 문장을 완성하시오.

1 see a. Did you _____ the parade yesterday?

b. It was amazing _____ the sunset.

2 be a. He hopes _____ a basketball player.

b. My father will _____ fifty years old next year.

3 get a. I want _____ good grades on the final exam.

b. Did you _____ my email this morning?

4 take a. James doesn't _____ piano lessons.

b. It is expensive _____ a taxi downtown.

5 learn a. Jessica's plan is _____ how to swim.

b. Did you _____ this song at school?

C 빈칸에 알맞은 말을 보기에서 골라 적절한 형태로 바꿔 문장을 완성하시오. (단, 한 번씩만 쓸 것)

[1-4]

보기	what/say	where/put	how/use	whether/invite

1 Jamie isn't sure _____ the mirror.

2 Julie taught me _____ the copy machine.

3 They didn't know _____ about the news.

4 Austin didn't decide _____ Emily to the party or not.

[5-8]

보기	when/water	what/wear	how/get	whom/choose

5 I don't know _____ this plant.

6 I'm not sure _____ as class president.

7 He didn't tell me _____ to his office.

8 Did you decide _____ to Jane's wedding?

D 밑줄 친 부분이 올바르면 ○표, 틀리면 바르게 고치시오.

1 I hope <u>see</u> you again soon. _____

2 It is hard <u>to trains</u> wild animals. _____

3 This sign shows us <u>where go</u>. _____

4 Kevin decided <u>to not watch</u> the game. _____

5 They are planning <u>to work</u> with us. _____

6 His job is <u>take</u> care of sick people. _____

7 Jason taught me <u>how to ride</u> a horse. _____

8 It is good <u>drink</u> a lot of water every day. _____

WRITING PRACTICE

Answer Key p.30

A 우리말과 일치하도록 ( ) 안의 말을 이용하여 문장을 완성하시오.

1 그들은 그 박물관을 방문하기로 계획했다. (plan, visit)

→ They _____ the museum.

2 우리는 늦었어. 서두를 필요가 있어. (need, hurry)

→ We're late. We _____.

3 그녀는 나와 영화관에 갈 것을 약속했다. (promise, go)

→ She _____ to the movie theater with me.

4 그 시를 암기하는 것은 어려웠다. (hard, memorize)

→ It was _____ the poem.

5 George는 우리 음악 동호회에 가입하길 원한다. (want, join)

→ George _____ our music club.

6 Sam은 키가 매우 커. 그를 찾는 건 쉬울 거야. (easy, find)

→ Sam is very tall. It will be _____ him.

7 Mark는 그 학교에 지원할지 말지 결정해야만 한다. (whether, apply for)

→ Mark has to decide _____ the school or not.

B 우리말과 일치하도록 ( ) 안에 주어진 말을 바르게 배열하시오.

1 다른 사람들을 돕는 것은 멋진 일이다. (wonderful, help, is, it, to)

→ _____ other people.

2 나는 치과에 가기로 결심했다. (to, the dentist, go to, decided)

→ I _____.

3 그들은 어디에 그 그림을 걸어야 할지 몰랐다. (hang, where, the painting, to)

→ They didn't know _____.

4 그의 목표는 최고의 축구선수가 되는 것이다. (to, soccer player, the best, be, is)

→ His goal _____.

5 그는 기차로 여행하는 것을 좋아한다. (to, by train, travel, likes)

→ He _____.

6 이 게임을 어떻게 하는지 내게 보여줄 수 있니? (to, this game, how, play)

→ Can you show me _____?

UNIT 02

to부정사의 형용사적, 부사적 용법

A 밑줄 친 to부정사가 꾸며주는 말에 동그라미 하시오.

1 I need a friend to help me.

2 You'll have a chance to see wild animals.

3 Peter is not a man to tell lies.

4 We don't have a plan to go there.

5 I don't have any money to lend you.

6 Do you want something warm to eat?

7 I'm looking for a person to teach me English.

8 There are a lot of places to visit in San Francisco.

B 자연스러운 문장이 되도록 알맞게 연결하시오.

[1-4]

1 I went to the bank •   • ⓐ to eat some pasta.

2 He sent Amy some flowers •   • ⓑ to travel around America.

3 We went to a restaurant •   • ⓒ to get some money.

4 Mina is studying English •   • ⓓ to make her happy.

[5-8]

5 I am sorry •   • ⓐ to find herself famous.

6 The singer woke up •   • ⓑ to bother you.

7 They were happy •   • ⓒ to be the president of Korea.

8 The boy grew up •   • ⓓ to get free movie tickets.

C 보기에서 알맞은 말을 골라 ( ) 안의 말과 함께 써서 문장을 완성하시오. (단, 한 번씩만 쓸 것)

[1-4]

보기	go	read	take	eat

1 This is a good _____ a picture. (place)

2 It's already 11:00 p.m. It's _____ to bed. (time)

3 We'll buy some _____ in this bookstore. (books)

4 Is there _____ in the refrigerator? I'm hungry. (anything)

[5-8]

보기	watch	open	solve	tell

5 These are the _____ this door. (keys)

6 Do you have a minute? I have _____ you. (something)

7 She looks serious. She must have some _____. (problems)

8 Are there any good _____? I'm bored. (videos)

D to부정사를 이용하여 두 문장을 연결하시오.

1 We were angry. We met some rude people.

→ We were angry _____.

2 I am saving money. I'm going to buy a laptop.

→ I am saving money _____.

3 She was surprised. She met Robin at the party.

→ She was surprised _____.

4 I came home early. I wanted to talk with my mom.

→ I came home early _____.

5 Dan wrote an email. He wanted to complain about the service.

→ Dan wrote an email _____.

6 Naomi and Charlie were excited. They had their first baby.

→ Naomi and Charlie were excited _____.

WRITING PRACTICE

🔍 Answer Key p-30

A 우리말과 일치하도록 ( ) 안의 말을 이용하여 문장을 완성하시오.

1 Henry는 산책을 하기 위해 밖에 나갔다. (take a walk)

→ Henry went out _____.

2 그는 백 살까지 살았다. (live, be)

→ He _____ a hundred years old.

3 그녀는 새 시계를 갖게 되어 기뻤다. (happy, get)

→ She was _____ a new watch.

4 그들은 그들과 함께 일할 사람을 찾고 있다. (someone, work)

→ They're looking for _____ with them.

5 나는 오늘 바빠. 해야 할 숙제가 많아. (homework, do)

→ I'm busy today. I have a lot of _____.

6 나는 크리스마스 선물을 사기 위해 쇼핑몰에 갈 것이다. (buy)

→ I'll go to the mall _____ Christmas presents.

B 우리말과 일치하도록 ( ) 안에 주어진 말을 바르게 배열하시오.

1 우리는 경기에 져서 슬펐다. (lose, to, were, the game, sad)

→ We _____.

2 그 남자는 자라서 요리사가 되었다. (be, grew up, to, a cook)

→ The man _____.

3 나는 겨울에 입을 따뜻한 것이 필요하다. (wear, warm, to, something)

→ I need _____ in winter.

4 Jane은 시험에 합격하기 위해 열심히 공부했다. (the exam, hard, pass, to, studied)

→ Jane _____.

5 그녀는 콘서트에 갈 시간이 없다. (go to, time, to, have, the concert)

→ She doesn't _____.

6 나는 회의에 대해 물어보기 위해 그에게 전화했다. (ask, him, to, called)

→ I _____ about the meeting.

7 우리는 그 사고에 대해 들어서 충격을 받았다. (hear, shocked, to, about the accident)

→ We were _____.

UNIT 03

동명사의 역할

Answer Key p-30

A

밑줄 친 동명사가 문장에서 주어, 목적어, 보어 중 어떤 역할을 하는지 쓰시오.

1 Learning science is fun. _____

2 Erica is afraid of being alone. _____

3 His favorite activity is riding a bicycle. _____

4 Going to a rock concert makes me excited. _____

5 Do you enjoy watching reality shows? _____

6 Robert has to keep smiling at the guests. _____

7 His hobby is writing poems. _____

8 She gave up solving the math problem. _____

9 You should quit using your smartphone in the dark. _____

B

( ) 안에서 알맞은 말을 고르시오.

1 We talked about (going, to go) to Africa.

2 The National Gallery is worth (visiting, to visiting).

3 His favorite activity is (paint, painting) pictures.

4 (Have, Having) breakfast is a healthy habit.

5 I feel (watching, like watching) an action movie.

6 My brother is busy (doing, to do) homework.

7 (Wearing not, Not wearing) a helmet is dangerous.

8 Would you mind (closing, to close) the window?

C 빈칸에 알맞은 말을 보기에서 골라 적절한 형태로 바꿔 문장을 완성하시오. (단, 한 번씩만 쓸 것)

보기	drink	bite	listen	turn	write	wait	sell

1 Do you enjoy _____ to the radio?

2 He finished _____ an essay.

3 Do you mind _____ off the light?

4 Maria was late, so I kept _____ for her.

5 She avoids _____ too much coffee.

6 You should quit _____ your nails.

7 They gave up _____ their house.

D 밑줄 친 부분이 올바르면 ○표, 틀리면 바르게 고치시오.

1 My hobby is <u>writing</u> posts on my blog. _____

2 Are you interested in <u>study</u> in Australia? _____

3 Adam often goes <u>surfing</u> in the sea. _____

4 Laura is good at <u>cook</u> Italian food. _____

5 They kept <u>talked</u> about the news. _____

6 I'm sorry for <u>coming not</u> to your party. _____

7 <u>Choose</u> a present for Dad was difficult. _____

8 He couldn't avoid <u>to hit</u> a tree. _____

9 How about <u>going shopping</u> this weekend? _____

WRITING PRACTICE

🔍 Answer Key p.31

A 우리말과 일치하도록 ( ) 안의 말을 이용하여 문장을 완성하시오.

1 나는 나쁜 성적을 받을 것이 걱정이 된다. (worried about, get)

→ I'm _____ poor grades.

2 이 제품은 살 만한 가치가 있다. (be worth, buy)

→ This product _____.

3 우리의 다음 단계는 해결책을 찾는 것이다. (find out, the solution)

→ Our next step is _____.

4 나는 오늘 저녁에 외식하고 싶다. (feel like, eat out)

→ I _____ tonight.

5 그는 신문 읽는 것을 끝마쳤다. (finish, read)

→ He _____ the newspaper.

6 Sarah는 나의 질문에 답하는 것을 피했다. (avoid, answer)

→ Sarah _____ my question.

7 우리는 비닐봉지를 사용하는 것을 중단할 것이다. (stop, use)

→ We will _____ plastic bags.

B 우리말과 일치하도록 ( ) 안에 주어진 말을 바르게 배열하시오.

1 Claire와 John은 토요일에 낚시를 갈 것이다. (fishing, go, will)

→ Claire and John _____ on Saturday.

2 저는 작은 방을 사용해도 상관없어요. (mind, I, using, don't)

→ _____ a small room.

3 Jason은 기타를 연주하는 것을 즐긴다. (playing, enjoys, the guitar)

→ Jason _____.

4 나는 중국어 배우는 것을 그만두지 않을 것이다. (learning, Chinese, quit)

→ I won't _____.

5 가족과 함께 시간을 보내는 것은 중요하다. (spending, with, time, family)

→ _____ is important.

6 Kate가 가장 좋아하는 활동은 공원에서 달리는 것이다. (the park, running, is, in)

→ Kate's favorite activity _____.

REVIEW TEST

[1-3] 빈칸에 들어갈 알맞은 말을 고르시오.

1

_____ is impossible to cancel the show.

① He   ② It   ③ This
④ That   ⑤ What

2

I want _____ in the race.

① run   ② runs   ③ ran
④ to run   ⑤ to runs

3

He kept _____ about his girlfriend.

① think   ② thinks   ③ thinking
④ to think   ⑤ to thinking

빈출

[4-5] 다음 중 보기의 밑줄 친 부분과 쓰임이 같은 것을 고르시오.

4   보기   I promised <u>to meet</u> her at 1:00 p.m.

① I'm sad <u>to leave</u>.
② I need <u>to fix</u> my computer.
③ His goal is <u>to become</u> a lawyer.
④ They sat down <u>to have</u> lunch.
⑤ It is difficult <u>to exercise</u> every day.

5   보기   Sandra's goal is <u>winning</u> the soccer game.

① <u>Making</u> a study plan is important.
② She stopped <u>reading</u> the newspaper.
③ My hobby is <u>collecting</u> movie posters.
④ He is avoiding <u>meeting</u> Rachel.
⑤ I'm afraid of <u>changing</u> my school.

서술형

[6-8] 빈칸에 알맞은 말을 보기에서 골라 대화를 완성하시오. (단, 한 번씩만 쓸 것)

보기   what   when   how

6

A: Can you tell me _____ to get to the subway station?
B: Sure. Just go straight.

7

A: I'm not sure _____ to buy for Mom's birthday.
B: How about a scarf? She'll like that.

8

A: I don't know _____ to visit Mr. Evans.
B: Why don't you call him first?

서술형

[9-10] 빈칸에 공통으로 들어갈 말을 쓰시오.

9
- My wish is _____ go to my favorite singer's concert.
- He doesn't have enough money _____ buy a VIP ticket.

10
- I'm not sure _____ to join the movie club or not.
- I don't know _____ to laugh or not.

빈출

[11-12] 밑줄 친 부분의 쓰임이 나머지 넷과 다른 것을 고르시오.

11
① There is no reason to hurry.
② We have a test to take tomorrow.
③ Will you have something to drink?
④ I read this book to write a report.
⑤ He didn't bring a sweater to wear.

12
① He wants to take a nap.
② Steve needs to wear glasses.
③ She decided to quit her job.
④ I promised to come home early.
⑤ My goal is to clean the whole house today.

[13-14] 다음 중 밑줄 친 부분이 잘못된 것을 고르시오.

13
① It is important doing your best.
② Do you have anything to tell me?
③ What do you want to be in the future?
④ We kept knocking on the door.
⑤ I went to Busan to see my cousin.

14
① It is time to start a new project.
② My hobby is updating my blog.
③ Do you know how make pizza?
④ He didn't give up looking for a job.
⑤ She grew up to become a famous dancer.

15 다음 중 고쳐 쓴 문장이 어법상 옳은 것은?
① That isn't easy to train a dog.
   → That isn't easy training a dog.
② I don't mind share the room.
   → I don't mind to share the room.
③ I was to tired too meet you.
   → I was too tired to meet you.
④ She was busy to helping her mom.
   → She was busy help her mom.
⑤ He's not enough old to drive a car.
   → He's not enough old driving a car.

서술형

[16-17] 대화가 성립되도록 ( ) 안에서 알맞은 말을 골라 쓰시오.

16
A: Thank you for ⓐ (visit, visiting) my house.
B: My pleasure. I'm happy ⓑ (coming, to come) here.

ⓐ _____ ⓑ _____

17
A: It wasn't easy ⓐ (get, to get) good grades on the final exams.
B: Right. I'm afraid of ⓑ (showing, to show) my report card to my parents.

ⓐ _____   ⓑ _____

[18-19] 다음 우리말을 영어로 바르게 옮긴 것을 고르시오.

18
나는 네게 보여줄 멋진 것을 갖고 있어.

① I have nice something to show you.
② I have something nice to show you.
③ I have something to show you nice.
④ I have to show nice something you.
⑤ I have to show something nice you.

19
우리는 많은 애플리케이션을 사용하는 것을 즐긴다.

① We enjoy use many applications.
② We enjoy many applications use.
③ We enjoy using many applications.
④ We enjoy many applications using.
⑤ We enjoy to use many applications.

서술형
[20-21] 우리말과 일치하도록 ( ) 안의 말을 이용하여 문장을 완성하시오.

20
너는 너무 많은 탄산음료를 마시는 것을 피해야 한다.
(avoid, drink)

→ You should _____ too much soda.

21
우리는 그들에게 작별 인사를 하게 되어 슬펐다.
(sad, say)

→ We were _____ goodbye to them.

서술형
[22-23] 우리말과 일치하도록 ( ) 안에 주어진 말을 바르게 배열하시오.

22
그녀는 신선한 공기를 쐬기 위해 창문을 열었다.
(get, opened, to, the window, some fresh air)

→ She _____.

23
그의 목표는 돈을 낭비하지 않는 것이다.
(not, money, is, wasting)

→ His goal _____.

서술형
[24-25] 밑줄 친 부분이 어법상 옳은지 판단하고, 틀리면 바르게 고치시오.

24
It is bad making fun of others.

(O / X) _____

25
This restaurant is worth visiting.

(O / X) _____

UNIT 01

장소를 나타내는 전치사

🔍 Answer Key p.31

A

( ) 안에서 알맞은 말을 고르시오.

1 Can you swim (in, on) the sea?

2 Noah is not (in, at) home right now.

3 The calendar is hanging (at, on) the wall.

4 Brian wasn't (at, on) school last week.

5 He is going to study music (in, on) Boston.

6 There are a lot of cars (at, on) the road.

7 Did you put your key (at, on) the table?

8 I was (at, on) Susan's birthday party last night.

9 I rode my bike from my house (in, to) the park.

10 (In, On) France, people have long breaks for their vacations.

B

( ) 안에서 알맞은 말을 골라 문장을 완성하시오.

1 (in, at)

a. Did you meet Paul _____ the airport?

b. My uncle has a clothing store _____ this building.

2 (at, under)

a. You should turn left _____ the next corner.

b. We sat _____ a tree to avoid the sun.

3 (on, behind)

a. Roy's apartment is _____ the eleventh floor.

b. Watch out! There is a big truck _____ you.

4 (near, from)

a. The young man traveled _____ Seoul to Busan.

b. There is an ice cream shop _____ the bookstore.

빈칸에 알맞은 말을 보기에서 골라 쓰시오. (단, 한 번씩만 쓸 것)

[1-4]

보기	in on over behind

1 He was lying _____ the beach.

2 Mickey threw the ball _____ the roof.

3 The supermarket is _____ the school.

4 You can see a big Christmas tree _____ New York.

[5-8]

보기	at on under near

5 City hall is _____ the fire station.

6 My cat was hiding _____ the sofa.

7 Nora dropped her pencil _____ the floor.

8 There were a few people _____ the bus stop.

다음 좌석표를 보고 빈칸에 알맞은 말을 보기에서 골라 쓰시오.

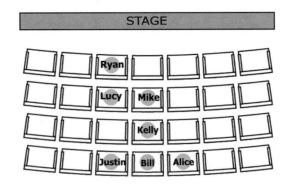

보기	in front of behind next to between

1 Ryan is sitting _____ Lucy.

2 Lucy is sitting _____ Mike.

3 Kelly is sitting _____ Mike.

4 Bill is sitting _____ Justin and Alice.

WRITING PRACTICE

🔍 Answer Key p-31

A 우리말과 일치하도록 ( ) 안의 말을 이용하여 문장을 완성하시오.

1 그 배는 다리 아래를 지나고 있다. (the bridge)

→ The ship is passing _____.

2 그녀는 팬케이크 위에 시럽을 조금 뿌렸다. (the pancakes)

→ She put some syrup _____.

3 그 비행기는 대서양 위를 날고 있다. (the Atlantic)

→ The plane is flying _____.

4 우리는 정원에 사과 나무 한 그루를 갖고 있다. (our garden)

→ We have an apple tree _____.

5 그들은 프런트 데스크에서 체크인했다. (the front desk)

→ They checked in _____.

6 Dan은 극장에서 그의 엄마와 아빠 사이에 앉았다. (his mom, dad)

→ Dan sat _____ in the theater.

7 집에서부터 지하철역까지 가는 데는 10분이 걸린다. (home, the subway station)

→ It takes ten minutes to get _____.

B 우리말과 일치하도록 ( ) 안에 주어진 말을 바르게 배열하시오.

1 그는 호수 근처에 산다. (the lake, lives, near, he)

→ _____.

2 그녀의 딸이 무대 위에서 노래하고 있다. (the stage, singing, on, is)

→ Her daughter _____.

3 경찰서는 제과점 맞은편에 있다. (from, the bakery, across, is)

→ The police station _____.

4 저 바구니 안에 빵이 조금 있다. (is, that basket, some bread, in)

→ There _____.

5 Andrew는 수업 시간에 내 뒤에 앉는다. (behind, in class, sits, me)

→ Andrew _____.

6 Susan은 거울 앞에 서 있다. (front, the mirror, in, of)

→ Susan is standing _____.

UNIT 02

시간을 나타내는 전치사

A ( ) 안에서 알맞은 말을 고르시오.

1 My birthday is (in, on) January.

2 It is very cold here (in, on) winter.

3 The movie will start (in, at) six o'clock.

4 We hope to see you (at, on) Sunday.

5 Last night, I slept (for, during) five hours.

6 The students have a lunch break (in, at) noon.

7 The sun rises (around, between) 6:00 a.m. these days.

8 I can meet you (between, from) 1:00 and 3:00 p.m. tomorrow.

9 They'll hold the contest (between, from) Monday to Friday.

10 Print this report (before, after) the meeting. We need it (around, during) the meeting.

B 빈칸에 알맞은 말을 보기에서 골라 쓰시오.

보기	in	at	on

1 I'm going to see a doctor _____ eleven o'clock.

2 Their wedding is _____ December 15.

3 Bell invented the telephone _____ 1876.

4 The science class finishes _____ 5:30 p.m.

5 The moon shines brightly _____ night.

6 Sometimes it snows _____ late March.

7 My father reads the newspaper _____ the morning.

8 We're going to have dinner with Dave _____ Friday.

C for 또는 during과 ( ) 안의 말을 함께 써서 문장을 완성하시오.

1 Cathy lived in London _____. (a year)

2 She went skiing _____. (the holidays)

3 He practiced the piano _____. (thirty minutes)

4 You can enjoy beautiful flowers _____. (the spring)

5 The science class lasted _____. (two hours)

6 Many people lost family members _____.
     (the Korean War)

7 You have to take this medicine _____. (three days)

8 The kids made a lot of noise _____. (the concert)

9 A man talked on his cell phone _____. (the movie)

10 I can hold my breath underwater _____. (sixty seconds)

D 밑줄 친 부분이 올바르면 ○표, 틀리면 바르게 고치시오.

1 I usually go out <u>in</u> Saturdays. _____

2 It is quite cold <u>at</u> the evening. _____

3 Steve leaves home <u>around</u> 8:00 a.m. _____

4 The election is <u>at</u> June 24. _____

5 You can see the fireworks <u>in</u> 9:00 p.m. _____

6 The song was a big hit <u>during</u> five months. _____

7 We're going to Carol's house <u>after</u> school. _____

8 The baseball season is from April <u>and</u> October. _____

9 Nick and I had dinner <u>before</u> the show. _____

10 The delivery man will come <u>from</u> 10:00 a.m. and noon. _____

WRITING **PRACTICE**

Q Answer Key p.31

A 우리말과 일치하도록 ( ) 안의 말을 이용하여 문장을 완성하시오.

1 가을에는 나뭇잎들이 빨갛고 노랗게 변한다. (autumn)

→ The leaves turn red and yellow _____.

2 나는 크리스마스 전에 선물들을 사야 한다. (Christmas)

→ I have to buy presents _____.

3 새 쇼핑몰은 11월 17일에 열 것이다. (November 17)

→ The new shopping mall will open _____.

4 많은 관광객들이 여름 동안 이 도시에 온다. (the summer)

→ Many tourists come to this city _____.

5 밤에 혼자 밖에 나가는 것은 위험하다. (night)

→ It is dangerous to go out alone _____.

6 Greg은 2019년에 그의 식당을 열었다. (2019)

→ Greg opened his restaurant _____.

7 그들은 토요일 아침에 우리를 방문할 것이다. (Saturday morning)

→ They will visit us _____.

B 우리말과 일치하도록 ( ) 안에 주어진 말을 바르게 배열하시오.

1 아빠는 저녁 7시경에 집에 오신다. (7:00 p.m., home, around, comes)

→ Dad _____.

2 오후에는 날이 흐릴 것이다. (be, in, cloudy, will, the afternoon)

→ It _____.

3 그 가수는 공연이 끝난 후 행복했다. (felt, after, happy, the show)

→ The singer _____.

4 우리는 이 시험을 한 시간 동안 볼 것이다. (take, an hour, this test, for)

→ We'll _____.

5 그 기차는 오후 5시 30분에 서울을 떠난다. (at, leaves, 5:30 p.m., Seoul)

→ The train _____.

6 당신은 수요일과 금요일 사이 어느 시점에 결과를 받아볼 것입니다.

(Friday, between, Wednesday, and)

→ You will have the results sometime _____.

108

UNIT 03

기타 전치사

🔍 Answer Key p.31

A

( ) 안에서 알맞은 말을 고르시오.

1 I gave a present to (he, him).

2 I'll do everything (by, for) you.

3 I don't want to fight (to, with) her.

4 Samuel spent his vacation with (we, us).

5 Can you carry these bags (about, for) me?

6 Do you know how to get (for, to) the library?

7 It will be faster to go there (by, with) subway.

8 Are you going to send an email (by, to) Sarah?

9 She bought some cookies (for, to) her children.

10 We have to write an essay (about, with) pollution.

B

자연스러운 문장이 되도록 알맞게 연결하시오.

[1-4]

1 They prepared lunch • • ⓐ by car.

2 We went to the beach • • ⓑ for their guests.

3 The boy is cutting the paper • • ⓒ about history.

4 Sally doesn't know much • • ⓓ with scissors.

[5-8]

5 I have information • • ⓐ to me.

6 I often play basketball • • ⓑ with my brother.

7 They recycle bottles • • ⓒ about the festival.

8 Jane showed her puppy • • ⓓ for the environment.

C 빈칸에 알맞은 말을 보기에서 골라 쓰시오. (단, 한 번씩만 쓸 것)

[1-4]

보기	about by for with

1 We voted for the winner _____ text message.

2 The morning news was _____ the flood.

3 Korean people eat _____ chopsticks.

4 This animation is _____ young children.

[5-8]

보기	about with to by

5 George gave me a book _____ a magician.

6 They traveled in the country _____ bike.

7 My sister went _____ school early today.

8 Will you watch the soccer game _____ us?

D 빈칸에 공통으로 들어갈 말을 보기에서 골라 쓰시오.

보기	about by for to with

1 Did you come here _____ taxi?

I'll send you this file _____ email.

2 I don't believe the rumors _____ him.

Last night, I dreamed _____ my grandfather.

3 I will show my report card _____ Mom today.

Robin came back _____ his office at 6:00 p.m.

4 Peter had dinner _____ me.

Dad always cleans the table _____ this cloth.

5 I bought a necklace _____ my mom.

We booked the restaurant _____ Julie's birthday party.

WRITING PRACTICE

Answer Key p.32

A 우리말과 일치하도록 ( ) 안의 말을 이용하여 문장을 완성하시오.

1 그들은 작년에 한국으로 돌아왔다. (Korea)

→ They came back _____ last year.

2 우리는 과학 수업 시간에 은하계에 대해 배웠다. (the galaxy)

→ We learned _____ in science class.

3 Jane은 반 친구들과 함께 많은 시간을 보낸다. (her classmates)

→ Jane spends a lot of time _____.

4 여러분의 안전을 위해 안전벨트를 매야 합니다. (your safety)

→ You should wear a seat belt _____.

5 우리는 비행기로 제주도에 갔다. (plane)

→ We went to Jeju Island _____.

6 너는 네 공책을 그에게 빌려줄 거니? (he)

→ Are you going to lend your notebook _____?

7 Bones 씨는 그 종이를 풀로 벽에 붙였다. (some glue)

→ Mr. Bones stuck the paper on the wall _____.

B 우리말과 일치하도록 ( ) 안에 주어진 말을 바르게 배열하시오.

1 당신은 이 책들을 전화로 주문할 수 있습니다. (by, order, phone, these books)

→ You can _____.

2 Victoria는 우리에게 친절했다. (was, us, kind, to)

→ Victoria _____.

3 나는 너에 대해 생각하고 있었어. (was, you, thinking, about)

→ I _____.

4 그녀는 그 아이를 담요로 덮었다. (the child, with, covered, a blanket)

→ She _____.

5 내가 모두를 위해 커피를 좀 가지고 올게. (some coffee, get, everyone, for)

→ I'll _____.

6 우리와 함께 영화를 보러 갈래? (the movies, us, to, with, go)

→ Will you _____?

[1-3] 빈칸에 들어갈 알맞은 말을 고르시오.

1 There is some juice _____ the glass.

① in   ② at   ③ on
④ to   ⑤ over

2 James told an interesting story _____ us.

① in   ② on   ③ from
④ to   ⑤ with

3 I heard _____ Jake's accident.

① for   ② about   ③ by
④ to   ⑤ with

[4-6] 빈칸에 공통으로 들어갈 말을 고르시오.

4
• I talked on the phone _____ two hours.
• Do you have a special menu _____ children?

① in   ② on   ③ for
④ during   ⑤ around

5
• Your wallet is _____ the table.
• This store will open _____ December 15.

① in   ② at   ③ on
④ to   ⑤ for

6
• My parents are _____ work now.
• We left the gym _____ 4:00 p.m.

① in   ② at   ③ on
④ from   ⑤ to

서술형

[7-8] 빈칸에 들어갈 알맞은 전치사를 쓰시오.

7 School finished at 5:30 p.m. We went to a shopping mall at 6:00 p.m.

→ We went to a shopping mall _____ school.

8 I'm going to make soup. I'll use some chicken.

→ I'm going to make soup _____ some chicken.

[9-10] 빈칸에 들어갈 말이 나머지 넷과 <u>다른</u> 것을 고르시오.

9 ① He lives _____ Chicago.
② The children sat _____ the floor.
③ I jump rope _____ the morning.
④ Molly entered middle school _____ 2020.
⑤ There are a few pencils _____ the pencil case.

10 ① My father gets up _____ 6:00 a.m.
② I met Diana _____ the bus stop.
③ They arrived _____ midnight.
④ I'll just stay _____ home today.
⑤ We will have a party _____ Sunday.

[11-13] 다음 여름 캠프 안내서를 보고 빈칸에 알맞은 전치사를 쓰시오.

Summer Camp Schedule
Student's name: Mike Anderson
Date: July 22 – August 12 (3 weeks)
Roommate: Danny Lewis

11 The summer camp is _____ July 22 to August 12.

12 Mike will go to the summer camp _____ three weeks.

13 Mike will share his room _____ Danny.

[14-15] 다음 중 밑줄 친 부분이 <u>잘못된</u> 것을 고르시오.

14 ① They will travel <u>by</u> car.
② I'm going <u>at</u> a supermarket.
③ There is a bridge <u>over</u> the river.
④ Billy took pictures <u>with</u> his new camera.
⑤ Susan felt disappointed <u>after</u> the exam.

15 ① I hid the letters <u>under</u> the bed.
② Can you make some tea <u>for</u> us?
③ Tom fell asleep <u>during</u> the class.
④ I'll finish this work <u>around</u> 6:00 p.m.
⑤ The festival is <u>between</u> Saturday to Wednesday.

16 다음 우리말을 영어로 바르게 옮긴 것은?

은행은 그의 회사 맞은편에 있다.

① The bank is across his company.
② The bank is from his company.
③ The bank is across to his company.
④ The bank is across from his company.
⑤ The bank is across about his company.

[17-18] 대화가 성립되도록 ( ) 안에서 알맞은 말을 골라 쓰시오.

17
A: I bought these books ⓐ (for, to) you.
B: Oh, they are ⓑ (about, with) dolphins. I like dolphins!

ⓐ _____ ⓑ _____

18
A: I will go on a trip ⓐ (in, on) May.
B: That's great! Will you go ⓑ (by, with) your family?

ⓐ _____ ⓑ _____

[19-20] 우리말과 일치하도록 ( ) 안의 말을 이용하여 문장을 완성하시오.

19 벽 뒤에 비밀의 방이 있었다. (the wall)

→ There was a secret room _____
_____ .

20 그녀는 유럽을 기차로 여행할지도 모른다. (train)

→ She may travel through Europe
_____ .

[21-22] 우리말과 일치하도록 ( ) 안에 주어진 말을 바르게 배열하시오.

21 당신은 신발 가게와 카페 사이의 길을 따라가야 합니다.
(the shoe store, the café, and, between)

→ You should follow the road _____
_____ .

22 그 서커스는 5월 1일부터 6월 30일까지이다.
(May 1, to, June 30, from)

→ The circus is _____ .

[23-24] 밑줄 친 부분이 어법상 옳은지 판단하고, <u>틀리면</u> 바르게 고치시오.

23 The hotel is <u>next to</u> the train station.

(O / X) _____

24 We are usually busy <u>at</u> Monday mornings.

(O / X) _____

UNIT 01

and, but, or, so

Answer Key p.32

A ( ) 안에서 알맞은 말을 고르시오.

1 Nick is kind and (gentle, gentleman).

2 The movie was sad, (but, so) I didn't cry.

3 My room looked messy, (or, so) I cleaned it.

4 I wanted to buy the doll, (but, so) I didn't have money.

5 Both Laura (and, but) Jihee are fans of K-pop.

6 We can talk either here (and, or) outside.

7 We went to the restaurant (and, but) had dinner there.

8 I forgot my umbrella, (but, so) I got wet in the rain.

9 Will you go to the beach, (and, or) will you stay at home?

10 Do you want to go to the museum today (but, or) tomorrow?

B ( ) 안에서 알맞은 말을 골라 문장을 완성하시오. (단, 한 번씩만 쓸 것)

1 (and, but, or)

a. These cookies look strange _____ taste nice.

b. He may be from Hong Kong _____ Taiwan.

c. You should wear a suit _____ tie for the interview.

2 (but, or, so)

a. My computer is new, _____ it doesn't work well.

b. Chris had a headache, _____ he took medicine.

c. You can put it on the sofa _____ on the table.

3 (and, or, so)

a. He drank too much coffee, _____ he couldn't sleep.

b. You can choose either ice cream _____ cake for dessert.

c. I took out a piece of paper _____ wrote his number on it.

C 빈칸에 알맞은 말을 보기에서 골라 두 문장을 연결하시오. (단, 한 번씩만 쓸 것)

보기	and but or so

[1-4]

1 Kimchi is delicious. It is healthy too.

→ Kimchi is delicious _____ healthy.

2 We can discuss it now. We can discuss it this afternoon.

→ We can discuss it now _____ this afternoon.

3 It was hot inside. We turned on the air conditioner.

→ It was hot inside, _____ we turned on the air conditioner.

4 They watched the movie. They didn't enjoy it.

→ They watched the movie _____ didn't enjoy it.

[5-8]

5 I can tell you by email. I can tell you by phone.

→ I can tell you by email _____ by phone.

6 She poured milk. She drank it.

→ She poured milk _____ drank it.

7 These flowers are pretty. They don't smell good.

→ These flowers are pretty _____ don't smell good.

8 Andy wasn't hungry this morning. He skipped breakfast.

→ Andy wasn't hungry this morning, _____ he skipped breakfast.

D 빈칸에 알맞은 말을 보기에서 골라 쓰시오.

보기	he didn't like it	Mark set the table
	his father will take him home	they went to the pool

1 Emily made dinner, and _____.

2 They wanted to swim, so _____.

3 His mom bought a T-shirt for him, but _____.

4 Ken will walk home with us, or _____.

WRITING PRACTICE

🔍 Answer Key p.32

A 우리말과 일치하도록 ( ) 안의 말을 이용하여 문장을 완성하시오.

1 그는 정직하고 예의 바르다. (honest, polite)

→ He _____.

2 제가 그 결과를 월요일이나 화요일에 받을 수 있나요? (Monday, Tuesday)

→ Can I get the results on _____?

3 Kelly는 테니스를 좋아하지만 잘 치지는 못한다. (can, play well)

→ Kelly likes tennis, _____.

4 그는 일을 끝마치고 집에 돌아왔다. (come back home)

→ He finished his work _____.

5 이 노래는 인기 있지만, 나는 그것을 좋아하지 않는다. (like, it)

→ This song is popular, _____.

6 내가 점심을 요리하거나 우리는 외식을 할 수 있다. (can, eat out)

→ I will cook lunch, _____.

7 Jenny가 내가 가장 좋아하는 책을 잃어버려서, 나는 화가 났다. (get angry)

→ Jenny lost my favorite book, _____.

B 우리말과 일치하도록 ( ) 안에 주어진 말을 바르게 배열하시오.

1 준수나 인혜가 학급 회장이 될 것이다. (or, be, Inhye, will, Junsu)

→ _____ class president.

2 그는 휴가 동안에 그리스와 터키를 방문했다. (Greece, he, Turkey, and, visited)

→ _____ during his vacation.

3 우리는 샌드위치가 하나밖에 없어서 그것을 나누어 먹었다. (shared, so, it, we)

→ We had only one sandwich, _____.

4 이 해변은 멋지지만 우리집에서 멀다. (nice, this beach, far, but, is)

→ _____ from my house.

5 William은 바빠서 저녁 식사에 올 수 없었다. (couldn't, so, to, come, he, dinner)

→ William was busy, _____.

6 그 가수는 밖으로 나와 그녀의 팬들에게 손을 흔들었다. (came out, waved, and)

→ The singer _____ to her fans.

when, before, after, until

A

( ) 안에서 알맞은 말을 고르시오.

1 (Before, After) I go to bed, I put on my pajamas.

2 I'm going to take a nap (when, after) I eat lunch.

3 I feel excited (when, until) I listen to dance music.

4 Please call me before you (visit, will visit) me.

5 I'll meet him after school (be, is) over.

6 Did you read many books (when, after) you were young?

7 We can't buy a new car until we (save, will save) some money.

8 Andrew was very thirsty (until, after) he ran in the marathon.

9 Robert will write you an email when he (goes, will go) to Boston.

10 The students waited (when, until) their teacher came into the classroom.

B

( ) 안에서 알맞은 말을 골라 문장을 완성하시오. (단, 한 번씩만 쓸 것)

1 (when, before)

 a. I felt sad _____ Sarah moved to another city.

 b. Greg wrote in his diary _____ he went to bed.

2 (when, after)

 a. I took a shower _____ I played soccer.

 b. _____ I have free time, I take a walk in the park.

3 (before, until)

 a. Dan will go on a diet _____ he loses 5 kg.

 b. _____ you come inside, you should take off your shoes.

4 (after, until)

 a. We should keep quiet _____ the movie ends.

 b. You should take this medicine _____ you eat dinner.

C 자연스러운 문장이 되도록 알맞게 연결하시오.

[1-4]

1 People screamed •   • ⓐ until I come back.

2 Nancy will work at a bank •   • ⓑ when the fire started.

3 You should stay here •   • ⓒ before I left home.

4 I checked the bus schedule •   • ⓓ after she graduates.

[5-8]

5 My family lived in London •   • ⓐ when I was thirteen.

6 His room looked nicer •   • ⓑ before your mom sees it.

7 You should clean the kitchen •   • ⓒ until she falls asleep.

8 Jessica always watches TV •   • ⓓ after he painted the wall.

D ( ) 안의 말을 이용하여 두 문장을 연결하시오.

1 It was snowy. We arrived at the lake. (when)

   → It was snowy _____.

2 We won't leave the stadium. The soccer game is over. (until)

   → We won't leave the stadium _____.

3 Peter was surprised. He saw his friend on TV. (when)

   → Peter was surprised _____.

4 I watched the movie. I wrote a review about it. (after)

   → _____, I wrote a review about it.

5 We go to Sydney. We have to book a hotel room. (before)

   → _____, we have to book a hotel room.

6 I have to wear contact lenses. I buy a new pair of glasses. (until)

   → I have to wear contact lenses _____.

WRITING PRACTICE

🔍 Answer Key p.32

A 우리말과 일치하도록 (   ) 안의 말을 이용하여 문장을 완성하시오.

1 나는 우리 팀이 경기에서 졌을 때 화가 났다. (my team, lose the game)

→ I was angry _____.

2 우리는 손님들이 오시기 전에 모든 것을 준비했다. (the guests, come)

→ We prepared everything _____.

3 네가 메인 요리를 다 먹은 후에 웨이터가 디저트를 내어줄 것이다. (finish, the main dish)

→ The waiter will serve dessert _____.

4 휴가철이 시작될 때, 이 해변은 붐빌 것이다. (the vacation season, start)

→ _____, this beach will be crowded.

5 저녁 식사가 준비될 때까지 우리는 이야기를 나누었다. (dinner, ready)

→ We talked _____.

6 너는 주문하기 전에 번호표를 받아야 한다. (order)

→ You should take a number _____.

7 나는 일곱 살 때까지 자전거를 어떻게 타는지 몰랐다. (be seven years old)

→ I didn't know how to ride a bike _____.

B 우리말과 일치하도록 (   ) 안에 주어진 말을 바르게 배열하시오.

1 Ryan은 어젯밤 집에 도착한 후 잠이 들었다. (home, last night, he, after, got)

→ Ryan fell asleep _____.

2 그 아이들은 그들의 부모님이 그들을 말릴 때까지 싸웠다. (stopped, their parents, them, until)

→ The children fought _____.

3 바다에서 수영할 때는 주의해야 한다. (swim, you, when, in the sea)

→ You should be careful _____.

4 나는 온라인으로 물건을 사기 전에, 항상 후기를 읽어본다. (I, online, buy things, before)

→ _____, I always read the reviews.

5 그녀는 고향을 떠난 후, 다시는 돌아오지 않았다. (she, after, her hometown, left)

→ _____, she never came back.

6 Betty가 대회에서 우승했을 때, 그녀는 겨우 열다섯 살이었다. (when, the contest, Betty, won)

→ _____, she was only fifteen.

UNIT 03

because, if, that

🔍 Answer Key p.32

A ( ) 안에서 알맞은 말을 고르시오.

1 Dan didn't believe (if, that) he won the lottery.

2 You'll get cold (if, that) you don't wear a coat.

3 If it (rains, will rain) tomorrow, we'll cancel our picnic.

4 Brian always says (that, because) he will be a doctor.

5 I'll make you some sandwiches (if, that) you're hungry.

6 It is strange (if, that) you don't remember Robin.

7 The problem is (if, that) Linda doesn't know Tom.

8 We had a party for Jake (that, because) it was his birthday.

9 If Susan (has, will have) free time this weekend, she will visit us.

10 (That, Because) Tim sings very well, he'll be the singer of our band.

B ( ) 안에서 알맞은 말을 골라 문장을 완성하시오. (단, 한 번씩만 쓸 것)

1 (if, that)

a. His problem is _____ he is too lazy.

b. _____ you meet Henry, you'll like him.

2 (because, if)

a. _____ you don't eat now, you will be hungry later.

b. She was tired _____ she worked very hard.

3 (if, that)

a. We hope _____ you will get better soon.

b. Tommy will be a great pianist _____ he practices harder.

4 (because, that)

a. We didn't know _____ Billy's grandfather was a general.

b. Angela is learning Spanish _____ her husband is from Spain.

C 빈칸에 알맞은 말을 보기에서 골라 쓰시오.

[1-3]

보기	because he is very kind if he doesn't get home early that he hurt his leg

1 It is unfortunate _____.

2 Everyone likes Sam _____.

3 _____, his father will be worried.

[4-6]

보기	that Suji likes you if Mark gets a C on the test because the bus came late

4 I was late for class _____.

5 Did you know _____?

6 _____, he has to take the test again.

D 밑줄 친 부분이 올바르면 ○표, 틀리면 바르게 고치시오.

1 I can't believe that she is thirty years old. _____

2 If you will do your best, your dream will come true. _____

3 This plant died that I didn't give water to it. _____

4 Is it true if there was water on Mars? _____

5 If the museum is closed, I will go to the park. _____

6 We didn't enjoy our vacation if the weather was terrible. _____

7 The important thing is that we are safe. _____

8 I'll be happy if we will be in the same class next year. _____

9 Do you think because this toy is dangerous for kids? _____

10 If the food is not good, you can get your money back. _____

WRITING PRACTICE

Q Answer Key p.33

A 우리말과 일치하도록 ( ) 안의 말을 이용하여 문장을 완성하시오.

1 네가 이번 주말에 나를 방문할 수 있으면 좋겠어. (can, visit me)
→ I hope _____ this weekend.

2 네가 오늘 영어 수업을 빠진다면, 너는 곤경에 처하게 될 거야. (miss English class)
→ _____ today, you will be in trouble.

3 시청은 여기와 가까우니까 걸어가도 돼. (it, close)
→ You can walk to city hall _____ to here.

4 우리가 올림픽에서 열 개의 금메달을 딴 것은 신나는 일이었다. (we, win ten gold medals)
→ It was exciting _____ at the Olympic Games.

5 방 안에서 나쁜 냄새가 났기 때문에 나는 창문을 열었다. (it, smell bad)
→ I opened the window _____ in the room.

6 이 셔츠가 당신에게 작다면 교환하실 수 있습니다. (it, small)
→ You can exchange this shirt _____ for you.

B 우리말과 일치하도록 ( ) 안에 주어진 말을 바르게 배열하시오.

1 나는 네가 옳다고 생각해. (that, right, you, think, are)
→ I _____.

2 네가 떡볶이를 맛본다면 너는 그것을 좋아할 거야. (you, if, it, taste)
→ You will like tteokbokki _____.

3 그녀는 구직 면접이 있었기 때문에 긴장했다. (a job interview, had, because, she)
→ She felt nervous _____.

4 네 컴퓨터가 작동하지 않으면, 내가 널 위해 그걸 고쳐줄게. (work, your computer, if, doesn't)
→ _____, I'll fix it for you.

5 엄마는 내게 짧은 머리가 어울린다고 말씀하신다. (look, I, with short hair, nice, that)
→ Mom tells me _____.

6 Peter는 책이 많아서 새 책장이 필요하다. (a lot of, has, because, he, books)
→ Peter needs a new bookshelf _____.

7 네가 무언가 잘못했다면, 미안하다고 말해야 한다. (something, you, if, wrong, did)
→ _____, you should say sorry.

REVIEW TEST

[1-3] 빈칸에 들어갈 알맞은 말을 고르시오.

1

It was too hot yesterday, _____ we had some ice cream.

① if   ② or   ③ so
④ that   ⑤ because

2

Our teacher said _____ we won't have our school festival this year.

① and   ② after   ③ if
④ that   ⑤ because

3

Mike and I live in the same apartment, _____ we hardly see each other.

① but   ② or   ③ so
④ until   ⑤ because

[4-5] 빈칸에 들어갈 말이 바르게 짝지어진 것을 고르시오.

4

• Is this bird a duck ___(A)___ a goose?
• George went out ___(B)___ he finished his homework.

	(A)		(B)
①	and	……	when
②	or	……	until
③	or	……	after
④	but	……	before
⑤	but	……	if

5

• Mia and Sam will stay in our house ___(A)___ they find a hotel.
• I didn't take any pictures ___(B)___ I didn't have my camera with me.

	(A)		(B)
①	when	……	if
②	if	……	because
③	if	……	if
④	until	……	because
⑤	until	……	that

서술형

[6-8] 빈칸에 알맞은 말을 보기에서 골라 쓰시오. (단, 한 번씩만 쓸 것)

보기	because if that

6

It is true _____ we will go to Europe this summer.

7

Raise your hand _____ you know the answer.

8

I couldn't print the file _____ there was no paper in the printer.

빈출

9 빈칸에 들어갈 말이 나머지 넷과 다른 것은?

① We hope _____ everyone is safe.

② I know _____ John is honest.

③ It was sad _____ the puppies lost their mom.

④ Both soccer _____ baseball are popular in Korea.

⑤ The truth is _____ she can't speak English.

[10-11] 다음 중 밑줄 친 부분이 잘못된 것을 고르시오.

10 ① Brenda is smart but lazy.

② He spoke loudly and clear.

③ We bought some lemons and cherries.

④ Alice is too young, so she can't read.

⑤ I waited for her until her class was over.

11 ① I'll be very sad if Nora will leave.

② I hope that we can meet again soon.

③ It was snowing heavily when we arrived in Moscow.

④ I turned on the lamp because it was dark.

⑤ After we had dinner, Peter did the dishes.

서술형

[12-14] 우리말과 일치하도록 빈칸에 알맞은 접속사를 쓰시오.

12 나는 우리가 서둘러야 한다고 생각해.

→ I think _____ we should hurry up.

13 그녀는 2년 동안 독일어를 배워서, 독일어를 잘 말한다.

→ She learned German for two years, _____ she speaks it well.

14 나는 아팠기 때문에 시험 공부를 하지 못했다.

→ I couldn't study for the exam _____ I was sick.

서술형

[15-16] 빈칸에 알맞은 접속사를 써서 대화를 완성하시오.

15 A: Do you want jam _____ butter on your toast?

B: Butter, please.

16 A: Victoria, did you live with your grandparents?

B: Yes. I lived with them _____ I was a child.

17 다음 중 밑줄 친 부분을 잘못 고친 것은?

① We packed our bags <u>so</u> left home.
→ and

② My brother loves science but <u>hate</u>
English. → hates

③ I believe <u>if</u> our project will be
successful. → but

④ Mom will not go to bed until I <u>will
come</u> back home. → come

⑤ <u>This</u> is clear that Lydia is hiding
something. → It

18 다음 우리말을 영어로 바르게 옮긴 것은?

나는 수프나 샐러드 중 하나를 먹을래.

① I'll have soup but salad.
② I'll have both soup and salad.
③ I'll have both soup or salad.
④ I'll have either soup and salad.
⑤ I'll have either soup or salad.

서술형

[19-21] 우리말과 일치하도록 ( ) 안의 말을 이용하여 문장을 완성하시오.

19 그가 록 음악을 좋아하는 것은 사실이다. (true)

→ _____ he likes rock music.

20 너는 그 정보를 이 책에서나 인터넷에서 찾을 수 있다.
(in this book, on the internet)

→ You can find the information _____
_____.

21 나는 무언가를 사기 전에 항상 가격을 물어본다.
(buy, something)

→ I always ask the price _____
_____.

서술형

[22-24] 밑줄 친 부분이 어법상 옳은지 판단하고, 틀리면 바르게 고치시오.

22 Kevin put on his shoes <u>but</u> started to
run.

(O / X) _____

23 You will get your ticket after you <u>will
sign</u> this form.

(O / X) _____

24 The problem was <u>if</u> you didn't follow
the rules.

(O / X) _____

UNIT 01

의문사 who, what, which

🔍 Answer Key p.33

A

( ) 안에서 알맞은 말을 고르시오.

1 A: (Who, Which) will you visit this afternoon?
   B: I will visit Mr. Jackman.

2 A: (What, Whose) were you listening to?
   B: I was listening to Maroon 5's new song.

3 A: (What, Whose) mistake was it?
   B: It was my mistake.

4 A: (Who, What) is waiting for you at the bus stop?
   B: My father is waiting there.

5 A: (Whom, Which) is your team, team A or team B?
   B: I'm on team A.

6 A: (What, Whose) do we need to buy at the store?
   B: We need to buy some milk.

B

자연스러운 대화가 되도록 알맞게 연결하시오.

[1-4]

1 Whose bus card is this? •   • ⓐ It's mine.

2 Who fixed this printer? •   • ⓑ I like cola better.

3 What are you eating? •   • ⓒ I'm eating a hamburger.

4 Which do you prefer, cola or lemonade? •   • ⓓ My brother did.

[5-8]

5 What kind of sports do you like? •   • ⓐ That one is mine.

6 What will we do in New York? •   • ⓑ I went with Tom.

7 Who did you go to the party with? •   • ⓒ I like baseball.

8 Which is your jacket, this one or that one? •   • ⓓ We'll watch a musical.

C 빈칸에 알맞은 말을 보기에서 골라 쓰시오. (단, 한 번씩만 쓸 것)

보기	who　　whose　　what　　which

1 A: _____ purse is it?

　 B: It may be Jena's.

2 A: _____ is Alice's phone number?

　 B: It's 555-2060.

3 A: _____ will you meet this weekend?

　 B: I will meet Brian.

4 A: _____ is faster, a cheetah or a lion?

　 B: A cheetah is much faster.

D 다음 문장의 밑줄 친 부분을 묻는 의문문을 완성하시오.

1 This is Danny's bat.

　 → _____?

2 Her mother is taking care of Emily.

　 → _____?

3 His name is Kevin Jones.

　 → _____?

4 They saw Jacob on the street.

　 → _____ on the street?

5 It is Mark's passport.

　 → _____?

6 The children are drawing giraffes.

　 → _____?

7 Susan got first prize in the contest.

　 → _____ in the contest?

8 I taught Mandy how to bake cookies.

　 → _____ how to bake cookies?

WRITING PRACTICE

🔍 Answer Key p.33

A 우리말과 일치하도록 ( ) 안의 말을 이용하여 문장을 완성하시오.

1 이것은 누구의 인형이니? (doll, this)

→ _____ ?

2 Julia가 너에게 뭐라고 말했니? (say)

→ _____ to you?

3 Jane은 어젯밤에 누구와 함께 외출했니? (go out)

→ _____ with last night?

4 누가 너에게 이 꽃들을 보냈니? (send)

→ _____ these flowers?

5 빨간 것과 파란 것 중 어느 것이 네 자전거니? (bike, yours)

→ _____ , the red one or the blue one?

6 너는 웅변 대회에서 무엇에 대해 이야기할 거니? (will, speak)

→ _____ about in the speech contest?

B 우리말과 일치하도록 ( ) 안에 주어진 말을 바르게 배열하시오.

1 무엇이 문제였니? (the problem, what, was)

→ _____ ?

2 너는 사과와 오렌지 중 어느 것을 더 좋아하니? (you, prefer, which, do)

→ _____ , apples or oranges?

3 누가 너희에게 이 도넛들을 사줬니? (these donuts, bought, who)

→ _____ for you?

4 그는 누구의 우산을 빌렸니? (he, borrow, whose, did, umbrella)

→ _____ ?

5 너는 오늘 아침에 누구에게 전화했니? (you, did, whom, call)

→ _____ this morning?

6 너는 아이스크림과 케이크 중 어떤 디저트를 원하니? (want, which, do, dessert, you)

→ _____ , ice cream or cake?

7 그녀는 어떤 종류의 소설을 쓰니? (novels, what, of, kind)

→ _____ does she write?

UNIT 02

의문사 when, where, why, how

A

( ) 안에서 알맞은 말을 고르시오.

1 A: (How, What) is the weather today?
   B: It's cloudy.

2 A: I have a toothache.
   B: Why (aren't, don't) you go to the dentist?

3 A: (When, Why) did you sleep so late this morning?
   B: Because my alarm didn't go off.

4 A: Why (do, don't) we have some coffee?
   B: That sounds great.

5 A: (When, Where) does he usually leave his office?
   B: At 7:00 p.m.

6 A: (Where, Why) should I upload my homework file?
   B: On our class webpage.

B

자연스러운 대화가 되도록 알맞게 연결하시오.

[1-4]

1 Where does Robert live? •

2 Why did you lie to me? •

3 How is your grandmother doing? •

4 When did the accident happen? •

• ⓐ She's doing fine.

• ⓑ At 10:00 a.m. this morning.

• ⓒ Because I was scared.

• ⓓ In Washington DC.

[5-8]

5 Why did you buy that book? •

6 Where do you want to eat dinner? •

7 When is the rock music festival? •

8 How can I get the cheapest tickets? •

• ⓐ It's this Saturday.

• ⓑ Because I liked its title.

• ⓒ You should buy them online.

• ⓓ I want to try this Italian restaurant.

C 빈칸에 알맞은 말을 보기에서 골라 대화를 완성하시오.

| 보기 | how old | how long | how far |
| | how often | how many | how much |

1 A: _____ is that backpack?

B: It's $30.

2 A: _____ is Mr. Robinson?

B: He is fifty years old.

3 A: _____ should I take this medicine?

B: Twice a day.

4 A: _____ can you hold your breath?

B: For a minute.

5 A: _____ students are in your class?

B: Thirty students are in my class.

6 A: _____ is it from LA to San Diego?

B: It's 195 km.

D 다음 문장의 밑줄 친 부분을 묻는 의문문을 완성하시오.

1 The movie was terrible.

→ _____ ?

2 She put her bag on the table.

→ _____ ?

3 They moved to Seattle in May.

→ _____ to Seattle?

4 Isabel loves Edward because he is nice to her.

→ _____ ?

5 The winter vacation will start next Monday.

→ _____ ?

6 Vincent is going to have his birthday party at his house.

→ _____ his birthday party?

WRITING PRACTICE

🔍 Answer Key p.33

A 우리말과 일치하도록 (   ) 안의 말을 이용하여 문장을 완성하시오.

1 스페인 여행은 어땠니? (your trip)

→ _____ to Spain?

2 이 근처에 은행이 어디에 있나요? (a bank)

→ _____ near here?

3 그녀는 얼마나 많은 골을 넣을까? (goal)

→ _____ will she score?

4 너는 어디서 그 소문에 대해 들었니? (hear)

→ _____ about the rumor?

5 그는 왜 선생님이 되고 싶어 하니? (want)

→ _____ to be a teacher?

6 그들은 언제 가장 친한 친구가 되었니? (become)

→ _____ best friends?

B 우리말과 일치하도록 (   ) 안에 주어진 말을 바르게 배열하시오.

1 그녀의 결혼식은 언제니? (is, her, when, wedding)

→ _____ ?

2 Daniel은 왜 속이 상했니? (Daniel, why, upset, was)

→ _____ ?

3 너는 어디서 이 열쇠를 찾았니? (find, where, this key, you, did)

→ _____ ?

4 너는 얼마나 많은 시간이 필요하니? (do, how, time, you, need, much)

→ _____ ?

5 제가 언제 그 소포를 받을 수 있나요? (I, when, can, the package, receive)

→ _____ ?

6 우리 피자를 좀 시키는 게 어때? (why, some pizza, we, order, don't)

→ _____ ?

7 그 아이들은 어떻게 이 문제를 풀었니? (did, the children, how, this problem, solve)

→ _____ ?

UNIT
03

부가의문문

🔍 Answer Key p.33

Ⓐ

( ) 안에서 알맞은 말을 고르시오.

1 This place is quite nice, (is, isn't) it?

2 He will not travel alone, (will, won't) he?

3 Your father doesn't smoke, (is, does) he?

4 You don't know his address, (do, don't) you?

5 Jacob was at home last night, wasn't (Jacob, he)?

6 You go to school by bus, (aren't, don't) you?

7 Karen can play the violin, (doesn't, can't) she?

8 These tomatoes are not fresh, (are, aren't) they?

9 We had a great time at the party, (don't, didn't) we?

10 You and Jason were classmates last year, (aren't, weren't) you?

Ⓑ

빈칸에 알맞은 말을 써서 부가의문문을 완성하시오.

1 He looks happy, _____ _____?

2 You should go now, _____ _____?

3 Mary isn't eighteen years old, _____ _____?

4 The train will arrive soon, _____ _____?

5 Rebecca doesn't eat meat, _____ _____?

6 Mark bought you this book, _____ _____?

7 Yesterday was your birthday, _____ _____?

8 They can't understand Korean, _____ _____?

9 Mom will not work late tonight, _____ _____?

10 We are going to meet him tomorrow, _____ _____?

C

빈칸에 알맞은 말을 써서 대화를 완성하시오.

1   A: The students miss Annie a lot, _____ _____?

   B: Yes, _____ _____.

2   A: Jack will leave on Saturday, _____ _____?

   B: Yes, _____ _____.

3   A: Chris can't swim in the sea, _____ _____?

   B: No, _____ _____.

4   A: You are the youngest in your family, _____ _____?

   B: No, _____ _____.

5   A: Susan was not interested in jazz music, _____ _____?

   B: No, _____ _____.

6   A: The department store didn't open yesterday, _____ _____?

   B: Yes, _____ _____.

D

밑줄 친 부분이 올바르면 ○표, 틀리면 바르게 고치시오.

1   It's hot in India, <u>is it</u>?   _____

2   We met in Rome two years ago, <u>did we</u>?   _____

3   You don't trust them, <u>do you</u>?   _____

4   This bag looks strange, <u>don't it</u>?   _____

5   Take me to the hospital, <u>don't you</u>?   _____

6   You were on TV last night, <u>aren't you</u>?   _____

7   Cats can climb trees well, <u>can't they</u>?   _____

8   Mr. Lee doesn't wear glasses, <u>doesn't he</u>?   _____

9   Emily is not going to have dinner, <u>is Emily</u>?   _____

10   Let's eat something sweet, <u>will we</u>?   _____

WRITING PRACTICE

🔍 Answer Key p.34

A 우리말과 일치하도록 ( ) 안의 말을 이용하여 문장을 완성하시오.

1 이 시계는 세일 중이야, 그렇지 않니? (be on sale)

→ This watch _____, _____?

2 이 바지는 멋져 보여, 그렇지 않니? (look good)

→ These pants _____, _____?

3 공항은 여기서 멀지 않아, 그렇지? (be far)

→ The airport _____ from here, _____?

4 Nick이 우리의 학급 회장이 될 거야, 그렇지 않니? (will, be our class president)

→ Nick _____, _____?

5 그녀는 경기 중에 팔을 다쳤어, 그렇지 않니? (hurt her arm)

→ She _____ during the game, _____?

6 너는 작년에 축구부에 있었지, 그렇지 않니? (be in the soccer club)

→ You _____ last year, _____?

7 Tom은 차를 운전할 수 있어, 그렇지 않니? (can, drive a car)

→ Tom _____, _____?

B 우리말과 일치하도록 ( ) 안에 주어진 말을 바르게 배열하시오.

1 밖에 눈이 내리고 있어, 그렇지 않니? (isn't, snowing, outside, it)

→ It's _____, _____?

2 너는 내 메시지를 못 받았지, 그렇지? (did, didn't, you, my message, get)

→ You _____, _____?

3 그들은 대회를 취소하지 않을 거야, 그렇지? (cancel, will, they, won't, the contest)

→ They _____, _____?

4 그녀는 노래를 매우 잘해, 그렇지 않니? (sings, doesn't, very well, she)

→ She _____, _____?

5 Owen은 학교에 늦지 않았어, 그렇지? (was, late for school, not, he, was)

→ Owen _____, _____?

6 그 아기들은 자고 있어, 그렇지 않니? (are, they, aren't, sleeping)

→ The babies _____, _____?

CHAPTER 12 의문문, 명령문, 감탄문

부정의문문, 선택의문문

A ( ) 안에서 알맞은 말을 고르시오.

1 (Don't, Doesn't) he work for a bank?

2 (Isn't, Aren't) their new house great?

3 Who did you meet yesterday, Kate (but, or) Sandra?

4 (Wasn't, Didn't) she crying when we saw her?

5 Do you like horror movies (so, or) action movies?

6 (How, Which) are you going to wear, sandals or sneakers?

7 A: Can't you remember his address?
   B: (Yes, I can., No, I can't.) I forgot.

8 A: Will you go there with Amy or with Carrie?
   B: (Yes, I will., I'll go with Amy.)

B ( ) 안의 말을 이용하여 부정의문문을 완성하시오.

1 A: _____ _____ _____ the movie? (you, watch)
   B: No, I didn't. But I'm going to watch it this weekend.

2 A: _____ _____ _____ this free meal coupon? (I, use)
   B: Yes, you can. Please show it when you order.

3 A: _____ _____ _____ a new cell phone? (James, buy)
   B: No, he won't. He doesn't need a new one.

4 A: _____ _____ _____ _____ of this singer? (you, a fan)
   B: Yes, I am. I love his music.

5 A: _____ _____ _____ _____ about your grades?
   (your parents, worry)
   B: No, they don't. They think that I'm doing well.

C 빈칸에 알맞은 대답을 써서 대화를 완성하시오.

1 A: Isn't your mother a teacher?

B: _____, _____ _____. She's a police officer.

2 A: Can't you teach me Japanese?

B: _____, _____ _____. I'm busy these days.

3 A: Aren't these shirts too expensive?

B: _____, _____ _____. I can't buy them.

4 A: Didn't they laugh at the jokes?

B: _____, _____ _____. The jokes were very funny.

5 A: Doesn't Sean go to the gym?

B: _____, _____ _____. He goes there twice a week.

D 보기와 같이 두 문장을 연결하여 선택의문문을 완성하시오.

보기	Will you order chicken? Will you order fish? → Will you order chicken or fish?

1 Did he call you before lunch? Did he call you after lunch?

→ _____?

2 Do you want to take a nap? Do you want to walk in the park?

→ _____?

3 Will they leave tonight? Will they leave tomorrow night?

→ _____?

4 Did she find this book here? Did she find this book at home?

→ _____?

5 Is Lucy going to have dinner alone? Is Lucy going to have dinner with us?

→ _____?

WRITING PRACTICE

🔍 Answer Key p.34

A 우리말과 일치하도록 ( ) 안의 말을 이용하여 문장을 완성하시오,

1 이 아이스크림은 너무 달지 않니? (this ice cream)

→ _____ too sweet?

2 너는 거기에 지하철로 가지 않았니? (go there)

→ _____ by subway?

3 너 나와 탁구를 치지 않을래? (will, play)

→ _____ table tennis with me?

4 Julie는 도서관에서 공부하고 있지 않았니? (study)

→ _____ in the library?

5 네 남동생은 영어로 자기 이름을 쓸 수 없니? (your little brother, write)

→ _____ his name in English?

6 너는 선물로 지갑과 가방 중 무엇을 원하니? (a wallet, a bag)

→ Which do you want for a gift, _____ ?

B 우리말과 일치하도록 ( ) 안에 주어진 말을 바르게 배열하시오.

1 저 두 여자아이들은 자매가 아니니? (the two girls, aren't, sisters)

→ _____ ?

2 너는 수영을 잘하지 않니? (you, swim, don't, well)

→ _____ ?

3 그들은 프랑스 출신이지 않니? (France, they, from, weren't)

→ _____ ?

4 네 친구들은 여기에 머무르지 않을 거니? (your friends, here, stay, won't)

→ _____ ?

5 그는 이 아파트에 살지 않니? (live, doesn't, he, in this apartment)

→ _____ ?

6 우리는 학교에서 만날 거니 Steve의 집에서 만날 거니? (at school, at Steve's house, or, meet)

→ Will we _____ ?

7 너는 야구를 하고 싶니 축구를 하고 싶니? (play, want, baseball, soccer, or, to)

→ Do you _____ ?

CHAPTER 12 의문문, 명령문, 감탄문

명령문, 감탄문

Answer Key p.34

A ( ) 안에서 알맞은 말을 고르시오.

1 How stupid (I was, was I)!

2 (What, How) a lovely song it is!

3 (Be, Do) quiet during the movie.

4 (What, How) slowly they cook!

5 (Don't please, Please don't) cry.

6 (Let's not, Let's don't) eat pasta today.

7 (What, What a) cute children they are!

8 (Not talk, Don't talk) much when you eat.

9 (Show, Shows) your passport to me, please.

10 (Let's turn, Let's turns) off the air conditioner.

B ( ) 안의 말을 이용하여 명령문을 완성하시오. (Let's는 사용하지 말 것)

1 _____ here. (not/smoke)

2 _____ to your friends. (nice)

3 _____ in the hallway. (not/run)

4 _____ two eggs in the pan. (fry)

5 _____ the guitar at night. (not/play)

6 _____ during the test. (not/cheat)

7 _____ the painting. (please, not/touch)

8 _____ the waste on the street. (not/throw)

9 _____ your teeth three times a day. (brush)

10 _____ these dishes for me. (please, clean)

다음 문장을 감탄문으로 바꿔 쓰시오.

1 It is a very exciting idea.

→ What _____ !

2 It is very cold.

→ How _____ !

3 Fred has a very wonderful voice.

→ What _____ !

4 She sings very beautifully.

→ How _____ !

5 This watch is very expensive.

→ How _____ !

6 These are very scary movies.

→ What _____ !

밑줄 친 부분이 올바르면 ○표, 틀리면 바르게 고치시오.

1 Don't nervous. _____

2 What handsome boy he is! _____

3 What quickly they talked! _____

4 Let's gets on the bus. _____

5 Don't enter my room! _____

6 Do play not with scissors. _____

7 What a smart students they are! _____

8 Orders a cup of coffee for me. _____

9 How generous your parents are! _____

10 Not let's turn on the heater. _____

WRITING PRACTICE

🔍 Answer Key p.34

Ⓐ 우리말과 일치하도록 ( ) 안의 말을 이용하여 문장을 완성하시오.

1 이 소파는 매우 편하구나! (comfortable)

→ _____ this sofa is!

2 실패를 두려워하지 마. (not, be afraid)

→ _____ of failure.

3 그는 매우 훌륭한 무용수구나! (a great dancer)

→ _____ he is!

4 그 소식은 매우 충격적이구나! (shocking)

→ _____ the news is!

5 그녀를 만날 때 그녀의 나이를 묻지 마라. (not, ask, her age)

→ _____ when you meet her.

6 그것에 대해서는 더 이상 이야기하지 말자. (not, talk)

→ _____ about it anymore.

7 네 여동생의 숙제를 도와라. (help, your little sister)

→ _____ with her homework.

Ⓑ 우리말과 일치하도록 ( ) 안에 주어진 말을 바르게 배열하시오.

1 다리를 꼬지 마라. (cross, legs, don't, your)

→ _____ .

2 우리 사진을 좀 찍자. (pictures, take, some, let's)

→ _____ .

3 그 차는 매우 빠르구나! (the car, how, is, fast)

→ _____ !

4 그에게 지금 전화하지 마. (call, him, don't, now)

→ _____ .

5 그것은 매우 쉬운 시험이구나! (test, it, what, is, easy, an)

→ _____ !

6 우리 거실을 청소하자. (the living room, clean, let's)

→ _____ .

[1-4] 빈칸에 들어갈 알맞은 말을 고르시오.

1

A: _____ you sleepy?
B: No, I'm not. I'm fine.

① Isn't　　② Aren't　　③ Don't
④ Can't　　⑤ Won't

2

A: _____ broke this window?
B: Helen did.

① Who　　② What　　③ When
④ Where　　⑤ How

3

A: _____ go on a picnic.
B: That sounds great.

① Be　　② Do　　③ Won't
④ Let　　⑤ Let's

4

A: _____ does he get up early?
B: Because he takes swimming
　　lessons in the morning.

① What　　② When　　③ Where
④ Why　　⑤ How

[5-6] 빈칸에 들어갈 말이 바르게 짝지어진 것을 고르시오.

5

• __(A)__ did you go on vacation
with?
• __(B)__ car do you like, the red
one or the white one?

	(A)		(B)
①	Who	······	How
②	Whom	······	Which
③	Whom	······	Why
④	Whose	······	Which
⑤	Whose	······	What

6

• The soccer game was exciting,
__(A)__ it?
• __(B)__ often do you go to the
movies?

	(A)		(B)
①	aren't	······	When
②	isn't	······	How
③	wasn't	······	How
④	doesn't	······	Why
⑤	didn't	······	Why

[7-8] 빈칸에 공통으로 들어갈 말을 쓰시오.

7

• _____ did you eat for lunch?
• _____ a rude person he is!

8

• A: _____ follow me!
　B: I was not following you.
• A: _____ they sell computers?
　B: No, they don't. They only sell cell
　　phones.

서술형

[9-11] 빈칸에 알맞은 말을 써서 부가의문문을 완성하시오.

9 Paul speaks both English and French,
_____?

10 You will go skating tomorrow,
_____?

11 Ms. Alison was your math teacher,
_____?

[12-13] 다음 중 밑줄 친 부분이 <u>잘못된</u> 것을 고르시오.

12 ① <u>Go to bed</u> right now.
② <u>Isn't this jacket</u> Dorothy's?
③ <u>Whom took</u> these photos?
④ <u>How old is</u> your grandfather?
⑤ <u>Where did you buy</u> the camera?

13 ① <u>Can't we sit</u> here?
② <u>Don't let's go</u> out today.
③ <u>Why did Jason call</u> you?
④ <u>What time did you meet</u> Andy?
⑤ <u>Open the door</u> for me, please.

빈출

14 다음 중 대화가 자연스럽지 <u>않은</u> 것은?

① A: How do we go to the airport?
B: We can take the shuttle bus.
② A: Isn't that card from Danny?
B: No, it's from Lewis.
③ A: Doesn't she look sad?
B: Yes, she doesn't. She looks happy.
④ A: How often do you check your
email?
B: Almost every day.
⑤ A: Why is this pen cheaper than that
one?
B: Because it's on sale.

서술형

[15-16] 대화가 성립되도록 ( ) 안에서 알맞은 말을 골라
쓰시오.

15 A: ⓐ (Whose, Which) is better, this
carpet or that one?
B: I like this one better. ⓑ (Let, Let's)
buy it.

ⓐ _____ ⓑ _____

16 A: We don't have homework today,
ⓐ (are, do) we?
B: I don't know. ⓑ (Why, How) don't
you ask Jenny?

ⓐ _____ ⓑ _____

17 다음 우리말을 영어로 바르게 옮긴 것은?

> 그는 외국 동전들을 모으지 않았니?

① Isn't he collect foreign coins?
② Wasn't he collect foreign coins?
③ Don't he collect foreign coins?
④ Doesn't he collect foreign coins?
⑤ Didn't he collect foreign coins?

서술형

[18-19] 다음 문장을 ( ) 안의 지시대로 바꿔 쓰시오.

18 They have a very cute baby. (감탄문으로)

→ _____ !

19 You should not make the same mistake again. (명령문으로)

→ _____ .

서술형

[20-22] 우리말과 일치하도록 ( ) 안에 주어진 말을 바르게 배열하시오.

20 우리의 약속에 대해 잊지 말자.
(about, let's, our promise, forget, not)

→ _____ .

21 저 새는 매우 높이 나는구나!
(how, flies, high, that bird)

→ _____ !

22 영어 수업은 몇 시에 시작하니?
(time, does, what, English class, begin)

→ _____ ?

서술형 고난도

[23-24] 어법상 틀린 부분을 찾아 바르게 고치시오.

23 A: Will you go to the library or home?
B: I will go to the library. I should study German today.
A: Isn't it difficult to learn?
B: Yes, it isn't. I have to memorize many things. (1개)

24 A: Let go to the concert. Pianist Isaac Dylan will play.
B: That sounds great. I like his music.
A: He is a great pianist, is he?
B: Yes, he is. What beautifully he plays! (3개)

GRAMMAR
Inside

workbook

A 4-level grammar course
with abundant writing practice

Compact and concise English grammar
간결하고 정확한 문법 설명

Extensive practice in sentence writing
다양한 유형의 영어 문장 쓰기

Full preparation for middle school tests
내신 완벽 대비

+ Workbook with additional exercises
풍부한 양의 추가 문제

GRAMMAR
Inside

LEVEL 1

CHAPTER 01 be동사

UNIT 01 **be동사의 현재형과 과거형**

CHECK UP p.12

1. ⓑ

PRACTICE p.13

STEP 1	**1.** It's **2.** I'm **3.** You're **4.** He's **5.** They're
STEP 2	**1.** am **2.** is **3.** were **4.** are **5.** was
STEP 3	**1.** There is **2.** There are **3.** There is **4.** There are **5.** There are
STEP 4	**1.** My favorite subject is **2.** The weather was **3.** Teddy and I are **4.** There was an email

UNIT 02 **be동사의 부정문과 의문문**

CHECK UP p.14

1. ⓒ 2. ⓑ

PRACTICE p.15

STEP 1	**1.** I'm not **2.** You're not / You aren't **3.** He's not / He isn't **4.** She wasn't **5.** They're not / They aren't
STEP 2	**1.** isn't **2.** aren't **3.** weren't **4.** aren't **5.** wasn't
STEP 3	**1.** Are you **2.** Am I **3.** Is Peter **4.** Were they
STEP 4	**1.** The meal isn't **2.** aren't busy **3.** Was the movie, was

GRAMMAR FOR WRITING pp.16-17

A **1.** is fresh **2.** There is a bus **3.** Are you cold **4.** They weren't[were not] there **5.** Mary isn't[is not] tall / Mary's not tall **6.** There are four seasons

7. was six years old

B **1.** We are middle school students **2.** You were a shy kid **3.** Is that street dangerous **4.** There were three children **5.** The book was not interesting **6.** Were you at the concert

C **1.** a. was tired b. am not tired **2.** a. was at school b. isn't[is not] at school **3.** a. were at home b. aren't[are not] at home **4.** a. weren't[were not] in the library b. are in the library

D **1.** There is a tree **2.** There are two birds **3.** There are three hats **4.** There is a bag

REVIEW TEST pp.18-21

1. ① **2.** ④ **3.** ⑤ **4.** are **5.** was **6.** There is **7.** There are **8.** ⑤ **9.** ② **10.** ② **11.** ② **12.** ③ **13.** ④ **14.** ③ **15.** ① **16.** ⑤ **17.** Is, is **18.** Are, aren't **19.** Is this movie funny **20.** Jack and Bill aren't[are not] twins **21.** There is a microphone **22.** is thick, isn't[is not] boring **23.** were in the swimming pool **24.** The ticket wasn't expensive **25.** ②, ④ **26.** ③ **27.** ③ **28.** X, were **29.** O **30.** X, are **31.** Two comedians was → Two comedians were **32.** My English teacher are → My English teacher is **33.** There is → There are, I were → I was

1 now로 보아 현재시제이고, 주어가 1인칭 단수이므로 am을 쓴다.

2 yesterday로 보아 과거시제이고, 주어가 3인칭 단수이므로 was를 쓴다.

3 last night으로 보아 과거시제이고, 주어가 3인칭 복수이므로 were를 쓴다.

4 this year로 보아 현재시제이고, 주어가 1인칭 복수(Andy and I)이므로 are를 쓴다.

5 two years ago로 보아 과거시제이고, 주어가 3인칭 단수이므로 was를 쓴다.

6 There is + 단수명사(a cat)

7 There are + 복수명사(twenty questions)

8 ① was ② is ③ were ④ are

9 주어가 3인칭 단수일 때 be동사 과거형의 부정문: 주어 + wasn't[was not]

10 ② Was Jenny ~?에 대한 답변: Yes, she was. / No, she wasn't.

11 ② I am의 부정형: I'm[I am] not

12 ③은 is, 나머지는 was

13 ④는 is, 나머지는 isn't

2

14 ③ the stores는 3인칭 복수이므로 Are가 되어야 한다.

15 ① There is + 단수명사, There are + 복수명사
(There is → There are)

16 There were + 복수명사: ~들이 있었다

17 주어가 3인칭 단수(this jacket)이므로 is를 쓴다.

18 현재시제이고 주어가 1인칭 복수이므로 are를 쓴다. 'Are we ~?'에 대한 부정의 대답은 'No, we aren't.'이다.

19 주어가 3인칭 단수일 때 be동사 현재형의 의문문: Is + 주어 ~?

20 주어가 3인칭 복수일 때 be동사 현재형의 부정문: 주어 + aren't[are not]

21 There is + 단수명사: ~가 있다

22 현재시제이고 주어가 3인칭 단수이므로 is를 쓴다. is의 부정형은 isn't[is not]이다.

23 과거시제이고 주어가 3인칭 복수일 때는 were를 쓴다.

24 주어가 3인칭 단수일 때 be동사 과거형의 부정형은 was not 이며, 줄임말은 wasn't이다.

25 ① 주어가 3인칭 단수이므로 be동사 과거형은 was
(were → was)
③ 주어가 3인칭 단수(Tokyo)이므로 be동사 현재형의 부정형은 isn't (aren't → isn't)
⑤ There are + 복수명사 (is → are)

26 c. 주어가 3인칭 단수일 때 be동사 과거형은 was
(were → was)
d. There is + 셀 수 없는 명사 (are → is)

27 · Jenny were hungry this morning.
→ Jenny was hungry this morning.
· The girls was noisy on the subway.
→ The girls were noisy on the subway.

28 last year로 보아 과거시제이고 주어가 1인칭 복수(Claire and I)이므로 were를 쓴다.

29 주어가 3인칭 단수(The dog)일 때 be동사 현재형은 is를 쓴다.

30 There are + 복수명사(a lot of books)

31 과거시제이고 주어가 3인칭 복수(Two comedians)이므로 were를 쓴다.

32 현재시제이고 주어가 3인칭 단수(My English teacher)이 므로 is를 쓴다.

33 첫 번째는 현재시제이고 복수명사(beautiful beaches)가 쓰 였으므로 there are를 쓴다. 두 번째는 last summer로 보 아 과거시제이고 주어가 I이므로 was를 쓴다.

02 일반동사

UNIT 01 일반동사의 현재형

CHECK UP p.24

1. ⓐ 2. ⓒ 3. ⓑ

PRACTICE p.25

STEP 1	1. eat 2. cries 3. have 4. sleeps 5. works 6. go
STEP 2	1. check 2. studies 3. washes 4. love 5. teaches 6. reads
STEP 3	1. has 2. tries 3. watches 4. speak
STEP 4	1. know that girl 2. live in London 3. goes to school

UNIT 02 일반동사의 과거형

CHECK UP p.26

1. ⓒ 2. ⓒ 3. ⓑ

PRACTICE p.27

STEP 1	1. spoke 2. put 3. made 4. slept 5. washed
STEP 2	1. planned 2. had 3. came 4. baked 5. bought 6. tried
STEP 3	1. worried 2. finished 3. invited 4. went
STEP 4	1. met Ann 2. taught English 3. got an email 4. watched the soccer game

UNIT 03 일반동사의 부정문

CHECK UP p.28

1. ⓑ 2. ⓒ 3. ⓐ 4. ⓒ

STEP 1	1. don't 2. doesn't 3. don't
	4. doesn't 5. doesn't 6. doesn't
STEP 2	1. didn't[did not] rain 2. didn't[did not] call 3. didn't[did not] pass
STEP 3	1. didn't come 2. don't like
	3. doesn't sell
STEP 4	1. doesn't work 2. don't listen
	3. didn't take 4. don't wear

UNIT 04   일반동사의 의문문

CHECK UP   p.30

1. ⓐ   2. ⓑ   3. ⓒ   4. ⓒ

PRACTICE   p.31

STEP 1	1. Does 2. Do 3. Does 4. Do
	5. Does
STEP 2	1. Did, enjoy 2. Did, go 3. Did, play
STEP 3	1. you don't 2. she does 3. I[we] did 4. they didn't
STEP 4	1. Does Susan sing 2. Do you like
	3. Did he buy 4. Did they plant

GRAMMAR FOR WRITING   pp.32-33

A   1. doesn't[does not] have a camera
2. opens at nine   3. didn't[did not] go to bed   4. hit my foot   5. Does Jack speak
6. don't[do not] remember his name
7. Did you buy

B   1. doesn't save money   2. do not watch that TV show   3. Did Jane fight with
4. I take piano lessons   5. Do they have pets   6. Emily visited her grandmother

C   1. gets up   2. goes to school   3. has lunch
4. comes home   5. watches TV   6. studies English

D   1. doesn't[does not] like   2. Does she have
3. didn't[did not] sleep   4. Did you read

REVIEW TEST   pp.34-37

1. ⑤   2. ③   3. ③   4. ⑤   5. ⑤   6. ④   7. ③
8. ⑤   9. ⓐ takes ⓑ brushes   10. ⓐ had
ⓑ didn't win   11. ⓐ don't[do not] ⓑ doesn't
[does not]   12. ⑤   13. ④   14. I didn't   15. they
don't   16. ⓐ didn't[did not] bring ⓑ gave
17. ④   18. ③   19. ①   20. doesn't[does not]
smoke   21. rained, stopped   22. cleans his room
23. read a book   24. didn't[did not] come to
school   25. ①, ⑤   26. ④   27. ④   28. X, walk
29. X, take   30. X, fixes   31. We eat → We ate
32. I doesn't → I don't, I find → I found
33. I writes → I write, I go → I went

1   ⑤ fly의 3인칭 단수 현재형: flies
2   ③은 동사원형과 3인칭 단수 현재형, 나머지는 현재형과 과거형
3   동사 likes의 형태로 보아 주어는 3인칭 단수가 되어야 한다.
4   주어가 3인칭 단수(Tim)일 때 일반동사 현재형의 의문문: Does + 주어 + 동사원형?
5   일반동사 과거형의 부정문: didn't[did not] + 동사원형
6   (A) 주어가 3인칭 단수(Karen)이므로 goes
   (B) 주어가 We이므로 take
7   (A) 주어가 3인칭 단수이므로 doesn't
   (B) 주어가 you이므로 Do
8   각각 ten minutes ago와 last night으로 보아 과거의 일을 나타내므로 과거형인 (A) washed (B) went를 쓴다.
9   주어가 3인칭 단수(Mina)이고 반복되는 습관을 나타내므로 현재형인 ⓐ takes ⓑ brushes를 쓴다.
10   last Friday로 보아 과거의 일을 나타내므로 과거형인 ⓐ had ⓑ didn't win을 쓴다.
11   문맥상 부정문이 자연스러우므로 ⓐ 주어가 I일 때는 don't ⓑ 주어가 3인칭 단수(Colin)일 때는 doesn't를 쓴다.
12   ⑤ last week로 보아 과거의 일을 나타내므로 동사의 과거형을 쓴다. (swims → swam)
13   일반동사 과거형의 의문문: ④ Did + 주어 + 동사원형? (came → come)
14   「Did + 주어 + 동사원형?」에 대한 부정의 대답: No, 주어 + didn't.
15   「Do + 주어 + 동사원형?」에 대한 부정의 대답: No, 주어 + don't.
16   ⓐ 일반동사 과거형의 부정문: didn't[did not] + 동사원형 ⓑ give의 과거형: gave
17   일반동사 과거형의 의문문: Did + 주어 + 동사원형?
18   주어가 3인칭 단수일 때 일반동사 현재형의 부정문: doesn't[does not] + 동사원형
19   질문이 과거형이므로 과거형으로 답한다.
20   주어가 3인칭 단수일 때 일반동사 현재형의 부정문: doesn't[does not] + 동사원형
21   과거의 일을 나타내므로 동사의 과거형을 쓴다.

22 주어가 3인칭 단수(Jeremy)이고 반복적인 습관을 나타내므로 「동사원형 + -(e)s」 형태로 쓴다.

23 과거의 일을 나타내므로 동사의 과거형을 쓴다.

24 일반동사 과거형의 부정문: didn't[did not] + 동사원형

25 ② 일반동사 과거형의 의문문: Did + 주어 + 동사원형?
(met → meet)
③ 주어가 3인칭 단수일 때 일반동사 현재형: 동사원형 + -(e)s
(cook → cooks)
④ last Friday로 보아 과거의 일을 나타내므로 동사의 과거형을 쓴다. (have → had)

26 a. 주어가 3인칭 단수이므로 현재형 부정문에는 doesn't를 쓴다. (don't → doesn't)
d. 일반동사 과거형의 부정문: didn't[did not] + 동사원형
(not played → didn't[did not] play)

27 ・This shirt does not has pockets.
→ This shirt does not have pockets.

28 주어가 3인칭 단수일 때 일반동사 현재형의 의문문: Does + 주어 + 동사원형?

29 일반동사 과거형의 부정문: didn't[did not] + 동사원형

30 fix의 3인칭 단수 현재형: fixes

31 last weekend로 보아 과거에 일어난 일이므로 동사 eat의 과거형인 ate을 쓴다.

32 첫 번째는 주어가 I이고 반복되는 습관을 나타내므로 현재형 부정문 don't를 쓴다. 두 번째는 편지를 발견한 것이 과거의 일이기 때문에 동사 find의 과거형인 found를 쓴다.

33 첫 번째는 every day를 보아 반복적인 습관을 나타내므로 동사의 현재형이 와야 하나, 주어가 I이므로 동사원형을 그대로 쓴다. 두 번째는 문맥상 '잠자리에 늦게 든 것'은 어제 있었던 일이기 때문에 과거형인 went를 쓴다.

CHAPTER 03 조동사

UNIT 01 can, may

CHECK UP   p.40

1. ⓑ 2. ⓑ

PRACTICE   p.41

STEP 1	1. ⓐ 2. ⓒ 3. ⓑ 4. ⓑ 5. ⓐ 6. ⓒ
STEP 2	1. can't sleep 2. Can, have 3. can solve 4. can draw
STEP 3	1. may be 2. may not come 3. May, see

STEP 4	1. can't[cannot] visit 2. May[Can] I use 3. couldn't reach 4. am able to lift

UNIT 02 must, have to, should

CHECK UP   p.42

1. ⓑ 2. ⓒ 3. ⓐ 4. ⓒ

PRACTICE   p.43

STEP 1	1. follow 2. not be 3. has to 4. don't have to 5. cannot 6. must not
STEP 2	1. have to 2. has to 3. have to 4. has to 5. has to
STEP 3	1. must not run 2. don't have to keep 3. must not cross 4. doesn't have to get up
STEP 4	1. should say 2. should not waste 3. doesn't have to help

GRAMMAR FOR WRITING   pp.44-45

A 1. must be happy 2. Can[May] I borrow 3. Can you answer / Are you able to answer 4. may be late 5. must[should] not make noise 6. should[must, have to] wear a seat belt 7. don't have to leave a tip

B 1. Can you play the cello 2. can't be a liar 3. May I try on these shoes 4. is able to use 5. should not fight with your brother 6. I have to call Gary

C 1. can buy 2. May I open 3. must be 4. You have to wear

D 1. can bring your pets 2. must not ride a bike 3. have to put trash in the bin 4. shouldn't[should not] pick the flowers

REVIEW TEST   pp.46-49

1. ③ 2. ④ 3. ⑤ 4. ③ 5. ③ 6. ③ 7. must
8. can't[cannot] 9. may 10. ② 11. ④ 12. ④
13. ③ 14. ⑤ 15. must not 16. don't have to
17. can't 18. ② 19. ② 20. has to[must,

should] take care of **21.** don't have to buy
22. may go   **23.** couldn't[could not] find
24. must be great   **25.** We shouldn't waste water
26. ①, ②   **27.** ②   **28.** ③   **29.** O   **30.** X, not
come   **31.** X, doesn't have to   **32.** must are →
must be   **33.** should say not → should not say
34. may is → may be, must knows → must know

1 may와 can은 '~해도 좋다(허가)'의 의미를 나타낸다.
2 must와 have to는 '~해야 한다(의무)'의 의미를 나타낸다.
3 can과 be able to는 '~할 수 있다(능력, 가능)'의 의미를 나타낸다.
4 허가를 나타내는 can이 와야 한다.
5 추측을 나타내는 may가 와야 한다.
6 must는 의무(~해야 한다)와 강한 추측(~임에 틀림없다)의 의미를 나타낸다.
7 must: ~임에 틀림없다(강한 추측)
8 can't[cannot]: ~할 수 없다
9 may: ~일지도 모른다(추측)
10 ②는 '~해도 좋다(허가)', 나머지는 '~할 수 있다(능력, 가능)'
11 ④는 '~임에 틀림없다(강한 추측)', 나머지는 '~해야 한다(의무)'
12 ④는 '~해도 좋다(허가)', 나머지는 '~일지도 모른다(추측)'
13 ③ 주어가 3인칭 단수이므로 has to를 쓴다.
14 ⑤ you must not → you don't have to (must not: ~해서는 안 된다, don't have to: ~할 필요가 없다)
15 '~해서는 안 된다'의 의미를 가진 must not이 와야 한다.
16 '~할 필요가 없다'의 의미를 가진 don't have to가 와야 한다.
17 '~할 수 없다'의 의미를 가진 can't가 와야 한다.
18 ② can't be는 '~일 리가 없다'는 의미로 문맥상 맞지 않는다.
19 may not: ~하지 않을지도 모른다
20 주어가 3인칭 단수이므로 has to를 쓴다. 의미상 must와 should도 가능하다.
21 don't have to: ~할 필요가 없다
22 may: ~일지도 모른다(추측)
23 가능을 나타내는 can의 과거 부정형은 couldn't[could not]이다.
24 must: ~임에 틀림없다(강한 추측)
25 should의 부정형은 shouldn't[should not]이다.
26 ③ 조동사 뒤에는 항상 동사원형을 쓴다. (cooks → cook)
④ can은 be able to와 같은 의미를 나타낸다.
(can → is 또는 able to pass → pass)
⑤ 조동사의 부정문은 조동사 뒤에 not을 붙여 나타낸다.
(must don't → must not)
27 b. be not able to: ~할 수 없다 (doesn't → isn't)
e. don't/doesn't have to + 동사원형: ~할 필요가 없다
(cleaning → clean)
28 · Claire and Sue has to study all night.
→ Claire and Sue have to study all night.
· The birthday cake don't have to be big.
→ The birthday cake doesn't have to be big.
29 허가를 나타내는 can

30 조동사의 부정문은 조동사 뒤에 not을 붙여 나타낸다.
31 주어가 3인칭 단수일 때 have to의 부정형은 doesn't have to이다.
32 조동사 뒤에는 항상 동사원형을 쓴다.
33 조동사의 부정문은 조동사 뒤에 not을 붙여 나타낸다.
34 조동사 뒤에는 항상 동사원형을 쓴다.

CHAPTER 04 진행형과 미래시제

UNIT 01   진행형

CHECK UP   p.52

1. ⓒ   **2.** ⓑ

PRACTICE   p.53

STEP 1	**1.** am eating **2.** waiting **3.** not working **4.** learning **5.** dancing **6.** is staying
STEP 2	**1.** are sitting **2.** am joking **3.** is crying **4.** isn't raining **5.** aren't dying
STEP 3	**1.** were watching **2.** was running **3.** were studying **4.** wasn't lying
STEP 4	**1.** are having **2.** isn't wearing **3.** Were you cutting **4.** was looking for

UNIT 02   **will, be going to**

CHECK UP   p.54

1. ⓑ   **2.** ⓑ   **3.** ⓒ

PRACTICE   p.55

STEP 1	**1.** be **2.** to take **3.** not forget **4.** change **5.** are going to
STEP 2	**1.** will help **2.** won't be **3.** will make
STEP 3	**1.** We're going to go **2.** I'm not going to eat **3.** He's going to clean

STEP 4 1. will have 2. won't break 3. is going to move 4. Are, going to study

---

GRAMMAR FOR WRITING pp.56-57

A 1. are wearing 2. Will you leave 3. was lying 4. won't[will not] be at home 5. Are you going to buy 6. wasn't[was not] listening to 7. am not going to watch

B 1. The train is arriving 2. Will you play chess 3. Nancy is going to bring 4. Is the musical going to start 5. Was he writing a letter 6. We are not speaking

C 1. is shining 2. aren't[are not] sleeping 3. is cooking 4. are standing 5. Were, taking

D 1. am going to post 2. will turn down 3. won't[will not] be 4. Are, going to read

---

REVIEW TEST pp.58-61

1. ④ 2. ③ 3. ③ 4. ④ 5. ⑤ 6. ④ 7. ⑤ 8. ③ 9. is drawing 10. was running 11. is going to water 12. are going to go 13. ④ 14. ② 15. Are they going to build 16. ⑤ 17. ③ 18. ⓐ are traveling ⓑ are going to visit 19. ⓐ will be ⓑ won't[will not] give up 20. is putting on his shoes 21. were taking a walk 22. am not reading a comic book 23. Will you buy the watch 24. We are not going to meet 25. ①, ②, ⑤ 26. ④ 27. ② 28. X, Are 29. X, were having 30. X, not going to 31. is sleep → is sleeping, will gets up → will get up 32. am studying → was studying 33. met → will[am going to] meet, His plane are going to → His plane is going to, he is going not to → he isn't[is not] going to

1 ④ see는 -e로 끝나는 동사지만 예외적으로 e를 빼지 않고 -ing를 붙인다. (seing → seeing)

2 지금 진행 중인 일을 나타내므로 현재진행형을 쓴다.

3 미래를 나타내므로 will이나 be going to를 쓴다. (주어가 I이므로 will see 또는 am going to see)

4 미래를 나타내므로 will이나 be going to를 쓴다. (주어가 We이므로 will go 또는 are going to go)

5 will + 동사원형: ~할 것이다
   will의 의문문: Will + 주어 + 동사원형?

6 과거진행형: be동사의 과거형 + v-ing
   과거진행형의 의문문: be동사의 과거형 + 주어 + v-ing?

7 ⑤ 주어가 3인칭 단수이므로 is going to play가 되어야 한다.

8 ③ 주어가 복수이므로 were making이 되어야 한다.

9 현재진행형: be동사의 현재형 + v-ing

10 과거진행형: be동사의 과거형 + v-ing

11 주어가 3인칭 단수이므로 is going to water가 되어야 한다.

12 주어가 복수이므로 are going to go가 되어야 한다.

13 ④ 진행형의 부정문: be동사 + not + v-ing (doesn't → isn't)

14 ② will의 의문문: Will + 주어 + 동사원형? (buys → buy)

15 be동사 + 주어 + going to + 동사원형?: ~할 예정이니?

16 과거의 한 시점에 진행 중이던 일을 나타내므로 과거진행형을 쓴다. (be동사의 과거형 + v-ing)

17 ③ 「Are you v-ing?」에 대한 대답: Yes, I am. / No, I'm not.

18 ⓐ 현재진행형: be동사의 현재형 + v-ing
   ⓑ be going to + 동사원형: ~할 예정이다

19 ⓐ will 뒤에는 동사원형을 쓴다. (will am → will be)
   ⓑ will의 부정문: won't[will not] + 동사원형

20 현재진행형: be동사의 현재형 + v-ing

21 과거진행형: be동사의 과거형 + v-ing

22 진행형의 부정문: be동사 + not + v-ing

23 will의 의문문: Will + 주어 + 동사원형?

24 be going to의 부정문: be not going to + 동사원형

25 ③ will의 의문문: Will + 주어 + 동사원형? (likes → like)
   ④ be going to의 부정문: be not going to + 동사원형 (is going not to → is not going to)

26 I'm not call Peter now.
   → I'm not calling Peter now.
   My sister and I was talking.
   → My sister and I were talking.

27 · I was knowing the answer.
      → I knew the answer.
   · She won't cries in front of people.
      → She won't cry in front of people.
   · Is Ben and Lily going to play the game?
      → Are Ben and Lily going to play the game?

28 be going to의 의문문: be동사 + 주어 + going to + 동사원형?

29 과거의 한 시점에 진행 중이던 일을 나타내므로 과거진행형을 쓰는데, 주어가 3인칭 복수이므로 were having을 쓴다.

30 be going to의 부정문: be not going to + 동사원형

31 첫 번째는 지금 진행 중인 일을 나타내므로 현재진행형인 「be동사 + v-ing」를 쓴다. 두 번째는 will 뒤에 동사원형이 와야 한다.

32 과거의 한 시점에 진행 중이던 일에 대해 이야기하고 있으므로 과거진행형을 써야 한다.

33 첫 번째는 미래시제이므로 will meet이나 am going to meet이, 두 번째는 주어가 3인칭 단수(His plane)이므로 is going to가, 세 번째는 be going to의 부정문 어순에 따라

CHAPTER 05 동사의 종류

UNIT 01 감각동사 + 형용사

CHECK UP p.64

1. ⓒ 2. ⓑ

PRACTICE p.65

STEP 1	1. warm 2. nice 3. lovely 4. sounds 5. good
STEP 2	1. strong 2. ○ 3. sleepy 4. ○ 5. salty
STEP 3	1. feel 2. sounds 3. look 4. smells
STEP 4	1. felt soft 2. sounds exciting 3. look beautiful

UNIT 02 목적어가 두 개 필요한 동사

CHECK UP p.66

1. ⓒ   2. ⓑ   3. ⓐ

PRACTICE p.67

STEP 1	1. for 2. to 3. for 4. for 5. of
STEP 2	1. passed 2. bought 3. cooked 4. sent
STEP 3	1. him an email 2. me some sandwiches 3. his cell phone to me
STEP 4	1. taught them math 2. brought me a newspaper 3. made gloves for her brother 4. sent a birthday card to David

UNIT 03 목적격 보어가 필요한 동사

CHECK UP p.68

1. ⓐ   2. ⓐ   3. ⓒ   4. ⓒ

PRACTICE p.69

STEP 1	1. rich 2. to help 3. warm 4. to answer
STEP 2	1. sad 2. easy 3. an angel 4. fresh
STEP 3	1. to be 2. to stop 3. to give 4. to read
STEP 4	1. keeps my juice cold 2. made him a millionaire 3. asked her to speak up 4. told me to finish

GRAMMAR FOR WRITING pp.70-71

A 1. looks expensive 2. made me a kite / made a kite for me 3. felt thirsty 4. taught me Japanese / taught Japanese to me 5. made him a great writer 6. advised me to eat 7. lent her his camera / lent his camera to her

B 1. showed my report card to my parents 2. This soap doesn't smell good 3. found the window open 4. make the world a better place 5. gives us useful information 6. asked me to explain the word

C 1. keep it cool 2. pass me the salt / pass the salt to me 3. call me Kim 4. feel terrible

D 1. felt hungry 2. asked my brother to make 3. made me pancakes / made pancakes for me, smelled great 4. tasted strange

REVIEW TEST pp.72-75

1. ④ 2. ③ 3. ④ 4. ⑤ 5. ③ 6. a fan letter to him 7. some napkins for you 8. ③ 9. ⑤ 10. ① 11. ③ 12. gave it to 13. want them to be 14. ③ 15. ⑤ 16. ⑤ 17. ② 18. ③ 19. tastes bitter 20. looks peaceful 21. asked me to carry her books 22. found the mailbox empty 23. make some cookies for you 24. He

allowed me to use his phone　**25.** ②, ④, ⑤
26. ③　**27.** ④　**28.** ○　**29.** X, useful　**30.** X, to his
brother　**31.** strangely → strange　**32.** Tori him →
him Tori, looks happily → looks happy　**33.** come
→ to come, to her? → for her?

1 간접목적어 앞에 전치사 for를 쓰는 동사는 buy이다.

2 B의 응답으로 미루어 보아 빈칸에는 긍정적인 내용이 들어가야
　한다. 또한 감각동사 뒤에는 형용사를 쓰므로 ③이 알맞다.

3 look + 형용사: ~해 보이다 (nicely → nice)

4 keep은 목적격 보어로 형용사를 쓴다. (quietly → quiet)

5 ③ make는 목적격 보어로 동사원형을 쓴다.

6 「send + 간접목적어 + 직접목적어」는 「send + 직접목적어 +
　to + 간접목적어」 형태로 바꿔 쓸 수 있다.

7 「get + 간접목적어 + 직접목적어」는 「get + 직접목적어 + for
　+ 간접목적어」 형태로 바꿔 쓸 수 있다.

8 ③은 목적어가 두 개 필요한 수여동사 make, 나머지는 목적격
　보어가 필요한 동사 make

9 ⑤ cook은 간접목적어 앞에 전치사 for를 쓴다.

10 show + 직접목적어 + to + 간접목적어,
　advise + 목적어 + to부정사

11 (A) sound + 형용사: ~하게 들리다
　(B) send + 직접목적어 + to + 간접목적어
　(C) tell + 목적어 + to부정사

12 give + 직접목적어 + to + 간접목적어

13 want + 목적어 + to부정사

14 ③ find + 목적어 + 형용사 (beautifully → beautiful)

15 ⑤ make는 간접목적어 앞에 전치사 for를 쓴다. (to → for)

16 ⑤ sound + 형용사: ~하게 들리다 (interestingly →
　interesting)

17 tell + 간접목적어(~에게) + 직접목적어(…을) 또는
　tell + 직접목적어 + to + 간접목적어

18 expect는 목적격 보어로 to부정사를 쓴다.

19 taste + 형용사: ~한 맛이 나다

20 look + 형용사: ~해 보이다

21 ask + 목적어 + to부정사

22 find + 목적어 + 형용사

23 make + 직접목적어 + for + 간접목적어

24 allow는 목적격 보어로 to부정사를 쓴다.

25 ① tell은 목적격 보어로 to부정사를 쓴다. (eat → to eat)
　③ sound + 형용사: ~하게 들리다 (nicely → nice)

26 c. teach는 간접목적어 앞에 to를 쓴다.
　(for Emma → to Emma)
　e. order는 목적격 보어로 to부정사를 쓴다.
　(finish → to finish)

27 ・I showed to my grandmother the painting.
　→ I showed the painting to my grandmother. /
　　I showed my grandmother the painting.

28 taste + 형용사: ~한 맛이 나다

29 find + 목적어 + 형용사

30 lend + 직접목적어 + to + 간접목적어

31 감각동사(smell) 다음에 형용사가 와야 하므로 strange가 되
　어야 한다.

32 첫 번째는 「name + 목적어 + 명사」 어순을 따라야 한다. 두 번
　째는 감각동사(look) 다음에 형용사가 와야 하므로 happy가
　되어야 한다.

33 첫 번째는 「ask + 목적어 + to부정사」이기 때문에 to come
　이 되어야 한다. 두 번째는 buy가 간접목적어 앞에 전치사 for
　를 쓰기 때문에 to her를 for her로 고쳐야 한다.

CHAPTER 06 명사와 관사

UNIT 01　셀 수 있는 명사 vs. 셀 수 없는 명사

CHECK UP　　　　　　　　　　　　　p.78

1. ⓑ　　**2.** ⓒ

PRACTICE　　　　　　　　　　　　　p.79

STEP 1	1. watches　2. songs　3. knives
	4. women　5. mice　6. photos
	7. buses　8. sheep　9. tomatoes
	10. toys　11. babies　12. feet
STEP 2	1. cats　2. cities　3. Health　4. ○
	5. teeth　6. bread
STEP 3	1. a cup of coffee　2. a bowl of soup
	3. two slices of cheese　4. three
	pieces of furniture
STEP 4	1. five classes　2. salt　3. a pair of
	shoes

UNIT 02　관사

CHECK UP　　　　　　　　　　　　　p.80

1. ⓒ　　**2.** ⓒ

PRACTICE　　　　　　　　　　　　　p.81

STEP 1	1. an　2. by bus　3. the　4. a
	5. The, the　6. The
STEP 2	1. a　2. an　3. ○　4. ○　5. The
STEP 3	1. X　2. an　3. the　4. a　5. X　6. the

<table>
<tr><td>STEP 4</td><td>1. the window   2. bed
3. plays tennis</td></tr>
</table>

GRAMMAR FOR WRITING   pp.82-83

A 1. has two watches   2. four women
3. turn on the air conditioner   4. a bottle of
water   5. went to the park by bike   6. saw
an elephant   7. two slices[pieces] of pizza

B 1. has breakfast at seven o'clock   2. The
world is changing   3. The picture on the
table is   4. goes to the dentist three times a
year   5. has ten pairs of shoes   6. bought
books on the internet

C 1. travel by train   2. saw the key   3. play
soccer   4. once a month   5. in the sky
6. play the drums

D 1. two bowls of cereal   2. a cup of tea
3. two slices of bread   4. a glass of
chocolate milk

REVIEW TEST   pp.84-87

1. ⑤   2. ③   3. ③   4. ②   5. ③   6. ④   7. ④
8. ②   9. leaves   10. tea   11. ⑤   12. ②   13. ③
14. an   15. X   16. the   17. the[The]   18. There
are many sheep, New Zealand   19. ④   20. health
21. The newspaper   22. ①   23. by taxi   24. a
piece of cake   25. ②, ④, ⑤   26. ③   27. ②
28. X, thieves   29. X, The pencil   30. X, the
internet   31. A supermarket → The supermarket,
a orange → an orange   32. to movies → to the
movies, a movie → the movie   33. teas → tea,
cheesecakes → cheesecake

1 ⑤ piano의 복수형: pianos
2 ③ knife의 복수형: knives
3 ③ sugar는 셀 수 없는 명사로 항상 단수형으로 쓴다.
4 ②는 관사 바로 다음 단어인 empty의 발음이 모음으로 시작하
므로 an을 쓰고, 나머지는 모두 a를 쓴다.
5 ③ money는 물질명사로 항상 단수형으로 쓴다.
(moneys → money)
6 ④ Australia는 고유명사로 앞에 a/an을 쓰지 않는다.
(an Australia → Australia)
7 ④ two cups of coffee: 커피 두 잔
8 ② 「by + 교통수단」을 나타낼 때는 관사를 쓰지 않는다.
(by a bus → by bus)
9 There were로 보아 빈칸에 복수명사가 와야 하므로 leaf의

복수형인 leaves를 쓴다.
10 tea는 셀 수 없는 명사이므로 앞에 a/an을 쓰지 않으며 항상
단수형으로 쓴다.
11 보기와 ⑤는 '~마다(= per)'의 의미이다.
12 (A) 특정하지 않은 하나를 나타내는 a
(B) 앞에 언급된 특정한 것을 나타내는 the
13 ③ 「by + 통신수단」을 나타낼 때는 관사를 쓰지 않는다.
(by a fax → by fax)
14 '하나의(= one)'의 의미를 갖는 부정관사 an을 쓴다.
15 장소가 본래의 목적으로 쓰일 때는 관사를 쓰지 않는다.
16 세상에 하나밖에 없는 것 앞에는 정관사 the를 쓴다.
17 정황상 무엇인지 알 수 있는 특정한 것을 나타낼 때나, 세상에
하나밖에 없는 것 앞에는 정관사 the를 쓴다.
18 sheep의 복수형은 sheep이고, New Zealand는 셀 수 없
는 명사(고유명사)로 복수형으로 쓰거나 앞에 a/an을 쓰지 않
는다.
19 play the + 악기 이름
20 health는 추상적인 개념을 나타내는 명사이므로 앞에 a/an을
쓰지 않으며 항상 단수형으로 쓴다.
21 명사 뒤에 수식어구가 있어 가리키는 대상이 분명할 때는 정관
사 the를 쓴다.
22 two slices of cheese: 치즈 두 장
(I need two slices of cheese.)
23 「by + 교통수단」을 나타낼 때는 관사를 쓰지 않는다.
24 a piece of cake: 케이크 한 조각
25 ① man의 복수형: men (mans → men)
③ help는 추상적인 개념을 나타내는 명사이므로 복수형으로
쓰지 않는다. (helps → help)
26 c. 세상에 하나밖에 없는 것 앞에는 정관사 the를 쓴다.
(A sun → The sun)
e. 식사 이름 앞에는 관사를 쓰지 않는다.
(the breakfast → breakfast)
27 ・Minho sent me pictures by the email.
→ Minho sent me pictures by email.
・I read the book for a hour.
→ I read the book for an hour.
・My foot are too cold in winter.
→ My feet are too cold in winter.
28 thief의 복수형: thieves
29 명사 뒤에 수식어구가 있어 가리키는 대상이 분명할 때는 정관
사 the를 쓴다.
30 일부 매체 앞에는 항상 정관사 the를 쓴다.
31 첫 번째는 supermarket이 앞 문장에서 이미 언급되었기 때
문에 앞에 정관사 The를 쓴다. 두 번째는 orange의 발음이
모음으로 시작하므로 an을 쓴다.
32 첫 번째는 movies가 go to와 함께 쓰일 때는 항상 정관사
the를 쓰므로 the movies가 되어야 한다. 두 번째는 앞에서
movie가 이미 언급되었기 때문에 정관사 the를 쓴다.
33 첫 번째 tea와 두 번째 cheesecake 모두 물질명사이므로
단수형으로 써야 한다. 복수형은 단위를 나타내는 표현을 써
서 나타내야 하므로 two cups of tea, two pieces of
cheesecake가 알맞다.

10

07 대명사

UNIT 01 인칭대명사, 재귀대명사

CHECK UP   p.90

1. ⓑ   **2.** ⓒ

PRACTICE   p.91

STEP 1	**1.** hers **2.** their **3.** himself **4.** you **5.** herself **6.** our
STEP 2	**1.** her **2.** They **3.** He **4.** Its **5.** them
STEP 3	**1.** introduce myself **2.** help yourself to **3.** by herself **4.** enjoy yourself
STEP 4	**1.** Daniel's phone number **2.** talks to herself **3.** use yours

UNIT 02   this, that, it

CHECK UP   p.92

1. ⓒ   **2.** ⓑ   **3.** ⓐ

PRACTICE   p.93

STEP 1	**1.** This **2.** It **3.** these **4.** It **5.** Those **6.** that
STEP 2	**1.** those **2.** that **3.** This
STEP 3	**1.** It's[It is] Tuesday **2.** It's[It is] windy **3.** It's[It is] 9:30 p.m **4.** It's[It is] November 15
STEP 4	**1.** these pictures **2.** That song **3.** It is bright

UNIT 03   one, some, any

CHECK UP   p.94

1. ⓐ   **2.** ⓑ   **3.** ⓒ   **4.** ⓒ

PRACTICE   p.95

STEP 1	**1.** some **2.** any **3.** one **4.** it **5.** some, any
STEP 2	**1.** ones **2.** it **3.** one **4.** one
STEP 3	**1.** any **2.** some **3.** some **4.** any
STEP 4	**1.** any flowers **2.** need one **3.** some magazines

---

GRAMMAR FOR WRITING   pp.96-97

A	**1.** It's[It is] rainy and windy **2.** This street **3.** You should love yourself **4.** any news **5.** We made some plans **6.** new one **7.** wrote us
B	**1.** Those are my cousins **2.** I will give these toys to Ronda **3.** It is dark here **4.** Will you have some cake **5.** We took a picture of ourselves **6.** Can I get yours
C	**1.** didn't bring it **2.** old ones don't fit **3.** borrow one
D	**1.** by himself **2.** hurt herself **3.** helped themselves **4.** made ourselves at home

---

REVIEW TEST   pp.98-101

1. ② **2.** ③ **3.** ② **4.** ⑤ **5.** ② **6.** ① **7.** ②
8. ⑤ **9.** ③ **10.** ④ **11.** his **12.** us **13.** ④
14. ③ **15.** ② **16.** ④ **17.** myself **18.** It **19.** ⓐ one ⓑ it **20.** This gift **21.** some tea **22.** It's[It is] two o'clock **23.** any snow **24.** trust yourself
25. ③, ④ **26.** ④ **27.** ③ **28.** O **29.** X, myself
30. X, hers **31.** purple one → purple ones
32. mine → me, its → it **33.** some food → any food, Help oneself → Help yourself

1   Jane을 대신하는 목적격 대명사는 her이다.
2   these + 복수명사(cookies)
3   앞에 나온 명사(a laptop)와 같은 종류의 불특정한 것을 가리 킬 때 one을 쓴다.
4   부정문에서 '조금도'의 의미를 나타내는 any를 쓴다.
5   ① This tomato ③ her email address ④ by himself ⑤ his dog
6   ② his wallet ③ It is ④ our English teacher ⑤ ourselves
7   ① me ③ you ④ hers ⑤ myself
8   (A)에는 소유격, (B)에는 소유대명사가 와야 한다.

9 ③ 날짜를 나타낼 때는 비인칭 주어 it을 쓴다. (This → It)

10 ④ this coat는 3인칭 단수 사물이므로 it을 쓴다. (they're → it's)

11 '그의 것'의 의미를 나타내는 소유대명사 his를 쓴다.

12 전치사의 목적어 자리이므로 목적격 대명사 us를 쓴다.

13 ④ 부정문에서 '조금도'의 의미를 나타내는 any를 쓴다.
(some pets → any pets)

14 ③ 앞에 나온 명사(a car)와 동일한 것을 가리키는 it을 쓴다.
(one → it)

15 ⓐ It ⓑ some ⓒ them ⓓ myself

16 ④ 앞에 나온 명사(pens)와 같은 종류의 불특정한 것을 가리키는 one을 쓴다. (a black it → a black one)

17 주어(I)의 행동을 강조하는 재귀대명사 myself를 쓴다.

18 첫 번째 빈칸에는 날씨를 나타내는 비인칭 주어 it을, 두 번째 빈칸에는 앞에 나온 the heater를 가리키는 대명사 it을 쓴다.

19 ⓐ 앞에 나온 명사(a bank)와 같은 종류의 불특정한 것을 가리키는 one, ⓑ 거리를 나타내는 비인칭 주어 it

20 this + 단수명사: 이 (~)

21 권유를 나타내는 의문문에서 '조금의'의 의미를 나타낼 때는 some을 쓴다.

22 시간을 나타낼 때는 비인칭 주어 it을 쓴다.

23 부정문에서 '조금도'의 의미를 나타낼 때는 any를 쓴다.

24 목적어가 주어와 같을 때는 목적어 자리에 재귀대명사를 쓴다.

25 ① 명암을 나타낼 때는 비인칭 주어 it을 쓴다. (This → It)
② 긍정문에서 '조금의'의 의미를 나타낼 때는 some을 쓴다. (any → some)
⑤ 명사 앞에 소유격이 와야 한다. (she → her)

26 a. 날짜를 나타낼 때는 비인칭 주어 it을 쓴다. (That → It)
c. 동사 뒤에 목적격이 와야 한다. (his → him)

27 · This gloves protect my hands.
→ These gloves protect my hands.
· Those are mine new toys.
→ Those are my new toys.

28 의문문에서 '조금', '아무'의 의미를 나타낼 때는 any를 쓴다.

29 목적어가 주어와 같을 때는 목적어 자리에 재귀대명사를 쓴다.

30 소유대명사 hers를 쓴다.

31 앞에 나온 복수명사(boots)와 같은 종류의 불특정한 것을 가리키므로 ones를 쓴다.

32 첫 번째는 '나에게'를 뜻하는 목적격 대명사 me를 쓴다. 두 번째는 '그것을'을 뜻하는 목적격 대명사 it을 쓴다.

33 첫 번째는 '조금도'의 의미를 나타내는 부정문이므로 any를 쓴다. 두 번째는 Help oneself를 상대방(you)에 알맞은 재귀대명사 형태로 고쳐 써야 한다.

CHAPTER
08 형용사와 부사

UNIT 01 형용사

CHECK UP p.104

1. ⓒ **2.** ⓐ

PRACTICE p.105

STEP 1	**1.** friendly **2.** lucky **3.** a few **4.** much **5.** something wrong
STEP 2	**1.** ⓒ **2.** ⓒ **3.** ⓑ **4.** ⓒ
STEP 3	**1.** little **2.** a lot of **3.** few **4.** much
STEP 4	**1.** was sick **2.** little coffee **3.** lots of sugar **4.** someone nice

UNIT 02 부사

CHECK UP p.106

1. ⓐ **2.** ⓒ

PRACTICE p.107

STEP 1	**1.** fast **2.** heavily **3.** Sadly **4.** late **5.** always eat
STEP 2	**1.** studied **2.** this tree is 500 years old **3.** spent **4.** long **5.** loudly **6.** I don't remember his name
STEP 3	**1.** should always lock the door **2.** is rarely absent from work **3.** will never tell your secret to others **4.** usually has strawberry ice cream for dessert
STEP 4	**1.** goes to bed early **2.** found, easily **3.** seldom stays up

UNIT 03 원급, 비교급, 최상급

CHECK UP p.108

1. ⓒ

PRACTICE

p.109

STEP 1	1. new 2. hotter 3. better
	4. longest 5. more comfortable
STEP 2	1. taller than 2. larger than
	3. thinner than 4. bigger than
	5. earlier than 6. more difficult than
STEP 3	1. the smartest 2. the strongest
	3. the worst 4. the most crowded
STEP 4	1. faster than 2. the best hotel 3. as
	nice as 4. more popular than

GRAMMAR FOR WRITING

pp.110-111

A 1. is honest 2. beautiful picture 3. the
door quietly 4. some[a few] students
5. much bigger than Venus 6. the most
famous scene 7. rarely has interviews

B 1. She felt sad about the news 2. He
spread a little butter 3. is the best player
on his team 4. studied as hard as Amy
5. much more interesting than science
6. Kevin often has a headache

C 1. older than 2. more expensive than
3. the fastest

D 1. many teeth 2. few cars 3. much time
4. little rain

REVIEW TEST

pp.112-115

1. ⑤ 2. ① 3. ⑤ 4. ② 5. as tall as 6. heavier
than 7. the biggest 8. ① 9. ② 10. ④ 11. ⑤
12. ⑤ 13. ④ 14. much 15. a few 16. little
17. ③ 18. ② 19. better than 20. the most
intelligent person 21. is as warm as last spring
22. We found something interesting 23. ④
24. is shorter than *Soul* 25. ①, ③, ④ 26. ①
27. ③ 28. X, little 29. X, high 30. drives
usually → usually drives, lately → late 31. greatly
→ great, more beautiful → most beautiful 32. the
most smart → the smartest, the funnyest → the
funniest, much → many[a lot of, lots of]

1 명사(baby)를 꾸며주는 형용사가 와야 한다.
2 much, even, far, a lot 등은 비교급 앞에 쓰여 비교급을 강
조한다.
3 ① fast ② quiet ③ expensive ④ large

4 ① nice ③ perfectly ④ good ⑤ quickly
5 as + 형용사의 원급 + as: ~만큼 ···한
6 형용사의 비교급 + than: ~보다 더 ···한
7 the + 형용사의 최상급: 가장 ~한
8 빈도부사는 일반동사 앞에 쓴다.
9 빈도부사는 조동사의 뒤, 일반동사의 앞에 쓴다.
10 ④ 명사(address)를 꾸며주는 형용사가 와야 한다. (newly
→ new)
11 ⑤ cold의 최상급: coldest (the most cold → the
coldest)
12 quickly의 비교급: more quickly
13 young의 최상급: youngest
14 much + 셀 수 없는 명사: 많은 ~
15 a few + 셀 수 있는 명사의 복수형: 약간의 ~
16 little + 셀 수 없는 명사: 거의 없는 ~
17 (A) 주어(A turtle)를 보충 설명하는 형용사 slow
(B) 동사(eat)를 꾸며주는 부사 slowly
18 (A) 명사(question)를 꾸며주는 형용사 hard
(B) 동사(know)를 꾸며주는 부사 hardly
19 good의 비교급: better
20 the + intelligent의 최상급: the most intelligent
21 as + 형용사의 원급 + as: ~만큼 ···한
22 -thing으로 끝나는 대명사는 형용사가 뒤에서 꾸며준다.
23 빈도부사는 조동사 뒤에 쓴다.
(They will often visit their grandparents.)
24 형용사의 비교급 + than: ~보다 더 ···한
25 ② 빈도부사는 일반동사 앞에 쓴다.
(buys sometimes → sometimes buys)
⑤ (a) few + 셀 수 있는 명사의 복수형 (a little → (a) few)
26 a. (a) little + 셀 수 없는 명사 (a few → (a) little)
d. 빈도부사는 일반동사 앞에 쓴다. (go rarely → rarely go)
e. nice의 비교급: nicer (more nice → nicer)
27 · Andy didn't put many salt in his soup.
→ Andy didn't put much[a lot of, lots of] salt in
his soup.
· Did you hear new anything?
→ Did you hear anything new?
28 little + 셀 수 없는 명사: 거의 없는 ~
29 high는 형용사와 부사의 형태가 같다. highly는 '매우'라는 다
른 뜻을 가진 부사이다.
30 첫 번째는 빈도부사가 일반동사의 앞에 와야 하므로 usually
drives의 어순으로 쓴다. 두 번째는 주어(he)를 보충 설명하는
형용사가 와야 하므로 late를 쓴다.
31 첫 번째는 명사(vacation)를 꾸며주는 형용사가 와야 하므로
great를 쓴다. 두 번째는 beautiful의 최상급인 most
beautiful을 쓴다.
32 첫 번째는 smart의 최상급인 smartest, 두 번째는 funny의
최상급인 funniest를 쓴다. 세 번째는 셀 수 있는 명사(funny
stories)와 함께 쓰는 many, a lot of 또는 lots of를 쓴다.

09 to부정사와 동명사

UNIT 01 · to부정사의 명사적 용법

CHECK UP　　　　　　　　　　p.118

1. ⓐ　2. ⓒ　3. ⓑ

PRACTICE　　　　　　　　　　p.119

STEP 1	1. 목적어　2. 주어　3. 보어　4. 목적어 5. 보어
STEP 2	1. a. go　b. to go　2. a. to walk b. walk　3. a. win　b. to win
STEP 3	1. whom to ask　2. when to take 3. whether to believe　4. where to stay
STEP 4	1. It, to find　2. what to say　3. is to read　4. needs to get

UNIT 02 · to부정사의 형용사적, 부사적 용법

CHECK UP　　　　　　　　　　p.120

1. ⓑ　2. ⓒ　3. ⓒ　4. ⓑ

PRACTICE　　　　　　　　　　p.121

STEP 1	1. time　2. an interesting city 3. something important　4. enough money
STEP 2	1. ⓓ　2. ⓒ　3. ⓑ　4. ⓐ
STEP 3	1. to read　2. to get good seats　3. to study music　4. to win the prize
STEP 4	1. something to give　2. glad to meet 3. plans to open　4. to buy clothes

UNIT 03 · 동명사의 역할

CHECK UP　　　　　　　　　　p.122

1. ⓑ　2. ⓒ　3. ⓑ

PRACTICE　　　　　　　　　　p.123

STEP 1	1. 목적어　2. 보어　3. 목적어　4. 보어 5. 주어
STEP 2	1. uploading　2. giving　3. not eating 4. skiing
STEP 3	1. Traveling　2. buying　3. writing 4. spending　5. making
STEP 4	1. are busy preparing　2. avoid eating 3. is worth trying　4. playing the violin

GRAMMAR FOR WRITING　　pp.124-125

A 1. hope to have　2. money to buy 3. opening the window　4. exciting to watch 5. went out to[in order to] get　6. riding the rollercoaster　7. how to use

B 1. is to have a house on the beach 2. Not wearing a seat belt　3. something special to show you　4. Solving the problem is impossible　5. turned on the TV to watch the news　6. what to do

C 1. difficult to answer　2. kept crying 3. go shopping　4. to[in order to] be a designer　5. watching[to watch] the parade 6. sorry to hear

D 1. to[in order to] interview　2. dancing 3. to[in order to] build　4. how to take care of

REVIEW TEST　　　　　　pp.126-129

1. ②　2. ④　3. ④　4. ⑤　5. ④　6. to　7. to be 8. painting　9. ⑤　10. ③　11. ②　12. ③　13. to leave her hometown　14. to pick up his friend 15. taking acting lessons　16. ④　17. ④　18. ⑤ 19. busy talking to the guests　20. to[in order to] rest on the grass　21. Listening[To listen]　22. It, to exercise　23. We hope to win the game 24. We stopped cheering for the players　25. ①, ③, ④　26. ④　27. ③　28. X, to take　29. X, studying　30. O　31. learn → to learn 32. decided stay → decided to stay, felt like to have → felt like having　33. where go to → where to go, places visit → places to visit, worth travel → worth traveling

1 to부정사가 주어로 쓰일 경우에는 보통 주어 자리에 가주어 It 을 사용하여 「It ~ to-v」 형태로 쓴다.

2 동사 enjoy는 목적어로 동명사를 쓴다.

3 앞의 명사(a person)를 꾸며주는 to부정사가 와야 한다.

4 whether to-v or not: ~할지 말지

5 보기와 ④는 동사의 목적어 역할을 하는 to부정사의 명사적 용법

6 감정의 원인과 목적을 나타내는 to부정사의 부사적 용법

7 동사 want는 목적어로 to부정사를 쓴다.

8 동사 finish는 목적어로 동명사를 쓴다.

9 ⑤는 to부정사의 부사적 용법(목적), 나머지는 명사적 용법(동사의 목적어)

10 ③은 to부정사의 부사적 용법(결과), 나머지는 형용사적 용법

11 ②는 보어 역할을 하는 동명사, 나머지는 동사의 목적어 역할

12 ③ to부정사의 부정형은 to 앞에 not을 붙인다.
(to not attend → not to attend)

13 감정의 원인을 나타내는 to부정사의 부사적 용법

14 목적을 나타내는 to부정사의 부사적 용법

15 전치사(in)의 목적어 역할을 하는 동명사

16 「-thing/-one/-body + 형용사 + to-v」의 어순

17 (A) 「It ~ to-v」 형태로 쓴 to부정사의 명사적 용법(주어 역할)
(B) a key를 꾸며주는 to부정사의 형용사적 용법

18 (A) when to start: 언제 시작할지
(B) how to make: 어떻게 만들지

19 be busy v-ing: ~하느라 바쁘다

20 목적을 나타내는 to부정사의 부사적 용법

21 주어 역할을 하는 동명사 또는 to부정사

22 to부정사가 주어로 쓰일 경우에는 보통 주어 자리에 가주어 It 을 사용하여 「It ~ to-v」 형태로 쓴다.

23 동사 hope는 목적어로 to부정사를 쓴다.

24 동사 stop은 목적어로 동명사를 쓴다.

25 ② 동명사가 주어로 쓰일 경우 3인칭 단수 취급한다.
(are → is)
⑤ 목적을 나타내는 to부정사의 부사적 용법
(enjoy → to enjoy)

26 b. to부정사가 형용사적 용법으로 쓰일 때는 꾸며주는 말 뒤에 위치한다.
(to wear something → something to wear)
d. 「It ~ to-v」 형태로 쓴 to부정사의 명사적 용법
(lose → to lose)

27 · He promised sending me presents.
→ He promised to send me presents.
· Robert went fish with his dad.
→ Robert went fishing with his dad.

28 too + 형용사 + to-v: 너무 ~해서 …할 수 없다

29 동사 give up은 목적어로 동명사를 쓴다.

30 감정의 원인을 나타내는 to부정사의 부사적 용법

31 「It ~ to-v」 형태로 쓴 to부정사의 명사적 용법이므로 to learn을 쓴다.

32 첫 번째는 동사 decide의 목적어로 to부정사를 써야 하므로 to stay를 쓴다. 두 번째는 '~하고 싶다'라는 표현인 「feel like

v-ing」를 써야 하므로 having을 쓴다.

33 첫 번째는 '어디로 ~할지'라는 뜻의 「where to-v」를 써야 하므로 to go를 쓴다. 두 번째는 명사(places)를 수식하는 형용사적 용법의 to부정사인 to visit을 쓴다. 세 번째는 '~할 가치가 있다'라는 표현인 「be worth v-ing」를 써야 하므로 traveling을 쓴다.

CHAPTER 10 전치사

UNIT 01 장소를 나타내는 전치사

CHECK UP p.132

1. ⓐ   2. ⓑ

PRACTICE p.133

STEP 1	1. in 2. on 3. on 4. at 5. in 6. at
STEP 2	1. in 2. on 3. at
STEP 3	1. in front of 2. behind 3. over
STEP 4	1. under a tree 2. next to my house 3. across from my school 4. from the hotel to downtown

UNIT 02 시간을 나타내는 전치사

CHECK UP p.134

1. ⓒ   2. ⓐ

PRACTICE p.135

STEP 1	1. at 2. in 3. at 4. on 5. in 6. on
STEP 2	1. at 2. after 3. before 4. for, in
STEP 3	1. during the summer 2. for two weeks 3. during our vacation 4. during class 5. for thirty minutes
STEP 4	1. around midnight 2. from Monday to Friday 3. between three and five o'clock

CHECK UP   p.136

1. ⓐ **2.** ⓑ **3.** ⓒ **4.** ⓐ

PRACTICE   p.137

STEP 1	**1.** me **2.** for **3.** by **4.** to **5.** about
STEP 2	**1.** ⓓ **2.** ⓑ **3.** ⓒ **4.** ⓐ
STEP 3	**1.** to **2.** by **3.** with
STEP 4	**1.** with a bat **2.** about the Second World War **3.** for her friends **4.** to the bookstore

GRAMMAR FOR WRITING   pp.138-139

A **1.** in the bottle **2.** before the game **3.** with my friends **4.** at 5:00 p.m **5.** under the seat **6.** during training **7.** on the second floor

B **1.** stood next to me **2.** sat in front of the TV **3.** will have a sale from Tuesday to Friday **4.** is between China and Japan **5.** planned a surprise party for Amy **6.** parked across from the restaurant

C **1.** in the park **2.** around 2:00 p.m. **3.** under a tree **4.** with a brush

D **1.** to 6:00 p.m **2.** on Mondays **3.** for two hours in the morning **4.** by telephone

REVIEW TEST   pp.140-143

1. ③ **2.** ① **3.** ② **4.** after **5.** between, and **6.** ④ **7.** ③ **8.** ⑤ **9.** from **10.** at **11.** for **12.** ① **13.** ② **14.** across from **15.** between, and **16.** next to **17.** ④ **18.** ② **19.** ③ **20.** ④ **21.** about, by **22.** for, after **23.** to, during **24.** between Kelly and Tim **25.** are in front of the bank **26.** ③, ④, ⑤ **27.** ③ **28.** ④ **29.** X, on **30.** X, him **31.** O **32.** in May 14 → on May 14, on 7:00 p.m. → at 7:00 p.m. **33.** next the beach → next to the beach, with taxi → by taxi **34.** at the morning → in the morning, at the sea → in the sea, In night → At night

1. 요일 앞에는 전치사 on을 쓴다.
2. 월 앞에는 전치사 in을 쓴다.
3. 장소의 한 지점을 나타내는 at을 쓴다. (at home: 집에)
4. after: ~ 후에
5. between A and B: A와 B 사이에
6. to: ~에게, ~로
7. for: ~을 위해, ~ 동안
8. with: ~와 함께, ~을 가지고
9. from A to B: A부터 B까지
10. 하루의 때를 나타내는 at을 쓴다. (at noon: 정오에)
11. for + 숫자를 포함한 구체적인 기간: ~ 동안
12. ①은 '~ 위에'를 의미하는 on, 나머지는 장소의 한 지점을 나타내는 at을 쓴다.
13. ②는 장소의 한 지점을 나타내는 at, 나머지는 공간의 내부나 도시, 국가를 나타내는 in을 쓴다.
14. across from: ~ 맞은편에
15. between A and B: A와 B 사이에
16. next to: ~ 옆에
17. ④ 날짜 앞에는 전치사 on을 쓴다. (in → on)
18. ② 공간의 내부를 나타내는 전치사 in을 쓴다. (at → in)
19. ③ '~을 위해'의 의미를 나타내는 for를 쓴다. (to → for)
20. from A to B: A부터 B까지
21. about: ~에 관하여, by: ~로(통신 수단)
22. for + 숫자를 포함한 구체적인 기간: ~ 동안, after: ~ 후에
23. to: ~로(목적지), during + 특정한 때를 나타내는 명사: ~ 동안
24. between A and B: A와 B 사이에
25. in front of: ~ 앞에
26. ① 하루의 때를 나타내는 at을 쓴다. (in → at)
    ② 오후를 나타낼 때는 in을 쓴다. (on → in)
27. c. for + 숫자를 포함한 구체적인 기간: ~ 동안 (during → for)
    e. between A and B: A와 B 사이에 (to → and)
28. • It is sunny and warm on spring.
    → It is sunny and warm in spring.
29. 요일 앞에는 전치사 on을 쓴다.
30. 전치사 뒤에 대명사가 올 때는 목적격을 쓴다.
31. near: ~ 근처에
32. 첫 번째는 날짜 앞이므로 전치사 on을 쓴다. 두 번째는 구체적인 시각 앞이므로 전치사 at을 쓴다.
33. 첫 번째는 '~ 옆에'를 나타내는 next to를 쓴다. 두 번째는 교통수단을 나타내는 전치사 by를 쓴다.
34. 첫 번째는 오전을 나타낼 때 쓰는 전치사 in, 두 번째는 공간의 내부를 나타내는 전치사 in, 세 번째는 하루의 때를 나타내는 전치사 at을 쓴다.

11 접속사

UNIT 01 and, but, or, so

CHECK UP   p.146

1. ⓑ 2. ⓐ 3. ⓑ 4. ⓒ

PRACTICE   p.147

STEP 1	1. and 2. interesting 3. or 4. so 5. or
STEP 2	1. and 2. or 3. but 4. so
STEP 3	1. he went to the doctor 2. he lost the game 3. he weighs 70 kg 4. he will go to the movies
STEP 4	1. both pizza and pasta 2. but I should leave

UNIT 02 when, before, after, until

CHECK UP   p.148

1. ⓐ 2. ⓒ 3. ⓑ 4. ⓐ

PRACTICE   p.149

STEP 1	1. When 2. get 3. After 4. until 5. before
STEP 2	1. ⓑ 2. ⓓ 3. ⓒ 4. ⓐ
STEP 3	1. When she saw me 2. until the storm is over 3. before he leaves Korea 4. After the party was over
STEP 4	1. until the bus came 2. After we had dinner 3. When I was young 4. before the movie starts

UNIT 03 because, if, that

CHECK UP   p.150

1. ⓐ 2. ⓒ 3. ⓑ

PRACTICE   p.151

STEP 1	1. that 2. If 3. that 4. because 5. doesn't come
STEP 2	1. that 2. If 3. that 4. because
STEP 3	1. that he is brilliant 2. If you need my help 3. because she was too busy
STEP 4	1. that he is right 2. because I studied hard 3. It is strange that 4. If you take a taxi

GRAMMAR FOR WRITING   pp.152-153

A 1. until I crossed the finish line 2. (that) this ticket is expensive 3. because he often tells lies 4. before she goes to bed 5. is old but useful 6. so he bought a new one 7. after the bus left

B 1. She bought meat and vegetables 2. when he heard the news 3. but I'm very busy 4. It is true that 5. if you have any questions 6. until we reach the top

C 1. but she lost the contest 2. or I will give you a hint 3. and he bought some clothes 4. so I made a reservation

D 1. after he left the office 2. before his wife got home 3. When his wife arrived 4. Because the food was delicious

REVIEW TEST   pp.154-157

1. ① 2. ② 3. ② 4. ④ 5. ② 6. ③ 7. ②
8. ① 9. ⑤ 10. or 11. but 12. that 13. ⑤
14. ① 15. ③ 16. ③ 17. because blue is my favorite color 18. when the doorbell rang 19. If you're[you are] free 20. until the rain stops
21. because my parents went out 22. It is surprising that he 23. after she plays tennis
24. ②, ④, ⑤ 25. ③ 26. ③ 27. X, that 28. X, gets 29. O 30. think it → think (that), will become → becomes 31. but → so, Peter or Pam → Peter and Pam, tired or happy → tired but happy 32. If I was → When I was, before → because

1 and: 그리고

2	or: 또는
3	but: 그러나
4	① and(그리고) ② both A and B(A와 B 둘 다) ③ but(그러나) ⑤ either A or B(A 또는 B 둘 중 하나)
5	② and로 연결된 것은 문법적으로 대등해야 한다. (quiet → quietly)
6	③ 조건을 나타내는 if절에서는 미래를 나타내더라도 현재시제 를 쓴다. (will hurry → hurry)
7	② '~할 때'의 뜻인 when을 쓴다. (if → when)
8	①은 but(그러나), 나머지는 so(그래서)
9	⑤는 or(또는), 나머지는 but(그러나)
10	or: 또는
11	but: 그러나
12	that절이 문장에서 보어로 쓰여 '~하는 것(이다)'의 의미를 나타 낸다.
13	because: ~하기 때문에
14	so: 그래서
15	after: ~한 후에
16	(A) or: 또는 (B) that절이 동사(think)의 목적어로 쓰여 '~하는 것을'의 의 미를 나타낸다.
17	because: ~하기 때문에
18	when: ~할 때
19	if: 만약 ~하다면
20	until: ~할 때까지
21	because: ~하기 때문에
22	that절이 문장에서 주어로 쓰일 때는 「It ~ that + 주어 + 동 사」 형태로 쓴다.
23	after: ~한 후에
24	① or: 또는 (and → or) ③ if는 절과 절을 연결하므로 if 뒤에 주어, 동사가 와야 한다. (if has → if she has)
25	a. if: 만약 ~하다면 (That → If) e. that절이 문장에서 주어로 쓰일 때는 「It ~ that + 주어 + 동사」 형태로 쓴다. (if → that)

26	· Both Ian or Mickey are great artists.
	  → Both Ian and Mickey are great artists.
	· I'll wait until the bus will come.
	  → I'll wait until the bus comes.

27	that절이 문장에서 보어로 쓰여 '~하는 것(이다)'의 의미를 나타 낸다.
28	시간을 나타내는 접속사가 이끄는 절에서는 미래를 나타내더 라도 현재시제를 쓴다.
29	if: 만약 ~하다면
30	첫 번째는 동사 think의 목적어로 '~하는 것을'의 의미를 나타 내는 that절을 쓴다. 이때의 that은 생략 가능하다. 두 번째는 조건을 나타내는 if절에서는 미래를 나타내더라도 현재시제를 쓰므로 becomes를 쓴다.
31	첫 번째는 '그래서'의 뜻인 so를, 두 번째는 '그리고'의 뜻인 and를, 세 번째는 tired와 happy가 상반된 내용이기 때문에 '그러나'의 뜻인 but을 쓴다.

32 첫 번째는 '~할 때'의 뜻인 when을, 두 번째는 이유를 나타내는 because를 쓴다.

CHAPTER
12 의문문, 명령문, 감탄문

UNIT 01 의문사 who, what, which

CHECK UP   p.160

1. ⓒ 2. ⓒ 3. ⓐ 4. ⓒ

PRACTICE   p.161

STEP 1	1. Who 2. Whom 3. Which	
STEP 2	1. ⓑ 2. ⓒ 3. ⓓ 4. ⓐ	
STEP 3	1. Whose 2. What 3. Who 4. Which	
STEP 4	1. Which is cheaper 2. Who[Whom] do you respect 3. What did he study	

UNIT 02 의문사 when, where, why, how

CHECK UP   p.162

1. ⓐ 2. ⓒ

PRACTICE   p.163

STEP 1	1. Where 2. How 3. When
STEP 2	1. ⓒ 2. ⓑ 3. ⓓ 4. ⓐ
STEP 3	1. How old 2. How much 3. How long 4. How far
STEP 4	1. Where does Erica 2. When did they 3. Why do you

UNIT 03 부가의문문

CHECK UP   p.164

1. ⓒ 2. ⓑ 3. ⓑ 4. ⓐ

STEP 1	**1.** he **2.** is **3.** won't **4.** did **5.** didn't
STEP 2	**1.** doesn't it **2.** didn't you **3.** should we **4.** wasn't he **5.** were they
STEP 3	**1.** can he, he can **2.** aren't they, they are **3.** didn't you, I didn't **4.** does it, it doesn't
STEP 4	**1.** will you **2.** won't you **3.** shall we

UNIT 04   부정의문문, 선택의문문

CHECK UP   p.166

1. ⓐ   **2.** ⓒ

PRACTICE   p.167

STEP 1	**1.** Don't **2.** or **3.** Which **4.** No **5.** They are French.
STEP 2	**1.** Isn't it cold **2.** Didn't she come **3.** Won't you join
STEP 3	**1.** Did you read a book or a newspaper **2.** Do you walk home or take the subway **3.** Will he come this Saturday or next Saturday
STEP 4	**1.** Doesn't she get up **2.** Which, summer or winter

UNIT 05   명령문, 감탄문

CHECK UP   p.168

1. ⓒ   **2.** ⓑ

PRACTICE   p.169

STEP 1	**1.** What **2.** Clean **3.** Don't leave **4.** How **5.** Let's not **6.** Please don't
STEP 2	**1.** Be quiet **2.** Don't[Do not] touch **3.** Don't[Do not] be **4.** Wear **5.** Please slow down / Slow down, please
STEP 3	**1.** lazy Susan is **2.** a great movie (it was) **3.** handsome the man is **4.** expensive shoes (these are)
STEP 4	**1.** Don't make noise **2.** What a cute puppy **3.** Let's eat ice cream

A   **1.** When was the festival **2.** How can I get **3.** Who made **4.** Where did you buy **5.** Tell me **6.** Isn't Ms. Jones **7.** will visit China, won't she

B   **1.** Let's go to the mountains **2.** How tall this building is **3.** How often do you eat out **4.** Why don't you read this book **5.** Do not enter that room **6.** Which did you like better

C   **1.** Where is **2.** Who told **3.** What did you eat **4.** When will you do **5.** Who[Whom] is she **6.** Which is more interesting

D   **1.** A. doesn't he B. No, he doesn't **2.** A. is she B. No, she isn't **3.** A. didn't they B. Yes, they did **4.** A. does he B. Yes, he does

1. ⑤ **2.** ① **3.** ⑤ **4.** ④ **5.** ④ **6.** Yes, I do **7.** No, isn't **8.** a fast runner (he is) **9.** boring this show is **10.** ② **11.** ⑤ **12.** ③ **13.** ⑤ **14.** ④ **15.** ③ **16.** ⑤ **17.** How **18.** Don't **19.** ④ **20.** Wear, or **21.** Let's find **22.** How much money do we have **23.** Don't park your car here **24.** What a nice plan it is **25.** ①, ②, ⑤ **26.** ② **27.** ③ **28.** X, Yes, she does. **29.** X, didn't he **30.** X, knows **31.** What dirty → How dirty, shall you → will you **32.** coffee and tea → coffee or tea, What do you → Why do you **33.** Looked → Look, is it → isn't it, Why do we → Why don't we

1 대답이 because로 시작하며 이유를 말하고 있으므로 의문사 why를 써서 묻는 것이 알맞다.

2 who: 누구

3 where: 어디에, 어디서

4 ④ Why don't you ~?는 '(너) ~하는 것이 어때?'의 의미이다.

5 ④ '~에 얼마나 오래 머무를 것이니?'에 대한 대답이므로 머무는 기간으로 답해야 한다.

6 대답하는 내용이 긍정이므로 Yes, I do.를 쓴다.

7 대답하는 내용이 부정이므로 No, she isn't.를 쓴다.

8 What + a(n) + 형용사 + 명사 (+ 주어 + 동사)!

9 How + 형용사/부사 (+ 주어 + 동사)!

10 ① doesn't he ③ won't you ④ does she ⑤ did they

11 ⑤ How many + 셀 수 있는 명사: 얼마나 많은 수의 ~
(How much countries → How many countries)

12 ③ Let's not + 동사원형 ~: (우리) ~하지 말자
(Not let's → Let's not)

13 ⑤ What + 형용사 + 복수명사 (+ 주어 + 동사)!
(How → What)

14 선택의문: Which ~, A or B?

15 yesterday를 묻는 의문사는 when이다.

16 with Jane을 묻는 의문사는 who이다.

17 how much: 얼마(의), how: 어떻게

18 Don't + 동사원형: ~하지 마라
Don't you ~?: 너는 ~하지 않니? (부정의문문)

19 Why don't you ~?: (너) ~하는 것이 어때?

20 명령문, or ~: ~해라, 그러지 않으면 …할 것이다

21 Let's + 동사원형: (우리) ~하자

22 how much + 셀 수 없는 명사: 얼마나 많은 양의 ~

23 Don't + 동사원형: ~하지 마라

24 What + a(n) + 형용사 + 명사 + 주어 + 동사!

25 ③ Let's not + 동사원형 ~: (우리) ~하지 말자
(Let's don't → Let's not)
④ How many + 셀 수 있는 명사: 얼마나 많은 수의 ~
(How much → How many)

26 b. What + 형용사 + 복수명사 (+ 주어 + 동사)!
(What a lucky → What lucky)
d. 명령문의 부가의문문은 항상 「~, will you?」로 쓴다.
(won't you → will you)

27 · How diligent are they!
→ How diligent they are!
· Don't turns off the air conditioner.
→ Don't turn off the air conditioner.

28 His name is Larry.라는 대답으로 보아 대답하는 내용이 긍
정이어야 하므로 Yes로 답해야 한다.

29 부가의문문: 긍정문 뒤에는 부정의 부가의문문을 쓰고, 주어는
대명사로 바꾸며, 시제는 앞의 평서문과 같은 시제를 쓴다. 일반
동사는 do/does/did로 바꾼다.

30 의문사가 주어일 때는 3인칭 단수 취급한다.

31 첫 번째는 How로 시작하는 감탄문 「How + 형용사 (+ 주어 +
동사)!」를 쓰며, 두 번째는 명령문의 부가의문문 「~, will you?」
를 쓴다.

32 첫 번째는 선택의문문 「Which ~, A or B?」이므로 or를 쓰고,
두 번째는 Because로 답하고 있으므로 의문사 why를 써서
묻는 것이 알맞다.

33 첫 번째는 명령문이므로 동사원형으로 시작하도록 Look을 쓰
고, 두 번째는 긍정문 뒤에는 부정의 부가의문문을 써야 하므로
isn't it?을 쓴다. 세 번째는 '우리 ~하지 않을래?'의 뜻을 나타
내는 「Why don't we ~?」를 쓴다.

GRAMMAR
Inside

LEVEL 1

GRAMMAR BASICS

 01 품사   p.2

A   1. with   2. may   3. at   4. never   5. friendly
    6. ask   7. bravo

B   1. 대명사   2. 접속사   3. 전치사   4. 감탄사   5. 부사
    6. 형용사   7. 명사   8. 동사   9. 형용사   10. 동사
    11. 명사   12. 부사

02 문장의 성분   **03** 구와 절   p.3

A   1. 목적어   2. 주어   3. 보어   4. 보어   5. 동사
    6. 보어   7. 주어   8. 수식어   9. 목적어   10. 동사

B   1. 구   2. 구   3. 절   4. 구   5. 구   6. 구   7. 구
    8. 절   9. 절   10. 절

CHAPTER 01 be동사

UNIT 01   be동사의 현재형과 과거형   pp.4-5

A   1. am   2. are   3. is   4. are   5. is   6. was
    7. are   8. were   9. are   10. was

B   1. I'm[I am]   2. We're[We are]   3. You're[You
    are]   4. They're[They are]   5. He's[He is]
    6. We were   7. I was   8. This song was
    9. Jenny was   10. Those boys were

C   1. am   2. was   3. are   4. is   5. were   6. are
    7. am   8. is   9. were   10. was

D   1. There are   2. There is   3. There are
    4. There is   5. There is   6. There are

WRITING PRACTICE   p.6

A   1. Your clothes are   2. There is an orange
    3. My father is   4. They were   5. It was
    cloudy   6. There are twelve months
    7. There was a coffee shop

B   1. He is a tennis player   2. It was a sad
    movie   3. There were five books   4. I was
    150 cm tall   5. We are in the classroom
    6. They were late for work

UNIT 02   be동사의 부정문과 의문문   pp.7-8

A   1. Are   2. isn't   3. Is   4. am not   5. Are
    6. aren't   7. Was   8. wasn't   9. is not
    10. weren't

B   1. wasn't   2. aren't   3. wasn't   4. isn't
    5. aren't   6. wasn't   7. weren't   8. isn't
    9. weren't   10. isn't

C   1. Are you   2. Is it   3. Are we   4. Am I   5. Is
    this cell phone   6. Was the hotel   7. Were
    you   8. Was Billy

D   1. isn't[is not]   2. Are   3. ○   4. Was
    5. aren't[are not]   6. Was   7. Are
    8. aren't[are not]

WRITING PRACTICE   p.9

A 1. I'm[I am] not 2. Are you 3. Is she
4. Were your parents 5. He wasn't[was not]
6. The museum isn't[is not]

B 1. He was not kind 2. We are not lazy
3. These comic books were not interesting
4. Susan isn't at the airport 5. Is that man
Mr. Woods 6. Was the restaurant open
7. Are they our new neighbors

REVIEW TEST   pp.10-12

1. ① 2. ② 3. ⑤ 4. ④ 5. ③ 6. ⑤ 7. There
are 8. There is 9. Were, were 10. Is, isn't
11. ③ 12. ④ 13. ③ 14. ⑤ 15. ③ 16. John
wasn't[was not] a shy student 17. The kids
aren't[are not] at school 18. Was Julia with her
family 19. Were Karen and Mark doctors
20. There were some photos 21. Are those pens
22. is Monday, was Sunday 23. isn't[is not]
healthy, is tasty 24. Are Mr. Bonds → Is Mr.
Bonds, he aren't → he isn't 25. It is → It was,
The party weren't → The party wasn't

CHAPTER
02 일반동사

UNIT 01 일반동사의 현재형   pp.13-14

A 1. live 2. opens 3. take 4. has 5. grows
6. tries 7. watches 8. learns 9. make
10. do

B 1. goes 2. smiles 3. comes 4. fixes
5. studies 6. brushes 7. meet 8. passes
9. flies 10. sells

C 1. have 2. sends 3. speak 4. washes
5. cries 6. drink 7. snows 8. love
9. teaches 10. runs

D 1. ○ 2. walks 3. catches 4. ○
5. cleans 6. starts 7. tells 8. ○

WRITING PRACTICE   p.15

A 1. Some wild animals live 2. My dog follows
3. He carries 4. Cherries have 5. Rachel
eats 6. Susan understands 7. A lot of
people use

B 1. know her uncle 2. goes around the earth
3. works in a restaurant 4. look like sisters
5. watches TV after dinner 6. leaves the
station at five o'clock

UNIT 02 일반동사의 과거형   pp.16-17

A 1. stayed 2. met 3. talked 4. live
5. bought 6. studied 7. invited 8. left
9. shared 10. comes

B 1. jumped 2. asked 3. put 4. worried
5. dropped 6. had 7. brought 8. ran
9. saw 10. took

C 1. stopped 2. sat 3. read 4. forgot
5. moved

D 1. went to bed after midnight 2. bought
some grapes 3. slept for four hours 4. met
in front of the school 5. played baseball
6. came in the afternoon 7. gave us
chocolate cake

WRITING PRACTICE   p.18

A 1. Steve told 2. He drew 3. It rained
4. They found 5. The bus schedule changed
6. Kevin gave 7. We tried

B 1. had a cold yesterday 2. called me at 6:00
a.m 3. left Toronto last weekend 4. sang a
song at the party 5. I washed my face
6. Joe broke my cell phone

UNIT 03 일반동사의 부정문   pp.19-20

A 1. don't 2. doesn't 3. didn't 4. don't
5. didn't 6. doesn't 7. didn't 8. doesn't
9. doesn't 10. didn't

B 1. didn't like 2. doesn't eat 3. didn't play
4. don't walk 5. didn't enjoy 6. doesn't
remember

C 1. don't[do not] need 2. don't[do not] bite 3. don't[do not] use 4. doesn't[does not] talk 5. doesn't[does not] work 6. didn't[did not] watch 7. didn't[did not] cry 8. didn't [did not] stop 9. didn't[did not] wash 10. didn't[did not] meet

D 1. doesn't like 2. ○ 3. didn't understand 4. ○ 5. didn't eat 6. didn't leave 7. ○ 8. didn't call

WRITING PRACTICE p.21

A 1. doesn't[does not] like 2. don't[do not] get up early 3. didn't[did not] save much money 4. don't[do not] fit me 5. didn't[did not] begin 6. doesn't[does not] fight with her sister

B 1. don't have a nickname 2. didn't answer my question 3. did not go to the theater 4. You don't look happy 5. I didn't bring my textbook 6. does not watch action movies 7. doesn't write with his right hand

UNIT 04 일반동사의 의문문 pp.22-23

A 1. Do 2. Does 3. Do 4. Did 5. Does 6. Did 7. Do 8. Did 9. Does 10. Did

B 1. Do, remember 2. Does, play 3. Did, forgive 4. Does, live 5. Did, lie 6. Do, eat 7. Did, have

C 1. Does your sister go 2. Did the man catch 3. Did you have 4. Do Amy and Dennis play 5. Does your father watch

D 1. Do you want 2. Does 3. Do 4. ○ 5. Did he come 6. write 7. Did you get up 8. ○ 9. Did Sam dance 10. Did you hear

WRITING PRACTICE p.24

A 1. Did he hear 2. Do we need 3. Does Anna believe 4. Do you know 5. Did they meet 6. Did you read

B 1. Do you want a red shirt 2. Did the kids break this window 3. Does Kate have a laptop 4. Did Lena pick her dress 5. Do we go to city hall 6. Did your brother bring his raincoat 7. Does your uncle work

REVIEW TEST pp.25-27

1. ④ 2. ① 3. ④ 4. ③ 5. ③ 6. we don't 7. he did 8. she doesn't 9. ⓐ works ⓑ goes 10. ⓐ watched ⓑ had 11. ④ 12. ⑤ 13. ③ 14. ② 15. ① 16. learned 17. doesn't[does not] buy 18. ④ 19. Did it rain 20. rode a bike 21. doesn't[does not] open 22. Does Billy exercise at the gym 23. Did you call me 24. X, give 25. ○

CHAPTER 03 조동사

UNIT 01 can, may pp.28-29

A 1. sleep 2. be 3. Can 4. answer 5. can't 6. may 7. are able to 8. may not 9. couldn't 10. may

B 1. can cook 2. can't buy 3. can lift 4. can't use 5. can draw 6. May, see 7. may not join 8. may leave 9. may be 10. may not like

C 1. am able to jump 2. aren't[are not] able to finish 3. aren't[are not] able to play 4. is able to get 5. are able to drive 6. isn't[is not] able to arrive

D 1. ○ 2. couldn't 3. not able to 4. ○ 5. may be 6. can solve 7. may not be 8. can't

WRITING PRACTICE p.30

A 1. Can[May] I leave 2. can[am able to] stand on my hands 3. can't[cannot, is not able to] ride a bike 4. can[may] go to bed 5. may move to New York 6. may not snow 7. couldn't[could not, were not able to] use the internet

B 1. We can see the lake 2. His office may not be open 3. May I read this magazine 4. Can I speak to Mr. Anderson 5. Neil may be in the library 6. Can your cat climb trees

must, have to, should

pp.31-32

A 1. has 2. be 3. have to 4. meet
5. doesn't have to 6. should 7. have to
8. must not 9. must 10. must not

B 1. have to make 2. must be 3. have to
hurry up 4. have to study 5. have to wear
6. must know 7. have to get up 8. must go

C 1. don't have to worry 2. must not play
3. must not hit 4. don't have to help
5. must not run 6. don't have to stay
7. must not touch 8. don't have to stand
9. must not park 10. doesn't have to work

D 1. must not 2. ○ 3. has to[must, should]
4. don't have to 5. must have 6. ○
7. doesn't have to 8. ○

WRITING PRACTICE

p.33

A 1. has to work 2. should wait for 3. don't
have to write the letter 4. have to go to bed
5. must like him 6. must not touch anything
7. must be

B 1. We should leave now 2. has to listen to
my advice 3. doesn't have to take medicine
4. Naomi must grow flowers 5. James
should not eat ice cream 6. must not enter
this building

REVIEW TEST

pp.34-36

1. ② 2. ③ 3. ⑤ 4. ④ 5. ③ 6. Can 7. may
not 8. have to 9. ④ 10. ③ 11. ④ 12. ②
13. ① 14. ② 15. is able to kick 16. has to
explain 17. may not like 18. can't[cannot] be
19. This must be the correct answer 20. don't
have to shout 21. Can I say something 22. X,
can[is able to] play 23. ○

CHAPTER
04 진행형과 미래시제

진행형

pp.37-38

A 1. blowing 2. Is 3. lying 4. was 5. sitting
6. changing 7. is sleeping 8. closes 9. is
10. is knocking

B 1. am parking 2. is talking 3. Is, learning
4. aren't fighting 5. were listening 6. are
tying 7. was jogging 8. is buying
9. Were, having 10. isn't using

C 1. is kicking 2. are wasting 3. is snowing
4. are planning 5. was baking 6. was
raising 7. was waiting 8. were walking

D 1. painting 2. isn't[is not] 3. ○ 4. isn't[is
not] crying 5. likes 6. Are 7. ○ 8. ○

WRITING PRACTICE

p.39

A 1. is singing 2. am packing 3. weren't[were
not] breaking 4. Are you coming 5. wasn't
[was not] smiling 6. Were you exercising
7. are counting

B 1. My parents are sitting 2. Kevin is not
brushing his teeth 3. I am collecting foreign
coins 4. Amelia is not asking 5. The man
was carrying books 6. They were not
swimming

will, be going to

pp.40-41

A 1. be 2. take 3. going 4. they 5. listen
6. isn't 7. to travel 8. not going 9. to
invite

B 1. will like 2. will be 3. won't buy 4. won't
come 5. won't start 6. will melt 7. won't
lose 8. will help

C 1. We're[We are] going to go 2. I'm[I am]
not going to see 3. She isn't[is not] going
to tell / She's not going to tell 4. Are you
going to buy 5. Are they going to borrow
6. Mark is going to pay

D 1. am going to 2. going to smoke 3. ○

4. ○ 5. will move 6. won't be 7. to print
8. will finish 9. ○ 10. ○

WRITING PRACTICE   p.42

A 1. are going to fix 2. is going to stay
3. Scarlett and Jack won't[will not] tell 4. Is
he going to bring 5. isn't[is not] going to
work 6. Will Grace be happy 7. Jim will
show

B 1. My brother will be twenty years old 2. Will
they help the old man 3. Victor is going to
make dinner 4. You will not believe 5. I'm
not going to watch 6. Are you going to
work for

REVIEW TEST   pp.43-45

1. ② 2. ③ 3. ⑤ 4. ⑤ 5. ③ 6. ⑤ 7. ④
8. Is, is 9. won't, will[is going to] 10. ② 11. ⓐ
going to give ⓑ she like 12. ⓐ not going to
ⓑ is cooking 13. ② 14. ⑤ 15. ② 16. ④
17. John will be fifteen next year 18. I'm[I am]
not going to eat this cake 19. is locking
20. won't[will not] have 21. I'm[I am] not going
to get 22. Will he score a goal 23. Are they
closing their eyes 24. is going to train her dog
25. ○ 26. X, will visit

CHAPTER
05 동사의 종류

UNIT 01 감각동사 + 형용사   pp.46-47

A 1. smells 2. sound 3. like coffee 4. feel
5. look 6. bitter 7. great 8. angry
9. happy 10. bad

B 1. feel cold 2. tastes spicy 3. sounds sad
4. smells sour 5. looks scary 6. sounds
nice 7. smell good 8. tastes delicious
9. feel safe 10. look beautiful

C 1. look expensive 2. tastes strange 3. feel
healthy 4. smell terrible 5. sounds serious
6. looks young

D 1. smells good 2. ○ 3. feel soft 4. look
lovely 5. smell fresh 6. looks easy 7. ○
8. feels sick

WRITING PRACTICE   p.48

A 1. look dangerous 2. tastes sweet 3. felt
bad 4. sounds familiar 5. looks great
6. smells strange 7. felt hungry

B 1. Time travel sounds exciting 2. Your body
lotion smells nice 3. These vegetables taste
fresh 4. My grandfather looks healthy
5. Her voice sounded sad 6. Linda felt
nervous

UNIT 02 목적어가 두 개 필요한 동사
pp.49-50

A 1. to 2. for 3. of 4. for 5. them 6. told
7. for 8. me 9. him an email 10. his sister
a new coat

B 1. bought 2. cooked 3. showed 4. taught
5. lent 6. told 7. got 8. wrote

C 1. you some fruit 2. me the ketchup
3. these sneakers for me 4. a favor of me
5. cards to me 6. a beautiful dress for her

D 1. bring me 2. get, for you 3. give, to the
waiter 4. a sandwich for me 5. her many
questions 6. it to my parents

WRITING PRACTICE   p.51

A 1. made us coffee / made coffee for us
2. tell Brenda the news / tell the news to
Brenda 3. give me your business card /
give your business card to me 4. writing my
friend an email / writing an email to my
friend 5. teach you English / teach English
to you 6. bought my brother ice cream /
bought ice cream for my brother

B 1. He sent us funny videos 2. give this
ticket to Cindy 3. lend you fifty dollars
4. showed her passport to us 5. get some
juice for me 6. asked me a difficult question
7. brought beautiful roses to her

A 1. call 2. to be 3. named 4. to stand
5. made 6. to win 7. healthy 8. to open
9. interesting

B 1. boring 2. a liar 3. strong 4. warm
5. Henry 6. exciting 7. fresh 8. angry

C 1. called me a fool 2. wanted you to meet
3. found Jenny friendly 4. expected him to
arrive 5. told her to leave 6. made me
happy 7. kept the room cool 8. asked us
to carry 9. made me the class president
10. advised me to get

D 1. amazing 2. to say 3. ○ 4. ○ 5. to
study 6. us to go 7. them to wait 8. ○

WRITING PRACTICE   p.54

A 1. keeps our house clean 2. want him to
join 3. made me a good player 4. told us
to follow him 5. call me Dan 6. named our
restaurant Lemon Tree 7. ordered him to
pay $100

B 1. made him famous 2. expect her to be
honest 3. find these shoes comfortable
4. made him a big star 5. He asked me to
have dinner 6. advised me to learn Chinese

REVIEW TEST   pp.55-57

1. ② 2. ② 3. ⑤ 4. ③ 5. ② 6. his ID card to
us 7. a scarf for me 8. that book to her 9. ③
10. ④ 11. ⑤ 12. ④ 13. ② 14. ④
15. ⓐ looked ⓑ interesting 16. ⓐ me ⓑ to be
17. ② 18. ① 19. sounds clear 20. feels rough
21. showed his room to me 22. Fresh air keeps
us healthy 23. The principal wants you to come
24. smells badly → smells bad, tastes greatly →
tastes great 25. for Rachel → to Rachel, keep →
to keep, angrily → angry

A 1. computers 2. shirts 3. glasses 4. flies
5. men 6. benches 7. boys 8. hands
9. dishes 10. lamps 11. potatoes 12. fish
13. teeth 14. ladies 15. deer 16. roofs

B 1. Air 2. California 3. paper 4. children
5. sugar 6. cities 7. boxes 8. classes
9. wolves 10. mice

C 1. days 2. thieves 3. Korea 4. stories
5. friendship 6. pianos 7. Money
8. Leaves 9. love 10. heroes

D 1. a cup of tea 2. two bottles of cola
3. four pieces of paper 4. three slices of
pizza 5. a glass of orange juice 6. a bowl
of chicken soup

WRITING PRACTICE   p.60

A 1. ate two tomatoes 2. Knives are
dangerous 3. looks after sheep 4. for
women 5. a cup of coffee 6. played with
sand 7. two slices of cheese

B 1. Edward lives in Osaka 2. We have three
fans 3. I bought six pairs of socks 4. Can I
see your photos 5. drink eight glasses of
water 6. two pieces of furniture

A 1. a 2. an 3. the 4. a 5. the 6. the
7. a 8. The 9. lunch 10. the

B 1. X 2. the 3. a 4. an 5. X 6. a 7. The
8. the

C 1. twice a week 2. by subway 3. put the
box 4. bring an umbrella 5. in the
refrigerator 6. went to bed

D 1. an 2. ○ 3. an 4. ○ 5. an
6. basketball 7. ○ 8. a 9. The 10. email

WRITING PRACTICE　　　　　p.63

A　1. read a book　2. have lunch　3. on the internet　4. by text message　5. three times a day　6. played badminton　7. The movie

B　1. Tom works for a bank　2. an apple and a sandwich　3. a bird in the sky　4. Can you play the clarinet　5. The sun gives us light　6. Mike goes to school

REVIEW TEST　　　　　pp.64-66

1. ④　2. ①　3. ④　4. ②　5. people　6. trees
7. feet　8. ⑤　9. ④　10. ④　11. ③　12. ②
13. the　14. a　15. X　16. go to the movies
17. a cup of green tea　18. ①　19. ③
20. thieves　21. by boat　22. three pieces of cake　23. a swimming pool twice a week　24. a water → water　25. A show → The show, once an week → once a week

CHAPTER 07 대명사

UNIT 01　인칭대명사, 재귀대명사　pp.67-68

A　1. my　2. herself　3. myself　4. its　5. their
6. her　7. They　8. Ours　9. mine　10. We

B　1. me　2. his　3. our　4. it　5. her　6. their
7. him　8. It　9. Its　10. They

C　1. introduce myself　2. help yourself to
3. burned[burnt] myself　4. enjoy yourself
5. by herself　6. make yourself at home

D　1. ○　2. our　3. me　4. She　5. ○　6. ○
7. himself　8. his

WRITING PRACTICE　　　　　p.69

A　1. I'm[I am]　2. He made us　3. herself
4. his pencil case　5. hurt himself　6. by myself

B　1. Is this your suitcase　2. I put it on the desk　3. She is our science teacher
4. Jennifer lost her earring　5. The man is talking to himself　6. I showed them my ticket　7. Molly lent me hers

UNIT 02　this, that, it　pp.70-71

A　1. This　2. these　3. that　4. These
5. those　6. It　7. That　8. it

B　1. these　2. That　3. This　4. It　5. those
6. It　7. that　8. This

C　1. It's[It is] 2:30 p.m　2. It's[It is] Thursday
3. It's[It is] very hot　4. It's[It is] eight o'clock
5. It's[It is] about 400 km　6. It's[It is] snowy
7. It's[It is] December 2

D　1. It　2. these　3. This　4. ○　5. that
6. bike　7. It　8. shirts

WRITING PRACTICE　　　　　p.72

A　1. It's[It is] twelve o'clock　2. These oranges
3. those photos　4. these clothes　5. that book　6. It's[It is] only a hundred meters　7. This poster

B　1. This is my little sister　2. Is it Saturday today　3. Those are not my gloves　4. It will be cloudy tomorrow　5. Is that Pam's report card　6. These people saved the children

UNIT 03　one, some, any　pp.73-74

A　1. any　2. some　3. it　4. any　5. any　6. it
7. one　8. some　9. one　10. some

B　1. it　2. ones　3. one　4. It　5. ones　6. one

C　1. any　2. some　3. any　4. some　5. some
6. any

D　1. any　2. ○　3. any　4. ○　5. it　6. ones
7. any　8. it　9. one

WRITING PRACTICE　　　　　p.75

A　1. any monkeys　2. some ice cream　3. new one　4. try some　5. black ones　6. is looking for it

B　1. My umbrella is that blue one　2. Will you have some chocolate　3. There were some children **4.** I am reading it **5.** There isn't any soup **6.** There is one in the sink **7.** Do you have any ideas

made me angry **6.** That restaurant was excellent

REVIEW TEST   pp.76-78

1. ⑤ **2.** ③ **3.** ③ **4.** ② **5.** ④ **6.** ③ **7.** ④
8. it **9.** one **10.** ones **11.** ⑤ **12.** ② **13.** ③
14. ④ **15.** ③ **16.** its **17.** his **18.** ⓐ one ⓑ it
19. ⓐ some ⓑ They **20.** It's[It is] March 25
21. help yourself to the donuts **22.** It is 300 meters from here **23.** These buildings are very tall **24.** wrote them → wrote it **25.** there is it → there is one, miss one → miss it

CHAPTER 08 형용사와 부사

UNIT 01 형용사   pp.79-80

A **1.** peaceful **2.** much **3.** wonderful **4.** a few **5.** healthy **6.** little **7.** Lots of
8. anything new **9.** many **10.** Someone strange

B **1.** soft **2.** long **3.** easy **4.** thirsty **5.** scary
6. cloudy **7.** perfect **8.** heavy

C **1.** a. much b. many **2.** a. a little b. a few
3. a. few b. little **4.** a. many b. much
5. a. a little b. a few **6.** a. Few b. little

D **1.** cute puppy **2.** ○ **3.** something important **4.** ○ **5.** interesting **6.** salty and spicy

WRITING PRACTICE   p.81

A **1.** dangerous animals **2.** keep you warm
3. much[a lot of, lots of] snow **4.** dry day
5. looks happy **6.** many[a lot of, lots of] paintings **7.** nothing special

B **1.** She has brown eyes **2.** Can I have something cold **3.** I got a few emails
4. are building a big bridge **5.** His jokes

UNIT 02 부사   pp.82-83

A **1.** very cold **2.** well **3.** quickly **4.** easily
5. late **6.** confidently **7.** never drinks
8. am always **9.** hard **10.** beautifully

B **1.** acted **2.** takes **3.** read **4.** hot **5.** the old man died alone **6.** hard **7.** touched
8. high **9.** came **10.** dangerous

C **1.** usually drinks milk in the morning
2. should always wash your hands before meals **3.** seldom talks about herself
4. John never wears jeans **5.** is always polite to her neighbors **6.** Sam often visits

D **1.** fast **2.** heavily **3.** ○ **4.** sometimes play
5. suddenly **6.** ○ **7.** often take **8.** ○
9. happily **10.** ○

WRITING PRACTICE   p.84

A **1.** brightly **2.** very lively **3.** rarely watches
4. bravely **5.** hit the ball high
6. Surprisingly **7.** often forgets

B **1.** It is quite cold **2.** Karen is always kind
3. The swimming lesson starts really early
4. is hardly late for school **5.** I will never forgive him **6.** He gained nearly 10 kg

UNIT 03 원급, 비교급, 최상급   pp.85-86

A **1.** hard **2.** better **3.** more slowly **4.** oldest
5. much **6.** as **7.** fastest **8.** bigger
9. later **10.** most intelligent

B **1.** as tall as **2.** as heavy as **3.** as high as
4. as well as **5.** as much as

C **1.** fatter than **2.** higher than **3.** worse than
4. dirtier than **5.** less than **6.** faster than
7. stronger than **8.** more exciting than
9. more useful than **10.** more interesting than

D **1.** the oldest **2.** the hottest **3.** the most expensive **4.** the most diligent **5.** the shortest **6.** the least

A
1. the deepest 2. much braver than 3. the worst typhoon 4. as important as 5. the most exciting 6. bigger than 7. more loudly than

B
1. is as crowded as New York 2. dances worse than you 3. Your idea is better than 4. This cake is the best dessert 5. is a lot lower than Mike's 6. rides a bike faster than me

REVIEW TEST
pp.88-90

1. ④ 2. ⑤ 3. ④ 4. ② 5. ① 6. a little 7. a few 8. many 9. ① 10. ② 11. ④ 12. ④ 13. ④ 14. ⓐ more ⓑ many 15. ⓐ hotter ⓑ less 16. ⑤ 17. ④ 18. better than 19. the highest mountain 20. ③ 21. We always wear school uniforms 22. Amy speaks Korean very well 23. X, quickly 24. X, something stupid

CHAPTER
09 to부정사와 동명사

UNIT 01 to부정사의 명사적 용법 pp.91-92

A
1. 목적어 2. 주어 3. 보어 4. 주어 5. 목적어 6. 주어 7. 목적어 8. 보어 9. 목적어 10. 주어

B
1. a. see b. to see 2. a. to be b. be 3. a. to get b. get 4. a. take b. to take 5. a. to learn b. learn

C
1. where to put 2. how to use 3. what to say 4. whether to invite 5. when to water 6. whom to choose 7. how to get 8. what to wear

D
1. to see 2. to train 3. where to go 4. not to watch 5. ○ 6. to take 7. ○ 8. to drink

A
1. planned to visit 2. need to hurry 3. promised to go 4. hard to memorize 5. wants to join 6. easy to find 7. whether to apply for

B
1. It is wonderful to help 2. decided to go to the dentist 3. where to hang the painting 4. is to be the best soccer player 5. likes to travel by train 6. how to play this game

UNIT 02 to부정사의 형용사적, 부사적 용법
pp.94-95

A
1. a friend 2. a chance 3. a man 4. a plan 5. any money 6. something warm 7. a person 8. a lot of places

B
1. © 2. ⓓ 3. ⓐ 4. ⓑ 5. ⓑ 6. ⓐ 7. ⓓ 8. ©

C
1. place to take 2. time to go 3. books to read 4. anything to eat 5. keys to open 6. something to tell 7. problems to solve 8. videos to watch

D
1. to meet some rude people 2. to[in order to] buy a laptop 3. to meet Robin at the party 4. to[in order to] talk with my mom 5. to[in order to] complain about the service 6. to have their first baby

A
1. to[in order to] take a walk 2. lived to be 3. happy to get 4. someone to work 5. homework to do 6. to[in order to] buy

B
1. were sad to lose the game 2. grew up to be a cook 3. something warm to wear 4. studied hard to pass the exam 5. have time to go to the concert 6. called him to ask 7. shocked to hear about the accident

UNIT 03 동명사의 역할 pp.97-98

A
1. 주어 2. 목적어 3. 보어 4. 주어 5. 목적어 6. 목적어 7. 보어 8. 목적어 9. 목적어

B
1. going 2. visiting 3. painting 4. Having 5. like watching 6. doing 7. Not wearing

8. closing

C **1.** listening **2.** writing **3.** turning **4.** waiting **5.** drinking **6.** biting **7.** selling

D **1.** ○ **2.** studying **3.** ○ **4.** cooking **5.** talking **6.** not coming **7.** Choosing[To choose] **8.** hitting **9.** ○

WRITING PRACTICE   p.99

A **1.** worried about getting **2.** is worth buying **3.** finding[to find] out the solution **4.** feel like eating out **5.** finished reading **6.** avoided answering **7.** stop using

B **1.** will go fishing **2.** I don't mind using **3.** enjoys playing the guitar **4.** quit learning Chinese **5.** Spending time with family **6.** is running in the park

REVIEW TEST   pp.100-102

1. ② **2.** ④ **3.** ③ **4.** ② **5.** ③ **6.** how **7.** what **8.** when **9.** to **10.** whether **11.** ④ **12.** ⑤ **13.** ① **14.** ③ **15.** ③ **16.** ⓐ visiting ⓑ to come **17.** ⓐ to get ⓑ showing **18.** ② **19.** ③ **20.** avoid drinking **21.** sad to say **22.** opened the window to get some fresh air **23.** is not wasting money **24.** X, to make **25.** ○

CHAPTER 10 전치사

UNIT 01   장소를 나타내는 전치사 pp.103-104

A **1.** in **2.** at **3.** on **4.** at **5.** in **6.** on **7.** on **8.** at **9.** to **10.** In

B **1.** a. at b. in **2.** a. at b. under **3.** a. on b. behind **4.** a. from b. near

C **1.** on **2.** over **3.** behind **4.** in **5.** near **6.** under **7.** on **8.** at

D **1.** in front of **2.** next to **3.** behind **4.** between

WRITING PRACTICE   p.105

A **1.** under the bridge **2.** on the pancakes **3.** over the Atlantic **4.** in our garden **5.** at the front desk **6.** between his mom and dad **7.** from home to the subway station

B **1.** He lives near the lake **2.** is singing on the stage **3.** is across from the bakery **4.** is some bread in that basket **5.** sits behind me in class **6.** in front of the mirror

UNIT 02   시간을 나타내는 전치사 pp.106-107

A **1.** in **2.** in **3.** at **4.** on **5.** for **6.** at **7.** around **8.** between **9.** from **10.** before, during

B **1.** at **2.** on **3.** in **4.** at **5.** at **6.** in **7.** in **8.** on

C **1.** for a year **2.** during the holidays **3.** for thirty minutes **4.** during the spring **5.** for two hours **6.** during the Korean War **7.** for three days **8.** during the concert **9.** during the movie **10.** for sixty seconds

D **1.** on **2.** in **3.** ○ **4.** on **5.** at **6.** for **7.** ○ **8.** to **9.** ○ **10.** between

WRITING PRACTICE   p.108

A **1.** in autumn **2.** before Christmas **3.** on November 17 **4.** during the summer **5.** at night **6.** in 2019 **7.** on Saturday morning

B **1.** comes home around 7:00 p.m **2.** will be cloudy in the afternoon **3.** felt happy after the show **4.** take this test for an hour **5.** leaves Seoul at 5:30 p.m **6.** between Wednesday and Friday

UNIT 03   기타 전치사   pp.109-110

A **1.** him **2.** for **3.** with **4.** us **5.** for **6.** to **7.** by **8.** to **9.** for **10.** about

B **1.** ⓑ **2.** ⓐ **3.** ⓓ **4.** ⓒ **5.** ⓒ **6.** ⓑ **7.** ⓓ **8.** ⓐ

C **1.** by **2.** about **3.** with **4.** for **5.** about **6.** by **7.** to **8.** with

D **1.** by **2.** about **3.** to **4.** with **5.** for

WRITING PRACTICE p.111

A **1.** to Korea **2.** about the galaxy **3.** with her classmates **4.** for your safety **5.** by plane **6.** to him **7.** with some glue

B **1.** order these books by phone **2.** was kind to us **3.** was thinking about you **4.** covered the child with a blanket **5.** get some coffee for everyone **6.** go to the movies with us

REVIEW TEST pp.112-114

1. ① **2.** ④ **3.** ② **4.** ③ **5.** ③ **6.** ② **7.** after **8.** with **9.** ② **10.** ⑤ **11.** from **12.** for **13.** with **14.** ② **15.** ⑤ **16.** ④ **17.** ⓐ for ⓑ about **18.** ⓐ in ⓑ with **19.** behind the wall **20.** by train **21.** between the shoe store and the café **22.** from May 1 to June 30 **23.** ○ **24.** X, on

CHAPTER
11 접속사

UNIT 01 and, but, or, so pp.115-116

A **1.** gentle **2.** but **3.** so **4.** but **5.** and **6.** or **7.** and **8.** so **9.** or **10.** or

B **1.** a. but b. or c. and **2.** a. but b. so c. or **3.** a. so b. or c. and

C **1.** and **2.** or **3.** so **4.** but **5.** or **6.** and **7.** but **8.** so

D **1.** Mark set the table **2.** they went to the pool **3.** he didn't like it **4.** his father will take him home

WRITING PRACTICE p.117

A **1.** is honest and polite **2.** Monday or Tuesday **3.** but she can't[cannot] play well **4.** and came back home **5.** but I don't[do not] like it **6.** or we can eat out **7.** so I got angry

B **1.** Junsu or Inhye will be **2.** He visited

Greece and Turkey **3.** so we shared it **4.** This beach is nice but far **5.** so he couldn't come to dinner **6.** came out and waved

UNIT 02 when, before, after, until pp.118-119

A **1.** Before **2.** after **3.** when **4.** visit **5.** is **6.** when **7.** save **8.** after **9.** goes **10.** until

B **1.** a. when b. before **2.** a. after b. When **3.** a. until b. Before **4.** a. until b. after

C **1.** ⓑ **2.** ⓓ **3.** ⓐ **4.** ⓒ **5.** ⓐ **6.** ⓓ **7.** ⓑ **8.** ⓒ

D **1.** when we arrived at the lake **2.** until the soccer game is over **3.** when he saw his friend on TV **4.** After I watched the movie **5.** Before we go to Sydney **6.** until I buy a new pair of glasses

WRITING PRACTICE p.120

A **1.** when my team lost the game **2.** before the guests came **3.** after you finish the main dish **4.** When the vacation season starts **5.** until dinner was ready **6.** before you order **7.** until I was seven years old

B **1.** after he got home last night **2.** until their parents stopped them **3.** when you swim in the sea **4.** Before I buy things online **5.** After she left her hometown **6.** When Betty won the contest

UNIT 03 because, if, that pp.121-122

A **1.** that **2.** if **3.** rains **4.** that **5.** if **6.** that **7.** that **8.** because **9.** has **10.** Because

B **1.** a. that b. If **2.** a. If b. because **3.** a. that b. if **4.** a. that b. because

C **1.** that he hurt his leg **2.** because he is very kind **3.** If he doesn't get home early **4.** because the bus came late **5.** that Suji likes you **6.** If Mark gets a C on the test

D **1.** ○ **2.** do **3.** because **4.** that **5.** ○ **6.** because **7.** ○ **8.** are **9.** that 또는 생략 **10.** ○

WRITING PRACTICE
p.123

A 1. (that) you can visit me 2. If you miss English class 3. because it's[it is] close 4. that we won ten gold medals 5. because it smelled bad 6. if it's[it is] small

B 1. think that you are right 2. if you taste it 3. because she had a job interview 4. If your computer doesn't work 5. that I look nice with short hair 6. because he has a lot of books 7. If you did something wrong

REVIEW TEST
pp.124-126

1. ③ 2. ④ 3. ① 4. ③ 5. ④ 6. that 7. if
8. because 9. ④ 10. ② 11. ① 12. that
13. so 14. because 15. or 16. when 17. ③
18. ⑤ 19. It is true that 20. (either) in this book or on the internet 21. before I buy something
22. X, and 23. X, sign 24. X, that

CHAPTER
12 의문문, 명령문, 감탄문

UNIT 01 의문사 who, what, which
pp.127-128

A 1. Who 2. What 3. Whose 4. Who 5. Which 6. What

B 1. ⓐ 2. ⓓ 3. ⓒ 4. ⓑ 5. ⓒ 6. ⓓ 7. ⓑ 8. ⓐ

C 1. Whose 2. What 3. Who 4. Which

D 1. Whose bat is this 2. Who is taking care of Emily 3. What is his name 4. Who[Whom] did they see 5. Whose passport is it 6. What are the children drawing 7. Who got first prize 8. Who[Whom] did you teach

WRITING PRACTICE
p.129

A 1. Whose doll is this 2. What did Julia say 3. Who[Whom] did Jane go out 4. Who sent you 5. Which bike is yours 6. What will you speak

B 1. What was the problem 2. Which do you prefer 3. Who bought these donuts 4. Whose umbrella did he borrow 5. Whom did you call 6. Which dessert do you want 7. What kind of novels

UNIT 02 의문사 when, where, why, how
pp.130-131

A 1. How 2. don't 3. Why 4. don't 5. When 6. Where

B 1. ⓓ 2. ⓒ 3. ⓐ 4. ⓑ 5. ⓑ 6. ⓓ 7. ⓐ 8. ⓒ

C 1. How much 2. How old 3. How often 4. How long 5. How many 6. How far

D 1. How was the movie 2. Where did she put her bag 3. When did they move 4. Why does Isabel love Edward 5. When will the winter vacation start 6. Where is Vincent going to have

WRITING PRACTICE
p.132

A 1. How was your trip 2. Where is a bank 3. How many goals 4. Where did you hear 5. Why does he want 6. When did they become

B 1. When is her wedding 2. Why was Daniel upset 3. Where did you find this key 4. How much time do you need 5. When can I receive the package 6. Why don't we order some pizza 7. How did the children solve this problem

UNIT 03 부가의문문
pp.133-134

A 1. isn't 2. will 3. does 4. do 5. he 6. don't 7. can't 8. are 9. didn't 10. weren't

B   **1.** doesn't he   **2.** shouldn't you   **3.** is she
4. won't it   **5.** does she   **6.** didn't he
7. wasn't it   **8.** can they   **9.** will she
10. aren't we

C   **1.** don't they, they do   **2.** won't he, he will
3. can he, he can't   **4.** aren't you, I'm not
5. was she, she wasn't   **6.** did it, it did

D   **1.** isn't it   **2.** didn't we   **3.** ○   **4.** doesn't it
5. will you   **6.** weren't you   **7.** ○   **8.** does
he   **9.** is she   **10.** shall we

WRITING PRACTICE   p.135

A   **1.** is on sale, isn't it   **2.** look good, don't
they   **3.** isn't[is not] far, is it   **4.** will be our
class president, won't he   **5.** hurt her arm,
didn't she   **6.** were in the soccer club,
weren't you   **7.** can drive a car, can't he

B   **1.** snowing outside, isn't it   **2.** didn't get my
message, did you   **3.** won't cancel the
contest, will they   **4.** sings very well, doesn't
she   **5.** was not late for school, was he
6. are sleeping, aren't they

UNIT 04   부정의문문, 선택의문문   pp.136-137

A   **1.** Doesn't   **2.** Isn't   **3.** or   **4.** Wasn't   **5.** or
6. Which   **7.** No, I can't.   **8.** I'll go with Amy.

B   **1.** Didn't you watch   **2.** Can't I use   **3.** Won't
James buy   **4.** Aren't you a fan   **5.** Don't
your parents worry

C   **1.** No, she isn't   **2.** No, I can't   **3.** Yes, they
are   **4.** Yes, they did   **5.** Yes, he does

D   **1.** Did he call you before lunch or after lunch
2. Do you want to take a nap or walk in the
park   **3.** Will they leave tonight or tomorrow
night   **4.** Did she find this book here or at
home   **5.** Is Lucy going to have dinner alone
or with us

WRITING PRACTICE   p.138

A   **1.** Isn't this ice cream   **2.** Didn't you go there
3. Won't you play   **4.** Wasn't Julie studying
5. Can't your little brother write   **6.** a wallet
or a bag

B   **1.** Aren't the two girls sisters   **2.** Don't you
swim well   **3.** Weren't they from France
4. Won't your friends stay here   **5.** Doesn't
he live in this apartment   **6.** meet at school
or at Steve's house   **7.** want to play baseball
or soccer

UNIT 05   명령문, 감탄문   pp.139-140

A   **1.** I was   **2.** What   **3.** Be   **4.** How   **5.** Please
don't   **6.** Let's not   **7.** What   **8.** Don't talk
9. Show   **10.** Let's turn

B   **1.** Don't[Do not] smoke   **2.** Be nice   **3.** Don't
[Do not] run   **4.** Fry   **5.** Don't[Do not] play
6. Don't[Do not] cheat   **7.** Please don't[do
not] touch   **8.** Don't[Do not] throw   **9.** Brush
10. Please clean

C   **1.** an exciting idea (it is)   **2.** cold (it is)   **3.** a
wonderful voice Fred has   **4.** beautifully she
sings   **5.** expensive this watch is   **6.** scary
movies (these are)

D   **1.** Don't be   **2.** What a handsome boy
3. How quickly   **4.** Let's get   **5.** ○   **6.** Don't
[Do not] play   **7.** What smart students
8. Order   **9.** ○   **10.** Let's not

WRITING PRACTICE   p.141

A   **1.** How comfortable   **2.** Don't[Do not] be
afraid   **3.** What a great dancer   **4.** How
shocking   **5.** Don't[Do not] ask her age
6. Let's not talk   **7.** Help your little sister

B   **1.** Don't cross your legs   **2.** Let's take some
pictures   **3.** How fast the car is   **4.** Don't
call him now   **5.** What an easy test it is
6. Let's clean the living room

REVIEW TEST   pp.142-144

1. ②   **2.** ①   **3.** ⑤   **4.** ④   **5.** ②   **6.** ③   **7.** What
8. Don't   **9.** doesn't he   **10.** won't you
11. wasn't she   **12.** ③   **13.** ②   **14.** ③   **15.** ⓐ
Which ⓑ Let's   **16.** ⓐ do ⓑ Why   **17.** ⑤
18. What a cute baby they have   **19.** Don't[Do
not] make the same mistake again   **20.** Let's not

forget about our promise   **21.** How high that bird flies   **22.** What time does English class begin   **23.** Yes, it isn't. → Yes, it is.   **24.** Let go → Let's go, is he → isn't he, What beautifully → How beautifully